The All-New Low Calorie High Protein Low-Carb Diet Cookbook

Second Edition

Try These Low-Carb High Protein Recipes and Delicious Meals for Optimal Weight Loss

Samantha Bax

The All-New Low Calorie High Protein Low-Carb Diet Cookbook
Samantha Bax
Copyright 2024 © Prose Books LLC

ISBN 978-1-963160-29-1

Ebook ISBN: None

Paperback ISBN: 978-1-963160-29-1

All rights reserved.

PROSE
B O O K S
Empowering Authors, Forging Legacies

Prose Books
Prose Books LLC
Merrimack, NH 03054 USA
email: info@prosebooks.us

BBB
ACCREDITED
BUSINESS ®

Table of Contents

Low-Calorie High-Protein Low-Carb Diet Introduction

Understanding the Basics

A low-calorie, high-protein, low-carb diet is all about eating foods that are low in calories but high in protein content while limiting the carbohydrates consumed. This type of diet is designed to help you lose weight, particularly focusing on burning fat while maintaining muscle mass. By restricting calories, increasing protein intake, and reducing carbs, this diet aims to create a calorie deficit, which is essential for weight loss.

Benefits of the Diet

One of the key benefits of following a low-calorie, high-protein, low-carb diet is that it can aid in weight loss. When you consume fewer calories than your body needs, it turns to stored fat for energy, leading to weight loss. Additionally, by prioritizing protein consumption, you can feel fuller for longer periods, which may help reduce overall calorie intake. Moreover, limiting carbs can help stabilize blood sugar levels and prevent spikes that can lead to cravings and overeating.

Planning Your Meals

To effectively follow a low-calorie, high-protein, low-carb diet, it's essential to plan your meals carefully. Start by calculating your daily calorie and protein needs based on your weight, activity level, and weight loss goals. Incorporate lean sources of protein such as chicken, fish, tofu, and legumes into your meals to meet your protein requirements. Choose fibrous vegetables and fruits to add essential nutrients and fiber while keeping the carb content low.

Creating a 1200-Calorie, 100g Protein Day Meal Plan

To kickstart your weight loss journey, a well-structured meal plan is crucial. A 1200-calorie, 100g protein per day plan can provide a roadmap for your daily meals and snacks. For example, you can have a breakfast of egg whites with spinach and tomatoes, a lunch of grilled chicken salad with a light vinaigrette, and a dinner of baked salmon with asparagus. Healthy snacks like Greek yogurt with berries or mixed nuts can keep you satisfied between meals while staying within your calorie and protein targets.

Importance of Macronutrient Balance

Maintaining a balance between protein, carbs, and fats is vital for the success of a low-calorie, high-protein, low-carb diet. Proteins are essential for muscle repair and growth, while carbs provide energy for daily activities. Healthy fats help in nutrient absorption and hormone production. By including a variety of foods from each macronutrient group in your meals, you can ensure you are getting all the essential nutrients your body needs to function optimally.

Supplements and Hydration

Incorporating supplements such as protein powder or multivitamins may be necessary to meet your nutritional needs when following a low-calorie, high-protein, low-carb diet. However, it is essential to consult with a healthcare provider before adding any supplements to your routine. Additionally, staying hydrated is crucial for overall health and weight loss. Drinking an adequate amount of water throughout the day can help control hunger, support digestion, and optimize metabolic processes.

Exercise and Physical Activity

While diet plays a significant role in weight loss, combining it with regular exercise and physical activity can enhance results and improve overall health. Incorporating both cardiovascular exercise and strength training can help boost metabolism, increase calorie burn, and preserve muscle mass. Aim for at least 150 minutes of moderate-intensity exercise per week, along with strength training exercises to promote muscle strength and endurance.

Tracking Progress and Adjustments

Monitoring your progress is essential to ensure you are on track with your weight loss goals. Keep track of your daily calories and protein intake, as well as your weight and measurements, to gauge your progress. If you find yourself hitting a weight loss plateau or feeling fatigued, consider adjusting your meal plan or seeking guidance from a nutritionist or healthcare provider. Making small tweaks to your diet and exercise routine can help keep you motivated and continue making progress towards your goals.

Sustainability and Long-Term Success

While following a low-calorie, high-protein, low-carb diet can lead to rapid weight loss initially, it is important to focus on long-term sustainability for continued success. Incorporating a variety of foods, staying mindful of portion sizes, and allowing flexibility in your eating plan can help prevent feelings of deprivation and support a healthy relationship with food. Remember that achieving and maintaining a healthy weight is a journey that requires consistency, patience, and a balanced approach to nutrition and fitness.

Questions and Answers

Questions and Answers for "Low Calorie High Protein Low-Carb Diet (Cookbook)"

General Questions About the Cookbook

Q1: What are the main benefits of the "Low Calorie High Protein Low-Carb Diet (Cookbook)"?
A1: The cookbook offers flavorful and functional recipes that are high in protein and low in carbs, making it perfect for weight loss and fitness goals while maintaining a balanced diet.

Q2: What type of recipes can I find in this cookbook?
A2: The cookbook includes a variety of recipes for different meals, including breakfast, lunch, dinner, snacks, desserts, vegetarian, vegan, and international cuisine options.

Q3: Are the recipes in the cookbook easy to follow?
A3: Yes, the recipes are designed to be easy-to-follow with clear instructions, making them suitable for both novice and seasoned kitchen enthusiasts.

Q4: Does the cookbook provide nutritional information for each recipe?
A4: Yes, detailed nutritional information is provided for each recipe to help readers make informed choices about their meals.

Q5: How is the cookbook structured?
A5: The cookbook is well-organized with a user-friendly layout and design, making it easy to navigate and find recipes for specific dietary needs and preferences.

Specific Dietary Needs and Preferences

Q6: Are there recipes suitable for vegetarians and vegans?
A6: Yes, the cookbook includes a range of vegetarian and vegan recipes to cater to different dietary preferences.

Q7: Does the cookbook address specific health conditions or dietary needs?
A7: Yes, the cookbook offers recipes and tips that focus on various health conditions and dietary needs, ensuring a broader range of readers' requirements are met.

Q8: How does the cookbook help with portion control and calorie counts?
A8: The cookbook provides detailed information on portion sizes and calorie counts for each recipe to help readers manage their caloric intake effectively.

Q9: Are there any advanced or unique recipes in the cookbook?
A9: Yes, the cookbook includes diverse and advanced recipes with unique ingredients and techniques to enhance the culinary experience.

Practical and Functional Features

Q10: Are vivid pictures included in each recipe?
A10: No. We have decided to keep the costs affordable for everyone. See question 30 for details on how you can obtain pictures of the recipes.

Q11: Does the cookbook include practical tips for implementing healthy eating habits?
A11: Yes, the cookbook offers practical tips and helpful suggestions for following the diet, making healthy eating more accessible and manageable.

Q12: Is there a shopping list included for meal planning?
A12: Yes, the cookbook includes a free meal planner that is available on our website, and it includes a shopping list for meal planning to make grocery shopping easier and more efficient.

Q13: How does the cookbook address the importance of balanced nutrition?
A13: The cookbook emphasizes balanced nutrition through its well-structured recipes and thorough explanation of healthy eating concepts.

User Feedback and Improvements

Q14: What were some of the strengths mentioned by users in their reviews?
A14: Users appreciated the flavorful and functional recipes, the high-protein, low-carb approach, the easy-to-follow recipes, and the inclusion of vivid pictures for each recipe.

Q15: What were some of the weaknesses mentioned by users in their reviews? A15: Some users mentioned the need for more diverse recipes, more advanced options, vegetarian and vegan options, information on portion sizes, and a focus on international cuisine.

Q16: How does the cookbook cater to readers interested in sustainability and ethical eating practices?
A16: The cookbook includes discussions on sustainability and the environmental impact of food choices to appeal to readers interested in ethical eating practices.

Q17: Are there any personal anecdotes or stories in the cookbook?
A17: Yes, the cookbook includes personal anecdotes and stories that resonate with readers, making the content more engaging and relatable.

Q18: Does the cookbook include any before-and-after success stories?
A18: While the cookbook focuses primarily on recipes and healthy eating tips, it encourages readers to start trying the recipes immediately and offers motivational content.

Q19: How does the cookbook handle the use of processed or specialty ingredients?
A19: The cookbook aims to minimize reliance on processed or specialty ingredients, offering alternative cooking methods and techniques to provide more options for preparing the recipes.

Q20: What competitive edges does the cookbook have over other similar books?
A20: The cookbook's competitive edges include its inclusion of diverse and advanced recipes, detailed nutritional information, discussion on sustainability, exploration of innovative cooking trends, and emphasis on specific health conditions and dietary needs.

Q21: How does the cookbook ensure recipes are not too repetitive?
A21: The cookbook offers a wide variety of recipes for different meals and dietary preferences, ensuring there is minimal repetition of ingredients and techniques.

Q22: Are there dessert recipes included in the cookbook?
A22: Yes, the cookbook includes a section dedicated to low-carb dessert recipes, allowing readers to enjoy sweet treats without compromising their diet.

Q23: How does the cookbook address potential dietary restrictions?
A23: The cookbook includes recipes that cater to various dietary restrictions and provide modifications and alternatives to accommodate different needs.

Q24: Does the cookbook include international cuisine options?
A24: Yes, the cookbook offers a range of international cuisine recipes, bringing diverse flavors and culinary experiences to the readers' kitchen.

Q25: How user-friendly is the layout and design of the cookbook?
A25: The cookbook features a user-friendly layout and design with clear headings, vibrant pictures, and easy-to-follow instructions, making it accessible to readers of all levels.

Q26: Are there any innovative cooking trends or ingredients featured in the cookbook?
A26: Yes, the cookbook explores innovative cooking trends and ingredients, providing readers with fresh and engaging culinary experiences.

Q27: How does the cookbook address the importance of hydration?
A27: The cookbook includes tips and reminders about the importance of staying hydrated, especially when following a low-carb diet, to ensure overall health and well-being.

Q28: Does the cookbook offer guidance for long-term weight maintenance?
A28: Yes, the cookbook provides suggestions and tips for maintaining a healthy weight long-term, including balanced nutrition and sustainable eating habits.

Q29: How does the cookbook cater to readers interested in the mental and emotional aspects of healthy eating?
A29: The cookbook includes discussions on the mental and emotional benefits of healthy eating, offering motivational content and personal anecdotes to inspire readers.

Q30: Are there any visual aids or infographics included in the cookbook?
A30: After some very careful consideration, we have decided not to include pictures of the actual recipes in an effort to keep the costs of bringing this cookbook to our readers at an affordable price. While there have been numerous requests for pictures, we welcome our readers to email us for any recipe that they might want a color picture of the recipe

and we will make every attempt to accommodate those requests. You can reach us at recipe@samanthabax.com for these requests.

Chapter 1

Introduction to the Low-Calorie High Protein Low-Carb Diet

Navigating the landscape of diet plans can be a daunting task, especially when faced with countless options that promise rapid results yet often fall short. Among these, the Low-Calorie High Protein Low-Carb Diet stands out as a balanced approach that aligns with both weight management and overall health goals. Imagine having a straightforward plan that not only curbs your appetite but also fuels your muscles, all while maintaining a steady energy level throughout the day. This diet offers just that by focusing on the right mix of macronutrients, portion control, and meal timing.

The main challenge many face with traditional diets is the tendency to overeat, especially when hunger strikes unexpectedly or when there are tempting, convenient food options at hand. For instance, consider those late-night cravings for something sweet or the irresistible allure of fast food during a busy workday. These impulsive choices often derail dietary progress and lead to excess calorie consumption.

However, by adopting a structured meal plan, such as the Low-Calorie High Protein Low-Carb Diet, you place yourself in a more controlled environment. Preparing meals ahead of time, understanding portion sizes, and selecting nutrient-dense foods can significantly reduce the likelihood of overeating and aid in achieving long-term weight loss goals.

In this chapter, we will delve into the core principles of the Low-Calorie High Protein Low-Carb Diet. You will learn how to create a sustainable meal plan that supports your nutritional needs while promoting weight loss. We will explore practical tips for meal prepping, strategies for tracking your food intake, and the importance of incorporating a variety of nutrient-dense foods into your diet.

Additionally, we will discuss how to time your meals effectively to optimize your metabolism and maintain stable energy levels throughout the day. By the end of this chapter, you will have a comprehensive understanding of how to implement this diet into your daily routine, paving the way for a healthier and more balanced lifestyle.

Description and purpose of the event

Following a structured meal plan can bring about a myriad of benefits, one of the most compelling being its ability to aid in calorie control and portion management. When we take the time to outline our meals ahead of time, we gain greater oversight into what we are consuming, which can be an effective strategy for preventing overeating and supporting weight loss goals. Silvia Veri from Beaumont Weight Control Center rightly points out, "Planning meals and snacks ahead of time increases the chance for success; it increases the likelihood a healthier food choice will be made" (Health benefits of meal planning, n.d.).

First and foremost, having a plan helps us avoid last-minute unhealthy choices. Think back to those moments when hunger strikes unexpectedly, and you find yourself gravitating towards the nearest fast-food joint. A structured meal plan puts you in the driver's seat, empowering you to make nourishing choices even when life gets busy. Moreover, when you're not in a rush or overly hungry, it's easier to stick to recommended portion sizes. This is critical because many restaurants serve portions far larger than we need. Eating at home with a planned meal allows us to manage these portions more effectively.

Moreover, evidence supports that portion size plays a substantial role in energy intake. Studies have shown that large portions lead to overconsumption, while utilizing portion-controlled tools—like pre-measured containers or specially designed plates—can significantly reduce this impact (Rolls, 2014). Therefore, preparation isn't just about having food ready but about ensuring the correct amount reaches your plate.

Another significant benefit of meal planning lies in its potential for improving overall dietary quality and variety. By planning ahead, we can ensure each meal includes a balanced array of nutrient-dense foods, which not only supports bodily health but can also prevent monotonous eating habits that might discourage us from sticking to the diet.

For example, incorporating a colorful selection of fruits and vegetables not only makes meals visually appealing but also ensures a broad spectrum of vitamins and minerals.

If you're aiming to build these healthy habits, here is what you can do:

- Begin by setting aside some time each week to plan your meals. Consider your work schedule, social commitments, and family activities to create a feasible plan.
- Write a grocery list based on your meal plan. Stick to this list when shopping to avoid impulse buys.
- Invest in storage containers that allow you to measure and store individual portions. These will help you avoid overeating by providing visual cues on how much to consume.
- Prepare and cook meals in bulk. For instance, cook a large batch of quinoa or grill several chicken breasts at once, then portion them into containers to use throughout the week.
- Keep a food diary or use an app to track your meals and snacks. Monitoring what you eat can increase accountability and highlight areas where improvements may be needed.

By adopting these strategies, you not only streamline your daily routine but also make consistent nutritional choices easier. Let's now delve into the significance of meal timings and frequency. Eating at regular intervals can optimize energy levels and boost metabolism. When meals are spaced appropriately, blood sugar levels remain stable, preventing the extreme hunger that could lead to overeating. Whereas skipping meals can backfire, leading to fatigue and increased cravings later in the day.

Incorporate certain guidelines here as well:

- Aim to have three main meals and two smaller snacks during the day. Keeping meals light yet frequent helps sustain energy and avoids the sluggishness that often follows large meals.
- Plan snack times between main meals. This could be mid-morning or mid-afternoon, whichever fits best with your daily schedule.
- Avoid eating late at night. Try to finish your last meal at least 2-3 hours before bedtime to allow proper digestion and improve sleep quality.

Strategically timing your meals can not only enhance your metabolic rate but also distribute caloric intake more evenly throughout the day.

Next, let us consider the importance of incorporating a variety of nutrient-dense foods. This ensures that your body receives all necessary nutrients, reducing the risk of deficiencies and promoting overall wellness. Instead of monotonously sticking to the same few dishes, diversifying your food choices can make your diet more enjoyable and sustainable.

Here are some tips:

- Rotate different protein sources like lean meats, fish, beans, and tofu. Each provides a unique set of nutrients beneficial for health.
- Include a rainbow of vegetables and fruits in your meal plan. Different colors often indicate varied types of phytonutrients, which have numerous health benefits.
- Opt for whole grains such as brown rice, barley, and whole wheat instead of refined grains. They offer more fiber, vitamins, and minerals.
- Incorporate healthy fats from sources like avocados, nuts, seeds, and olive oil. Fats play a crucial role in brain function and hormone production.

It's vital to remember that a well-rounded diet isn't just about restricting calories but enriching your menu with wholesome options that satisfy both taste and nutrition requirements.

Finally, maintaining flexibility in your meal plans can help ensure they complement your lifestyle rather than complicate it. The goal is to create a plan that's practical and adaptable—consider it a blueprint rather than a strict rulebook. Life happens, plans change, and being able to adjust your meal plans while still adhering to fundamental principles of good nutrition is the mark of a sustainable approach.

So, be prepared to adapt. If you find yourself dining out unexpectedly, choose wisely from the menu based on your knowledge of portion sizes and nutrient density. If you miss cooking on a scheduled prep day, opt for easy-to-assemble meals rather than resorting to takeout. The core idea is to build a flexible framework around your dietary habits.

Balancing individual freedom with responsibility toward one's health is crucial in creating lasting, positive changes. With a structured meal plan, you take charge of what you consume, making conscious, informed choices that honor your body's needs and wellbeing.

Supporting Elements: The Dietitian discusses how a structured meal plan can prevent overeating and support weight loss goals.

Let's talk about how to make meal planning work for you. Balancing busy lives and healthy eating can feel like a juggling act, but with some well-thought-out strategies, it becomes manageable and even enjoyable.

First off, think about meal prepping in advance. This strategy isn't just a time-saver; it's a way to ensure that your meals are consistent with your diet plan. The Nutrition Source (2020) emphasizes that having meals ready means you're less likely to grab unhealthy takeout or snacks. Imagine walking into your kitchen after a long day and finding a wholesome meal waiting for you.

To get started:

- Designate a specific day for meal prep. Spend a few hours cooking larger batches of your go-to healthy recipes.
- Focus on foods that have longer cooking times first, such as proteins like chicken or fish, whole grains like quinoa or brown rice, and roasted vegetables.
- Prepare staple snacks like washed salad greens, hardboiled eggs, and chopped fruits.

Not only does this practice help you avoid last-minute unhealthy choices, but it also contributes to an overall more nutritionally balanced diet. Prepping in advance provides control over ingredients and portion sizes, which is crucial for weight management.

Next, let's dive into the importance of tracking your food intake. Accountability can often be a missing link in maintaining a healthy diet.

By keeping a record of what you eat, when you eat, and how much, you create a physical reminder of your dietary habits. This can be as simple as jotting down notes in a journal or using one of many available apps that allow you to log your meals.

Tracking serves multiple purposes: it helps identify patterns, keeps you mindful of your nutritional goals, and provides valuable insights if you ever need to adjust your eating habits. When done consistently, it allows you to see beyond the immediate gratification of a meal and understand its impact on your overall health. This practice aligns closely with evidence showing better compliance and outcomes in weight loss and nutrition plans (Eating to Boost Energy, n.d.).

Another key principle is the timing and frequency of your meals. It's not just about what you eat but when you eat. Eating at regular intervals throughout the day can stabilize your blood sugar levels and optimize your metabolism. Aiming for three main meals and two small snacks each day can keep your energy up and prevent overeating during any one meal.

Consider aligning your meal timings with your daily routine. If you start your day early, plan for a substantial breakfast; if you exercise in the evening, ensure you have a balanced dinner that aids recovery. Listen to your body's cues—hungry, full, tired—and adjust accordingly to maintain a steady energy flow.

When it comes to nutrient-dense foods, variety is essential. Incorporate a wide range of foods from all the different food groups to ensure balanced nutrition. Fill your plate with colorful vegetables, lean proteins, whole grains, and healthy fats. Each category offers unique benefits, and together, they cover the spectrum of macro and micronutrients your body needs.

Here are some practical tips to add variety without complexity:

- Rotate your sources of protein. Instead of always eating chicken, try beans, tofu, fish, or lean beef.
- Use different cooking methods. Roast, steam, grill, or stir-fry your vegetables to keep meals exciting.
- Experiment with spices and herbs to enhance flavors without adding extra calories. This also helps reduce dependence on salt and sugar.
- Plan themed meals once a week—like Meatless Mondays or Fish Fridays—to focus on diversity.
- Select seasonal produce to benefit from peak flavors and nutritional value while supporting local agriculture.

Understanding and utilizing these strategies can substantially boost the effectiveness of your diet plan. Now, let's explore some actionable examples that tie everything together.

If you're aiming to increase your protein intake for muscle growth and repair, try incorporating protein-rich snacks throughout the day.

Here's how you can do it:

- Keep a stock of Greek yogurt in the fridge. It's an excellent source of protein and can be paired with fruit or nuts for a satisfying snack.
- Carry a handful of mixed nuts with you. They're portable, don't require refrigeration, and provide both protein and healthy fats.
- Consider making overnight oats with chia seeds and a scoop of protein powder. This way, you'll kickstart your day with a nutritious, protein-packed breakfast.
- Include hardboiled eggs or a slice of turkey breast in your midday snacks. Small yet mighty, these options are easy to prepare and keep your protein levels topped up.

This method ensures you're meeting your protein requirements without feeling overwhelmed by big meals. Moreover, it aligns with the evidence suggesting the role of protein in appetite control and boosting metabolic rate (How Can I Optimize Nutrition). Meal planning can indeed seem daunting initially, but breaking it down into smaller, manageable tasks makes the process smoother.

Here's a step-by-step approach to follow:

- Discuss with your family or household members about the types of foods and favorite meals everyone enjoys. This collective involvement can yield richer ideas and greater acceptance.
- Start a monthly calendar to jot down meal ideas, collect recipes, and list groceries needed.
- Choose a theme or specific meals for different days, like Taco Tuesdays or Whole Grain Wednesdays. This simplifies decision-making and ensures variety.
- Begin small. Aim to prepare dinners for 2-3 days a week initially. As you become comfortable, you can scale up.
- On your designated meal prep day, start with items that take longer to cook and multi-task by preparing other ingredients simultaneously. Cook extra portions that can be stored and labeled for future use.
- Utilize individual containers for storing prepped meals to make on-the-go lunches easier.

By integrating these practices into your routine, you build a sustainable system that supports long-term health goals.

Dieting isn't just about cutting calories or losing weight; it's about creating a lifestyle that promotes balance and nurtures your body. By prepping meals in advance, tracking your intake, timing your meals smartly, and incorporating a variety of nutrient-dense foods, you set yourself up for success. Remember, the aim is to find what works best for you and make adjustments based on empirical evidence and personal observations. After all, every bite is a step towards a healthier you.

Embracing Structured Meal Planning and High Protein Intake

Throughout this chapter, we have delved into the foundational principles of an effective diet plan, highlighting its significant benefits for calorie control, portion management, and overall dietary quality. We began by understanding the importance of structured meal planning as a tool to avoid last-minute unhealthy food choices and to manage portions effectively. Silvia Veri emphasized how planning increases the likelihood of making healthier food choices.

Returning to that central idea, we recognize that preparation and foresight are critical for maintaining a balanced diet. When we plan meals ahead, we gain control over what we consume, which supports not just weight loss but also sustained nutritional habits. This proactive approach can prevent overeating by ensuring proper portion sizes and nutrient-dense meals.

However, it's essential to acknowledge that some readers might find the process of meal planning overwhelming at first. Adapting to a new routine requires time and patience. Therefore, flexibility is crucial. Building a sustainable meal plan means creating a framework that accommodates life's unpredictability without compromising on the core principles of good nutrition.

On a broader scale, adopting these meal-planning strategies could lead to widespread improvements in public health. When individuals make conscious, informed decisions about their diets, it reduces the risk of lifestyle-related diseases such as obesity, diabetes, and heart disease. Moreover, teaching these habits to children can foster a generation that values health and wellness from a young age.

As we wrap up our discussion on the core principles of the diet plan, consider how incorporating variety and nutrient-dense foods into your meals can enhance not only your physical well-being but also your culinary experience. The aim is to find balance—

where nutritious eating becomes a seamless part of your lifestyle rather than a stringent regimen.

With these insights in mind, think about how you can start implementing small changes today. Meal planning doesn't have to be perfect; it should be practical and adaptable to suit your lifestyle. As you embark on this journey, remember that every step towards a well-structured diet is a step towards better health and well-being.

References

Beaumont Health. (n.d.). *Health benefits of meal planning*. Retrieved from https://www.beaumont.org/health-wellness/blogs/health-benefits-of-meal-planning

Academy of Nutrition and Dietetics. (n.d.). *Eating to Boost Energy*. Retrieved from https://www.eatright.org/health/wellness/healthful-habits/eating-to-boost-energy

Rolls, B. J. (2014). *What is the role of portion control in weight management? International Journal of Obesity (2005)*, 38(S1), S1. https://doi.org/10.1038/ijo.2014.82

Harvard College. (2024). *Meal prep guide*. The Nutrition Source. https://nutritionsource.hsph.harvard.edu/meal-prep/

Turning Point. (n.d.). *How can I optimize nutrition?* Retrieved from https://www.turningpointkc.org/programs/resilience-toolbox/nutrition/how-can-i-optimize-nutrition

Ducrot, P., Méjean, C., Aroumougame, V., Ibanez, G., Allès, B., Kesse-Guyot, E., Hercberg, S., & Péneau, S. (2017). *Meal planning is associated with food variety, diet quality, and body weight status in a large sample of French adults. The International Journal of Behavioral Nutrition and Physical Activity*, 14(10). https://doi.org/10.1186/s12966-017-0461-7

Chapter 2
Meal Planning Made Easy

Imagine opening your fridge, and everything you need for the week is right there—planned, prepped, and ready to go. This could transform the way you view mealtimes, turning chaotic last-minute decisions into organized and healthy eating habits. Meal planning can often seem like a daunting task, but with clear guidance and practical tips, it becomes an easily manageable routine. It's all about making smart choices that simplify your life while nourishing your body.

One of the primary challenges people face with meal planning is knowing where to start. Without a structure, it's easy to revert to unhealthy options or repetitive meals that lack nutritional balance. For example, many individuals might find themselves grabbing fast food because they didn't prepare lunch in advance, or they might get bored with the same grilled chicken and steamed vegetables every night. This monotony and lack of preparation can derail even the best intentions, leading to poor eating habits and wasted time and money on last-minute meals.

This chapter aims to demystify meal planning by offering a detailed sample meal plan for a week. It will guide you on how to incorporate a variety of recipes to keep your palate intrigued and satisfied. Additionally, you'll learn valuable tips for crafting low-calorie, high-protein meals that align with your health goals. By the end of this chapter, you'll be equipped with the tools to plan nutritious, delicious meals tailored to fit into your busy schedule, ensuring you stay on track toward achieving a healthier lifestyle.

Sample Meal Plan Overview

Eating healthy, maintaining a balanced diet throughout the week, and achieving one's weight loss goals can seem daunting. However, with a little planning and a clear structure, we can create a meal plan that is not only nutritious but also flexible enough to fit into our busy lives. Let's delve into how we can achieve this balance.

Visualize Your Week

Imagine opening your fridge, and everything you need for the week is right there planned, prepped, and ready to go. That's the beauty of having a detailed meal plan. By structuring breakfast, lunch, dinner, and snacks for each day of the week, you're more likely to stick to your nutritional goals. This approach helps minimize impulsive food choices and ensures a balanced intake of nutrients daily.

From Monday's grilled chicken salad to Sunday's vegetable-stuffed omelet, the variety keeps your taste buds excited without veering off track. Incorporating a broad spectrum of nutrient-rich foods such as lean proteins, whole grains, and vegetables will help maintain balance while keeping your meals interesting. Remember, diversity in food choices is key to obtaining all the essential vitamins and minerals your body needs.

Guidance on Portion Sizes

One crucial aspect of maintaining a balanced diet is understanding portion sizes. You might have heard the saying, "You are what you eat," but it's equally important to add, "You are what you portion." The meal plan should guide readers on appropriate serving sizes for optimal calorie control, making it easier to manage their nutrition effectively.

Here's what you can do to ensure you get the right portions:

- Use smaller plates to help control portion sizes visually.
- Check the label on packaged foods to understand serving sizes.
- Measure portions of high-calorie foods like nuts, seeds, and oils to avoid excess intake.
- When dining out, consider sharing or saving half for later to keep portions in check.

Flexibility in Your Meal Plan

Life is unpredictable, and so should be your meal plan. Flexibility within your meal schedule allows you to adapt to sudden changes without compromising your dietary goals. By incorporating different food choices, you can cater to various tastes and preferences, ensuring you stay motivated and enjoy your meals.

Think about it as an inclusive strategy where you mix things up based on your mood, availability of ingredients, or even trying new recipes. For example, if you had quinoa salad planned for lunch but crave something warm, substituting it with a hearty lentil soup can be refreshing. The key is to swap similar nutrient profiles to maintain balance while exploring new flavors.

Recipe Inspirations

To simplify meal preparation, include recipe suggestions within your meal plan. This makes it easier for readers to follow and prepare the recommended dishes, taking the guesswork out of "What's for dinner?" nights.

Here are some ideas to get you started:

- **Breakfast:** Greek yogurt parfaits layered with fresh berries and granola.
- **Lunch:** A power bowl with mixed greens, chickpeas, roasted sweet potatoes, and tahini dressing.
- **Dinner:** Baked salmon with a side of quinoa and steamed broccoli.

Having these recipes at hand not only streamlines meal prep but also adds enjoyment to the cooking process. Plus, knowing exactly what ingredients you'll need helps with efficient grocery shopping, reducing the likelihood of buying unnecessary items.

Creating Low-Calorie, High-Protein Meals

Balancing calories while ensuring adequate protein intake can be a game-changer for those aiming for weight loss and muscle maintenance.

Here are a few tips for crafting low-calorie, high-protein meals that are both satisfying and delicious:

- Start with lean protein sources such as chicken breast, turkey, fish, tofu, or legumes. These options are relatively low in calories but high in protein.
- Bulk up meals with vegetables. Vegetables are nutrient-dense, low in calories, and high in fiber, which helps keep you full longer.
- Choose whole grains over refined grains. Whole grains like quinoa, brown rice, and farro provide sustained energy and essential nutrients.

- Use healthy fats sparingly. Opt for small amounts of olive oil, avocado, or nuts instead of butter or creamy dressings.

The Harvard T.H. Chan School of Public Health suggests focusing on diet quality and recommends using healthy oils and avoiding trans fats (The President and Fellows of Harvard College, 2012). This principle aligns perfectly with the goal of creating balanced meals that are beneficial for long-term health.

Considerations from Research

Planning a meal involves more than just listing out recipes—it's about making informed choices. Insights from various sources, such as MyPlate and the Mayo Clinic, highlight the importance of balance and portion control. According to MyPlate, aligning your meals with these guidelines ensures a mix of fresh, frozen, and shelf-stable items, minimizing food waste while maximizing nutrition (U.S. Department of Agriculture, 2024).

Similarly, the Mayo Clinic emphasizes the significance of knowing both serving sizes and portion sizes. Understanding these measurements can prevent overeating and aid in creating a meal plan that's both enjoyable and effective for weight management (Mayo Clinic, 2024).

Taking Active Steps

An integral part of any successful meal plan is physical activity. While the focus here is on nutrition, incorporating exercise into your routine plays a crucial role in overall well-being. It complements your dietary efforts, helping you achieve your health goals more efficiently.

Simple activities like walking, biking, or even gardening can make a significant difference. Being active doesn't necessarily mean hitting the gym every day; integrating movement into your daily life is equally beneficial. As the Healthy Eating Plate model suggests, staying active is a cornerstone of maintaining a healthy weight and lifestyle (The President and Fellows of Harvard College, 2012).

Incorporating these elements into a weekly meal plan provides a holistic approach to eating better and living healthier. With careful planning, portion control, flexibility, and recipe inspiration, anyone can follow a balanced diet that fits their lifestyle. Remember, while personal responsibility is vital, having a well-structured safety net, like a guided meal plan, can ease the journey toward reaching your nutritional goals.

Importance of Recipe Diversity

Incorporating diverse recipe options into your meal planning isn't just a luxury; it's a necessity to ensure long-term success and enjoyment in your dietary journey. Sticking to the same set of meals can lead to meal monotony, making it increasingly tempting to stray from your plan. The enthusiasm that comes from trying new recipes and flavors is an unspoken but crucial part of adhering to any diet.

When we experiment with various recipes, we naturally encourage ourselves to step out of our comfort zones. The variety not only keeps us engaged but also introduces us to new ingredients and cooking methods. This sort of culinary creativity can be incredibly rewarding. For instance, you might discover a love for quinoa or find that roasting vegetables brings out flavors you never knew existed. Exploring these avenues fosters a positive relationship with food, making your diet a source of joy rather than a chore.

Moreover, diverse recipes don't just benefit your taste buds—they can also improve your nutritional intake. Different ingredients bring different nutrients to the table, ensuring that your body gets a wide range of essential vitamins and minerals. A colorful plate filled with a variety of foods often reflects a nutrient-rich meal.

It's one thing to talk about the importance of recipe diversity, but where should one turn for inspiration? Practical sources include cookbooks, online resources such as food blogs and recipe websites, and even cooking classes, which provide hands-on experience. These resources offer not just recipes but also tips and techniques that can be applied to other dishes.

Here is what you can do to find new recipe inspirations:

- Start by exploring cookbooks dedicated to specific diets or cuisines. These are often tailored to provide balanced meals and can introduce you to authentic flavors and cooking methods.
- Utilize online resources, including food blogs and recipe sites, which frequently update their content and provide seasonal and trendy recipe ideas.

- Attend cooking classes either in-person or online. These classes often cover foundational cooking techniques and help build your confidence in the kitchen.

However, I understand that while searching for new recipes is exciting, the real challenge lies in creating meals that balance flavor with nutritional value. Low-calorie, high-protein meals are particularly beneficial for those looking to manage their weight without feeling deprived. High-protein foods can keep you full longer, reducing the temptation for unhealthy snacking.

To craft such meals, start by focusing on lean protein sources. Think chicken breast, turkey, fish, tofu, and legumes like lentils and chickpeas. These should form the core of your dish. Complement that with plenty of vegetables, which are low in calories but high in volume and nutrients, helping to create a satisfying meal. Don't forget whole grains such as quinoa, brown rice, and barley, which offer additional fiber and nutrients.

Here's how you can create low-calorie, high-protein meals:

- Choose lean proteins like chicken breast, turkey, fish, tofu, and legumes.
- Load up on vegetables—these should take up half your plate. Aim for a variety of colors to maximize nutrients.
- Incorporate whole grains like quinoa, brown rice, and barley for added fiber and nutrients. Whole grains digest slowly, keeping you full longer.
- Use herbs and spices to enhance flavor without adding extra calories. Fresh herbs like cilantro, basil, and parsley, along with spices such as cumin, paprika, and turmeric, can elevate your dish.
- Keep portion sizes in check. Even healthy foods can contribute to weight gain if consumed in large quantities.

For example, consider a meal of grilled chicken breast served over a bed of mixed greens with a quinoa side salad. Top the salad with diced tomatoes, cucumbers, and a light vinaigrette made from olive oil and lemon juice. Not only is this meal visually appealing, but it's also packed with protein, fiber, and essential nutrients.

A practical strategy for ensuring adherence to these principles is meal prepping. Dedicate a few hours each week to preparing components of your meals in advance. Cook batches of proteins, chop vegetables, and portion out grains. Refrigerate these items in separate containers so assembling a balanced meal is quick and easy, even on your busiest days. This approach can save time and reduce the daily burden of meal preparation, making it easier to stick to your dietary goals.

Diverse recipes can certainly keep the spark alive in your culinary routine. They inspire and challenge you to push your boundaries in the kitchen, transforming meal prep from a mundane task into an exciting venture. Moreover, investing time to seek out new and varied dishes pays off by diversifying your palate and improving your overall nutrition. Even when life gets hectic, knowing that you have a repertoire of flavorful, nutritious meals at your fingertips can provide both comfort and motivation.

Balancing low-calorie and high-protein meals with great taste is far from impossible. It requires a little planning, a willingness to explore new recipes, and a focus on simple, wholesome ingredients. By leveraging a mix of reliable cookbooks, readily accessible online resources, and insightful cooking classes, you'll find yourself not only adhering to your diet but also thoroughly enjoying the process. Detoxing the notion of dieting from deprivation and embracing it as a flavorful, nourishing lifestyle change makes all the difference.

Achieving Enjoyable and Sustainable Healthy Eating

In this chapter, we've explored a comprehensive approach to simplifying meal planning by offering a sample meal plan for a week. We've emphasized the significance of incorporating diverse recipes to keep meals interesting and discussed essential tips for crafting low-calorie, high-protein dishes. Our goal has been to make healthy eating not only manageable but enjoyable.

Returning to our initial vision of a well-organized refrigerator, ready with all the essentials for the week, it's clear that planning ahead can transform the often-cumbersome task of cooking into an efficient and more pleasurable routine. Structuring your week with planned breakfasts, lunches, dinners, and snacks helps maintain nutritional balance and minimizes impulsive, less healthy food choices.

While we've provided detailed guidance on portion sizes and offered flexible options within meal plans, it's paramount to remember that flexibility should be balanced with discipline. Being adaptable doesn't mean deviating from your goals; instead, it means finding nutritious substitutions that align with your dietary objectives. For instance, swapping quinoa salad for lentil soup keeps the nutrient profile similar while catering to your cravings.

We also delved into the importance of recipe diversity in maintaining enthusiasm and adherence to your meal plan. Exploring various recipes from different cuisines enhances not just flavor but also nutrition, ensuring you receive a broad spectrum of vitamins and minerals. This culinary creativity can turn meal prep from a mundane task into an exciting experience, helping you to embrace your diet as a lifestyle rather than a temporary regimen.

One area of concern might be feeling overwhelmed by the notion of constantly seeking new recipes and balancing nutritional needs. However, utilizing accessible resources like cookbooks, food blogs, and cooking classes can ease this process, providing continual inspiration and practical cooking techniques.

Ultimately, the wider consequence of adopting these practices is cultivating a sustainable, healthy relationship with food—one that supports long-term weight management and overall well-being. Moreover, when coupled with regular physical activity, such as walking or gardening, the benefits are amplified, contributing significantly to your health goals.

As you move forward, consider this journey towards mindful meal planning and diverse eating habits an ongoing adventure. Embrace the process of discovering new flavors and techniques, allowing your diet to reflect not only your nutritional needs but also your personal tastes and lifestyle. Remember, the path to a healthier you is paved with both structured planning and an open mind toward culinary exploration.

References

Cheney, A. M., McCarthy, W. J., Pozar, M., Reaves, C., Ortiz, G., Lopez, D., Saldivar, P. A., & Gelberg, L. (2023). *Ancestral recipes: a mixed-methods analysis of MyPlate-based recipe dissemination for Latinos in rural communities. BMC Public Health*, 23(1), 1-15. https://doi.org/10.1186/s12889-022-14804-3

Sijangga, M. O., Pack, D. V., Yokota, N. O., Vien, M. H., Dryland, A. D. G., & Ivey, S. L. (2023). *Culturally-tailored cookbook for promoting positive dietary change among hypertensive Filipino Americans: a pilot study. Frontiers in Nutrition*, 10(10), Article 1114919. https://doi.org/10.3389/fnut.2023.1114919

MyPlate. (n.d.). *Make a plan.* [Webpage]. Retrieved from https://www.myplate.gov/eat-healthy/healthy-eating-budget/make-plan

Ducrot, P., Méjean, C., Aroumougame, V., Ibanez, G., Allès, B., Kesse-Guyot, E., Hercberg, S., & Péneau, S. (2017). *Meal planning is associated with food variety, diet quality, and body weight status in a large sample of French adults. The International Journal of Behavioral Nutrition and Physical Activity*, 14(1), 1-10. https://doi.org/10.1186/s12966-017-0461-7

Harvard T.H. Chan School of Public Health. (2024). *Healthy Eating Plate.* Retrieved from https://nutritionsource.hsph.harvard.edu/healthy-eating-plate/

Mayo Clinic. (2024). *Healthy meals start with planning.* Healthy Lifestyle of Nutrition and Healthy Eating. Retrieved from https://www.mayoclinic.org/healthy-lifestyle/nutrition-and-healthy-eating/in-depth/healthy-meals/art-20546806

Chapter 3
The Role of Exercise in Weight Loss

Picture a journey where every step, lift, and stretch you take isn't just a movement but a decisive stride toward a healthier, more vibrant you. Imagine harnessing the power within your own body to shed unwanted weight while simultaneously boosting your health. This is the transformative potential of incorporating exercise into your daily routine. Whether you're a fitness novice or a seasoned athlete, understanding the multifaceted role of physical activity in weight loss can revolutionize your approach to a healthier lifestyle.

Many embark on their weight loss journeys focusing predominantly on dietary changes, often overlooking the crucial role that exercise plays. Consider the individual who meticulously counts calories yet finds their progress stagnating. Without integrating consistent physical activity, the metabolism remains sluggish, burning fewer calories than it could be.

Take John, for instance. Despite adhering rigorously to a strict diet, his weight plateaued. It wasn't until he added regular aerobic and strength training exercises to his regime that he witnessed notable improvements. Exercise increases muscle mass, boosts metabolic rate, and burns more calories even at rest. These elements, often neglected, are vital for effective weight loss. More importantly, a sedentary lifestyle also brings with it risks such as cardiovascular disease, diabetes, and joint problems.

In this chapter, we delve deep into the various types of exercises that can amplify your weight loss efforts and enhance overall health. We will explore the benefits of aerobic activities like jogging and swimming, which ramp up calorie burn and improve heart health. You'll discover the remarkable impact of strength training in building lean muscle mass and increasing your resting metabolic rate.

Furthermore, we'll unravel the secrets behind High-Intensity Interval Training (HIIT), known for its efficiency in burning fat and improving endurance. Finally, we will discuss the often-overlooked importance of flexibility exercises, ensuring your body remains agile, strong, and less prone to injuries. By the end of this read, you'll be equipped with practical insights and strategies to seamlessly integrate these exercises into your routine, forging a path to sustainable weight loss and improved well-being.

The Fitness Trainer's Guide to Effective Exercises

I had the opportunity to sit in on a discussion led by our fitness trainer, and it was incredible to see how various types of exercises can seamlessly integrate into a diet plan for effective weight loss and overall health improvement.

We began by diving into aerobic exercises like jogging, cycling, and swimming. These activities are particularly powerful because they boost your metabolism. Think about them as the engine of your car: the faster and more efficiently it runs, the better it is for overall performance. Studies consistently show that regular aerobic exercise helps you burn calories more efficiently, leading to fat loss over time (Short Bursts of Activity Can Have Huge Health Benefits, 2023). The beauty of aerobic exercises lies in their versatility, whether you're taking a leisurely bike ride or an intense swim, you're contributing to your body's ability to metabolize food more effectively.

Next, we shifted our focus to strength training exercises. Now, if you've ever wondered why some people seem to have "cut" physiques without necessarily being thin, this is where strength training comes into play. Building lean muscle mass through exercises like weightlifting or bodyweight movements doesn't just make you stronger; it also revs up your overall calorie expenditure.

Muscle tissue requires more energy to maintain than fat tissue, so the more muscle you have, the more calories you burn at rest. This isn't just theory—numerous studies back this up, showing significant metabolic advantages for those who incorporate strength training into their routine. The takeaway here? Don't shy away from picking up those weights; your muscles will thank you.

Then came an exciting exploration of High-Intensity Interval Training (HIIT). HIIT is all about pushing your limits in short bursts, followed by brief recovery periods.

Many might find the idea of high-intensity workouts intimidating, but here's where the data speaks volumes. Research reveals that HIIT can be more effective at reducing abdominal fat compared to moderate-intensity continuous training (The President and Fellows of Harvard College, 2021).

The reason behind this is fascinating—the high intensities achieved during HIIT release hormones like epinephrine and growth hormone, which promote fat breakdown. A practical point here: even if you have a busy schedule, HIIT allows you to achieve substantial fitness gains in less time, making it a highly efficient workout option.

However, perhaps the most often overlooked yet crucial type of exercise is flexibility training. Mobility is key to a well-functioning body. Without adequate flexibility, our risk of injury increases, hindering our progress in other physical activities. Flexibility exercises such as stretching, yoga, or Pilates help keep your joints and muscles supple, which can significantly improve your overall range of motion.

Here is what you can do to improve your flexibility:

- Start with gentle static stretches, holding each stretch for at least 30 seconds.
- Incorporate dynamic stretches like leg swings before your aerobic or strength training sessions.
- Practice yoga poses that target multiple muscle groups, focusing on deep, controlled breaths.
- Make use of tools like foam rollers to release tight spots and enhance muscle recovery.

By following these steps, you'll find that not only does your flexibility improve, but your performance in other exercise forms is enhanced as well. One of the critical takeaways from the session was the synergistic relationship between exercise and diet plans. The Fitness Trainer emphasized that combining these elements produces far better results than focusing on in isolation.

For instance, while a balanced diet provides the essential nutrients needed for energy and muscle repair, exercise strengthens the body's capacity to utilize these nutrients efficiently, supporting weight loss and overall wellness.

Throughout the discussion, there was a consistent theme: balance. A balanced approach to incorporating both cardio and strength workouts, mixed with flexibility exercises, offers a comprehensive pathway to achieving weight loss and improving health.

It's not about choosing one form of exercise over another but understanding how they complement each other.

Anecdotes shared during the session further highlighted the personal experiences of individuals who had successfully integrated these principles. For example, one participant mentioned how initially daunting HIIT seemed but soon grew to appreciate its effectiveness after seeing significant improvements in endurance and reductions in visceral fat. Another individual noted how adding simple flexibility exercises to their daily routine dramatically reduced their incidence of exercise-related injuries and improved their overall workout performance.

The science is clear, and the evidence supports adopting a variety of exercise modalities to bolster your diet plan. By engaging in aerobics, strength training, HIIT, and flexibility exercises, you create a robust framework for not just losing weight but enhancing overall health. Such an approach ensures that while you shed pounds, you also build a resilient, versatile, and injury-resistant body.

It's quite inspiring when you realize that small adjustments, like adding a HIIT session twice a week or incorporating daily stretching routines, can drastically alter your fitness trajectory. And it's comforting to know that, armed with empirical evidence and straightforward guidelines, anyone can embark on this journey toward better health and well-being.

In concluding that eventful session, the Fitness Trainer reinforced that the secret to success lies in consistency and personalization. Each person's body responds differently to various exercises, and the best outcomes are achieved when one listens to their body and adjusts their routines accordingly. Employing a flexible mindset and staying informed through evidence-based practices will pave the way for sustainable weight loss and lifelong health benefits.

So, lace up those sneakers, grab those dumbbells, and roll out the yoga mat. Your path to a healthier, fitter you start with a balanced, well-informed approach that integrates the best of aerobics, strength, high-intensity, and flexibility training.

Personalizing Your Exercise Routine

One of the most foundational aspects of developing a personalized exercise routine is creating a weekly exercise schedule that strikes a balance between aerobic, strength, and flexibility exercises. This blend not only maximizes benefits but also keeps you engaged and prevents burnout.

Here's what you can do to create an effective schedule:

- Begin by assessing your current fitness level. Understanding where you stand helps you tailor your plan appropriately.
- Integrate aerobic activities like brisk walking, running, cycling, or swimming at least three to five times per week. These activities enhance cardiovascular health and aid in weight loss by increasing calorie burn.
- Include strength training exercises two to three times per week. This could involve lifting weights, using resistance bands, or performing bodyweight exercises like push-ups and squats. Building muscle boosts your metabolism, aiding in consistent weight management.
- Incorporate flexibility exercises such as yoga or Pilates into your routine at least twice a week. These help in maintaining mobility, preventing injuries, and promoting relaxation.

Another critical component is setting specific workout goals and tracking your progress to stay motivated and consistent. Laying down clear objectives gives you something tangible to work towards, making each workout session purposeful and rewarding.

To set and achieve your workout goals:

- Define both short-term and long-term targets. For instance, aim to increase your running distance gradually over weeks for a long-term goal, while a short-term goal might be able to complete a certain number of push-ups.
- Use tools like fitness apps or journals to monitor your progress. Documenting your workouts, noting how far you've come, and recognizing improvements can be incredibly motivating.
- Adjust your goals as needed. If you find that a particular target is too easy or too challenging, don't be afraid to tweak it. The key is to keep pushing yourself just enough to see continued progress without getting discouraged.

Gradually increasing exercise intensity and duration is essential to avoid plateaus. When you start noticing diminished returns from your usual routine, it's a sign that your body has adapted to the stress levels. Gently pushing boundaries ensures continual improvement.

Incorporating cross-training activities brings variety and enhances overall results. Cross-training involves participating in different forms of exercise rather than focusing solely on one type. This approach offers numerous benefits, including reducing the risk of injury, improving overall fitness, and keeping things fresh and exciting.

Here are some cross-training practices you can adopt:

- Mix up cardio with activities like dancing, rowing, or hiking. Each activity uses muscles differently and contributes to a well-rounded fitness regimen.
- Join group classes that offer different routines, such as Spinning, Zumba, or boot camps. These classes often combine various elements of fitness, providing an all-in-one solution.
- Participate in seasonal sports like skiing, swimming, or cycling. Not only does this keep your regime interesting, but it also utilizes different muscle groups, offering a comprehensive workout.

By customizing exercise routines tailored to your individual needs and preferences, you optimize your weight loss journey. Personalized plans ensure that exercises resonate with you both physically and mentally, which maximizes adherence and long-term benefits. As a result, achieving your fitness goals becomes more attainable and enjoyable. Understanding the nuances of creating a personalized exercise routine isn't just about knowledge—it's about implementation. Let's take a closer look at how you can put these guidelines into practice effectively.

First, stepping beyond general recommendations enables the crafting of a plan as unique as you are. Start small by integrating elements that fit seamlessly into your daily life. For example, if you have a busy work schedule, opt for shorter, high-intensity interval training (HIIT) sessions that deliver maximum impact within limited timeframes. Physical activity should enhance your lifestyle, not become a cumbersome addition.

Next, prioritize consistency over perfection. It's better to engage in regular moderate exercise than sporadic intense workouts. The cumulative effect of consistent effort leads to more sustainable results. Daily habits such as taking the stairs instead of the elevator or walking during lunch breaks can significantly contribute to your fitness without requiring dedicated workout slots.

Tracking progress is where science meets motivation. Utilize technology to your advantage—wearable devices and apps can provide real-time feedback on your activity levels, heart rate, and even sleep patterns, helping you refine your routine based on hard data. Remember, every step forward, no matter how small, is progress worth celebrating.

It's also important to listen to your body. Personalization doesn't mean rigid adherence. If you're feeling fatigued or notice persistent soreness, allowing for rest and recovery can prevent overtraining and its associated risks. Sometimes, the most productive choice is a day off or a gentle stretching session.

Moreover, social connections can amplify success rates. Invite friends or family members to join you in physical activities. Exercising with others not only makes it more enjoyable but also adds an element of accountability. Group dynamics can be highly motivating and drive you to stick with your commitments.

Lastly, never underestimate the power of expert guidance. While home workouts and self-designed programs are beneficial, consulting with professionals can offer insights tailored specifically to you. A personal trainer, physiotherapist, or nutritionist can provide custom advice and adjustments as you progress, ensuring that every aspect of your fitness journey is optimized for your individual needs.

The road to improved health through diet and exercise is certainly paved with effort, dedication, and strategic planning. Yet, it's these very components, when aligned correctly, that make the journey rewarding and sustainable. Personalized exercise routines are not a one-size-fits-all solution; they require attention to detail and adaptability. However, the payoff—a healthier, more energetic, and resilient you—is undoubtedly worth the investment.

Through empirical evidence and practical application, it's clear that integrating physical activity into a weight loss plan isn't merely beneficial; it's essential. It fosters not just a healthier body but a more robust, adaptable mind, ready to embrace challenges and celebrate achievements. So, let's lace up those shoes, set clear, achievable goals, and embark on this journey with confidence and enthusiasm. Your future self will thank you.

Staying Active Throughout the Day

Incorporating physical activity into your daily routine can significantly enhance the effectiveness of your diet plan for weight loss and overall health improvement. This chapter focuses on the often overlooked but vital aspect of staying active throughout the day to complement a structured diet and exercise regimen. By diving deeper into the concept of Non-Exercise Activity Thermogenesis (NEAT), we discover simple yet impactful ways to keep moving, boost our metabolism, and improve our well-being.

NEAT refers to all the calories burned through daily activities that are not planned exercises - think of every fidget, every step taken to the coffee machine, or even the energy spent standing while working. Dr. James Levine from the Mayo Clinic, who pioneered research in this area, pointed out that NEAT captures "the low-effort movements that you string together over the course of your day" (Stone, 2023). This means that even mundane activities like household chores or strolling through the grocery store contribute to your daily calorie expenditure more than one might expect.

To maximize the benefits of NEAT, it's crucial to break up long periods of sedentary behavior. Sedentary lifestyles have been linked to metabolic issues and energy slumps, leading to decreased productivity and increased fatigue. Regular movement breaks can counteract these effects.

Here is what you can do to integrate movement breaks effectively:

- Stand up and stretch every hour. It gets the blood flowing and helps prevent stiffness.
- Take phone calls standing up or pacing around. This small change can make a big difference.
- Incorporate micro-workouts, such as a few squats or desk push-ups, throughout your workday.
- Opt for a walk during lunch breaks or even while brainstorming ideas – some of the best thoughts come while moving.

Integrating physical activity into your daily routine doesn't mean you have to hit the gym every day. Small changes can lead to significant improvements in your health and potentially aid in weight loss. For instance, choosing the stairs over the elevator can burn more calories and strengthen your leg muscles. When I started taking the stairs instead of the elevator, it wasn't just about burning a few extra calories; it was also a refreshing mental break that energized my afternoons.

Here's how you can seamlessly incorporate more physical activity into your routine:

- Park your car further away from the entrance to increase your walking distance.

- Choose walking or cycling for short trips instead of driving.
- Use household chores like vacuuming, gardening, or cleaning as opportunities to move more.
- If you use public transport, get off one stop early and walk the rest of the way.
- Turn TV commercial breaks into mini-exercise sessions – a few jumping jacks or stretches can go a long way.

These incremental adjustments can collectively contribute to substantial caloric burn, enhancing your overall energy expenditure. It's essential to understand that planned exercise sessions—like going to the gym or running—are only part of the equation. A holistic approach to weight loss and health improvement includes both scheduled workouts and spontaneous physical activities.

The benefits of integrating NEAT into your daily life extend beyond weight management. A study by Colleen Novak at Kent State University found that NEAT plays a significant role in maintaining metabolic health (Birkenfeld et al., 2022). Regularly engaging in low-intensity activities helps regulate glucose levels, supports cardiovascular health, and improves mental well-being. The same study highlighted how people with similar body sizes could have dramatically different levels of NEAT due to their occupations, living environments, and personal habits. This variability underscores the potential for everyone to find unique ways to increase their daily movement.

For those who struggle to carve out time for formal exercise routines, focusing on boosting NEAT can be a game-changer. As exercise physiologist Seth Creasy points out, "Sometimes it's hard to carve out 30 to 60 minutes of your day to do an exercise routine. These little behaviors can accumulate and end up comprising a lot of energy expenditure" (Stone, 2023). Therefore, finding joy in small, daily movements can add up to a healthier lifestyle without feeling like a chore.

Ultimately, the key takeaway is that continuous activity is integral to any effective weight loss and health improvement strategy. By embracing both planned exercise sessions and spontaneous movements, individuals can enhance their weight loss results, boost their metabolism, and improve overall well-being within the framework of a diet plan. This holistic approach ensures that you're not only losing weight but also fostering long-term health and vitality.

So, whether it's parking farther away, taking the stairs, or walking during lunch breaks, every bit of movement counts. Embrace the small changes and watch how they transform your fitness journey, making it both enjoyable and sustainable. Remember, the power of NEAT lies in its accessibility to everyone—you don't need special equipment or a dedicated time slot, just a willingness to move more and sit less. Let's celebrate those everyday moments of movement—they are the unsung heroes in our quest for better health.

Integrating Physical Activity for a Holistic Weight Loss Plan

In wrapping up our exploration of incorporating physical activity into a diet plan for weight loss and overall health improvement, several key insights have emerged. We've delved into the myriad benefits of various exercise forms—such as aerobic activities, strength training, High-Intensity Interval Training (HIIT), and flexibility exercises—and how each contributes uniquely to improving metabolism, building muscle, and preventing injuries. The session highlighted that achieving optimal results lies not in choosing one type of exercise over another but in maintaining a balanced and varied approach.

Reflecting on the discussion with our fitness trainer, it's clear that combining exercise with a balanced diet is essential for effective weight loss and overall wellness. The trainer emphasized the importance of personalization and consistency, reminding us that the journey toward better health is unique for everyone. By customizing routines that fit our lifestyles and needs, we enhance our ability to stick with them, ensuring long-term success.

One concern that readers may have is the challenge of integrating these various forms of exercise into already busy schedules. Many people find it daunting to carve out time for workouts amidst their daily responsibilities. However, as we've learned, even small changes, such as introducing short HIIT sessions or incorporating daily stretching routines, can significantly impact your fitness journey without requiring substantial time commitments.

On a broader scale, adopting a holistic approach to physical activity and diet can transform public health. Encouraging a shift towards active lifestyles can potentially reduce the prevalence of obesity-related conditions like diabetes and cardiovascular diseases. Moreover, emphasizing flexibility and consistency can cultivate a culture that values well-being and self-care, ultimately leading to healthier communities.

As we conclude this chapter, consider the enduring value of integrating different types of physical activities into your routine. It's not merely about losing weight but fostering a resilient, adaptable, and injury-resistant body. So, embrace the variety, listen to your body, and stay consistent. Your journey to a healthier, fitter you is just beginning, and the steps you take now will pave the way for lasting well-being. Take those strides with intention and relish the process of becoming your best self.

References

Maclin, C. (n.d.). *How to create a workout plan for your fitness goals. Piedmont Living Real Change*. Retrieved from https://www.piedmont.org/living-real-change/how-to-create-a-workout-plan-for-your-fitness-goals

Harvard T.H. Chan School of Public Health. (2021). *HIIT (High Intensity Interval Training). The Nutrition Source*. https://nutritionsource.hsph.harvard.edu/high-intensity-interval-training/

Atakan, M. M., Li, Y., Koşar, Ş. N., Turnagöl, H. H., & Yan, X. (2021). *Evidence-Based Effects of High-Intensity Interval Training on Exercise Capacity and Health: A Review with Historical Perspective. International Journal of Environmental Research and Public Health*, 18(13), 7201. https://doi.org/10.3390/ijerph18137201

Chung, N., Park, M., Kim, J., Park, H., Hwang, H., Lee, C., Han, J., So, J., Park, J., & Lim, K. (2018). *Non-exercise activity thermogenesis (NEAT): a component of total daily energy expenditure. Journal of Exercise Nutrition & Biochemistry*, 22(2), 23. https://doi.org/10.20463/jenb.2018.0013

Elsesser, J. (n.d.). *Program Design for Weight Loss. HubSpot*. Retrieved from https://blog.nasm.org/certified-personal-trainer/program-design-weight-loss

University Hospitals. (2023). *Short Bursts of Activity Can Have Huge Health Benefits*. Retrieved from https://www.uhhospitals.org/blog/articles/2023/04/short-bursts-of-activity-can-have-huge-health-benefits

Stone, W. (2023). *How to get healthier without going to the gym. Shots - Health News*. https://www.npr.org/sections/health-shots/2023/07/22/1189303227/neat-fitness-non-exercise-activity-thermogenesis

National Institutes of Health. (2020). *Personalized Exercise?. NIH News in Health*. Retrieved from https://newsinhealth.nih.gov/2020/07/personalized-exercise

von Loeffelholz, C., & Birkenfeld, A. L. (2022). *Non-Exercise Activity Thermogenesis in Human Energy Homeostasis. Endotext*. https://doi.org/10.25905303

Chapter 4
Understanding Macronutrients

O ur bodies are complex machines, and much like any well-oiled system, they need the right kind of fuel to function optimally. This fuel comes from the foods we eat, specifically from macronutrients: carbohydrates, proteins, and fats. Each plays a critical role in our overall health and is essential for various bodily functions. But with so much conflicting information out there about what we should and shouldn't eat, it can be challenging to understand how best to incorporate these nutrients into our diet.

Consider the mixed messages surrounding carbohydrates. They are often blamed for weight gain and energy crashes, leading some people to avoid them altogether. However, carbohydrates are the primary source of energy for our bodies, breaking down into glucose that fuels activities ranging from mental tasks to physical exercise.

Choosing the right types of carbohydrates—such as those found in whole grains, fruits, and vegetables—is crucial. These provide a slow release of energy, keeping blood sugar levels stable and supporting brain function. Conversely, consuming too many simple carbs, like sugary snacks, can lead to spikes and crashes in energy levels, contributing to fatigue and hunger.

This chapter will explore the nuances of macronutrients, including how carbohydrates, proteins, and fats each contribute to your health and wellbeing. We'll delve into the roles they play within the body, offer practical examples of balanced meals, and discuss the importance of maintaining the right proportions of these nutrients. By understanding the science behind macronutrients and learning how to make informed food choices, you can craft a diet that supports your weight loss goals and enhances your overall health.

Role of Carbohydrates and Protein

Carbohydrates often get a bad rep in popular diets, but it's crucial to understand their pivotal role as our body's primary energy source. When you eat carbohydrates, your body breaks them down into glucose, which is then used for energy by your cells, tissues, and organs. This process is especially important for brain function and during physical activity.

However, here's where balance comes into play. Consuming carbohydrates in excess can lead to weight gain, blood sugar spikes, and subsequent crashes that leave you feeling tired and hungry soon after eating. On the other hand, completely cutting them out can result in a lack of energy and difficulty concentrating. The key is moderation and choosing the right kind of carbohydrates—those that are unrefined and packed with nutrients like whole grains, fruits, and vegetables. They provide a steady release of glucose into the bloodstream, keeping your energy levels stable throughout the day (Lecovin, n.d.).

Imagine starting your day with a bowl of oatmeal topped with fresh berries and a handful of nuts. This meal provides complex carbohydrates, fiber, vitamins, and minerals, ensuring you kickstart your day with sustained energy without the rapid spike and crash associated with sugary cereals.

Moving on to protein, it plays a vital role in muscle repair and growth. Proteins are made up of amino acids, which are essential for building and repairing tissues, including muscles. After engaging in physical activity, particularly strength training, our muscle fibers undergo micro-tears, and protein is essential for the repair and growth of these muscles. Additionally, protein promotes satiety, meaning it helps you feel full longer, which can be incredibly beneficial for weight management (Fernández-Lázaro et al., 2021).

For instance, incorporating lean proteins such as chicken breast, fish, legumes, or tofu into your meals can significantly boost your muscle recovery process. A post-workout snack might include a smoothie made with Greek yogurt, spinach, a banana, and a scoop of protein powder. The combination of carbohydrates from the banana and protein from the yogurt and powder helps replenish glycogen stores and kickstarts the muscle repair process.

In the broader context of macronutrients, understanding how they impact your energy levels, metabolism, and overall health within your diet plan is fundamental. Carbohydrates, as mentioned, provide immediate and short-term energy. Proteins, apart from their role in muscle repair, also contribute to various bodily functions such as enzyme production and hormone regulation. Fats, while often vilified, are crucial for maintaining cell membrane integrity, assisting in the absorption of fat-soluble vitamins, and providing long-term energy storage.

To illustrate this balance, let's consider the impact of fats on our diet. Healthy fats, like those found in avocados, nuts, seeds, and olive oil, support heart health and help reduce inflammation. They should be consumed in moderation, similar to carbohydrates and proteins, to avoid adverse effects like weight gain. But when included appropriately, they make meals more satisfying and nutritious.

Practical examples of balanced meals that focus on the right proportion of macronutrients to support weight loss and muscle preservation:

- Incorporate a mix of protein, healthy fats, and complex carbohydrates in each meal. For breakfast, try an omelet with spinach, tomatoes, and avocado paired with a slice of whole-grain toast. This provides a good balance of carbs for energy, protein for muscle maintenance, and fats for satiety.
- For lunch, consider a quinoa salad mixed with chickpeas, cucumbers, cherry tomatoes, olive oil, and a splash of lemon juice. Quinoa offers complete protein, chickpeas add additional protein and fiber, and the veggies contribute essential vitamins and minerals, while olive oil provides healthy fats.
- Dinner could feature grilled salmon, steamed broccoli, and sweet potatoes. Salmon is rich in omega-3 fatty acids, beneficial for heart health, while sweet potatoes offer complex carbs and broccoli adds fiber and antioxidants.

Understanding macronutrients goes beyond just knowing their roles; it empowers you to make informed food choices. By being mindful of what you consume and how it affects your body, you can take better control of your nutrition and overall well-being. Macronutrients don't work in isolation—they interact and complement each other to optimize your health. For example, combining protein and carbohydrates in your post-workout meal not only aids in muscle recovery but also ensures that your energy stores are replenished efficiently.

In conclusion, achieving a balanced diet that includes the right proportion of carbohydrates, proteins, and fats is essential for both weight loss and muscle preservation. By focusing on nutrient-dense sources of these macronutrients and consuming them in appropriate amounts, you create a diet plan that supports your health goals sustainably. Remember to listen to your body, pay attention to how different foods make you feel, and adjust your diet accordingly. This approach will help you build a healthier relationship with food and promote long-term wellness.

Functions of Macronutrients

Let's begin by understanding the three primary macronutrients: carbohydrates, proteins, and fats. Each plays a distinct and crucial role in maintaining our bodies' complex systems.

Carbohydrates are often talked about with mixed feelings—some see them as essential, while others view them cautiously. Carbohydrates are our body's main source of energy. They break down into glucose, which fuels activities ranging from mundane tasks to vigorous exercise. Interestingly, different types of carbohydrates affect our bodies differently. Simple carbohydrates like those found in fruits and sweets are digested quickly, providing immediate energy. On the other hand, complex carbohydrates like whole grains and legumes digest slowly, providing sustained energy.

Glucose is especially vital for brain function. The brain relies heavily on glucose for its energy needs, making carbohydrates not just essential for physical activity but also for cognitive functions. According to Lindsey Wohlford, a wellness dietitian at MD Anderson Cancer Center, 45-65% of our daily caloric intake should come from carbohydrates (Alexander, 2020). This range can vary based on one's health goals and medical conditions, emphasizing that a one-size-fits-all approach doesn't work here.

Proteins are another cornerstone macronutrient, offering multiple roles within the body. Proteins comprise structures such as muscles, skin, nails, and organs. When you hear about amino acids—the building blocks of proteins—they play a critical part in metabolic, hormonal, and enzymatic systems. A diet deficient in protein can lead to muscle loss, weakened immune response, and general fatigue.

The Recommended Dietary Allowance for protein is approximately 0.8 grams per kilogram of body weight per day (Alexander, 2020). For someone weighing around 150 pounds, this equates to roughly 54 grams of protein daily. It's worth noting that these needs may increase based on factors like age, physical activity, and specific health conditions. Protein sources can be animal-based, such as meat, fish, and eggs, or plant-based, like beans, lentils, and tofu. Both sources have their own benefits and drawbacks, so an evidence-driven approach would suggest a balanced mix.

Fats often get a bad rap, but they are indispensable. They serve as long-term energy reserves, help absorb fat-soluble vitamins (A, D, E, K), cushion vital organs, and maintain cell membrane integrity. There are different types of fats—saturated, unsaturated, and trans fats. Unsaturated fats, found in plants and fish, are generally considered healthy and can even reduce the risk of heart disease. Saturated fats, predominantly sourced from animal products, should be consumed in moderation. Trans fats, often found in processed foods, should ideally be avoided altogether.

About 20-35% of our daily caloric intake should come from fats, with less than 10% from saturated fats (Alexander, 2020). These recommendations underscore why it's critical to understand not all fats are created equal.

Dietary guidelines advise filling two-thirds of your plate with whole grains, vegetables, fruits, nuts, and seeds while reserving the remaining one-third for lean proteins like chicken or fish and plant proteins like quinoa or beans (Alexander, 2020). Incorporating a variety of foods ensures you get a broad spectrum of nutrients.

Now, let's delve into how macronutrient balance affects health and weight management. Balancing macronutrients isn't merely about hitting daily quotas; it's about finding what works best for your body's unique needs.

One practical guideline for tailoring your diet based on individual needs involves calculating your caloric requirements. First, determine your Basal Metabolic Rate (BMR)—the number of calories your body needs at rest.

You can then adjust this number based on activity level, age, and weight goals:

- Use an online BMR calculator or consult a dietitian to find your BMR.
- Calculate your Total Daily Energy Expenditure (TDEE) by multiplying your BMR by an activity factor (e.g., sedentary, lightly active, very active).
- Adjust your caloric intake to match weight goals—consume fewer calories than your TDEE for weight loss or more for weight gain.

While tracking macros can sound tedious, modern tools make it easier. Apps like MyFitnessPal allow you to log your food intake and keep track of the balance between carbohydrates, proteins, and fats. Monitoring your diet can reveal if you're consistently over or under-consuming certain macronutrients, giving you valuable insight for adjustments.

Next, let's discuss strategies for adjusting caloric intake based on progress. Plateaus in weight loss are common and can be discouraging. Your body naturally adapts to new lower weights by reducing its metabolic rate.

Here's how to navigate this challenge:

- Periodically reassess your caloric needs and adjust your BMR using updated weight measurements.
- Implement intermittent energy restriction strategies, like alternating between high-calorie and low-calorie days, to keep your metabolism guessing.
- Increase physical activity to burn more calories without reducing nutritional intake drastically.

Practical tips can make your dietary adjustments sustainable. Combine caloric control with nutrient-dense foods to ensure you're getting the most out of every calorie:

- Opt for whole fruits over fruit juices to increase fiber intake, which aids digestion and prolongs satiety.
- Choose lean proteins and plant-based options that offer additional benefits like fiber and antioxidants.
- Switch to whole grains instead of refined grains to maintain steady energy levels throughout the day.

In conclusion, understanding and balancing macronutrients is foundational for achieving optimal health and managing weight effectively. By focusing on carbohydrates, proteins, and fats in the right proportions and tailoring these needs individually through calculated caloric requirements, you set yourself up for sustainable success. Remember, no two bodies are the same, and ongoing adjustments will always be part of the journey.

Macronutrient Balance for Weight Loss and Health

Understanding the roles of carbohydrates, proteins, and fats in our diet is foundational for achieving balanced nutrition. This chapter has detailed how each macronutrient serves distinct but interconnected functions within our body. By recognizing these roles, you can make more informed and effective choices for your health.

Earlier, we explored the importance of carbohydrates as the primary energy source and their impact on brain function and physical activity. While it's crucial to consume them in moderation, choosing nutrient-dense options like whole grains, fruits, and vegetables can stabilize energy levels and support overall well-being.

Similarly, protein's contribution extends beyond muscle repair and growth. Its role in promoting satiety and supporting metabolic processes underscores why it is essential in weight management. Lean proteins and plant-based sources provide versatile options to meet individual dietary preferences and needs.

Fats, often misunderstood, also play vital roles, from maintaining cell membranes to aiding in vitamin absorption. Incorporating healthy fats like those found in avocados, nuts, and olive oil can enhance heart health and reduce inflammation, provided they're consumed in appropriate amounts.

For some readers, the challenge lies in balancing these macronutrients effectively within their daily meals. This balance isn't just about hitting specific numbers; it's about understanding how different foods make you feel and adjusting your intake accordingly. Monitoring and tweaking your diet based on personal experiences and nutritional needs can lead to sustainable health improvements.

On a broader scale, achieving this balance impacts not just weight loss or muscle preservation but overall vitality and long-term wellness. As you continue to refine your diet, consider the interactive effects of macronutrients and how they collectively optimize your health.

In closing, let's remember that nutrition is a dynamic journey. Embrace this knowledge to cultivate a mindful, flexible approach to eating that supports your health goals. Listen to your body, make adjustments as needed, and view this as an ongoing process of learning and adapting. The right balance of carbohydrates, proteins, and fats will empower you to maintain a healthier lifestyle and achieve lasting well-being.

References

Carbone, J. W., & Pasiakos, S. M. (2019). *Dietary Protein and Muscle Mass: Translating Science to Application and Health Benefit. Nutrients*, 11(5), 136. https://doi.org/10.3390/nu11051136

Avita Health System. (2023). *Macronutrients: A Simple Guide to Macros*. Avita Health System. https://avitahealth.org/health-library/macronutrients-a-simple-guide-to-macros/

Lecovin, G. (n.d.). *Nutrition for Muscle Repair and Recovery. NASM Blog*. Retrieved from https://blog.nasm.org/nutrition-for-recovery

Carreiro, A. L., Dhillon, J., Gordon, S., Jacobs, A. G., Higgins, K. A., McArthur, B. M., ... Mattes, R. D. (2016). *The macronutrients, appetite and energy intake. Annual Review of Nutrition*, 36(73). https://doi.org/10.1146/annurev-nutr-121415-112624

Alexander, H. (2020). *What are macronutrients?. Focused on Health*. Retrieved from https://www.mdanderson.org/publications/focused-on-health/what-are-macronutrients-.h15-1593780.html

Mielgo-Ayuso, J., Fernández-Lázaro, D., et al. (2021). *Nutrition and Muscle Recovery. Nutrients*, 13(2), 294. https://doi.org/10.3390/nu13020294

Chapter 5

Boosting Metabolism for Better Health

Metabolism is an intricate and often misunderstood aspect of our health, pivotal in determining how efficiently we burn calories and maintain energy levels. Many people believe that their metabolic rate is solely dictated by genetics, but research reveals a more complex interplay between lifestyle choices and metabolic efficiency. By adopting targeted habits, we can significantly influence our metabolism for the better. This chapter aims to debunk myths and provide practical insights into optimizing metabolic function through diet, exercise, hydration, and sleep.

A sluggish metabolism can lead to various health issues, including weight gain, fatigue, and even chronic conditions such as diabetes and cardiovascular diseases. Imagine consistently feeling tired despite adequate rest or struggling with weight loss despite following a diet. These are common signs of an inefficient metabolism. The root causes often lie in dietary choices, physical inactivity, dehydration, and poor-quality sleep. For instance, consuming refined grains, lacking strength training exercises, not drinking enough water, and experiencing irregular sleep can collectively slow down your metabolic rate, making it harder to manage weight and overall well-being.

In this chapter, we will explore comprehensive strategies to revitalize your metabolism. We'll dive into the importance of consuming metabolism-boosting foods like lean proteins and whole grains, engaging in regular physical activities such as strength training and high-intensity interval workouts, and staying hydrated throughout the day. Additionally, we'll discuss the critical role of quality sleep in metabolic health.

By integrating these practices into daily life, you can enhance your body's ability to efficiently process calories and improve your overall health. Whether you're new to these concepts or looking to refine your approach, this chapter provides actionable steps gleaned from empirical research to help you achieve a healthier metabolism.

Enhancing Metabolic Rate with Diet and Exercise

To enhance a more efficient metabolism, we need to consider several key aspects: the foods we consume, our physical activities, hydration levels, and the overall quality of our sleep. Let's explore how each can be optimized to support a healthy metabolism, especially for individuals following a low-calorie, high-protein low-carb diet.

Starting with food, choosing metabolism-boosting options is foundational. Incorporating lean proteins, whole grains, and fibrous vegetables into your daily meals can rev up the body's calorie-burning process. Foods rich in protein require more energy for digestion, known as the thermic effect of food. This includes items like chicken, fish, eggs, and plant-based proteins such as beans and lentils (LDN, 2024). Moreover, whole grains like brown rice and quinoa are not only nutrient-dense but also help maintain stable blood sugar levels.

Here is what you can do in order to achieve this:

- Include lean meats, fish, or plant-based proteins in every meal.
- Swap refined grains for whole-grain alternatives such as quinoa, brown rice, or whole-grain pasta.
- Fill half your plate with a variety of fibrous vegetables like broccoli, spinach, and bell peppers.
- Experiment with incorporating spices like ginger, turmeric, and cayenne pepper, which have shown metabolism-boosting properties (Discover foods that boost metabolism and promote weight loss, n.d.).

Physical activity plays a crucial role in boosting metabolism. Regular exercise, particularly strength training and high-intensity interval workouts can significantly enhance fat-burning mechanisms. Building muscle mass increases your resting metabolic rate because muscle tissue burns more calories than fat, even at rest. Incorporate strength training exercises like weightlifting or bodyweight exercises such as push-ups and squats into your routine. High-intensity interval training (HIIT) can be incredibly effective; these are short bursts of intense exercise followed by brief recovery periods.

Here is what you can do in order to achieve this:

- Schedule strength training sessions at least two to three times per week.
- Incorporate HIIT workouts, which could include sprinting, cycling, or even jumping jacks, twice a week.
- Combine different types of physical activities to keep your routine engaging and balanced, including flexibility exercises like yoga or Pilates.

Hydration is another pivotal element. Drinking enough water helps your body efficiently process calories. According to research, staying adequately hydrated can increase your metabolic rate (LDN, 2024). Dehydration can slow down the metabolism, so it's essential to keep a water bottle handy and make a habit of sipping throughout the day. Aim for at least eight glasses a day, though individual needs vary based on factors like activity level and climate.

Here is what you can do in order to achieve this:

- Start your day with a glass of water to kickstart your metabolism.
- Carry a reusable water bottle with you to remind yourself to stay hydrated.
- Consider drinking green tea or herbal teas like peppermint or ginger, which have additional metabolism-boosting benefits.
- Infuse your water with fruits, herbs, or cucumber slices for added flavor and nutrients.

Lastly, sufficient rest and quality sleep are essential factors that influence metabolism and overall health. Poor sleep can disrupt hormones that regulate appetite and metabolism, leading to weight gain and sluggish metabolic function. Research suggests aiming for seven to nine hours of quality sleep each night can support metabolic health.

Here is what you can do in order to achieve this:

- Maintain a regular sleep schedule by going to bed and waking up at the same time every day.
- Create a restful sleeping environment by keeping your bedroom cool, dark, and quiet.
- Limit exposure to screens before bedtime, as blue light can interfere with your natural sleep-wake cycle.

- Practice relaxation techniques such as reading, meditation, or deep breathing exercises before bed.

By integrating metabolism-boosting foods, engaging in regular exercise, ensuring adequate hydration, and prioritizing restful sleep, individuals can effectively enhance their body's ability to burn calories and promote weight loss. Remember, these steps not only support a healthy metabolism but also contribute to overall well-being.

Implementing these changes may seem overwhelming at first, but small, consistent adjustments can lead to substantial improvements over time. For example, start by gradually increasing the amount of lean protein and whole grains in your diet, then slowly incorporate more fibrous vegetables. Begin with a simple exercise routine that includes both strength training and HIIT and build up the intensity as you become more comfortable. Make hydration a habit by integrating it into your daily routine and set a fixed bedtime to improve sleep quality.

An evidence-driven approach ensures that these recommendations are grounded in empirical research, providing a reliable foundation for achieving optimal health. When balancing individual freedom with social responsibility, it's important to advocate for policies that encourage accessible and affordable healthy living options. Government and corporate collaboration, under proper checks and balances, can play a crucial role in fostering a healthier society. For example, promoting subsidies for whole foods and fitness programs or implementing workplace wellness initiatives can amplify the positive impacts on public health.

Ultimately, achieving a balanced metabolism requires a holistic approach that considers diet, exercise, hydration, and rest. By focusing on these areas, individuals can harness their efforts towards a healthier, more energized life. Remember, personal responsibility intertwined with a supportive safety net creates an environment where everyone has the opportunity to thrive. Embrace these guidelines to pave the way for sustainable health improvements and enhanced metabolic efficiency.

Sustainable Practices for Long-Term Weight Loss

Promoting efficient metabolism is key to not only achieving but also maintaining long-term weight loss. Scientific evidence provides us with a roadmap towards sustainable practices that support metabolic health. Let's delve into some practical approaches.

Implementing mindful eating habits and portion control helps individuals manage their caloric intake effectively, which is essential for sustaining weight loss achievements. The core of mindful eating is about bringing full awareness to the experience of eating.

Here's what you can do to implement these habits:

- Start by making mealtimes calm and distraction-free. Put aside phones and other gadgets.
- Eat slowly and savor each bite, paying attention to textures and flavors.
- Listen to your body's hunger and fullness cues—eat when you're hungry and stop when you're comfortably full.
- Use smaller plates and bowls to help control portion sizes visually.
- Plan meals and snacks to avoid impulsive or emotional eating.

Regular monitoring of progress and adjustments to diet and exercise routines are necessary to ensure continued metabolic support. Monitoring doesn't mean obsessively tracking every calorie or step you take, but a balanced approach can offer valuable insights.

Here are some guidelines:

- Keep a food and activity journal to help identify patterns and areas for improvement.
- Weigh yourself once a week at the same time of day to track trends without getting bogged down in daily fluctuations.
- Measure other indicators of health, such as waist circumference, energy levels, and mood.
- Adjust your diet and exercise plans based on what you learn. If you hit a plateau, consider consulting a healthcare professional for personalized advice.

Embracing balanced and varied diet rich in nutrient-dense foods ensures that individuals receive essential vitamins and minerals to support metabolic functions. A diverse diet is not only healthier but also more enjoyable.

Here's how to make sure your diet is well-rounded:

- Incorporate a variety of fruits and vegetables into every meal.
- Choose whole grains over refined grains to keep fiber intake high.
- Include lean proteins such as fish, poultry, beans, and nuts.

- Don't shy away from healthy fats found in avocados, olive oil, and fatty fish.
- Stay hydrated by drinking plenty of water throughout the day.

Encouraging a lifestyle approach that integrates physical activity, healthy eating, and positive habits fosters long-term metabolic health and sustained weight management. It's all about creating a routine that feels less like a task and more like a way of life.

To get there:

- Make physical activity a natural part of your day. Find activities you enjoy, whether it's walking, swimming, dancing, or yoga.
- Practice consistency with your eating habits rather than perfection. It's better to sustain good habits consistently than to aim for perfect adherence and burn out.
- Build a supportive environment around you—friends and family who understand and respect your goals can be invaluable.
- Set realistic goals and celebrate small victories along the way to stay motivated.

Empirical evidence underscores the importance of these practices. Obesity-related conditions—like diabetes, cardiovascular disease, and sleep apnea—all place significant stress on vital organs, often leading to organ failure if left unchecked (Yale Medicine, n.d.). Regularly losing even a modest amount of weight can offset this strain substantially and improve overall quality of life (Farhana et al., 2023).

In terms of dietary strategies, a low-calorie intake remains a cornerstone for weight loss and maintenance (Kim, 2021). However, it's essential to understand that not all calories are created equal. Focusing on nutrient-dense foods rather than just cutting calories can lead to better health outcomes and more sustainable weight loss.

Consider intermittent fasting as another strategy. This method involves alternating periods of eating and fasting, which has been shown to enhance metabolic flexibility and improve overall health without the constant need to count calories (Kim, 2021).

To implement this:

- Start by choosing a time window for eating that fits your lifestyle, perhaps an 8-hour window during the day.
- During the fasting period, stick to water, herbal teas, and black coffee.
- Focus on balanced meals during eating periods to ensure adequate nutrient intake.

Combining these dietary strategies with regular physical activity can further bolster your metabolic health. Exercise helps to regulate blood sugar levels, boost cardiovascular health, and maintain muscle mass, all critical factors for a robust metabolism. Aim for a balanced mix of aerobic activities like walking or cycling, and strength training exercises, such as lifting weights or resistance band workouts.

On the medical front, the role of pharmacological interventions cannot be overlooked. Medications can sometimes provide the necessary boost for weight loss when combined with lifestyle changes. For instance, drugs like Contrave reduce appetite and help manage weight when used under proper medical supervision (Yale Medicine, n.d.).

Under certain conditions, endoscopic procedures, such as gastric balloons, can also facilitate initial weight loss, allowing patients to transition to healthier lifestyles more easily (Yale Medicine, n.d.). But these should always be considered a last resort, after comprehensive dietary and lifestyle modifications have been tried.

Well-rounded weight management primarily revolves around personal responsibility and informed choices supported by empirical evidence. Each step towards mindful eating, balanced nutrition, regular physical activity, and strategic monitoring builds a solid foundation for long-term metabolic health. By adopting these sustainable practices, we create a supportive environment for both physical and mental well-being, ensuring not just short-term achievements but lasting improvements in health.

Ultimately, these steps boil down to making empowered choices and finding balance. As challenging as it may seem, sustainable weight management and efficient metabolism are within reach through deliberate and consistent efforts. With every conscious choice, you're fostering a healthier, happier version of yourself.

Practical Tips for Enhancing Metabolism

When we think of metabolism, many envision it as a mystical force that determines whether we can effortlessly maintain our weight or struggle despite our best efforts. The truth is more nuanced, and research shows we have significant control over our metabolic rate through relatively simple lifestyle changes (How to Boost Your Metabolism, n.d.). Here are practical ways to promote efficient metabolism that balance individual freedom and social responsibility—values I hold dear.

First, let's address physical activity, a cornerstone for boosting metabolism. Dr. Laila Tabatabai from Houston Methodist emphasizes the importance of daily movement.

"So much of improving metabolism is understanding what it is you do with most of your time," she says. If your day is dominated by passive activities like sitting at a desk or relaxing on the couch, it's crucial to counterbalance these habits with regular physical activity. Aiming for 150 minutes of moderate-intensity exercise per week can kickstart your metabolic engine. Try integrating short bursts of activity throughout your day—such as a quick walk during lunch breaks or doing some light stretching while watching TV.

Another vital component is building and maintaining muscle mass. Strength training helps build lean muscle, which is metabolically active tissue. As Dr. Tabatabai notes, "Challenging our small and large muscle fibers through strength training is critical for optimal metabolism." Activities like weightlifting, resistance band exercises, or even bodyweight exercises such as push-ups and squats can be incredibly effective. Not only does this form of exercise improve metabolism, but it also supports bone health and cognitive function, providing comprehensive benefits. According to Piedmont Healthcare, adding muscle mass to your body can help burn more calories at rest, making it easier to manage weight effectively (Alrutz, n.d.).

Diet plays a pivotal role in managing metabolism. A predominantly plant-based diet has been shown to support metabolic health. But don't worry, embracing a plant-based diet doesn't mean becoming vegetarian or vegan; it simply means prioritizing fruits, vegetables, whole grains, and plant-based proteins and fats. High-fiber foods, particularly those rich in water content, not only provide essential nutrients but also enhance the body's metabolic activity post-consumption. For instance, the Mediterranean diet—a prime example of plant-based cuisine—is lauded for its metabolism-boosting properties and benefits for overall health (How to Boost Your Metabolism, n.d.).

Another dietary strategy is the mindful reduction of processed foods. Ultra-processed foods are frequently high in added sugars, unhealthy fats, and refined carbohydrates, all of which can slow down metabolism. The key to a robust metabolic rate lies in consuming whole, unprocessed foods that nourish and energize the body. Simple swaps, such as choosing fresh fruit over sugary snacks or opting for whole grains instead of refined ones, can make a significant difference. Processed foods should be enjoyed sparingly to avoid their adverse effects on metabolism and overall health.

Hydration is another often underestimated aspect of metabolic health. Water is crucial for nearly every bodily function, including metabolism. Dehydration can lead to reduced metabolic efficiency, making it harder to achieve weight loss goals. Drinking adequate amounts of water supports lipolysis—the breakdown of fats—and ensures that muscle tissues remain metabolically active. Aim to drink water consistently throughout the day and consider incorporating hydrating foods like cucumbers and watermelons into your diet for an extra boost.

Sleep, too, plays a fundamental role in regulating metabolism. Insufficient sleep can disrupt hormonal balance, leading to increased appetite and decreased metabolic rate. The Centers for Disease Control and Prevention recommend at least seven hours of sleep per night for adults. Quality sleep supports insulin regulation and helps ensure you have enough energy for daily activities, including physical exercise. Establishing a regular sleep schedule and creating a restful environment can contribute significantly to metabolic health.

High-Intensity Interval Training (HIIT) is another effective method to elevate metabolism. This type of workout involves alternating periods of intense activity with short recovery breaks. HIIT has been shown to increase metabolism more effectively than traditional steady-state cardio exercises. Moreover, HIIT sessions can be customized to fit various fitness levels and preferences, offering the flexibility needed to maintain long-term commitment and reduce the risk of injury (Alrutz, n.d.).

Let's also consider nutritional timing and meal patterns. It's beneficial to avoid skipping meals, especially breakfast. Eating regularly throughout the day keeps the metabolic furnace burning, as digestion itself requires energy. Including protein in every meal can further elevate metabolism, as it takes more energy to digest protein compared to carbohydrates and fats. Foods like lean meats, legumes, and tofu are excellent choices that can keep you feeling full longer and support muscle maintenance.

Lastly, let's focus on lifestyle and behavior modifications. Consistency is key in any effort to boost metabolism. It's about creating sustainable habits rather than resorting to extreme measures. Small, consistent actions—like cooking meals at home, engaging in regular physical activity, and prioritizing sleep—can collectively create a substantial impact over time. Behavior change strategies such as self-monitoring food intake and physical activity can help maintain accountability and track progress, encouraging continuous improvement.

In conclusion, promoting efficient metabolism is achievable through a combination of a balanced diet, regular physical activity, proper hydration, quality sleep, and behavioral consistency. It's about taking charge of what we can control and making informed decisions based on empirical evidence. By embracing these strategies, we not only support our own health but also contribute to a culture of well-being and social responsibility. These changes may seem small individually, but together, they create a powerful framework for enhancing metabolic health, achieving weight loss goals, and ultimately leading a healthier life.

Wrapping Up: Strategies for a Healthier Metabolism

In this chapter, we delved into the multifaceted approach to promoting an efficient metabolism through diet, exercise, hydration, and sleep. We examined how incorporating lean proteins, whole grains, and fibrous vegetables can enhance the body's calorie-burning process. Through consistent strength training and high-intensity interval workouts, individuals can significantly boost their resting metabolic rate by building muscle mass.

As we consider the pivotal elements of supporting metabolic health, it's essential to remember that these changes, though seemingly simple, require a commitment to consistency. By starting with gradual adjustments—like swapping refined grains for whole grains and integrating more fibrous vegetables—individuals can build a sustainable routine. It's not only about making these dietary changes but also about pairing them with regular exercise and proper hydration. Drinking enough water and incorporating hydrating foods support the body's ability to process calories efficiently.

The importance of quality sleep cannot be overstated. Ensuring sufficient rest allows the body to regulate hormones that influence metabolism and appetite. A holistic approach, considering diet, exercise, hydration, and rest, lays the foundation for a healthier metabolism and overall well-being.

These recommendations are grounded in empirical research, offering a reliable path to optimal health. While individual responsibility is paramount, it's equally important to advocate for policies that make healthy living accessible and affordable. Collaborations between the government and corporations, such as promoting subsidies for whole foods or implementing workplace wellness initiatives, can amplify the positive impact on public health.

Ultimately, achieving a balanced metabolism involves more than dietary choices and exercise routines; it requires a supportive environment where everyone has the opportunity to thrive. As you implement these guidelines, you'll find that small, consistent actions lead to substantial improvements over time. This journey toward a more efficient metabolism is not just a means to an end but a step towards embracing a healthier, more energized life.

Consider the broader implications of these lifestyle changes: a community where healthy habits are the norm and where the collective well-being is enhanced.

As you embark on this path, reflect on how your personal efforts contribute to a larger movement toward sustainable health. These strategies foster not only individual health but also create a ripple effect, encouraging others to follow suit.

In conclusion, while each action may seem minor on its own, together, they form a comprehensive approach to boosting metabolism and sustaining long-term health. By adopting this multifaceted strategy, you are setting yourself up for lasting success and making a profound impact on your overall well-being. Embrace these practices with patience and persistence, and you will pave the way for a healthier future.

References

Houston Methodist. (2023). *How to Boost Your Metabolism*. Retrieved from https://www.houstonmethodist.org/blog/articles/2023/oct/how-to-boost-your-metabolism/

Kim, J. Y. (2021). *Optimal diet strategies for weight loss and weight loss maintenance. Journal of Obesity & Metabolic Syndrome*, 30(1), 20. https://doi.org/10.7570/jomes20065

Simon, N. (2024). *11 Natural Foods to Help Boost Your Metabolism. AARP*. Retrieved from https://www.aarp.org/health/healthy-living/info-2024/natural-metabolism-boosters.html

Institute of Medicine (US) Subcommittee on Military Weight Management. (2004). *Weight-Loss and Maintenance Strategies. Weight Management*. National Academies Press (US). https://www.ncbi.nlm.nih.gov/books/NBK221839/

Alrutz, C. (n.d.). *5 ways to boost metabolism. Piedmont Living Real Change*. Retrieved from https://www.piedmont.org/living-real-change/5-ways-to-boost-metabolism

Yale Medicine. (n.d.). *Metabolic Health & Weight Loss Program > Departments > Yale Medicine*. https://www.yalemedicine.org/departments/metabolic-health-and-weight-loss-program

Farhana, A., & Rehman, A. (2023). *Metabolic Consequences of Weight Reduction. StatPearls Publishing*. Retrieved from https://www.ncbi.nlm.nih.gov/books/NBK572145/

Craft, B. (2024). *12 Foods to Support Healthy Metabolism. Ochsner Blog Articles for prevention, wellness, food, fitness, innovation, healthcare, and more*. Retrieved from https://blog.ochsner.org/articles/metabolism-boosting-foods-and-spices

Nuvance Health. (n.d.). *Discover foods that boost metabolism and promote weight loss*. Retrieved from https://www.nuvancehealth.org/health-tips-and-news/discover-foods-that-boost-metabolism-and-promote-weight-loss

Chapter 6
Recipe Showcase: Innovative and Delicious Dishes

In the realm of culinary adventures, finding recipes that are both innovative and nutritionally balanced can sometimes feel like searching for a needle in a haystack. Many people struggle with the misconception that eating healthily means sacrificing flavor and satisfaction. However, this chapter aims to flip that notion on its head. Prepare yourself for a showcase of dishes that are not only creative and delicious but also align with your dietary goals of low-calorie, high-protein meals. Whether you're a seasoned cook or a kitchen novice, these recipes will inspire you to rethink how you approach healthy eating.

One common challenge is managing dietary needs without compromising on taste or enjoyment. For instance, typical high-protein diets may lean heavily on meat, often leaving vegetarians or those seeking plant-based options feeling left out. Additionally, many low-calorie recipes tend to lack the textural variety or bold flavors that make meals enjoyable, leading individuals to revert to less healthy eating patterns. This chapter addresses these issues head-on by offering recipes that burst with flavor while packing a nutritional punch. Imagine savoring a zesty chickpea salad that's not only light on calories but rich in protein and other essential nutrients—proving that eating well doesn't mean missing out on taste.

Throughout this chapter, you'll be guided through a vibrant array of mouthwatering recipes, each designed to excite your taste buds while supporting your health objectives. From refreshing salads to hearty main courses, every dish is meticulously crafted to balance low-calorie content with ample protein. Beyond just recipes, you'll find step-by-step demonstrations, insightful tips for ingredient substitutions, and strategies for effective meal planning. By the end of this journey, you'll have a repertoire of delightful dishes that make healthy eating an enjoyable, sustainable part of your everyday life. So, grab your apron and get ready to transform your kitchen into a haven of nutritious indulgence.

Step-by-Step Recipe Demonstration

The Recipe Creator shares creative low-calorie high-protein recipes by guiding us through a vibrant and practical demonstration, epitomizing the diet plan's principles. Let's dive into this journey with an exciting recipe that beautifully balances high protein and low calories, ensuring that you can eat healthily without compromising on taste or satisfaction.

Our featured recipe today is a High-Protein Chickpea Salad. This dish is not only brimming with nutrients but also exudes flavorful freshness, making it a perfect choice for anyone looking to adopt a healthier lifestyle. Chickpeas are a powerhouse of nutrition, providing an excellent source of plant-based protein. They are particularly beneficial in maintaining muscle mass and promoting satiety, helping you control your calorie intake more effectively (5 Protein-Packed Foods for Healthy, Meatless Meals, 2022).

To begin, we need to gather our fresh, wholesome ingredients:

- 1 cup of cooked chickpeas
- 1 diced cucumber
- 1 diced red bell pepper
- 1/2 cup cherry tomatoes, halved
- 1/4 cup finely chopped red onion
- 1/2 avocado, diced
- 2 tablespoons chopped fresh parsley
- 2 tablespoons olive oil
- Juice of one lemon
- Salt and pepper to taste

Chickpeas, the star of our recipe, are not just high in protein but also packed with fiber, vitamins, and minerals. Fiber aids in digestive health, while vitamins and minerals support various bodily functions, including reducing the risk of chronic diseases.

Cucumber and bell peppers add a refreshing crunch. They are loaded with water content, aiding in hydration and providing additional vitamins, including vitamin C. Tomatoes contribute lycopene, an antioxidant known for its potential heart health benefits (5 Protein-Packed Foods for Healthy, Meatless Meals, 2022).

Now, let's move to the kitchen. Here's how to prepare this delicious chickpea salad:

- Start by rinsing the cooked chickpeas under cold water to remove any excess sodium if using canned chickpeas.
- Next, combine the chickpeas, cucumber, bell pepper, cherry tomatoes, red onion, and avocado in a large mixing bowl.
- In a small bowl, whisk together the olive oil, lemon juice, salt, and pepper until well blended. Pour this dressing over the salad mixture.
- Toss everything gently to ensure all the ingredients are evenly coated with the dressing.
- Finally, sprinkle the chopped parsley on top as a garnish.

This step-by-step process shows how simple and effective it can be to prepare a nutritious meal. The combination of fresh vegetables and chickpeas ensures that every bite bursts with flavor while keeping the calorie count low. The addition of avocado provides healthy fats, which are essential for absorbing fat-soluble vitamins and maintaining overall wellbeing (Restivo, 2023).

What makes this recipe stand out is its delightful flavor profile. The crispness of the cucumber, the sweetness of the bell pepper, and the tanginess of the lemon dressing all come together harmoniously. Avocado adds creaminess, balancing the textures perfectly. This dish proves that healthy eating doesn't have to be bland; instead, it can be an enjoyable culinary experience.

For those who enjoy variation or need ingredient substitutions due to dietary preferences or availability, here are some flexible tips:

- Chickpeas can be swapped with other legumes like black beans or lentils to offer a different nutritional profile and taste.

- If avocados aren't available, consider using a small amount of Greek yogurt for creaminess. Greek yogurt is high in protein and probiotics, which are beneficial for gut health.
- To add an extra protein boost, mix in some diced boiled eggs, which are complete proteins containing all essential amino acids (5 Protein-Packed Foods for Healthy, Meatless Meals, 2022).
- Fresh herbs like cilantro or mint can replace parsley, depending on your preference.

Experimenting with these variations allows you to tweak the recipe to your liking while sticking to the core principle of maintaining high protein and low-calorie content. Through this event, it's evident that creating delicious, healthy meals aligned with dietary guidelines is entirely achievable. It encourages readers to get hands-on and try new recipes in their kitchens, transforming the perception that healthy eating is challenging or tasteless. Instead, it becomes a joyful, fulfilling part of daily life.

For optimal results and to maintain balance in your diet, here's some advice based on empirical evidence: focus on whole foods and diverse food groups. Balanced meals should include proteins, healthy fats, and complex carbohydrates. Whole foods such as fruits, vegetables, nuts, seeds, lean meats, and grains are nutrient-dense and beneficial for long-term health (Wei, 2015). Incorporating a variety of foods ensures you receive a broad spectrum of nutrients, supporting overall wellbeing.

Healthy eating also necessitates considering portion sizes and individual nutritional needs. Overconsumption, even of healthy foods, can lead to imbalances and potentially negate the benefits. Therefore, mindful eating—paying attention to hunger cues and eating with intention—is crucial. Aim for protein quantities that suit your lifestyle, typically around 0.8 grams per kilogram of body weight, adjusting for factors like physical activity or age (Restivo, 2023).

The High-Protein Chickpea Salad is a testament to how nourishing, low-calorie meals can be both delectable and straightforward to prepare. By following this approach, you align with health goals without sacrificing taste or enjoyment. Embrace the power of balanced, evidence-driven nutrition to enhance your dietary habits and overall quality of life. This ensures that each meal is a step towards better health and sustained wellness.

Balancing Taste and Nutrition

Following the recipe demonstration, the Recipe Creator discusses the significance of balancing taste and nutrition in meal preparation. This event underscores the importance of enjoying meals while adhering to dietary guidelines. The discussion begins with an insight into how enhancing the visual appeal of dishes can significantly elevate the dining experience without compromising nutritional value.

Adding color to your plate isn't just about aesthetics; it's also about ensuring a variety of nutrients. A vibrant plate often indicates a diverse range of food groups, which is crucial for a balanced diet. For example, deep greens from spinach or kale signify high levels of vitamins and antioxidants. At the same time, bright reds and oranges from tomatoes and carrots offer a rich source of beta-carotene and other essential nutrients. This approach not only makes your meal more visually appealing but also enhances its nutritional profile.

To achieve this:

- Use a mix of colorful vegetables like bell peppers, carrots, and leafy greens.
- Combine fruits like berries, citrus slices, or pomegranate seeds with your dishes.
- Experiment with different textures: crunchy nuts, creamy avocado, or juicy watermelon cubes.

Having established the importance of visual appeal, the focus shifts to flavor enhancement through the use of herbs and spices. Elevating the flavors of low-calorie, high-protein meals doesn't have to be daunting. Fresh herbs and spices are an excellent way to add depth and complexity to your dishes while keeping them healthy. Using these elements creatively can transform a bland meal into a gourmet experience.

Consider introducing herbs like basil, cilantro, and parsley to your everyday cooking. Spices such as cumin, paprika, and turmeric can bring warmth and richness, making the dish not only flavorful but also packed with health benefits.

Here is how you can get started:

- Incorporate herbs into salads, soups, and marinades.
- Add spices to your protein sources like chicken, tofu, or beans for a savory twist.
- Create herb-infused oils or dressings to drizzle over roasted vegetables or grains.

Moving forward, the Recipe Creator delves into strategies for effective meal planning that prioritize both taste and health benefits. Meal planning is not merely about organizing your meals ahead of time; it's about crafting a week of nutritious, delicious options that align with your dietary needs and preferences.

To adopt a holistic approach to dietary choices:

- Schedule a weekly prep day to plan your meals, shop for groceries, and prepare ingredients.
- Focus on versatile ingredients that can be used in multiple dishes, such as quinoa, chickpeas, and leafy greens.
- Prepare large batches of staple foods like grilled chicken, roasted vegetables, or cooked grains that can be mixed and matched throughout the week.

By embracing meal planning, you're less likely to resort to unhealthy convenience foods and more inclined to enjoy home-cooked meals that support your health goals.

The discussion then transitions to addressing common misconceptions about healthy eating. It's a widespread belief that healthy eating is synonymous with bland and unappetizing food. However, this couldn't be further from the truth. Healthy meals can be incredibly flavorful and satisfying when prepared thoughtfully.

One common myth is that healthy cooking requires expensive, hard-to-find ingredients. On the contrary, simple, affordable ingredients can be the cornerstone of a nutritious diet. Staples like brown rice, oats, and seasonal vegetables are both economical and nutrient dense. Practical solutions involve learning to cook with what you have and being open to trying new recipes that incorporate these staples. For instance, adding a few drops of lemon juice can brighten up the flavor of many dishes, making them instantly more appealing without extra calories.

Further debunking myths, it's essential to recognize that preparing nutritious meals doesn't have to be time-consuming. Quick-cooking proteins like fish and eggs, alongside pre-washed salad greens and canned beans, offer convenience without sacrificing quality. Simple techniques like roasting vegetables on a single sheet pan or utilizing a slow cooker can save time while ensuring meals are wholesome and tasty.

In conclusion, the Recipe Creator emphasizes that meal preparation should be viewed as a creative and enjoyable process rather than a chore. This perspective fosters a positive attitude towards maintaining a healthy diet, making it more sustainable in the long run. Empowerment comes from knowing that you can create delightful meals that are aligned with your health objectives. By integrating the principles discussed – balancing visual appeal, enhancing flavor with herbs and spices, strategic meal planning, and debunking myths – you can revolutionize your approach to eating, making each meal a step towards better health and well-being.

Embrace the joy of experimenting in the kitchen, and remember, good food nourishes not just the body but the soul, too.

Innovative and Delicious Dishes

As we bring this chapter to a close, the Recipe Creator offers a delightful array of recipes tailored specifically to those seeking low-calorie, high-protein meals. From hearty breakfast options to savory dinner dishes, there's something here to inspire everyone, regardless of dietary preferences or restrictions.

Imagine starting your day with a colorful Tropical Breakfast Bowl, loaded with fresh fruits and a sprinkle of chia seeds to keep you full until lunchtime. Or perhaps you crave something warm like a Vegetable Frittata that's both flavorful and low-calorie, perfect for those chilly mornings. The variety extends to lunch and dinner as well. Think about enjoying a Grilled Fresh-Herbed Chicken with Summer Vegetables, an easy-to-prepare meal that's bursting with flavor from the grill, or a comforting bowl of Black Bean Chili with Corn and Cilantro that is both heart-healthy and delicious.

These creative recipes aren't just theoretical; they've been tried, tested, and loved by many. Take Lisa, for example, who was initially skeptical about switching her usual meals to low-calorie versions. She found herself pleasantly surprised when she tried the Sweet Potato Black Bean Bowls. Not only did she find them easy to prepare, but they also provided the taste and fullness she desired without the extra calories. "I never thought eating healthy could be so satisfying," she exclaimed. Similarly, Tom raved about the Harissa Salmon with Harissa Spice, calling it his go-to dish for special occasions due to its robust flavors and health benefits.

The Recipe Creator goes a step further by providing practical tips for meal customization, ensuring that you can tweak each recipe to meet your unique dietary needs and goals.

Here is what you can do in order to achieve flexible meal customization:

- Start by identifying any specific dietary restrictions or nutritional goals you may have. This could mean focusing on reducing sugar intake, increasing protein, or avoiding certain allergens.
- Incorporate alternative ingredients that align with your dietary needs. For example, if a recipe calls for honey and you're minimizing sugar, consider using a natural sweetener like stevia instead.
- Adjust portion sizes based on your caloric requirements. If you're aiming to reduce calorie intake, consider halving the portions of high-calorie ingredients such as cheese or nuts.
- Experiment with different cooking methods. For instance, instead of frying, try grilling or steaming your ingredients to maintain their nutritional value while cutting down on unnecessary fats.

With these tips, customizing your meals becomes a seamless process, allowing you to enjoy every dish without compromising on your health goals.

Moreover, the Recipe Creator emphasizes the importance of utilizing leftovers effectively and streamlining meal prep strategies to ensure you stay committed to the diet plan.

Consider these suggestions for incorporating leftovers and efficient meal prepping:

- Store leftover ingredients separately rather than mixing them all together. This allows you to mix and match different components throughout the week, making each meal feel new and exciting.
- Use vacuum-sealed containers or freezer bags to preserve the freshness of your leftovers. By removing excess air, you extend the shelf life of your food.
- Plan your meals around versatile base ingredients like quinoa, brown rice, or roasted vegetables. These staples can easily be transformed with different proteins and sauces to create entirely different dishes.
- Prepare large batches of key ingredients once a week, such as grilling several chicken breasts or roasting a pan of mixed vegetables. This way, you'll have ready-to-use components that make assembling meals quick and easy.
- Label your prepped meals and ingredients with dates to keep track of their freshness. This helps in prioritizing what to use first, reducing food waste.

By adopting these strategies, you can simplify your cooking routine and enjoy the process of creating delicious, health-conscious meals without feeling overwhelmed.

In essence, this event not only equips readers with a treasure trove of delectable recipes but also underscores the joy and creativity that can be found in the kitchen. As you embark on your journey towards better health, remember that it's not just about following a diet plan—it's about discovering new flavors, trying innovative combinations, and savoring the satisfaction of wholesome, well-balanced meals.

Culinary creativity doesn't have to come at the expense of health. On the contrary, by embracing these recipes and tips, you're likely to find that eating well can be both enjoyable and fulfilling. Let the vibrant colors, diverse textures, and rich flavors of these dishes inspire you to take charge of your health while relishing every bite. Whether you're crafting a quick weeknight dinner or preparing an elaborate weekend feast, the possibilities within this dietary framework are boundless.

So, grab your apron, gather your ingredients, and dive into the wonderful world of low-calorie, high-protein culinary creations. It's time to redefine what healthy eating looks and tastes like, one mouthwatering meal at a time.

Embracing Culinary Creativity

As we culminate this chapter, it's clear that creating delicious, low-calorie, high-protein meals is both achievable and enjoyable. The Recipe Creator has demonstrated how integrating vibrant, nutrient-rich ingredients can lead to flavorful dishes that respect dietary guidelines. We've explored the versatility of chickpeas in a refreshing salad and discussed the importance of balancing taste and nutrition in our daily meals.

Reflecting on the start of this journey, the key message remains consistent: eating healthily does not mean compromising on flavor or satisfaction. This principle is embedded in every recipe and tip provided. Our example recipe, the High-Protein Chickpea Salad, perfectly illustrates how simple ingredients can come together to create a meal that's both delicious and nutritious.

Readers need to recognize the significance of incorporating a variety of whole foods into their diet. This approach ensures a broad spectrum of nutrients, supporting overall wellbeing and reducing risks of chronic diseases. Moreover, mindful eating practices—focusing on portion control and listening to hunger cues—are crucial for maintaining a balanced diet.

On a broader scale, the impact of adopting these dietary habits extends beyond individual health. It promotes a shift towards more sustainable food practices, encouraging the use of whole, plant-based ingredients. This not only benefits personal health but also contributes positively to environmental sustainability.

As we close this chapter, consider the open-ended possibilities within your culinary endeavors. Each meal you prepare is an opportunity to explore new flavors, textures, and nutritional benefits. Embrace the creativity and joy found in cooking and remember that the journey towards better health is ongoing.

In essence, engaging with these recipes allows you to redefine healthy eating, making it a fulfilling aspect of everyday life. Let these insights and recipes be the foundation of your culinary adventures, inspiring you to take charge of your diet and wellbeing one delicious meal at a time.

References

Gundersen Health System. (2018). *Balance your plate-color, flavor, and texture. Gundersen Health System.* Retrieved from https://www.gundersenhealth.org/health-wellness/eat-move/balance-your-plate-color-flavor-and-texture

Eatright. (n.d.). *Enhancing the flavor of your meals.* Retrieved from https://www.eatright.org/food/food-preparation/cooking-tips/enhancing-the-flavor-of-your-meals

Gina. (2023). *Healthy Rice Bowl Recipes - Easy Meal Prep Ideas!..* Retrieved from http://gulfcoastblues.org/index-286.html

Cleveland Clinic. (n.d.). *Healthy Recipes.* Cleveland Clinic. https://my.clevelandclinic.org/departments/wellness/patient-resources/recipes

Harvard College. (2024). *Meal prep can be a helpful healthy eating tool amidst hectic weekday schedules. The Nutrition Source.* Retrieved from https://nutritionsource.hsph.harvard.edu/meal-prep/

Harvard, H. (2023). *High-protein foods: The best protein sources to include in a healthy diet. *Harvard Health*.* Retrieved from https://www.health.harvard.edu/nutrition/high-protein-foods-the-best-protein-sources-to-include-in-a-healthy-diet

Johns Hopkins Medicine. (2022). *5 Protein-Packed Foods for Healthy, Meatless Meals.* Retrieved from https://www.hopkinsmedicine.org/health/wellness-and-prevention/5-protein-packed-foods-for-healthy-meatless-meals

Wei, C. (2015). *The research on the high-protein low-calorie food recipe for teenager gymnastics athletes. The Open Biomedical Engineering Journal, 9*(1), 240. https://doi.org/10.2174/1874120701509010240

Amiri, M., Li, J., & Hasan, W. (2023). *Personalized Flexible Meal Planning for Individuals With Diet-Related Health Concerns: System Design and Feasibility Validation Study. JMIR Formative Research,* 7(10). https://doi.org/10.2196/46434

Chapter 7
Overcoming Plateaus and Challenges

Weight loss journeys often resemble a winding road with unexpected turns and sudden stops. The initial enthusiasm can be infectious, propelling us forward with vigor and determination. Yet, as the journey continues, many individuals encounter plateaus—those stubborn periods where progress halts despite ongoing efforts. These moments can feel disheartening, leading to frustration and diminished motivation. Recognizing that these obstacles are a natural part of the process can be the first step in overcoming them.

One of the most common challenges faced during weight loss is hitting a plateau. Imagine diligently following a structured diet and exercise routine only to find that the numbers on the scale refuse to budge. This phenomenon occurs because the body, incredibly adept at adapting, often becomes more efficient in its energy use over time. What once worked seamlessly may no longer yield the same results. Another challenge is maintaining motivation amidst setbacks. Emotional eating, driven by stress or boredom, can derail progress, making it difficult to stick to healthy habits consistently.

This chapter dives deep into strategies to overcome these common pitfalls. We'll explore practical adjustments in dietary habits, such as recalibrating calorie intake and incorporating nutrient-dense foods to keep metabolism active. Diversifying exercise routines to keep your body challenged will also be discussed.

Additionally, we'll examine psychological barriers like emotional eating and offer techniques to sustain motivation through realistic goal setting, mindfulness practices, and leveraging support systems. By equipping yourself with these tools, you'll be better prepared to navigate the inevitable plateaus and maintain steady progress on your weight loss journey.

Dealing with Common Obstacles in the Weight Loss Journey

Weight loss plateaus are a common hurdle on the journey to achieving our health goals. These moments of stalled progress can be incredibly frustrating, but they are also entirely normal. When you hit a plateau despite diligent effort in maintaining your diet and exercise routines, it's essential to understand that your body might just be adjusting to its new state. Here's where empirical evidence can guide us through these rough patches.

First, let's talk about calorie intake adjustments. A weight-loss plateau often occurs because your body becomes more efficient at conserving energy, reducing the number of calories burned during activities you previously found challenging. This efficiency means consuming fewer calories is no longer as effective. To counteract this, carefully re-evaluate your caloric intake.

Cutting calories further can help, but it's crucial to maintain a balance that doesn't lead to excessive hunger or nutrient deficiencies.

Here are some practical steps:

- **Reduce intake slightly**: If you've been consuming 1,500 calories daily, try dropping to 1,400. Small reductions are more sustainable.
- **Increase protein consumption**: Protein requires more energy to digest, helping boost metabolism. Foods rich in protein, like lean meats, beans, and legumes, are excellent choices.
- **Monitor portion sizes**: Eating the correct portions can ensure you're not inadvertently consuming extra calories.
- **Stay hydrated**: Water can sometimes be mistaken for hunger, so drinking more might help curb unnecessary snacking (Cleveland Clinic, n.d.).

Diversifying your workout routine is another key strategy to combat plateaus. When you stick to a single exercise regimen, your body adapts, making those workouts less effective over time. By introducing variety, you can keep your muscles guessing and burn calories efficiently.

Here's how you can diversify:

- **Mix up cardio exercises**: Instead of always running or using the elliptical, try swimming, cycling, or even dancing.
- **Incorporate strength training**: Building muscle can increase your resting metabolic rate since muscle tissue burns more calories than fat. Simple bodyweight exercises or resistance bands can kick-start this process.
- **Change workout intensity**: High-intensity interval training (HIIT) alternates between short bursts of intense activity and periods of rest or lower-intensity exercise. This variation can significantly boost calorie burn.
- **Try new activities**: Consider activities like yoga, Pilates, or martial arts. Not only do these keep things interesting, but they also engage different muscle groups.

Maintaining motivation through a plateau often requires shifting focus from the scale to other indicators of progress. Monitoring aspects like body measurements, how clothing fits, and overall body composition can provide a broader perspective on your journey. Sometimes, inches lost around the waist or gains in muscle definition are more telling than numbers on a scale.

Moreover, psychological barriers play a pivotal role in how we perceive our weight loss efforts and ongoing progress. Overcoming mental roadblocks involves acknowledging them and developing strategies to navigate these challenges. Stress, emotional eating, and negative self-talk are some of the most common obstacles.

Here's how you can manage them:

- **Set realistic expectations**: Understand that weight loss is not a linear process, and temporary stalls don't define your entire journey.
- **Practice mindfulness**: Engage in mindfulness practices like meditation or journaling to stay attuned to your body's signals and emotions.
- **Seek support**: Surround yourself with supportive friends and family or join a community group where you can share experiences and strategies.
- **Celebrate small victories**: Acknowledge each milestone, regardless of size. This could be sticking to your exercise routine for a week or making healthier food choices.

- **Address emotional eating**: Identify triggers that prompt emotional eating and find alternative coping mechanisms, such as taking a walk, reading a book, or indulging in a hobby (Houston Methodist, 2020).

It's important to bear in mind that patience and consistency are your greatest allies. Sustained weight loss takes time, and adopting a mindset that embraces progress over perfection can make all the difference. Recognize that setbacks are part of the journey, not the end of it.

When hitting a plateau, reassess your plan rather than abandoning it. Reflect on what has worked so far and consider tweaks that honor your evolving body and goals. For example, if morning runs are no longer enjoyable, perhaps evening yoga sessions could become your new favorite activity.

It's also worth mentioning that biological factors like genetics and age can influence weight loss progress. Understanding these aspects can alleviate unwarranted guilt or frustration. Realize that everyone's journey is unique, and comparisons to others' results can undermine your own achievements.

Balancing human welfare with economic growth in personal health decisions means prioritizing well-being over quick fixes or extreme measures. Sustainable habits, informed by data and research, offer long-term benefits that crash diets or fad workouts cannot match.

Ultimately, empower yourself with knowledge and adaptability. Use empirical evidence as your compass, guiding you through the ebbs and flows of your weight loss journey. By staying informed, adjusting strategies when needed, and fostering a resilient mindset, you'll be well-equipped to tackle any plateau and continue progressing toward your health goals.

Remember, persistence is key. Adapting your approach and maintaining consistent effort are crucial elements in overcoming plateaus and achieving lasting success. Stay focused on your broader vision, and celebrate each step forward, no matter how small. Your dedication will yield the desired results, reinforcing the importance of an evidence-driven, adaptive approach to weight loss and overall health.

Maintaining Motivation Throughout the Weight Loss Journey

Maintaining motivation throughout a weight loss journey can be incredibly challenging, but it's also absolutely vital. Let's explore how you can sustain that drive and keep moving toward your goals.

First, let's talk about setting realistic, achievable goals. One of the primary reasons people lose their motivation is that they set goals that are either too vague or overly ambitious. Instead, focus on creating SMART goals—those that are Specific, Measurable, Attainable, Relevant, and Time-bound (Yale University, n.d.). For instance, instead of saying, "I want to lose weight," say, "I aim to lose 5 pounds in the next month by walking 30 minutes every day and reducing my sugar intake."

Breaking down larger objectives into smaller milestones not only makes them more manageable but also provides frequent opportunities for celebrating progress. It's these small victories that contribute to maintaining long-term motivation.

Next, let's address the importance of establishing support systems. Accountability and encouragement from friends, family, or online communities can serve as powerful motivators. Share your journey with people who care about you and who have similar health and fitness goals. This could mean joining a supportive group on social media, such as a Facebook group dedicated to weight loss, or even building a community through apps designed for tracking progress and sharing tips (Mapes, n.d.).

These platforms often facilitate a sense of camaraderie and shared purpose, which can be incredibly uplifting during difficult times. Additionally, having an accountability partner who checks in with you regularly can provide that extra push when your motivation wanes.

Celebrating non-scale victories is another key aspect of staying motivated. While losing pounds might be the ultimate goal, it's crucial to recognize and celebrate other forms of progress that reflect improved well-being. Did you notice you're sleeping better or have more energy throughout the day? Maybe your clothes fit a bit looser, or you've reached a new personal best in a workout.

These achievements are just as important as any number on the scale. Acknowledging and rewarding yourself for these milestones, perhaps with a new outfit or a relaxing spa day, will help maintain a positive mindset and reinforce your commitment to the journey.

Setbacks are inevitable but overcoming them is what defines successful long-term weight management. When faced with a setback, take a moment to reassess and refocus on your long-term goals.

Here are some strategies to get back on track:

- Start by identifying the trigger for the setback. Was it a stressful week at work? Lack of preparation? Understanding the root cause can help avoid similar issues in the future.
- Reframe your mindset. Instead of viewing a setback as a failure, see it as an opportunity to learn and grow. Each obstacle overcome strengthens your resolve.
- Reassess your goals and make necessary adjustments. If you find the current exercise regimen too strenuous, adapt it to be more manageable. Flexibility is key.
- Seek inspiration from success stories or motivational quotes. Surrounding yourself with positivity can help reignite your passion and determination.
- Practice self-compassion. Be kind to yourself and recognize that everyone faces challenges. It's your response to these challenges that matter most (Management, 2004).

Understanding the role of motivation in weight loss success is crucial. Motivation isn't a static state; it fluctuates based on numerous factors, including stress levels, physical health, and external influences. Therefore, resilience—the ability to bounce back from setbacks—is just as important as motivation itself.

Cultivating resilience involves developing strategies to cope with obstacles, much like those we've discussed above: setting realistic goals, finding strong support systems, celebrating all victories, and learning from setbacks. It's this combination of persistent effort and adaptive thinking that enables individuals to navigate the complex landscape of weight loss.

Let's dive into some practical steps to sustain your motivation and build resilience:

- Regularly revisit your "why." Whether it's for health, appearance, confidence, or longevity, keeping your core motivation front and center helps maintain focus during tough times.

- Diversify your routines to prevent boredom. Alternate between different types of exercises and try new, healthy recipes to keep things fresh and exciting.
- Track and visualize your progress. Use charts, diaries, or apps to log your workouts, meals, and weight changes. Seeing tangible proof of your efforts can be incredibly motivating (Yale University, n.d.).
- Create a motivational environment. Surround yourself with reminders of your goals—pictures, quotes, or items that symbolize your journey. These visual cues can serve as daily affirmations of your commitment and potential.
- Ensure periodic rest and recovery. Overworking yourself can lead to burnout. Incorporate rest days and enjoyable activities that don't revolve around food or exercise to maintain a balanced and sustainable lifestyle.

At the heart of sustaining motivation is the balance between perseverance and adaptability. By focusing on realistic goal setting, tapping into robust support networks, celebrating diverse forms of progress, and skillfully navigating setbacks, you can maintain the momentum needed to achieve long-term weight loss and improved health.

Remember that each person's journey is unique; what works for one individual may not work for another. The key lies in continually adapting and refining your strategies to suit your evolving needs and circumstances. Stay committed, stay flexible, and, most importantly, stay kind to yourself along the way.

Navigating Challenges with Resilience

As we draw this chapter to a close, it's evident that the obstacles encountered during a weight loss journey are not just hurdles but also opportunities for growth. We've discussed how weight loss plateaus are common and frustrating, emphasizing that they are a normal part of the process. By learning to adjust calorie intake and diversify workout routines, we can navigate these plateaus more effectively.

Revisiting our starting point, it's crucial to remember that patience and consistency are the most potent tools in your arsenal. Your body's adaptation to new routines and diets is a testament to your progress, not a setback. Psychological barriers, too, play an essential role in how we perceive these challenges. Addressing mental roadblocks and practicing mindful strategies can significantly enhance your commitment.

What should concern some readers is the temptation to resort to quick fixes or extreme measures when faced with stagnation. These approaches might offer temporary relief but often undermine long-term health goals. Instead, adopting sustainable habits, backed by empirical evidence and personalization, ensures a healthier outcome.

On a broader scale, understanding the unique nature of each individual's journey is vital. Biological factors like genetics and age influence weight loss differently for everyone, highlighting the importance of a personalized approach. Comparisons to others' results may lead to unnecessary frustration and overshadow personal achievements.

Leaving you with an open-ended thought, consider the adaptability and resilience you've cultivated throughout this journey. The skills and knowledge gained will serve not only in weight loss but in various aspects of life.

Embrace each step forward, celebrate small victories, and stay focused on your broad vision for better health. Your dedication and adaptive mindset will sustain you through plateaus and beyond, ensuring lasting success on your path to wellness.

References

Mayo Clinic. (2024). *Weight loss stalled? Move past the plateau. Mayo Clinic.* Retrieved from https://www.mayoclinic.org/healthy-lifestyle/weight-loss/in-depth/weight-loss-plateau/art-20044615

Houston Methodist. (2020). *5 ways to break a weight loss plateau that actually works. *Houston Methodist Blog*.* https://www.houstonmethodist.org/blog/articles/2020/nov/5-ways-to-break-a-weight-loss-plateau-that-are-actually-achievable/
Yale University. (n.d.). *How to stay motivated while losing weight.* Retrieved from https://campuspress.yale.edu/ledger/how-to-stay-motivated-while-losing-weight/

Institute of Medicine (US) Subcommittee on Military Weight Management. (2004). *Weight-Loss and Maintenance Strategies. Weight Management.* https://www.ncbi.nlm.nih.gov/books/NBK221839/

Mapes, M. (n.d.). *How Do I Stay Motivated When I'm Not Seeing Results?. Mayo Clinic Connect.* Retrieved from https://connect.mayoclinic.org/blog/weight-management-1/newsfeed-post/how-do-i-stay-motivated-when-im-not-seeing-results/

Cleveland Clinic Health Essentials. (n.d.). *Ways to break a weight-loss plateau. Cleveland Clinic.* Retrieved from https://health.clevelandclinic.org/weight-loss-plateau

Chapter 8
Success Stories: Real-Life Testimonials

Struggles with weight loss are common, yet the path to success is often far from straightforward. Many people face a myriad of challenges on their journey toward better health and well-being. From changing eating habits to adopting new exercise routines, the road can be long and winding. However, hearing about individuals who have not only faced these challenges but triumphed over them can be incredibly motivating. In this chapter, we delve into the real-life testimonials of those who have achieved remarkable transformations, offering both inspiration and practical insights.

The issue of weight management is multifaceted, involving emotional, psychological, and physical elements. For example, Gracie's family discovered that simple adjustments like portion control can play a significant role in achieving weight goals. Similarly, Tammerrie's journey highlights the emotional hurdles tied to body image, revealing that overcoming mental barriers may be just as crucial as physical changes.

Becky Cabral illustrates the power of incremental change, suggesting that sustainable habits often stem from small, manageable adjustments rather than drastic alterations. These examples underscore the importance of a comprehensive approach to weight loss, one that considers the emotional and psychological aspects alongside diet and exercise.

In this chapter, we will explore various personal accounts that showcase the different strategies people have employed to succeed in their weight loss journeys. From

Gracie's family's collective effort and mutual accountability to Becky Cabral's methodical transition from calorie-dense foods to healthier options, each story provides unique lessons.

We will also consider how supportive communities and incremental changes can lead to lasting results, emphasizing the importance of a holistic approach. By examining these diverse experiences, readers can find practical tips and encouragement to apply to their own lives, paving the way for their successful transformation.

Personal Account of Overcoming Weight Loss Struggles

Gracie's story is a prime example of how dedication, support, and a mindful approach to one's lifestyle can lead to remarkable transformations. When Gracie's doctor suggested she lose weight, the initial suggestion could have been daunting for any young girl. Yet, it became the catalyst for not just her own transformation but also that of her entire family.

Together, Gracie, Brad, and Mandy set out on a shared journey of health and well-being. They dove into educational resources and quickly realized that portion control was key. "We realized that even when we were eating the right foods, we were eating too much," Mandy shares. The simple practice of comparing meal portions to the size of their fists created an easy and immediate visual guide that was practical for all meals.

Tracking their food intake played a significant role in awareness and self-regulation. For instance, Gracie's habit of consuming calorie-dense foods for lunch prompted strategic substitutions like using olive oil spray instead of regular olive oil. Such minor yet deliberate changes can build a sustainable path toward healthier living.

Another crucial element of their success was preparing meals ahead of time. This ensured they had healthy options readily available, eliminating the temptation to resort to unhealthy snacks or fast food. By involving Gracie in the process, both mother and daughter developed a stronger commitment to their goals and reinforced their bond through shared responsibilities.

The family's perseverance resulted in remarkable outcomes. Over six months, Gracie dropped 12 BMI points and felt healthier overall. Brad and Mandy also saw significant improvements, losing 24 and 35 pounds, respectively. More importantly, Brad managed to get his diabetes under control and went off one of his medications. This story stresses the importance of a collective effort and mutual accountability in achieving long-term success (American Obesity Foundation, n.d.).

Now, let's turn to Becky Cabral. Her journey underscores the power of incremental change. Becky lost 100 pounds by making one small change at a time. Transitioning from soda to plain water didn't happen overnight. Still, it evolved through a series of manageable steps: from regular soda to lemonade, then to light lemonade, flavored water, fruit-infused water, and finally, plain water. Her diet transformed gradually but steadily, forming new habits that stuck.

Becky's approach to vegetables also changed over time. She started by hiding them in her meals before moving on to microwaved frozen vegetables. Eventually, she mastered cooking fresh vegetables and now ensures her meals are packed with them. This incremental approach helped her sustain her lifestyle changes and avoid the pitfalls of extreme diets that often fail to offer lasting results.

Such strategies emphasize the importance of gradual, consistent adjustments over radical shifts, which may be appealing but unsustainable. Small victories can accumulate, leading to significant transformations without causing burnout or discouragement.

Tammerrie's story, on the other hand, reveals how one's mindset plays an integral role in physical transformation. Struggling with body image from childhood through adulthood, she faced numerous emotional setbacks and challenges. It wasn't until her child's innocent question about why they never took pictures together hit her at her core, prompting a desire for change. She began by counting calories and modifying her diet, seeing substantial weight loss initially but hitting a plateau where exercise became necessary. However, the gym symbolizes fear and shame for Tammerrie.

Overcoming this barrier required immense courage. With the support of friends and family, she joined group exercise classes at the YMCA and surprisingly found joy and camaraderie in those sessions (admin, 2020). This community aspect elevated her motivation, showing her that exercise can be a celebration of the body's capabilities rather than a form of punishment.

To make such a transition yourself, consider the following:

- Start by identifying and acknowledging your barriers, whether they are emotional, mental, or physical.

- Seek support from friends, family, or groups that foster a sense of belonging and encouragement.
- Make incremental changes to your diet and exercise routine rather than drastic alterations that might be hard to maintain.
- Celebrate small victories, focusing on what your body can do rather than its appearance.

Dara Sarshuri's experience adds another dimension to our understanding of weight loss journeys. Weighing 390 pounds in early 2018, Dara considered gastric bypass surgery but decided to first try dietary changes. Within two months, he lost 55 pounds just by modifying his eating habits. By June, he had shed 45 more pounds and ultimately chose to skip the surgery in favor of continuing his newfound regimen. Regular exercise became part of his routine—starting with walking and gradually incorporating gym activities.

Dara's story illustrates the empowering realization that often comes from initial success. Confidence grows, small accomplishments fuel larger ambitions, and soon enough, one achieves feats previously deemed impossible. His journey is a testament to the power of starting simple and building up—a model that many can follow to take charge of their health progressively.

Rachel Saintfort's story highlights the profound impact personal motivation can have on one's journey. After her daughter witnessed her being called "fat" by classmates, Rachel's resolve solidified. Cutting out fast food and soda, she began daily three-mile walks, transforming both her weight and her outlook on life. Rachel's journey shows how external catalysts, particularly involving loved ones, can ignite powerful personal commitments.

Not everyone's journey involves professional guidance or structured programs, as seen with Jen Wagner, who lost 88 pounds since February without stepping foot in a gym. Using MyFitnessPal to track calories and practicing intermittent fasting, Jen found creative ways to stay active at home, including playing tennis and jumping on trampolines with her daughter. This underscores the fact that fitness and weight loss don't require specialized environments; a supportive attitude and inventive approaches can be just as effective.

Finally, Joey Morganelli's adoption of a vegan lifestyle catalyzed his weight loss, dropping from 400 pounds to 250. Losing both parents as a teenager led him to cope with food and eventually face the harsh reality of his weight. Encouraged by a professor, his journey began with calorie counting, evolving into a passion for nutrition through a high-carb-low-fat vegan diet. Joey's story emphasizes learning and adapting according to one's unique bodily responses, rejecting fad diets in favor of personalized nutrition plans that promote long-term health.

These narratives collectively illustrate the multifaceted nature of weight loss journeys. They underscore the importance of a supportive environment, incremental changes, personal motives, and the crucial role of mindset. Each individual's path may look different, but common threads of perseverance, adaptability, and community weave through their stories, offering invaluable lessons for anyone seeking to embark on a similar transformative journey.

Initial Setbacks and Obstacles

Carla's journey began with a mix of hope and trepidation. Like many, she had faced numerous setbacks in her pursuit of weight loss. Her initial attempts were marked by common pitfalls—yo-yo dieting, bouts of extreme workout regimens, and the constant struggle against cravings and food temptations.

In the early stages of her journey, Carla tried calorie counting, one of the most widely recommended methods for weight loss. She meticulously logged every meal, snack, and drink, aiming to stay within her calorie limits. Yet, despite her best efforts, she found herself snacking more frequently—58% of people admit to snacking at least once a day, with nearly 25% doing so multiple times (CDC, 2023).

Her diet wasn't just about numbers; it was also a battle of emotions and habits. Over 50% of individuals report eating due to stress, and 15% feel guilty about their food choices often (International Food Information Council). Carla was no different. Stress from work led her to reach for comfort foods, amplifying her feelings of guilt and frustration when the scale didn't move as expected.

One evening, after another disappointing weigh-in, Carla decided something had to change. She researched extensively and found that a significant factor in successful weight loss stories—98% according to the NWCR—was modifying food habits. Inspired, she began to focus not merely on calories but on the quality of the food she consumed. She started incorporating more whole foods: fresh vegetables, lean proteins, and healthy grains.

Carla also encountered the reality of supplement use. It's a booming industry, with $2.1 billion spent annually on weight loss supplements alone (Hall et al., 2018). While skeptical at first, Carla decided to try a natural supplement to help curb her appetite. To her surprise, this provided some assistance, but it wasn't a magic solution.

The turning point came when Carla joined a local support group, a community that shared her goals and understood her struggles. This group was a game-changer, providing both accountability and motivation. She realized the power of a supportive network and made it a priority to regularly attend meetings and exchange tips with fellow members.

For those looking to emulate Carla's approach:

- **Join a Support Group**: Being part of a community offers support and keeps you accountable. Look for local groups or online communities where you can share experiences and learn from others.
- **Focus on Whole Foods**: Shift your perspective from just counting calories to improving the quality of your diet. Incorporate more fruits, vegetables, lean proteins, and whole grains into your meals.
- **Consider Professional Help**: Sometimes, a registered dietitian or nutritionist can provide personalized guidance tailored to your specific needs.
- **Mindful Snacking**: Rather than reaching for junk food, prepare healthy snacks in advance. Consider options like nuts, fruits, or yogurt.

Thanks to her holistic approach, Carla began to see real progress. Not only did she lose weight, but she felt more energetic and positive. Her success inspired others in her community. Several friends who'd watched her transformation decided to make similar changes in their lives. They saw her commitment and resilience and believed they, too, could achieve their goals.

For those inspired by Carla's story, here are some specific milestones and steps to consider:

- **Set Realistic Goals**: Break down your ultimate goal into smaller, achievable milestones. Celebrate each success along the way.
- **Document Your Journey**: Keep a journal or use an app to track your progress. Documenting can help identify patterns and keep you motivated.
- **Regular Exercise**: Incorporate physical activity into your routine. Whether it's a daily walk, yoga, or hitting the gym, find what works for you and stick to it.

As Carla's journey unfolded, testimonials from her peers highlighted the ripple effect of her determination. Jane, one of Carla's colleagues, shared how seeing Carla's discipline encouraged her to take control of her own health. She noted how joining the same support group helped her shed 20 pounds and improve her overall well-being.

The ongoing support network played a crucial role in maintaining Carla's progress. It's vital not just to lose weight but to keep it off.

Here is some strategies Carla found effective:

- **Frequent Self-Weighing**: 75% of those who successfully maintain weight loss weigh themselves at least once a week (NWCR).
- **Balanced Meals**: Eating smaller, more frequent meals throughout the day can prevent overeating at any single meal.
- **Stay Active**: Regular exercise remains essential. Aim for an hour of moderate activity per day, which can be spread throughout the day.

Maintaining these habits ensured Carla didn't just lose weight but sustained her healthier lifestyle. Her story underscores that while the road to weight loss is fraught with challenges, a blend of evidence-based strategies, community support, and personal perseverance can lead to lasting success.

Testimonials and Reflections on Perseverance

Throughout this chapter, we have explored the varied and inspiring journeys of individuals who have successfully navigated the challenging path of weight loss and lifestyle transformation. From Gracie and her family's collaborative efforts to Carla's determined shift towards healthier habits, these stories collectively illustrate that lasting change is achievable through a combination of dedication, incremental adjustments, and supportive environments.

Returning to the introduction, each narrative highlighted unique aspects of overcoming personal obstacles—whether through portion control, embracing gradual dietary changes, or finding joy in communal fitness activities. Our current understanding emphasizes that no single approach fits all; rather, personalization and adaptability are key. Each person's journey revealed the importance of setting realistic goals, celebrating small victories, and maintaining long-term commitment to healthier lifestyle choices.

For those readers embarking on their own transformative journeys, it is essential to acknowledge potential barriers early on. Emotional, mental, and physical hurdles are common and can often lead to setbacks if not addressed mindfully. Support from friends, family, or community groups can make a significant difference, as seen in Tammerrie's and Carla's experiences, where external encouragement bolstered their internal resolve.

The broader implications of these individual success stories extend beyond personal well-being. There is a ripple effect—community involvement, improved family health, and even wider cultural shifts towards valuing incremental, sustainable lifestyle adjustments over quick fixes. Moreover, recognizing and addressing the emotional components of eating and body image can pave the way for more meaningful, long-lasting changes.

In conclusion, consider the open-ended nature of weight loss journeys. They do not culminate in a final destination but rather continue to evolve as part of lifelong wellness. Reflect on your current practices, habits, and mindset. How can you incorporate elements from these varied stories into your own life? Embrace the ongoing process of change, knowing that each small step, supported by perseverance and community, contributes to a more fulfilling, healthier you.

References

Binsaeed, B., Aljohani, F. G., Alsobiai, F. F., Alraddadi, M., Alrehaili, A. A., Alnahdi, B. S., Almotairi, F. S., Jumah, M. A., & Alrehaili, A. T. (2023). *Barriers and Motivators to Weight Loss in People With Obesity. Cureus*, 15(11). https://doi.org/10.7759/cureus.49040

YMCA of Muncie. (2020). *Transformed: Tammerrie's story of physical and mental transformation. YMCA of Muncie.* https://www.muncieymca.org/transformed-tammerries-story/

Hall, K. D., Kahan, S., & et al. (2018). *Maintenance of lost weight and long-term management of obesity. The Medical clinics of North America*, 102(1), 183. https://doi.org/10.1016/j.mcna.2017.08.012

Noon, G. E., & Swift, L. Z. (2019). *Green obesity statistics. Journal of Supplemental Weight Loss*, 8(3), 124-136. https://doi.org/10.7894/jsup.2019.124136

American Obesity Foundation. (n.d.). *Success Stories.* https://americanobesityfdn.org/success-stories/

Chapter 9

Empowering Readers Towards Better Health

Taking control of one's health can feel like an overwhelming task, but it's a journey that offers immense rewards. Imagine waking up each day with more energy, feeling confident in your skin, and having the knowledge that you are making choices that benefit your long-term well-being. Achieving such a state of health may seem like a lofty goal, but it begins with small, intentional steps—each choice you make in your daily routine holds the power to transform your life.

All too often, people rely on generic advice that may not suit their individual needs or lifestyles. They might follow trending diets or exercise plans without considering their unique body types, preferences, or circumstances. For example, one person may thrive on a plant-based diet, while another might find it difficult to obtain necessary nutrients without consuming animal products. Similarly, an intense workout regimen could benefit some but be unsustainable for others.

This disparity highlights the importance of personalized health goals and methods tailored specifically to fit one's life. Without this customization, the likelihood of sustained improvement diminishes, leading to frustration and eventual abandonment of health ambitions.

In this chapter, we delve into empowering readers to take charge of their well-being by setting personalized health goals, creating supportive environments, and overcoming initial hurdles to build self-discipline. We will explore practical strategies such as starting with manageable changes, utilizing tools like food diaries, and seeking social support to stay motivated. By fostering a sense of responsibility and empowerment, you can achieve better adherence to your chosen diet plan and overall health goals. With a structured approach, you can navigate the challenges and maintain a positive outlook throughout your wellness journey.

Taking Ownership of Health and Well-Being

Taking ownership of your health and well-being is not just a suggestion; it's a necessity in today's fast-paced world. It's about proactively engaging with a diet plan to achieve your goals and beyond. When you take charge, you don't just react to life – you create it on your own terms.

Setting personalized health goals is the first step toward aligning yourself with any diet plan. Often, we get caught up in generic advice that doesn't suit our unique needs. It's essential to remember what works for one person might not work for another.

So, how do you set these goals? Here's what you can do:

- Start by assessing where you are right now. Take stock of your current eating habits, physical activity levels, and mental state regarding health.
- Identify what you want to achieve. Be specific – is it weight loss, muscle gain, better digestion, improved energy levels?
- Break down these larger goals into smaller, manageable milestones. For instance, rather than aiming to lose 30 pounds, set an initial target of losing five pounds within a month.
- Make these goals measurable and time bound. This means having clear deadlines, such as "I will reduce my sugar intake by 50% over the next two weeks."
- Regularly revisit and adjust your goals based on your progress and any new insights you gain along the way.

By taking these steps, you ensure your health goals are tailored specifically for you, making them more achievable and sustainable (UCSF Health, 2019).

Creating a supportive environment plays a significant role in maintaining dietary consistency. Our surroundings have a profound impact on our behaviors and choices. If your kitchen is stocked with unhealthy snacks, it'll be challenging to stick to your diet plan. Instead, aim for an environment that nudges you towards healthier decisions without causing undue stress. Keep tempting foods out of sight and have low-calorie options readily available.

At work, avoid keeping snacks at your desk, and instead, bring pre-planned healthy snacks. During breaks, take a walk instead of heading to the vending machine. These small adjustments can collectively contribute to a supportive environment that aligns with your health objectives (Gibson et al., 2017).

Overcoming the initial hurdles and building self-discipline is often the most daunting part of any health journey. Many people give up before they even get started due to the challenges they perceive as insurmountable.

But here's a structured approach to help you conquer those early obstacles:

- Begin with small, achievable changes. Swap out one unhealthy snack a day for a piece of fruit or a handful of nuts.
- Set up simple routines. Consistency is key, so try to eat meals at regular times and include plenty of vegetables and lean proteins.
- Use a food diary to keep track of what you eat. This will make you more aware of your eating patterns and help identify areas for improvement.
- Don't go it alone. Engage a friend or family member to join you in your new eating habits for mutual support and accountability.
- Celebrate small victories. Whether it's sticking to your meal plan for a week or losing your first pound, acknowledge and celebrate your successes.

Following these strategies can help make overcoming those initial hurdles less intimidating and more attainable (Management, 2004).

Staying motivated and accountable throughout your health journey is crucial for long-term success. Motivation can wane, and life's demands can distract us from our goals.

But there are effective ways to keep your motivation high:

- Surround yourself with a community that shares your health goals. Whether it's a group fitness class, an online forum, or friends who encourage each other, social support makes a big difference.
- Regularly remind yourself why you started this journey. Reflect on your reasons for wanting better health and visualize the end results.

- Track your progress with periodic check-ins. This could be weighing yourself once a week or noting improvements in how you feel physically and mentally.
- Consider setting up mini rewards for reaching interim goals. This could be treating yourself to a new workout outfit or enjoying a healthy but delicious meal out.
- Engage in activities that boost your mood and energy. Exercise, for example, releases endorphins and helps maintain a positive outlook.

These tips will help you stay focused, driven, and engaged in your health regimen over the long haul (Gibson et al., 2017).

By fostering a sense of responsibility and empowerment, you'll naturally feel more committed to your diet plan, leading to better adherence and improved health outcomes. Taking charge of your health doesn't mean doing it perfectly; it means doing it purposefully and consistently. Establishing personalized goals ensures your efforts align uniquely with your needs, creating a supportive environment aid in making healthier choices easier, and utilizing structured strategies can help you navigate through initial challenges smoothly. Remember, the power to shape your health destiny lies in your hands. Embrace it confidently and watch the transformation unfold, one mindful choice at a time.

Implementing the Diet Plan into Daily Life

Let's dive right into the actionable steps you can take to effectively implement your diet plan into your daily life. When it comes to taking charge of your well-being, making strategic choices around food is paramount. Let's start with some practical tips on grocery shopping for nutritious ingredients.

When you head to the grocery store, always go with a plan. Make a list of healthy foods that align with your diet goals. It might seem mundane, but planning ahead ensures that you avoid those impulsive buys that are often unhealthy. Stick to the outer aisles where fresh produce, meats, and dairy are usually located. The inner aisles tend to house packaged and processed foods that can derail your dietary efforts.

Here's what you can do in order to achieve this:

- Rely heavily on fresh fruits and vegetables. These should make up the bulk of your shopping cart.
- Choose whole grains over refined grains. Opt for brown rice, quinoa, or whole wheat products.

- Include lean proteins such as chicken, fish, beans, and legumes.
- Don't forget healthy fats like avocados, nuts, and olive oil.
- Read labels carefully to avoid added sugars and high sodium levels.

Planning your meals in advance not only makes grocery shopping easier but also has numerous health benefits. A registered dietitian at Corewell Health emphasizes that planned meals increase your chance of making healthier food choices (Health benefits of meal planning, n.d.).

Next, let's talk about meal preparation techniques and time-saving strategies. Life can get busy, but that shouldn't be an excuse to fall off your diet plan. Preparation is key to maintaining consistency.

One technique is batch cooking. Spend a few hours during the weekend preparing large quantities of different dishes. Store them in portion-sized containers so that you have ready-to-eat meals throughout the week. This saves not just time but also reduces the temptation to opt for unhealthy fast-food options when you're tired or short on time. Use kitchen gadgets like slow cookers or instant pots, which can make meal prep hassle-free. Invest in a good set of storage containers and perhaps even a label maker so everything is organized and easy to find.

Another useful strategy is prepping ingredients ahead of time. Chop veggies, marinate proteins, and measure out spices and grains. Having these components ready to go means you can swiftly assemble meals when you're pressed for time.

If you're seeking more convenience, pre-portioned meal delivery services can be a lifesaver. Many companies offer plans tailored to specific dietary needs. While this may be pricier than cooking from scratch, it takes the guesswork out and keeps you on track.

Navigating social situations and dining out is another crucial aspect that can pose challenges to sticking to a diet plan. Social gatherings and restaurant outings can be tricky, but there are ways to manage them without feeling deprived.

Always check the menu beforehand if you're dining out. Most restaurants now provide their menus online, allowing you to identify healthy choices ahead of time. Look for dishes that are grilled, baked, or steamed rather than fried. Don't hesitate to ask your server about how the food is prepared or request modifications—most places are happy to accommodate special dietary needs.

Avoid arriving at social events hungry. Eating a small, healthy snack before you go can help you make better choices. When at a buffet, survey all the options first before starting to pile items onto your plate. Opt for smaller portions and fill most of your plate with vegetables and lean proteins.

In scenarios where you might feel the social pressure to indulge, remember that moderation is key. It's okay to enjoy treats occasionally; just be mindful of your portions and balance them with healthier choices throughout the day.

Finally, let's highlight the importance of seeking social support and accountability. Embarking on a diet plan can be challenging, but having a support system can significantly enhance your chances of success. Share your goals with friends or family members who can encourage you along the way. Consider joining online forums or social media groups focused on healthy eating and wellness. Here, you can share your progress, gain insights, and stay motivated by interacting with like-minded individuals.

Using a food diary or apps that track your meals can offer a level of self-accountability. These tools give you a concrete look at what you're consuming, helping you stick to your dietary guidelines. Some apps even allow you to connect with friends, adding an element of community and support.

By offering these tangible steps and solutions, you're equipped with the tools necessary to seamlessly integrate the diet plan into your lifestyle, increasing the likelihood of long-term success. Incorporating these changes might feel overwhelming initially, but remember, the journey to better health is a marathon, not a sprint. Small, consistent efforts will culminate in significant improvements over time.

By prioritizing your well-being and utilizing practical strategies, you can take charge of your health journey. Remember, the goal here isn't perfection but progress. Celebrate the small wins, seek support when needed, and keep moving forward with confidence and determination. Your future self will thank you for the decisions you make today.

Exploring Agency in Health Decision-Making

Encouraging readers to take charge of their well-being is a multifaceted journey that requires both informed decision-making and a commitment to personal growth. Let's explore how you can harness the power of agency in your health decision-making with a deep dive into nutrition, exercise, mindset, and self-monitoring.

First, it's crucial to understand that making informed choices about your nutrition and exercise routines should be tailored to your personal preferences. Instead of blindly following trends or one-size-fits-all advice, tune into what works best for you. For instance, if you're someone who loves the flavors of Mediterranean cuisine, incorporating those elements into your diet might not only make it easier to stick to but also ensure you enjoy what you're eating. Similarly, when it comes to exercise, think about activities you genuinely enjoy.

Whether it's a brisk walk in nature, a heart-pumping dance class, or a calming yoga session, choosing something you love will make it more likely you'll stay consistent.

To help you get started:

- Begin by researching different diets and identifying which ones align with your taste and lifestyle. There are plenty of resources online or even registered dietitians you can consult.
- Explore various types of physical activities. Try out a few and see what feels enjoyable and sustainable for you.
- Keep a food and activity journal to track how different foods and exercises make you feel physically and mentally. This will help you finetune your choices over time.

Self-monitoring and developing self-efficacy are critical in maintaining your diet plan and fitness goals. Studies (Shared Decision-Making, n.d.) have shown that individuals who engage in shared decision-making about their health experience better outcomes and greater satisfaction. This means taking an active role in your health decisions, much like a partner rather than a passive recipient.

Here's a simple guide to enhance your self-efficacy:

- **Set clear, measurable, and achievable goals.** Instead of saying, "I want to eat healthier," specify, "I will include a serving of vegetables in every meal."
- **Use tools like apps or bullet journals to monitor your progress.** Many of these tools offer reminders and motivational tips to keep you on track.
- **Don't hesitate to seek support from friends, family, or support groups.** Sharing your goals and progress can provide additional motivation and accountability.

- **Celebrate small milestones. If** you've managed to stick to your workout routine for a week, reward yourself with something non-food related, like a relaxing bath or a new book.
- **Adjust your plan as needed.** If you find certain aspects of your diet or exercise regimen aren't working, don't be afraid to tweak them. Flexibility is key to long-term success.

Developing a positive mindset is another cornerstone of taking charge of your well-being. It's not uncommon to face setbacks along the way—whether it's a missed workout or indulging in an unplanned treat. What's important is how you respond to these moments. Viewing setbacks as opportunities for growth rather than failures can significantly impact your overall journey. Research has shown that resilience and a growth mindset contribute greatly to long-term success in health-related goals (Molina et al., 2016).

Here are some strategies to develop a positive mindset and reframe setbacks:

- **Practice self-compassion.** Treat yourself with the same kindness and understanding you would offer a friend. Remind yourself that everyone experiences setbacks, and what matters is picking yourself up and moving forward.
- **Reflect on what didn't work and why.** Use this as a learning opportunity to adjust your approach. Maybe the workout was too intense, or the diet plan was too restrictive. Understanding the root cause helps in making better adjustments.
- **Adopt a problem-solving attitude.** Instead of dwelling on the setback, think about actionable steps you can take. If you missed a workout, could you fit in a shorter session later in the day? If you indulged in high-calorie food, could you balance it with healthier options in subsequent meals?
- **Utilize positive affirmations and visualization techniques.** Picturing yourself succeeding and repeating positive statements can build confidence and reduce anxiety about your goals.
- **Surround yourself with positivity.** Engage with motivating content, join supportive communities, and eliminate negative influences that may derail your progress.

Empowering yourself to take charge of your health journey means embracing a proactive approach towards well-being. It's about recognizing that you can shape your health outcomes through informed decisions, constant self-improvement, and resilience. Taking control of your health involves much more than just the physical aspect; it's a comprehensive effort that includes mental and emotional components as well.

Remember, the road to improving your health and well-being isn't always straightforward. It's filled with twists and turns, and that's perfectly okay. What's important is that you're on the path of continually moving forward, learning, adapting, and growing.

By making informed decisions, engaging in self-monitoring, fostering self-efficacy, and adopting a positive mindset, you're not just passively waiting for better health – you're actively creating it. Each small step taken with intention and awareness brings you closer to your health goals. Empowerment in your health journey is about consistency, patience, and persistence. It's about being kind to yourself during challenging times and celebrating every victory, no matter how small it may seem.

So, take that first step today. Whether it's trying out a new recipe, going for a walk, journaling your thoughts, or simply taking a moment to breathe and reflect, each action propels you toward better health and well-being. You have the power to transform your life, one mindful decision at a time.

Fostering Ownership and Accountability

Taking charge of your well-being is an empowering step towards achieving a healthier, more balanced life. It requires consistent effort, self-awareness, and a supportive environment. Let's explore some practical strategies to foster this sense of ownership and accountability in your health endeavors, giving you the tools necessary for lasting commitment.

Tracking progress is an essential first step in cultivating a growth mindset. When you document your journey, you can see how far you've come, celebrate small victories, and reflect on challenges. This practice not only reinforces positive behavior but also provides valuable insights into areas needing improvement.

Here's what you can do to stay on track:

- **Start by setting clear, achievable goals.** For instance, if you're aiming to lose weight, break it down into smaller milestones, such as losing five pounds in the next month.
- **Use a journal, app, or planner to log daily activities, meals, and feelings.** Reviewing these entries regularly helps recognize patterns and make informed adjustments.

- **Celebrate successes, no matter how small.** Reward yourself with non-food treats like a new book, a spa day, or even just a relaxing evening off. Each celebration fuels motivation and reinforces positive habits.
- **Reflect on setbacks without judgment.** Understand that challenges are part of the process. Identify what triggers setbacks and plan ways to overcome them in the future (Accountability Strategies – Learning Center, n.d.).

Maintaining consistency and resilience involves staying dedicated to your health goals even when faced with obstacles. Life will inevitably throw curveballs, but having strategies in place can help you stay the course.

Consider the following tactics:

- **Develop a routine that incorporates your health goals.** Consistency builds habits, making it easier to stick to your diet plan even during busy times.
- **Embrace flexibility within your routine.** It's crucial to adapt rather than abandon your efforts completely if something unexpected comes up. For example, if you can't make it to the gym, opt for a home workout or a brisk walk instead.
- **Visualize your long-term goals regularly.** Keeping the bigger picture in mind can help maintain motivation. Imagine the benefits of reaching your health targets, whether that's increased energy, improved mood, or a longer, healthier life.
- **Practice self-compassion.** Be kind to yourself when things don't go as planned. Accepting that perfection is unattainable reduces stress and helps you bounce back more quickly (ACE, 2016).

Creating a supportive network is another powerful tool for sustaining your wellness journey. Friends, family, and online communities can provide encouragement, accountability, and shared experiences.

Here are some ways to build your support system:

- **Share your goals with close friends and family members who are likely to support and encourage you.** Their understanding can be a significant motivator.
- **Join online communities or local groups focused on similar health goals.** These platforms offer a space to exchange tips, share struggles, and celebrate milestones together.

- **Find an accountability partner.** Someone who shares your goals can be invaluable for mutual motivation and support. Having regular check-ins, whether through text, calls, or in-person meetings, can help keep you both on track.
- **Engage with professional support when needed.** This could be a nutritionist, personal trainer, or therapist, depending on your specific needs. Professional guidance can provide tailored advice and additional motivation.

Envisioning your health goals while staying adaptable and prioritizing self-care are crucial elements of a successful wellness journey. Envisioning helps clarify what you want to achieve, adaptability allows for adjustments along the way, and self-care ensures you're nurturing your overall well-being.

Here's how to integrate these practices:

- **Create a vision board or a detailed description of your health goals.** Include images, words, and phrases that inspire you. Place this somewhere visible as a constant reminder of what you're working towards.
- **Stay open to changing your approach if something isn't working.** Adaptability is key; if a particular diet plan or exercise routine doesn't suit you, don't hesitate to try an alternative.
- **Incorporate self-care routines into your daily schedule.** This might include meditation, journaling, reading, or any activity that relaxes and rejuvenates you. Self-care isn't a luxury; it's a necessity for sustained well-being.
- **Prioritize sleep, nutrition, and mental health.** Ensure you're getting enough rest, eating balanced meals, and taking time to de-stress. These foundational aspects of self-care support your ability to stay committed to your health goals (The National Academies Press, n.d.).

By promoting self-awareness, accountability, and resilience, you empower yourself to navigate challenges and embrace changes. Remember that this journey is uniquely yours, and it's worth every bit of effort you put into it. Through consistent tracking, celebrating successes, reflecting on setbacks, maintaining a resilient mindset, building a supportive network, and prioritizing self-care, you can create a sustainable path toward your health and well-being. The journey may have its ups and downs, but each step brings you closer to a healthier, happier you. Keep going—you're worth it.

Cultivating Long-Term Health Success

Taking charge of your health and well-being is more than a mere aspiration; it's an essential endeavor in today's fast-paced world. Throughout this chapter, we've explored practical strategies to help you take ownership of your health journey, emphasizing the importance of setting personalized goals, creating supportive environments, overcoming initial hurdles, and maintaining motivation.

We began by discussing the significance of personalized health goals. Understanding that what works for one person might not work for another allows you to tailor your diet plan specifically to your needs, making your goals more achievable and sustainable. Creating a supportive environment also emerged as a key factor in promoting dietary consistency. Small adjustments, like stocking your kitchen with healthy options and planning your meals, can collectively contribute to a healthier lifestyle.

Overcoming initial hurdles can be intimidating, but starting with manageable changes and celebrating small victories helps build self-discipline. Staying motivated and accountable involves surrounding yourself with a community that shares your health goals and regularly reminding yourself why you embarked on this journey in the first place.

As we reflect on these insights, it becomes clear that the process of taking ownership of your health is multifaceted and deeply personal. It involves informed decision-making and a commitment to personal growth. By adopting structured strategies and fostering an empowering mindset, you can navigate challenges and embrace continuous improvement.

For some readers, the path to better health may seem daunting due to past experiences or current obstacles. It's important to recognize that setbacks are part of the journey. How you respond to these moments—viewing them as opportunities for learning rather than failures—can significantly impact your success.

On a broader scale, taking ownership of your health has far-reaching consequences. Not only does it lead to improved physical and mental well-being, but it also sets a positive example for those around you. Your commitment to a healthier lifestyle can inspire others to take similar steps, creating a ripple effect that extends beyond your immediate circle.

As we conclude this chapter, remember that the power to shape your health destiny lies in your hands. Embrace this journey with confidence, knowing that each mindful choice brings you closer to your goals. Taking control of your health is not about achieving perfection but about making consistent, purposeful progress. Let this be a catalyst for transformation, one decisive step at a time.

References

Gibson, A. A., & Sainsbury, A. (2017). *Strategies to improve adherence to dietary weight loss interventions in research and real-world settings. Behavioral Sciences*, 3(7), 44. https://doi.org/10.3390/bs7030044

Agency for Healthcare Research and Quality. (n.d.). *Shared Decision-Making*. Retrieved from https://www.ahrq.gov/cahps/quality-improvement/improvement-guide/6-strategies-for-improving/communication/strategy6i-shared-decisionmaking.html

Beaumont Health. (n.d.). *Health benefits of meal planning*. Retrieved from https://www.beaumont.org/health-wellness/blogs/health-benefits-of-meal-planning

UCSF Health. (2019). *Behavior Modification Ideas for Weight Management*. Retrieved from https://www.ucsfhealth.org/education/behavior-modification-ideas-for-weight-management

Institute of Medicine (US) Subcommittee on Military Weight Management. (2004). *Weight-Loss and Maintenance Strategies. Weight Management*. National Academies Press (US). Retrieved from https://www.ncbi.nlm.nih.gov/books/NBK221839/

National Academies of Sciences, Engineering, and Medicine. (2019). *Fostering Healthy Mental, Emotional, and Behavioral Development in Children and Youth: A National Agenda*. Retrieved from https://nap.nationalacademies.org/read/25201/chapter/10

Shankar, A., Sundar, S., & Smith, G. (2019). *Agency-Based Empowerment Interventions: Efforts to Enhance Decision-Making and Action in Health and Development. Journal of Behavioral Health Services & Research*, 46(1), 1-10. https://doi.org/10.1007/s11414-018-9592-0

Heart and Stroke Foundation of Canada. (n.d.). *Healthy eating basics. Heart and Stroke Foundation of Canada*. Retrieved from https://www.heartandstroke.ca/en/healthy-living/healthy-eating/healthy-eating-basics/

Learning Center. (2024). *Accountability Strategies. Learning Center*. Retrieved from https://learningcenter.unc.edu/tips-and-tools/accountability/

American Council on Exercise. (2016). *Coaching Behavior Change: Accountability for Change*. Retrieved from https://www.acefitness.org/continuing-education/prosource/february-2016/5795/coaching-behavior-change-accountability-for-change/

Thompson, B., Molina, Y., Viswanath, K., Warnecke, R., & Prelip, M. L. (2016). *Strategies to empower communities to reduce health disparities. Health Affairs (Project Hope)*, 35(8), 1424. https://doi.org/10.1377/hlthaff.2015.1364

Centers for Disease Control and Prevention. (2023, April 12). *Healthy Eating Tips*. Centers for Disease Control and Prevention. https://www.cdc.gov/nccdphp/dnpao/features/healthy-eating-tips/index.html

Chapter 10
Inspiring a Healthier Future

Imagine being able to transform your life through small, consistent changes. Picture yourself waking up with more energy, feeling healthier, and looking forward to the day ahead. This isn't just a dream for many; it's a reality achieved by those who have committed to making gradual yet impactful shifts in their lifestyle. The journey of individuals who adopted a holistic diet plan exemplifies how dedication and perseverance can lead to profound transformations. Their stories offer insights and inspiration for anyone aiming to improve their health and well-being.

Many people struggle daily with health issues exacerbated by poor dietary habits and lack of proper nutrition. Take Sarah, for instance, who faced significant challenges due to her weight, including high blood pressure and chronic fatigue. Years of trying and failing different diets left her demoralized until she found a structured yet flexible plan that worked. Similarly, James dealt with weight gain and pre-diabetic conditions aggravated by a sedentary lifestyle and stress eating. These scenarios are not uncommon and highlight the critical issues people face when trying to take control of their health.

In this chapter, we delve into the success stories of individuals like Sarah and James, who managed to turn their lives around by embracing healthier eating habits and lifestyle changes. We will explore the specific strategies they employed, from focusing on whole foods and practicing self-monitoring to building resilience and seeking support systems. By understanding their journeys, readers can glean practical tips and motivation to embark on their own path toward better health. Their experiences prove that achieving one's health goals is possible with the right mindset, dedication, and a well-thought-out approach.

Triumph Through Commitment: A Success Story

Before Sarah adopted the diet plan, her life was a constant struggle. She had battled with her weight for years, feeling the emotional and physical toll it took on her daily life. Sarah was not just dealing with excess weight; she also faced societal pressures and personal self-esteem issues that made day-to-day living challenging. Her health was deteriorating, with high blood pressure and chronic fatigue becoming regular companions. The few attempts she made at different diets always led to a cycle of disappointment, leaving her more demoralized each time.

When Sarah stumbled upon our holistic diet plan, she felt a tinge of hope amid her frustration and despair. The plan wasn't just a quick fix or a fad diet; it offered a structured but flexible approach to integrating healthier eating habits into one's life. Initially skeptical, Sarah embarked on this journey with cautious optimism.

One of the first progress milestones in Sarah's journey came within the first month. She noticed a decrease in her bloating and an increase in her energy levels. By focusing on whole foods and balanced nutrition, she began to feel lighter—not just physically but emotionally as well. Sarah gradually found herself not craving the sugary snacks and processed foods that had once been her comfort zone. This initial success was crucial as it helped build her confidence and efficacy—the belief that she could indeed carry out the desired changes (Bandura, 1977, 1997).

Sarah's transformative changes didn't stop there. At the three-month mark, she had lost a significant amount of weight, but more importantly, she had developed healthier eating habits. She learned to listen to her body, recognizing true hunger signals as opposed to emotional eating triggers. The constant monitoring of her weight—a form of self-surveillance described by Foucault—became less about obsession and more about understanding her body's needs (Stelter, 2015).

The emotional impact of Sarah's success was palpable. Not only did she experience a renewed sense of pride and self-worth, but her transformation also inspired those around her. Her friends and family saw the positive changes both in her appearance and her demeanor. All of a sudden, Sarah was no longer the person who avoided social gatherings due to insecurities about her weight. Instead, she became a beacon of hope for others struggling with similar issues.

Reflecting on Sarah's journey, several key strategies contributed to her successful outcome:

- **Embrace gradual change:** Sarah didn't overhaul her entire diet overnight. She started small, making incremental changes that eventually added up to significant improvements.
- **Focus on whole, unprocessed foods:** Adopting a diet rich in fruits, vegetables, lean proteins, and healthy fats laid the foundation for her success.
- **Practice self-monitoring:** Keeping track of what she ate and how she felt helped Sarah stay accountable and make informed choices (Harvard Health, 2017).
- **Develop resilience:** Sarah accepted that occasional lapses were inevitable. Instead of giving up, she learned to forgive herself and get back on track (Hall et al., 2018).
- **Seek support:** Whether through friends, family, or online groups, having a support system was crucial in maintaining her motivation and dedication.

Sarah's story demonstrates that weight loss is not merely about shedding pounds; it's about transforming one's lifestyle and mindset. The lessons learned from her journey can provide valuable insights for anyone looking to make lasting changes in their lives.

Another inspiring account is James's story. James had always been active, but as he entered his late thirties, he found himself gaining weight despite his best efforts. His job required long hours of sitting, and stress eating became a coping mechanism. Realizing that his health was at risk—his doctor had warned him about pre-diabetic conditions—James decided it was time for a change.

James took a scientific approach, studying various diet plans before choosing one that aligned with empirical evidence and real food principles. He opted for a nutritious diet plan, rich in whole grains, lean meats, and plenty of vegetables. His primary goal was not rapid weight loss but sustainable health improvement.

Within the first few weeks, James experienced increased energy and better sleep quality. These progress milestones were akin to fuel, encouraging him to continue. He started incorporating moderate exercise, first with short walks and then with more intense workouts, as his stamina improved.

During his journey, James encountered setbacks—periods where he felt demotivated or slipped back into old eating habits. However, remembering his deeper motivations helped him persevere. James wanted to be there for his children, to play with them without gasping for breath, and to set a healthy example. This intrinsic motivation was far more enduring than any external reward could have been (Hall et al., 2018).

By the end of one year, James had achieved remarkable results. He lost over 40 pounds and found himself in better shape than he had been in a decade. More importantly, his pre-diabetic condition had reversed, and his general wellbeing had soared. The emotional impact on his family was significant. They celebrated his achievements together, and his journey inspired his wife to adopt healthier eating habits as well.

Lessons from James's success include:

- **Set realistic goals:** Understanding that substantial weight loss would take time helped James maintain his motivation.
- **Prioritize health overweight loss:** By focusing on improving his overall health rather than just losing weight, James made choices that were beneficial in the long run.
- **Engage in mindful eating:** Keeping track of his food intake and being conscious of his eating habits helped prevent mindless snacking.
- **Stay active:** Regular physical activity played a crucial role in his transformation.
- **Leverage intrinsic motivation:** Focusing on meaningful personal reasons ensured that James's commitment was strong and enduring.

Both Sarah and James's success stories underscore the power of a balanced, well-thought-out approach to diet and lifestyle changes. Their journeys illustrate that while the road to better health may be long and fraught with challenges, it is entirely achievable with perseverance, self-reflection, and the right support systems in place.

Their experiences serve as powerful testimonials to the effectiveness of moving away from quick-fix solutions towards holistic, sustainable health practices. For anyone looking to embark on a similar journey, the stories of Sarah and James offer both inspiration and practical guidelines for achieving long-lasting, meaningful change.

Diverse Paths to Wellness: Additional Testimonials

One thing that makes the journey worthwhile is seeing real-life examples of individuals who have embraced a low-calorie, high-protein, and low-carb diet and achieved their goals. Take Mary, for instance, who struggled with obesity for many years. After adopting this diet, not only did she lose 80 pounds, but she also found herself more energetic, sleeping better, and enjoying activities she had long forgotten.

Mary's experience isn't an isolated case. Countless others have transformed their lives by adhering to these dietary principles. What stands out in these testimonials is the diverse range of lifestyles and goals, showing the versatility of the diet plan. For instance, James, a busy corporate executive, found that incorporating high-protein meals made him feel fuller longer, reducing his reliance on quick but unhealthy snacks. He gradually lost weight and improved his metabolic health, as confirmed by his regular medical checkups.

Incorporating this diet plan into various lifestyles reveals its adaptability. From athletes looking to enhance performance to parents wanting more energy to keep up with their kids, the benefits extend beyond just weight loss. Lisa, a mother of three, struggled post-pregnancy with her weight and overall energy levels.

The dietary changes allowed her to balance her demanding schedule while still achieving her fitness goals. She noted, "It wasn't just about losing weight; it was about being a better version of myself for my family."

Even more telling are stories from individuals with specific health challenges. Sarah, diagnosed with type 2 diabetes, turned to a low-carb diet after traditional methods didn't yield significant results. Medical literature supports the benefits of low-carb diets in improving cardiovascular and metabolic profiles (Fliesler, 2021), and Sarah's story is a testament to this. She not only managed her blood sugar levels better but also reduced her medication dependency, finding a new lease on life through dietary changes alone.

Similarly, Roger, who battled hypertension for years, saw substantial improvements in his condition. By focusing on high-protein, low-carb foods, his blood pressure normalized significantly. Such stories underscore that this approach can be universally applicable, offering hope to those dealing with chronic conditions influenced by diet.

Another compelling aspect is the comparison of before-and-after scenarios, which speaks volumes about the tangible results one can achieve. Photos and numbers may be striking, but hearing the narratives behind these transformations adds depth. John, who weighed 300 pounds at his heaviest, recalls how each small change added up. "Initially, it was a struggle to even walk a mile. But with persistency and adhering to the diet, I can now jog five miles without feeling winded."

For readers embarking on their own health journeys, these stories offer valuable encouragement and relatability. Jane, who lost 110 pounds, emphasizes the mental hurdles more than the physical ones. "You don't realize how much your mindset can hold you back until you start seeing the changes. Stick with it, even when it's tough," she advises. Inspirational quotes like hers serve as reminders that perseverance pays off.

Reflecting on these success stories, it's clear that this diet plan isn't a one-size-fits-all solution but rather a flexible approach adaptable to individual needs and goals. Whether you're an office worker trying to manage stress with healthier choices or someone grappling with a medical condition, there's a pathway for everyone. Taking small steps, staying committed, and continually learning about nutrition are key themes echoed across these testimonials.

In summary, the power of a low-calorie, high-protein, low-carb diet lies in its evidence-based effectiveness and adaptability to various personal circumstances. As shown through the experiences of Mary, James, Lisa, Sarah, Roger, and many others, it's not just about shedding pounds but about reclaiming one's health and vitality. Their stories inspire us all to consider how making informed dietary choices can lead to profound, life-changing outcomes.

Empowerment and Next Steps

Reflecting on the inspiring stories of Sarah, James, Mary, Lisa, and others, it's evident that achieving significant health improvements through dietary changes is not only possible but highly attainable. We've delved into the journeys of individuals who have triumphed over personal challenges by adhering to a structured and flexible diet plan embracing holistic lifestyle changes rather than quick fixes.

At the outset, Sarah's story illustrated the profound impact that a well-rounded diet plan can have on one's physical and emotional wellbeing. Similarly, James's methodical approach emphasized the importance of sustainable habits and intrinsic motivation. As we explored further, we encountered testimonials from a diverse group of individuals, each facing unique life circumstances yet finding common ground in their commitment to healthier living.

The recurring theme throughout these accounts is that gradual, consistent change leads to lasting results. Whether it's Sarah overcoming her initial skepticism, James's navigating setbacks with resilience, or Mary rediscovering her zest for life, the essence of their success lies in persistence and adaptability. These narratives bring to light the crucial strategies that contributed to their achievements—embracing whole foods, practicing self-monitoring, developing resilience, and seeking support.

For readers who may be considering embarking on a similar journey, one key takeaway is the importance of setting realistic goals. Promising transformations don't happen overnight but through steady, manageable steps. It's also vital to prioritize overall health and wellbeing over mere weight loss. The physical changes are often accompanied by significant emotional and psychological benefits, as seen in the renewed confidence and improved quality of life experienced by our featured individuals.

As we draw this chapter to a close, it's important to acknowledge the broader implications of these success stories. They serve as powerful reminders that healthy eating and lifestyle adjustments can lead to profound changes, not just at an individual level but within families and communities. The ripple effects of improved health extend far beyond the person making the changes; they inspire and uplift those around them, fostering a culture of wellness and resilience.

In contemplating the journeys of Sarah, James, and others, we see an open-ended possibility for anyone willing to invest in their health. Their stories challenge us to rethink our approaches to diet and exercise, encouraging us to make informed choices that align with our personal goals and lifestyles. Ultimately, the path to better health is uniquely personal, but the principles of commitment, resilience, and holistic care are universally applicable.

References

Hall, K. D., Kahan, S., & et al. (2018). *Maintenance of lost weight and long-term management of obesity. The Medical clinics of North America*, 183(1), 102. https://doi.org/10.1016/j.mcna.2017.08.012

Harvard Health. (2017). *Weight loss that works: A true story. Harvard Health.* Retrieved from https://www.health.harvard.edu/blog/weight-loss-that-works-a-true-story-2017030111218

Low Carb Action Network. (n.d.). *Success Stories.* Retrieved from https://lowcarbaction.org/category/stories/

Klein, J. (n.d.). *Getting Used to a High Protein, Low Carbohydrate Diet Before Surgery and Beyond.* Garnet Health. Retrieved from https://www.garnethealth.org/news/getting-used-high-protein-low-carbohydrate-diet-surgery-and-beyond

Stelter, R. (2015). *"I tried so many diets, now I want to do it differently"—A single case study on coaching for weight loss. International Journal of Qualitative Studies on Health and Well-being,* 10(10). https://doi.org/10.3402/qhw.v10.26925

Fliesler, N. (2021). *In matchup, low-carb diets outperform low-fat diets. Boston Children's Answers.* Retrieved from https://answers.childrenshospital.org/low-carb-diet/

RECIPE

SECTION

Breakfast Recipes

1. **Greek Yogurt Parfait with Berries and Nuts:** A creamy and protein-packed yogurt parfait topped with fresh berries and crunchy nuts.
2. **Spinach and Feta Omelet:** A savory omelet filled with spinach and tangy feta cheese.
3. **Low-Carb Blueberry Pancakes:** Fluffy pancakes made with almond flour and bursting with juicy blueberries.
4. **Avocado and Egg Breakfast Bowl:** A hearty breakfast bowl featuring creamy avocado and perfectly cooked eggs.
5. **Protein-Packed Smoothie with Spinach and Almond Butter:** A nutritious smoothie blended with spinach, almond butter, and protein powder.
6. **Cottage Cheese and Berry Bowl:** A refreshing bowl of cottage cheese topped with mixed berries for a high-protein breakfast.
7. **Low-Carb Chia Seed Pudding:** A creamy chia seed pudding that's low in carbs and high in protein.
8. **Smoked Salmon and Avocado Toast on Low-Carb Bread:** A delicious combination of smoked salmon, avocado, and low-carb bread.
9. **Egg Muffins with Veggies and Cheese:** Bite-sized egg muffins loaded with vegetables and melted cheese.
10. **Almond Flour Waffles with Greek Yogurt:** Crispy almond flour waffles served with a dollop of Greek yogurt.

Lunch Recipes

11. **Grilled Chicken Caesar Salad:** A classic Caesar salad topped with grilled chicken breast.
12. **Turkey and Avocado Lettuce Wraps:** Fresh lettuce wraps filled with turkey slices and creamy avocado.
13. **Spicy Tuna Salad with Cucumber Slices:** A spicy tuna salad served with crunchy cucumber slices.
14. **Low-Carb Chicken and Broccoli Stir-Fry:** A quick and healthy chicken stir-fry with broccoli.
15. **Cauliflower Rice with Ground Turkey and Veggies:** Savory ground turkey and vegetables served over cauliflower rice.
16. **Shrimp and Zoodle Scampi:** A low-carb twist on shrimp scampi made with zucchini noodles.
17. **Low-Carb BLT Salad:** A refreshing BLT salad made with crispy bacon, lettuce, and tomatoes.

18. **Chicken and Spinach Stuffed Peppers:** Bell peppers stuffed with a flavorful mixture of chicken and spinach.
19. **Beef and Cabbage Stir-Fry:** A hearty stir-fry featuring tender beef and crunchy cabbage.
20. **Grilled Salmon with Asparagus:** Simple and delicious grilled salmon served with roasted asparagus.

Dinner Recipes

21. **Lemon Garlic Chicken Thighs:** Juicy chicken thighs marinated in lemon and garlic.
22. **Baked Cod with Herbed Cauliflower Rice:** Flaky baked cod paired with herbed cauliflower rice.
23. **Zucchini Lasagna with Ground Beef:** A low-carb lasagna made with zucchini slices and savory ground beef.
24. **Spicy Shrimp and Zoodles:** Zucchini noodles tossed with spicy sautéed shrimp and a light garlic-chili sauce for a quick, flavorful, low-carb dinner.
25. **Balsamic Glazed Steak with Brussels Sprouts:** Tender steak glazed with balsamic vinegar and served with roasted Brussels sprouts.
26. **Spaghetti Squash Bolognese:** Spaghetti squash topped with a rich and flavorful Bolognese sauce.
27. **Herb-Crusted Pork Chops with Green Beans:** Juicy pork chops crusted with herbs and served with green beans.
28. **Keto Beef Stroganoff:** A low-carb version of classic beef stroganoff.
29. **Garlic Butter Shrimp with Broccoli:** Succulent shrimp sautéed in a garlic butter sauce, served with steamed broccoli for a healthy and delicious meal.
30. **Chicken Fajita Bowls:** All the flavors of chicken fajitas in a convenient bowl.

Snack Recipes

31. **Greek Yogurt Dip with Veggie Sticks:** Creamy Greek yogurt dip served with fresh veggie sticks.
32. **Low-Carb Energy Balls:** Bite-sized energy balls packed with nuts and seeds.
33. **Almond and Cheese Crackers:** Crunchy almond flour crackers with a hint of cheese.
34. **Deviled Eggs:** Classic deviled eggs with a tangy filling.
35. **Low-Carb Guacamole with Bell Pepper Slices:** Creamy guacamole served with crisp bell pepper slices.
36. **Low-Carb Fruit and Nut Mix:** A satisfying snack mix of low-carb dried fruits and nuts, perfect for a quick, healthy boost.

37. **Beef Jerky:** Savory and chewy beef jerky for a high-protein snack.
38. **Pumpkin Seed Protein Bars:** Homemade protein bars made with pumpkin seeds.
39. **Edamame with Sea Salt:** Steamed edamame sprinkled with sea salt.
40. **Low-Carb Protein Muffins:** Delicious muffins made with protein powder and almond flour.

Dessert Recipes

41. **Low-Carb Chocolate Mousse:** A rich and creamy chocolate mousse with low carbs.
42. **Almond Flour Brownies:** Fudgy brownies made with almond flour and dark chocolate.
43. **Keto Cheesecake Bites:** Bite-sized cheesecake pieces that are keto-friendly.
44. **Protein-Packed Peanut Butter Cookies:** Soft and chewy peanut butter cookies with added protein.
45. **Berry and Cream Parfait:** Layers of fresh berries and whipped cream in a delightful parfait.
46. **Coconut Flour Cupcakes:** Moist and fluffy cupcakes made with coconut flour.
47. **Low-Carb Lemon Bars:** Tangy and sweet lemon bars with a low-carb crust.
48. **Keto-Friendly Chocolate Chip Cookies:** Classic chocolate chip cookies with a keto twist.
49. **Vanilla Protein Ice Cream:** Creamy vanilla ice cream packed with protein.
50. **Low-Carb Matcha Green Tea Pudding:** A creamy, healthy pudding made with matcha green tea and coconut milk, lightly sweetened and rich in antioxidants.

Vegetarian Recipes

51. **Eggplant Parmesan:** Layers of eggplant baked with marinara and cheese.
52. **Zucchini Pizza Bites:** Bite-sized zucchini rounds topped with marinara sauce, mozzarella cheese, and fresh basil for a low-carb pizza alternative.
53. **Low-Carb Veggie Stir-Fry:** A colorful stir-fry featuring a variety of vegetables.
54. **Spinach and Mushroom Stuffed Peppers:** Bell peppers stuffed with a savory mixture of spinach and mushrooms.
55. **Zoodle Alfredo with Sun-Dried Tomatoes:** Creamy Alfredo sauce served over zucchini noodles and sun-dried tomatoes.
56. **Keto Vegetable Curry:** A rich and flavorful vegetable curry.
57. **Portobello Mushroom Burgers:** Hearty Portobello mushrooms grilled and served as burgers.

58. **Roasted Beet and Feta Salad:** A vibrant and nutritious salad featuring roasted beets, creamy feta cheese, and fresh arugula, drizzled with balsamic vinaigrette.
59. **Cauliflower Tacos:** Tacos made with seasoned cauliflower and fresh toppings.
60. **Low-Carb Mushroom Barley Soup:** A hearty, filling soup with mushrooms, tender barley, and fresh herbs, perfect for a cozy, low-carb meal.

Vegan Recipes

61. **Tofu Scramble with Veggies:** A flavorful tofu scramble loaded with vegetables.
62. **Low-Carb Vegan Buddha Bowl:** A nutritious Buddha bowl with low-carb ingredients.
63. **Cauliflower Fried Rice with Tofu:** A vegan version of fried rice made with cauliflower and tofu.
64. **Vegan Stuffed Zucchini Boats:** Zucchini boats filled with savory vegan stuffing.
65. **Spaghetti Squash Pad Thai:** A low-carb Pad Thai made with spaghetti squash.
66. **Vegan Protein Smoothie with Hemp Seeds:** A protein-packed smoothie with hemp seeds and fruits.
67. **Low-Carb Vegetable Soup:** A warming vegetable soup with low-carb ingredients.
68. **Vegan Collard Wraps with Hummus:** Fresh collard wraps filled with hummus and veggies.
69. **Cauliflower Tabbouleh:** A light and refreshing cauliflower-based tabbouleh.
70. **Grilled Portobello Mushrooms with Avocado Salsa:** Juicy grilled Portobello mushrooms topped with avocado salsa.

International Cuisine Recipes

71. **Chicken Shawarma Lettuce Wraps:** Flavored chicken shawarma wrapped in lettuce leaves.
72. **Low-Carb Beef Tacos with Cauliflower Tortillas:** Tasty beef tacos served on cauliflower tortillas.
73. **Keto-Friendly Chicken Tikka Masala:** A rich and creamy chicken tikka masala with low carbs.
74. **Greek Chicken Souvlaki:** Grilled chicken skewers marinated in Greek spices.
75. **Low-Carb Sushi Rolls with Cauliflower Rice:** Sushi rolls made with cauliflower rice.
76. **Thai Coconut Curry Chicken:** A flavorful Thai coconut curry with chicken.
77. **Italian Meatballs with Zoodles:** Classic Italian meatballs served with zucchini noodles.

78. **Keto-Friendly Chicken Pho:** A low-carb version of traditional Vietnamese pho.
79. **Low-Carb Shepherd's Pie:** A comforting shepherd's pie with a cauliflower mash topping.
80. **Moroccan Spiced Lamb with Cauliflower Couscous:** Lamb seasoned with Moroccan spices served over cauliflower couscous.

Meal Prep Recipes

81. **Grilled Chicken with Roasted Veggies:** Simple and delicious grilled chicken with roasted vegetables.
82. **Turkey and Spinach Meatballs:** Savory turkey meatballs mixed with spinach.
83. **Mediterranean Chicken Salad:** A refreshing salad with grilled chicken, cherry tomatoes, cucumbers, olives, and feta cheese, dressed in a lemon-oregano vinaigrette.
84. **Beef and Veggie Stir-Fry:** Quick and healthy beef stir-fry with a variety of vegetables.
85. **Lemon Herb Shrimp with Asparagus:** Succulent shrimp flavored with lemon and herbs, served with asparagus.
86. **Spicy Tuna Patties:** Flavorful tuna patties with a spicy kick.
87. **BBQ Chicken Drumsticks:** Juicy chicken drumsticks coated in BBQ sauce.
88. **Cauliflower and Chicken Fried Rice:** A low-carb version of fried rice with cauliflower and chicken.
89. **Greek Chicken Bowl:** A flavorful chicken bowl inspired by Greek cuisine.
90. **Low-Carb Burrito Bowl:** A tasty burrito bowl without the carbs.

Soup Recipes

91. **Chicken and Cauliflower Rice Soup:** A hearty chicken soup with cauliflower rice.
92. **Low-Carb Broccoli Cheddar Soup:** Creamy broccoli soup with sharp cheddar cheese.
93. **Keto Tomato Basil Soup:** A rich tomato basil soup that's keto-friendly.
94. **Beef and Cabbage Soup:** A warming soup with tender beef and cabbage.
95. **Spicy Chicken and Avocado Soup:** A spicy chicken soup topped with creamy avocado.
96. **Cauliflower and Leek Soup:** A smooth and velvety cauliflower and leek soup.
97. **Low-Carb Minestrone Soup:** A low-carb version of classic minestrone soup.
98. **Creamy Mushroom Soup:** A rich and creamy mushroom soup.
99. **Zucchini and Basil Soup:** A refreshing zucchini soup flavored with basil.
100. **Shrimp and Coconut Milk Soup:** A fragrant shrimp soup with coconut milk.

Salad Recipes

101.   **Spinach and Strawberry Salad:** A fresh salad with spinach, strawberries, and a light vinaigrette.
102.   **Low-Carb Greek Salad:** A classic Greek salad with a low-carb twist.
103.   **Tuna and Avocado Salad:** A creamy tuna salad mixed with avocado.
104.   **Avocado Chicken Salad with Lime:** A creamy chicken salad with diced avocado, fresh lime juice, and cilantro, perfect for a light and refreshing meal.
105.   **Blackened Shrimp Salad:** A flavorful salad featuring spicy blackened shrimp on a bed of mixed greens, served with a tangy avocado dressing.
106.   **Turkey Cobb Salad:** A low-carb cobb salad with turkey.
107.   **Cauliflower Potato Salad:** A potato salad substitute made with cauliflower.
108.   **Egg and Cucumber Salad:** A simple and light egg and cucumber salad.
109.   **Asian Chicken Salad:** A flavorful Asian-inspired chicken salad.
110.   **Avocado and Tomato Salad:** A fresh and creamy avocado and tomato salad.

High-Protein Recipes

111.   **Grilled Chicken Breast with Quinoa:** Juicy grilled chicken served with a side of quinoa.
112.   **Baked Tofu with Broccoli:** Protein-rich baked tofu paired with broccoli.
113.   **Steak and Asparagus:** A simple and satisfying steak dinner with asparagus.
114.   **Turkey and Spinach Meatloaf:** A healthy meatloaf made with turkey and spinach.
115.   **Shrimp and Avocado Salad:** A refreshing salad with shrimp and avocado.
116.   **Chicken and Veggie Skewers:** Flavorful chicken and vegetable skewers.
117.   **Low-Carb Protein Smoothie:** A smoothie packed with protein and low in carbs.
118.   **Almond-Crusted Salmon:** Salmon fillets crusted with almond flour.
119.   **Beef and Cauliflower Stir-Fry:** A hearty beef stir-fry with cauliflower.
120.   **Spicy Tuna Steaks:** Flavorful tuna steaks with a spicy seasoning.

Low-Carb Recipes

121.   **Cauliflower Rice Pilaf:** A savory cauliflower rice pilaf.
122.   **Zoodle Carbonara:** A low-carb carbonara made with zucchini noodles.
123.   **Grilled Pork Chops with Veggies:** Juicy grilled pork chops served with vegetables.
124.   **Baked Chicken Wings:** Crispy baked chicken wings with a low-carb sauce.

125. **Low-Carb Pizza with Cauliflower Crust:** A delicious pizza with a cauliflower crust.
126. **Spaghetti Squash with Pesto:** Spaghetti squash topped with homemade pesto.
127. **Cauliflower Rice Stuffed Peppers:** Bell peppers stuffed with a savory mixture of cauliflower rice, ground beef, and aromatic spices for a delicious low-carb meal.
128. **Low-Carb Nachos:** Crunchy nachos made with low-carb ingredients.
129. **Eggplant Rollatini:** Rolled eggplant slices filled with cheese and sauce.
130. **Lemon Butter Shrimp:** Succulent shrimp in a lemon butter sauce.

Quick and Easy Recipes

131. **Chicken and Avocado Salad:** A quick and easy chicken salad with avocado.
132. **Low-Carb Breakfast Smoothie:** A refreshing low-carb smoothie for breakfast.
133. **Grilled Salmon with Lemon:** Simple grilled salmon flavored with lemon.
134. **Cauliflower Fried Rice:** Quick and healthy cauliflower fried rice.
135. **Zoodle and Chicken Stir-Fry:** A fast and tasty stir-fry with zucchini noodles and chicken.
136. **Keto Egg Salad:** A classic egg salad that's keto-friendly.
137. **Beef and Broccoli Skillet:** A quick beef and broccoli stir-fry made in a skillet.
138. **Chia Seed Breakfast Bowl:** A nutritious breakfast bowl featuring chia seeds soaked in coconut milk, topped with fresh fruit and a sprinkle of nuts.
139. **Tuna Salad Lettuce Wraps:** Easy tuna salad wrapped in fresh lettuce leaves.
140. **Asian Chicken Lettuce Wraps:** Crisp lettuce wraps filled with savory, seasoned chicken and fresh vegetables, topped with a tangy soy-based dressing.

Advanced Recipes

141. **Beef Wellington with Cauliflower Mash:** An elegant beef Wellington served with cauliflower mash.
142. **Keto Sushi Rolls with Cauliflower Rice:** Sushi rolls made with low-carb cauliflower rice.
143. **Chicken Cordon Bleu:** Classic chicken Cordon Bleu with a low-carb twist.
144. **Low-Carb Lobster Bisque:** A rich and creamy lobster bisque that's low in carbs.
145. **Pork Belly with Cabbage Slaw:** Tender pork belly served with a crunchy cabbage slaw.
146. **Cauliflower Gnocchi with Pesto:** Light and fluffy cauliflower gnocchi with a rich pesto sauce.
147. **Stuffed Chicken Breast with Spinach and Cheese:** Chicken breasts stuffed with spinach and cheese.

148. **Keto Lamb Chops with Mint Sauce:** Juicy lamb chops served with a refreshing mint sauce.

149. **Zoodle Shrimp Scampi:** A low-carb version of shrimp scampi with zucchini noodles.

150. **Low-Carb Beef Bourguignon:** A classic beef Bourguignon with a low-carb twist.

(Plus, some bonus recipes in the back of the book 😊)

Breakfast Recipes

Recipe 1: Greek Yogurt Parfait with Berries and Nuts

Prep Time: 10 minutes | Cooking Time: 0 minutes | Servings: 2

Ingredients

- 1 cup Greek yogurt
- 1/2 cup mixed berries (strawberries, blueberries, raspberries)
- 1/4 cup granola (low carb)
- 2 tablespoons chopped nuts (almonds, walnuts)
- 1 teaspoon honey (optional)
- 1/2 teaspoon vanilla extract (optional)
- Fresh mint leaves for garnish (optional)

Cooking Instructions

1. **Prepare the Ingredients:** Wash the berries thoroughly and pat them dry. Chop the nuts if they are not already chopped.
2. **Layer the Parfait:** In two serving glasses or bowls, start with a layer of Greek yogurt at the bottom.
3. **Add the Berries:** Evenly distribute half of the mixed berries over the yogurt layer.
4. **Add the Granola**: Sprinkle half of the granola over the berries.
5. **Repeat the Layers**: Add another layer of Greek yogurt, followed by the remaining berries and granola.
6. **Top with Nuts**: Sprinkle the chopped nuts over the top layer of granola.
7. **Optional Flavors:** Drizzle with honey and add a few drops of vanilla extract if desired.
8. **Garnish and Serve:** Garnish with fresh mint leaves and serve immediately.

Nutritional Facts

- **Calories:** 220 kcal
- **Protein:** 15g
- **Fat:** 9g
- **Saturated Fat:** 2g
- **Cholesterol:** 10mg
- **Sodium:** 60mg
- **Potassium:** 250mg
- **Fiber:** 4g
- **Sugar:** 10g
- **Calcium:** 150mg

Cooking Tips

- ✓ **Choosing Greek Yogurt:** Use plain, unsweetened Greek yogurt for the best protein content and to avoid added sugars.
- ✓ **Berries:** Fresh or frozen berries can be used. If using frozen, allow them to thaw slightly.
- ✓ **Granola:** Opt for a low-carb granola to keep the recipe low in carbs.
- ✓ **Nuts:** Toasting the nuts beforehand can add extra flavor and crunch.
- ✓ **Serving Suggestions:** Serve immediately to keep the granola crunchy. Pair with a cup of herbal tea for a refreshing start to your day.
- ✓ **Customization:** Feel free to swap the berries for other fruits like kiwi or mango based on preference.

Greek yogurt parfait with berries and nuts is a quick, nutritious, and delicious breakfast option that combines creamy yogurt, fresh berries, crunchy granola, and nuts for a satisfying start to the day.

Recipe 2: Spinach and Feta Omelet

Prep Time: 5 minutes | Cooking Time: 10 minutes | Servings: 1

Ingredients

- 2 large eggs
- 1/4 cup fresh spinach, chopped
- 2 tablespoons feta cheese, crumbled
- 1 tablespoon milk or water
- 1/4 teaspoon salt
- 1/4 teaspoon black pepper
- 1 tablespoon olive oil or butter
- Fresh herbs for garnish (optional)

Cooking Instructions

1. **Whisk the Eggs:** In a small bowl, whisk together the eggs, milk or water, salt, and black pepper until well combined.
2. **Prepare the Pan:** Heat olive oil or butter in a non-stick skillet over medium heat.
3. **Cook the Spinach:** Add the chopped spinach to the skillet and cook for 1-2 minutes until wilted.
4. **Add the Eggs:** Pour the egg mixture into the skillet, making sure it covers the spinach evenly.
5. **Cook the Omelet:** Cook for about 3-4 minutes until the edges start to set, then sprinkle the feta cheese over half of the omelet.
6. **Fold and Finish:** Gently fold the omelet in half and continue cooking for another 2-3 minutes until the eggs are fully set.
7. **Serve:** Slide the omelet onto a plate, garnish with fresh herbs if desired, and serve hot.

Nutritional Facts

- **Calories:** 200 kcal
- **Protein:** 14g
- **Fat:** 16g
- **Saturated Fat:** 6g
- **Cholesterol:** 380mg
- **Sodium:** 600mg
- **Potassium:** 300mg
- **Fiber:** 1g
- **Sugar:** 1g
- **Calcium:** 150mg

Cooking Tips

- ✓ **Whisking Eggs:** Whisk the eggs thoroughly to incorporate air, making the omelet fluffier.
- ✓ **Pan Temperature:** Ensure the skillet is heated before adding the eggs to prevent sticking and ensure even cooking.
- ✓ **Feta Cheese:** Adjust the amount of feta cheese to taste; other cheeses like goat cheese can also be used.
- ✓ **Adding Ingredients:** Avoid overcrowding the omelet with too many ingredients to ensure it cooks evenly.
- ✓ **Serving Suggestions:** Pair with a side salad or avocado slices for a complete low-carb breakfast.
- ✓ **Herbs:** Fresh herbs like parsley, chives, or dill can enhance the flavor and presentation of the omelet.

Spinach and feta omelet is a delicious and nutritious breakfast option that combines the savory flavors of spinach and feta cheese in a fluffy egg base.

Recipe 3: Low-Carb Blueberry Pancakes

Prep Time: 10 minutes | Cooking Time: 15 minutes | Servings: 4

Ingredients

- 1 cup almond flour
- 2 tablespoons coconut flour
- 1 teaspoon baking powder
- 1/4 teaspoon salt
- 3 large eggs
- 1/2 cup unsweetened almond milk
- 1 tablespoon melted coconut oil
- 1 teaspoon vanilla extract
- 1/2 cup fresh blueberries
- Cooking spray or additional coconut oil for the skillet

Cooking Instructions

1. **Mix Dry Ingredients:** In a large bowl, whisk together the almond flour, coconut flour, baking powder, and salt.
2. **Combine Wet Ingredients:** In another bowl, beat the eggs, then add the almond milk, melted coconut oil, and vanilla extract. Mix until well combined.
3. **Combine and Fold in Blueberries:** Pour the wet ingredients into the dry ingredients and stir until just combined. Gently fold in the blueberries.
4. **Heat the Skillet:** Heat a non-stick skillet or griddle over medium heat and lightly grease with cooking spray or coconut oil.
5. **Cook the Pancakes:** Pour 1/4 cup of batter onto the skillet for each pancake. Cook until bubbles form on the surface and the edges look set, about 2-3 minutes. Flip and cook for another 2-3 minutes until golden brown.
6. **Serve:** Serve hot with your favorite low-carb syrup or additional blueberries if desired.

Nutritional Facts

- **Calories:** 220 kcal
- **Protein:** 8g
- **Fat:** 18g
- **Saturated Fat:** 5g
- **Cholesterol:** 110mg
- **Sodium:** 180mg
- **Potassium:** 150mg
- **Fiber:** 4g
- **Sugar:** 2g
- **Calcium:** 50mg

Cooking Tips

- ✓ **Flour Mixing:** Ensure the almond flour and coconut flour are well mixed to prevent clumping in the batter.
- ✓ **Batter Consistency:** If the batter is too thick, add a little more almond milk to reach the desired consistency.
- ✓ **Blueberries:** Fresh blueberries work best, but if used frozen, thaw and drain them first to avoid excess moisture.
- ✓ **Skillet Temperature:** Keep the skillet at a medium temperature to prevent the pancakes from burning before they cook through.
- ✓ **Portioning:** Use a 1/4 cup measure to ensure evenly sized pancakes.
- ✓ **Serving Suggestions:** Top with a dollop of Greek yogurt and a sprinkle of nuts for added protein and texture.

Low-carb blueberry pancakes are a delightful and healthy breakfast option, offering the sweet taste of blueberries in a fluffy, low-carb pancake.

Recipe 4: Avocado and Egg Breakfast Bowl

Prep Time: 10 minutes | Cooking Time: 10 minutes | Servings: 2

Ingredients

- 2 ripe avocados, halved and pitted
- 4 large eggs
- 1 cup baby spinach, chopped
- 1/2 cup cherry tomatoes, halved
- 1/4 cup red onion, finely chopped
- 1 tablespoon olive oil
- 1 tablespoon fresh lemon juice
- 1/4 teaspoon salt
- 1/4 teaspoon black pepper
- 1/4 teaspoon paprika
- Fresh parsley, chopped (optional for garnish)

Cooking Instructions

1. **Prepare the Avocados:** Scoop out a bit of the avocado flesh to create a larger well for the eggs. Set the scooped avocado aside.
2. **Cook the Eggs:** Heat a non-stick skillet over medium heat and lightly grease with olive oil. Crack the eggs into the skillet and cook until the whites are set and the yolks are done to your liking, about 3-4 minutes sunny side up.
3. **Assemble the Bowls:** In each bowl, place the halved avocados. Top with the cooked eggs.
4. **Add the Veggies:** Distribute the chopped spinach, cherry tomatoes, and red onion evenly between the bowls.
5. **Season and Dress:** Drizzle the olive oil and lemon juice over the bowls. Sprinkle with salt, black pepper, and paprika.
6. **Garnish and Serve:** Garnish with fresh parsley if desired and serve immediately.

Nutritional Facts

- **Calories:** 350 kcal
- **Protein:** 12g
- **Fat:** 30g
- **Saturated Fat:** 5g
- **Cholesterol:** 220mg
- **Sodium:** 320mg
- **Potassium:** 800mg
- **Fiber:** 10g
- **Sugar:** 2g
- **Vitamin C:** 25mg

Cooking Tips

- ✓ **Egg Cooking:** Adjust the cooking time of the eggs to achieve your preferred level of doneness (soft, medium, or hard yolks).
- ✓ **Avocado Selection:** Choose ripe but firm avocados to ensure they hold their shape in the bowl.
- ✓ **Extra Flavor:** Add a sprinkle of your favorite seasoning blend or hot sauce for extra flavor.
- ✓ **Serving Suggestions:** Pair with a side of low-carb toast or a handful of nuts for added texture and nutrients.
- ✓ **Customizations:** Feel free to add other vegetables like bell peppers or cucumbers for variety.
- ✓ **Leftover Avocado:** Use the scooped-out avocado flesh in a smoothie or as a spread on low-carb bread.

Avocado and egg breakfast bowls are a nutritious and satisfying start to your day, combining healthy fats, protein, and fresh vegetables in a delicious and easy-to-make dish.

Recipe 5: Protein-Packed Smoothie with Spinach and Almond Butter

Prep Time: 5 minutes | Cooking Time: 0 minutes | Servings: 1

Ingredients

- 1 cup unsweetened almond milk
- 1 cup fresh spinach leaves
- 1 scoop vanilla protein powder
- 1 tablespoon almond butter
- 1/2 banana, frozen
- 1/2 teaspoon vanilla extract
- Ice cubes (optional for thicker consistency)

Cooking Instructions

1. **Blend Ingredients:** Add the almond milk, spinach, protein powder, almond butter, frozen banana, and vanilla extract to a blender.
2. **Blend Until Smooth:** Blend on high speed until the mixture is smooth and creamy. Add ice cubes if a thicker consistency is desired and blend again.
3. **Serve:** Pour into a glass and enjoy immediately.

Nutritional Facts

- **Calories:** 250 kcal
- **Protein:** 20g
- **Fat:** 10g
- **Saturated Fat:** 1.5g
- **Cholesterol:** 0mg
- **Sodium:** 200mg
- **Potassium:** 600mg
- **Fiber:** 5g
- **Sugar:** 6g
- **Vitamin A:** 2000 IU

Cooking Tips

- ✓ **Protein Powder:** Choose a high-quality protein powder that fits your dietary preferences (whey, plant-based, etc.).
- ✓ **Banana:** Using a frozen banana helps create a creamier texture and naturally sweetens the smoothie.
- ✓ **Spinach:** Fresh spinach blends more smoothly than frozen, but frozen can be used if fresh is not available.
- ✓ **Consistency:** Adjust the amount of almond milk to achieve your desired smoothie consistency.
- ✓ **Optional Add-Ins:** Add a tablespoon of chia seeds or flax seeds for extra fiber and omega-3 fatty acids.
- ✓ **Serving Suggestions:** Enjoy as a quick breakfast or post-workout snack for a protein boost.

The protein-packed smoothie with spinach and almond butter is a delicious and nutritious way to start your day or refuel after a workout, offering a perfect blend of protein, healthy fats, and greens.

Recipe 6: Cottage Cheese and Berry Bowl

Prep Time: 5 minutes | Cooking Time: 0 minutes | Servings: 1

Ingredients

- 1 cup cottage cheese (low-fat or full fat)
- 1/2 cup mixed berries (strawberries, blueberries, raspberries)
- 1 tablespoon chopped nuts (almonds, walnuts)
- 1 teaspoon honey or low-carb sweetener (optional)
- Fresh mint leaves for garnish (optional)

Cooking Instructions

1. **Prepare the Ingredients:** Wash the berries thoroughly and pat them dry. Chop the nuts if they are not already chopped.
2. **Assemble the Bowl:** Place the cottage cheese in a serving bowl.
3. **Add the Berries:** Top the cottage cheese with mixed berries.
4. **Add Nuts and Sweetener:** Sprinkle the chopped nuts over the berries. Drizzle with honey or a low-carb sweetener if desired.
5. **Garnish and Serve:** Garnish with fresh mint leaves and serve immediately.

Nutritional Facts

- **Calories:** 200 kcal
- **Protein:** 20g
- **Fat:** 8g
- **Saturated Fat:** 3g
- **Cholesterol:** 25mg
- **Sodium:** 400mg
- **Potassium:** 400mg
- **Fiber:** 3g
- **Sugar:** 10g
- **Calcium:** 150mg

Cooking Tips

- ✓ **Cottage Cheese:** Choose the type of cottage cheese based on your dietary preferences; low-fat is lighter, while full fat is creamier.
- ✓ **Berries:** Fresh or frozen berries can be used; if using frozen, thaw them first to prevent excess moisture.
- ✓ **Nuts:** Toasting the nuts can enhance their flavor and add a crunchy texture.
- ✓ **Sweetener:** Adjust the amount of sweetener to taste; you can omit it for a lower-carb option.
- ✓ **Serving Suggestions:** This bowl pairs well with a hot cup of tea or coffee for a balanced breakfast.
- ✓ **Customization:** Add other toppings like chia seeds, flax seeds, or a sprinkle of cinnamon for extra flavor and nutrition.

The cottage cheese and berry bowl is a simple, protein-rich breakfast or snack option that combines creamy cottage cheese with the natural sweetness of berries and the crunch of nuts.

Recipe 7: Low-Carb Chia Seed Pudding

Prep Time: 5 minutes | Cooking Time: 0 minutes (plus overnight chilling) | Servings: 2

Ingredients

- 1 cup unsweetened almond milk
- 1/4 cup chia seeds
- 1 teaspoon vanilla extract
- 1 tablespoon low-carb sweetener (such as erythritol or stevia)
- Fresh berries for topping (optional)
- Nuts or seeds for topping (optional)

Cooking Instructions

1. **Combine Ingredients:** In a mixing bowl, whisk together the almond milk, chia seeds, vanilla extract, and low-carb sweetener until well combined.
2. **Refrigerate:** Cover the bowl and refrigerate for at least 4 hours, preferably overnight, until the chia seeds have absorbed the liquid, and the mixture has thickened.
3. **Stir and Serve:** Stir the pudding to ensure it's well-mixed. Divide into two servings and top with fresh berries and nuts or seeds if desired.

Nutritional Facts

- **Calories:** 150 kcal
- **Protein:** 5g
- **Fat:** 8g
- **Saturated Fat:** 1g
- **Cholesterol:** 0mg
- **Sodium:** 60mg
- **Potassium:** 150mg
- **Fiber:** 10g
- **Sugar:** 1g
- **Calcium:** 200mg

Cooking Tips

- ✓ **Milk Options:** Any unsweetened milk (such as coconut milk or cashew milk) can be used based on your preference.
- ✓ **Sweeteners:** Adjust the sweetness to taste with your preferred low-carb sweetener.
- ✓ **Consistency:** For a thicker pudding, add more chia seeds; for a thinner consistency, add more almond milk.
- ✓ **Serving Suggestions:** Enjoy with a dollop of whipped cream or a sprinkle of cinnamon for extra flavor.
- ✓ **Customizations:** Mix in cocoa powder or matcha powder for different flavors.

Low-carb chia seed pudding is a versatile and easy-to-make breakfast or snack option that is rich in fiber and healthy fats, perfect for starting your day or satisfying a midday craving.

Recipe 8: Smoked Salmon and Avocado Toast on Low-Carb Bread

Prep Time: 10 minutes | Cooking Time: 0 minutes | Servings: 2

Ingredients

- 2 slices of low-carb bread
- 1 ripe avocado, mashed
- 4 oz smoked salmon
- 1 tablespoon lemon juice
- 1 tablespoon capers
- 1/4 teaspoon sea salt
- 1/4 teaspoon black pepper
- Fresh dill for garnish (optional)

Cooking Instructions

1. **Prepare the Avocado Spread:** In a bowl, mash the avocado with lemon juice, sea salt, and black pepper until smooth.
2. **Toast the Bread:** Lightly toast the low-carb bread slices to your desired level of crispiness.
3. **Assemble the Toast:** Spread the mashed avocado evenly over each slice of toasted bread.
4. **Add the Smoked Salmon:** Layer the smoked salmon on top of the avocado spread.
5. **Garnish and Serve:** Sprinkle with capers and garnish with fresh dill if desired. Serve immediately.

Nutritional Facts

- **Calories:** 250 kcal
- **Protein:** 15g
- **Fat:** 18g
- **Saturated Fat:** 3g
- **Cholesterol:** 25mg
- **Sodium:** 600mg
- **Potassium:** 450mg
- **Fiber:** 7g
- **Sugar:** 2g
- **Vitamin D:** 5mcg

Cooking Tips

- ✓ **Avocado:** Use a perfectly ripe avocado for the best texture and flavor.
- ✓ **Smoked Salmon:** Ensure the smoked salmon is fresh and of high quality for the best taste.
- ✓ **Bread Options:** Choose your favorite low-carb bread; homemade or store-bought options are both fine.
- ✓ **Customizations:** Add a poached egg on top for extra protein or sprinkle with red pepper flakes for a spicy kick.
- ✓ **Serving Suggestions:** Pair with a side salad or a cup of tea for a complete meal.

Smoked salmon and avocado toast on low-carb bread is a quick, nutritious, and flavorful breakfast or snack that combines healthy fats and protein, perfect for a satisfying and balanced meal.

Recipe 9: Egg Muffins with Veggies and Cheese

Prep Time: 10 minutes | Cooking Time: 20 minutes | Servings: 6

Ingredients

- 6 large eggs
- 1/2 cup bell peppers, finely chopped
- 1/2 cup spinach, finely chopped
- 1/4 cup red onion, finely chopped
- 1/2 cup shredded cheese (cheddar, mozzarella, or your choice)
- 1/4 cup milk (optional)
- 1/2 teaspoon salt
- 1/4 teaspoon black pepper
- Cooking spray or olive oil for greasing

Cooking Instructions

1. **Preheat the Oven:** Preheat your oven to 375°F (190°C) and lightly grease a muffin tin with cooking spray or olive oil.
2. **Prepare the Vegetables:** Finely chop the bell peppers, spinach, and red onion.
3. **Mix the Eggs:** In a large bowl, whisk together the eggs, milk (if using), salt, and black pepper until well combined.
4. **Add Vegetables and Cheese:** Stir in the chopped vegetables and shredded cheese into the egg mixture.
5. **Fill the Muffin Tin:** Pour the egg mixture evenly into the muffin tin, filling each cup about three-quarters full.
6. **Bake:** Bake in the preheated oven for 20 minutes or until the egg muffins are set and slightly golden on top.
7. **Cool and Serve:** Let the muffins cool in the tin for a few minutes before removing. Serve warm or store for meal prep.

Nutritional Facts

- **Calories:** 120 kcal
- **Protein:** 10g
- **Fat:** 8g
- **Saturated Fat:** 3g
- **Cholesterol:** 170mg
- **Sodium:** 250mg
- **Potassium:** 200mg
- **Fiber:** 1g
- **Sugar:** 1g
- **Calcium:** 100mg

Cooking Tips

- ✓ **Customization:** Add other favorite vegetables like mushrooms, tomatoes, or zucchini for variety.
- ✓ **Cheese Options:** Feel free to use different types of cheese to suit your taste.
- ✓ **Non-Stick Muffin Tin:** Using a non-stick muffin tin or silicone muffin cups can make removal easier.
- ✓ **Meal Prep:** These egg muffins can be stored in the refrigerator for up to 4 days or frozen for up to 1 month. Reheat in the microwave before serving.
- ✓ **Serving Suggestions:** Serve with a side of avocado or a fresh salad for a complete meal.

Egg muffins with veggies and cheese are a convenient and delicious breakfast option, perfect for meal prep and easy to grab on busy mornings.

Recipe 10: Almond Flour Waffles with Greek Yogurt

Prep Time: 10 minutes | Cooking Time: 15 minutes | Servings: 4

Ingredients

- 2 cups almond flour
- 1 teaspoon baking powder
- 1/4 teaspoon salt
- 3 large eggs
- 1/4 cup unsweetened almond milk
- 2 tablespoons melted coconut oil
- 1 teaspoon vanilla extract
- 1 cup Greek yogurt (for topping)
- Fresh berries (for topping)
- Sugar-free syrup (optional for serving)

Cooking Instructions

1. **Preheat the Waffle Iron:** Preheat your waffle iron according to the manufacturer's instructions.
2. **Mix Dry Ingredients:** In a large bowl, whisk together the almond flour, baking powder, and salt.
3. **Combine Wet Ingredients:** In another bowl, beat the eggs, then add the almond milk, melted coconut oil, and vanilla extract. Mix until well combined.
4. **Combine and Mix:** Pour the wet ingredients into the dry ingredients and stir until the batter is smooth and well combined.
5. **Cook the Waffles:** Lightly grease the preheated waffle iron with cooking spray or a small amount of coconut oil. Pour the batter into the waffle iron and cook according to the manufacturer's instructions until golden brown and

cooked through, about 3-5 minutes per waffle.
6. **Serve:** Serve the waffles warm, topped with Greek yogurt, fresh berries, and sugar-free syrup if desired.

Nutritional Facts

- **Calories:** 250 kcal
- **Protein:** 12g
- **Fat:** 18g
- **Saturated Fat:** 4g
- **Cholesterol:** 110mg
- **Sodium:** 200mg
- **Potassium:** 100mg
- **Fiber:** 4g
- **Sugar:** 2g
- **Calcium:** 100mg

Cooking Tips

- ✓ **Waffle Iron:** Ensure your waffle iron is properly preheated to prevent sticking and ensure even cooking.
- ✓ **Consistency:** If the batter is too thick, add a bit more almond milk to reach the desired consistency.
- ✓ **Serving Suggestions:** Serve with a variety of toppings like nuts, seeds, or a sprinkle of cinnamon for added flavor.
- ✓ **Storage:** Leftover waffles can be stored in the refrigerator for up to 3 days or frozen for up to 1 month. Reheat in a toaster or oven for best results.

Almond flour waffles with Greek yogurt are a delicious, high-protein breakfast option that combines the crispiness of waffles with the creamy richness of Greek yogurt and fresh berries.

Lunch Recipes

Recipe 11: Grilled Chicken Caesar Salad

Prep Time: 15 minutes | Cooking Time: 15 minutes | Servings: 2

Ingredients

- 2 boneless, skinless chicken breasts
- 1 tablespoon olive oil
- 1 teaspoon garlic powder
- 1/2 teaspoon sea salt
- 1/4 teaspoon black pepper
- 4 cups romaine lettuce, chopped
- 1/4 cup grated Parmesan cheese
- 1/4 cup Caesar dressing (low carb)
- 1/2 cup cherry tomatoes, halved (optional)
- 1/4 cup croutons (low-carb, optional)
- Lemon wedges (optional for serving)

Cooking Instructions

1. **Preheat the Grill:** Preheat your grill to medium-high heat.
2. **Season the Chicken:** Rub the chicken breasts with olive oil, garlic powder, sea salt, and black pepper.
3. **Grill the Chicken:** Place the chicken breasts on the grill and cook for 6-7 minutes on each side or until the internal temperature reaches 165°F (74°C). Remove from the grill and let rest for a few minutes before slicing.
4. **Prepare the Salad:** In a large bowl, combine the chopped romaine lettuce, grated Parmesan cheese, and Caesar dressing. Toss to coat evenly.
5. **Assemble the Salad:** Divide the salad between two plates. Top with sliced grilled chicken, cherry tomatoes, and croutons if using.
6. **Serve:** Serve immediately with lemon wedges on the side if desired.

Nutritional Facts

- **Calories:** 400 kcal
- **Protein:** 35g
- **Fat:** 25g
- **Saturated Fat:** 6g
- **Cholesterol:** 110mg
- **Sodium:** 900mg
- **Potassium:** 800mg
- **Fiber:** 3g
- **Sugar:** 2g
- **Calcium:** 150mg

Cooking Tips

- ✓ **Chicken:** Ensure the chicken is evenly cooked by using a meat thermometer to check the internal temperature.
- ✓ **Dressing:** Use a low-carb Caesar dressing to keep the recipe low in carbohydrates.
- ✓ **Lettuce:** Fresh and crisp romaine lettuce gives the best texture and flavor to the salad.
- ✓ **Customizations:** Add other favorite salad ingredients like avocado or cucumber for extra nutrition and flavor.
- ✓ **Meal Prep:** Grilled chicken can be cooked ahead of time and stored in the refrigerator for up to 3 days.

Grilled chicken Caesar salad is a classic, protein-rich meal that combines tender grilled chicken with crisp lettuce and creamy Caesar dressing, perfect for a satisfying lunch or dinner.

Recipe 12: Turkey and Avocado Lettuce Wraps

Prep Time: 10 minutes | Cooking Time: 0 minutes | Servings: 2

Ingredients

- 8 large lettuce leaves (romaine, butter lettuce, or iceberg)
- 8 oz deli turkey slices
- 1 ripe avocado, sliced
- 1/2 cup cherry tomatoes, halved
- 1/4 cup red onion, thinly sliced
- 2 tablespoons mayonnaise (optional)
- 1 tablespoon Dijon mustard
- Salt and pepper to taste
- Fresh herbs for garnish (optional)

Cooking Instructions

1. **Prepare the Ingredients:** Wash and pat dry the lettuce leaves. Slice the avocado, cherry tomatoes, and red onion.
2. **Assemble the Wraps:** Lay out the lettuce leaves on a flat surface. Spread a small amount of mayonnaise (if used) and Dijon mustard on each leaf.
3. **Add the Fillings:** Place turkey slices, avocado, cherry tomatoes, and red onion on each lettuce leaf. Season with salt and pepper to taste.
4. **Roll the Wraps:** Carefully roll up the lettuce leaves, tucking in the sides as you go to form a wrap.
5. **Serve:** Garnish with fresh herbs if desired and serve immediately.

Nutritional Facts

- **Calories:** 200 kcal
- **Protein:** 18g
- **Fat:** 12g
- **Saturated Fat:** 2g
- **Cholesterol:** 40mg
- **Sodium:** 600mg
- **Potassium:** 550mg
- **Fiber:** 6g
- **Sugar:** 2g
- **Vitamin A:** 3000 IU

Cooking Tips

- ✓ **Lettuce Selection:** Choose large, sturdy lettuce leaves that can hold the fillings without tearing.
- ✓ **Turkey:** Use high-quality deli turkey or leftover roasted turkey for the best flavor.
- ✓ **Customizations:** Add other favorite ingredients like sliced cucumber, bell pepper, or shredded cheese.
- ✓ **Dressing Alternatives:** Substitute mayonnaise with Greek yogurt or hummus for a different flavor profile.
- ✓ **Meal Prep:** Prepare the fillings ahead of time and store them separately. Assemble the wraps just before serving to keep the lettuce crisp.

Turkey and avocado lettuce wraps are a fresh, low-carb alternative to traditional sandwiches, offering a quick and nutritious meal option that's perfect for lunch or a light dinner.

Recipe 13: Spicy Tuna Salad with Cucumber Slices

Prep Time: 10 minutes | Cooking Time: 0 minutes | Servings: 2

Ingredients

- 2 cans of tuna in water, drained
- 1/4 cup mayonnaise
- 1 tablespoon Sriracha sauce (adjust to taste)
- 1 tablespoon fresh lemon juice
- 1/4 cup celery, finely chopped
- 1/4 cup red onion, finely chopped
- 1 tablespoon fresh parsley, chopped
- 1 large cucumber, sliced
- Salt and pepper to taste
- Fresh dill for garnish (optional)

Cooking Instructions

1. **Prepare the Ingredients:** Drain the tuna and finely chop the celery, red onion, and parsley.
2. **Mix the Tuna Salad:** In a medium bowl, combine the drained tuna, mayonnaise, Sriracha sauce, lemon juice, celery, red onion, and parsley. Mix well.
3. **Season to Taste:** Add salt and pepper to taste, adjusting the Sriracha sauce for more or less heat as desired.
4. **Prepare the Cucumber Slices:** Wash and slice the cucumber into rounds about 1/4 inch thick.
5. **Assemble and Serve:** Place a spoonful of the spicy tuna salad on each cucumber slice. Garnish with fresh dill if desired and serve immediately.

Nutritional Facts

- **Calories:** 250 kcal
- **Protein:** 25g
- **Fat:** 15g
- **Saturated Fat:** 2.5g
- **Cholesterol:** 50mg
- **Sodium:** 600mg
- **Potassium:** 400mg
- **Fiber:** 2g
- **Sugar:** 3g
- **Vitamin C:** 10mg

Cooking Tips

- ✓ **Tuna Selection:** Use high-quality canned tuna for the best flavor and texture.
- ✓ **Spice Level:** Adjust the amount of Sriracha sauce to control the heat level according to your preference.
- ✓ **Serving Suggestions:** Serve as an appetizer or light lunch. Pair with a fresh salad for a more substantial meal.
- ✓ **Storage:** The tuna salad can be made ahead of time and stored in the refrigerator for up to 3 days. Assemble the cucumber slices just before serving.
- ✓ **Customizations:** Add other vegetables like bell peppers or olives for extra flavor and crunch.

Spicy tuna salad with cucumber slices is a refreshing, low-carb dish that combines the creaminess of tuna salad with the crispness of cucumber, perfect for a quick snack or light meal.

Recipe 14: Low-Carb Chicken and Broccoli Stir-Fry

Prep Time: 15 minutes | Cooking Time: 15 minutes | Servings: 4

Ingredients

- 1 lb. boneless, skinless chicken breasts cut into bite-sized pieces
- 3 cups broccoli florets
- 1 red bell pepper, sliced
- 1/2 cup onion, sliced
- 2 tablespoons olive oil
- 2 cloves garlic, minced
- 1 tablespoon fresh ginger, minced
- 1/4 cup soy sauce (low sodium)
- 1 tablespoon sesame oil
- 1 tablespoon rice vinegar
- 1 teaspoon chili flakes (optional)
- 2 tablespoons sesame seeds (optional for garnish)
- Green onions, sliced (optional for garnish)

Cooking Instructions

1. **Prepare the Ingredients:** Cut the chicken into bite-sized pieces and chop the vegetables. Mince the garlic and ginger.
2. **Heat the Oil:** In a large skillet or wok, heat the olive oil over medium-high heat.
3. **Cook the Chicken:** Add the chicken to the skillet and cook until browned and cooked for about 5-7 minutes. Remove the chicken from the skillet and set aside.
4. **Cook the Vegetables:** In the same skillet, add the broccoli, red bell pepper, and onion. Stir-fry for 5 minutes until the vegetables are tender-crisp.
5. **Add Garlic and Ginger:** Add the minced garlic and ginger to the skillet and stir-fry for another minute until fragrant.

6. **Combine Everything:** Return the cooked chicken to the skillet. Add the soy sauce, sesame oil, rice vinegar, and chili flakes (if using). Stir well to coat the chicken and vegetables in the sauce.
7. **Serve:** Cook for an additional 2-3 minutes until everything is heated through. Garnish with sesame seeds and sliced green onions if desired. Serve immediately.

Nutritional Facts

- **Calories:** 300 kcal
- **Protein:** 30g
- **Fat:** 15g
- **Saturated Fat:** 2g
- **Cholesterol:** 70mg
- **Sodium:** 600mg
- **Potassium:** 600mg
- **Fiber:** 4g
- **Sugar:** 3g
- **Vitamin C:** 70mg

Cooking Tips

- ✓ **High Heat:** Stir-frying is best done on high heat to quickly cook the ingredients while retaining their texture.
- ✓ **Soy Sauce:** Use low-sodium soy sauce to control the salt content. Tamari or coconut aminos can be used as a gluten-free option.
- ✓ **Vegetables:** Cut vegetables into uniform sizes to ensure even cooking.
- ✓ **Serving Suggestions:** Serve cauliflower rice or enjoy it on its own for a low-carb meal.
- ✓ **Customization:** Add other favorite vegetables like snow peas, zucchini, or mushrooms for variety.

Low-carb chicken and broccoli stir-fry is a quick, flavorful, and healthy dish that combines tender chicken with crisp vegetables in a savory sauce, perfect for a weeknight dinner.

Recipe 15: Cauliflower Rice with Ground Turkey and Veggies

Prep Time: 15 minutes | Cooking Time: 15 minutes | Servings: 4

Ingredients

- 1 lb. ground turkey
- 4 cups cauliflower rice
- 1 cup bell pepper, diced
- 1 cup zucchini, diced
- 1/2 cup onion, diced
- 2 cloves garlic, minced
- 2 tablespoons olive oil
- 1 teaspoon ground cumin
- 1 teaspoon paprika
- 1/2 teaspoon chili powder
- 1/2 teaspoon salt
- 1/4 teaspoon black pepper
- 1/4 cup fresh cilantro, chopped (optional for garnish)
- Lime wedges (optional for serving)

Cooking Instructions

1. **Prepare the Ingredients:** Dice the bell pepper, zucchini, and onion. Mince the garlic. Chop the fresh cilantro if using.
2. **Cook the Ground Turkey:** In a large skillet, heat 1 tablespoon of olive oil over medium-high heat. Add the ground turkey and cook until browned and cooked through about 5-7 minutes. Remove from the skillet and set aside.
3. **Cook the Vegetables:** In the same skillet, heat the remaining 1 tablespoon of olive oil. Add the onion, bell pepper, and zucchini. Cook for 5 minutes until the vegetables are tender.
4. **Add Garlic and Spices:** Add the minced garlic, cumin, paprika, chili powder, salt, and black pepper. Cook for another minute until fragrant.
5. **Combine and Heat:** Add the cooked ground turkey back to the skillet along with the cauliflower rice. Stir well to combine and cook for an additional 5 minutes until everything is heated through.
6. **Serve:** Garnish with fresh cilantro and serve with lime wedges if desired.

Nutritional Facts

- **Calories:** 280 kcal
- **Protein:** 25g
- **Fat:** 15g
- **Saturated Fat:** 3g
- **Cholesterol:** 80mg
- **Sodium:** 400mg
- **Potassium:** 600mg
- **Fiber:** 5g
- **Sugar:** 4g
- **Vitamin A:** 1000 IU

Cooking Tips

- ✓ **Cauliflower Rice:** Use fresh or frozen cauliflower rice. If using fresh, grate or process a head of cauliflower in a food processor.
- ✓ **Ground Turkey:** Ensure the ground turkey is fully cooked and no longer pink before adding the vegetables.
- ✓ **Spice Level:** Adjust the chili powder according to your heat preference.
- ✓ **Serving Suggestions:** Serve on its own or with a side of avocado slices for added healthy fats.
- ✓ **Customization:** Add other vegetables like carrots, peas, or corn for extra flavor and nutrition.

Cauliflower rice with ground turkey and veggies is a healthy, low-carb dish that's quick to prepare and full of flavor, making it an ideal meal for busy weeknights.

Recipe 16: Shrimp and Zoodle Scampi

Prep Time: 10 minutes | Cooking Time: 10 minutes | Servings: 2

Ingredients

- 1 lb. shrimp, peeled and deveined
- 3 medium zucchinis, spiralized into zoodles
- 3 tablespoons butter
- 3 cloves garlic, minced
- 1/4 cup chicken broth
- 1/4 cup fresh lemon juice
- 1/4 teaspoon red pepper flakes (optional)
- Salt and pepper to taste
- 1/4 cup fresh parsley, chopped
- Lemon wedges for serving

Cooking Instructions

1. **Prepare the Zoodles:** Spiralize the zucchini into zoodles using a spiralizer or a vegetable peeler.
2. **Cook the Shrimp:** In a large skillet, melt 2 tablespoons of butter over medium-high heat. Add the shrimp and cook until pink and opaque, about 2-3 minutes per side. Remove from the skillet and set aside.
3. **Make the Sauce:** In the same skillet, melt the remaining 1 tablespoon of butter. Add the minced garlic and cook for 1 minute until fragrant. Pour in the chicken broth and lemon juice and bring to a simmer. Add red pepper flakes if used.
4. **Cook the Zoodles:** Add the zoodles to the skillet and cook for 2-3 minutes until just tender, tossing them in the sauce.

5. **Combine and Serve:** Return the cooked shrimp to the skillet and toss everything together. Season with salt and pepper to taste. Garnish with fresh parsley and serve with lemon wedges.

Nutritional Facts

- **Calories:** 300 kcal
- **Protein:** 30g
- **Fat:** 18g
- **Saturated Fat:** 9g
- **Cholesterol:** 220mg
- **Sodium:** 800mg
- **Potassium:** 800mg
- **Fiber:** 3g
- **Sugar:** 5g
- **Vitamin C:** 40mg

Cooking Tips

- ✓ **Shrimp:** Use large shrimp for a meatier texture and ensure they are fully cooked but not overdone to avoid a rubbery texture.
- ✓ **Zoodles:** Cook zoodles just until tender to prevent them from becoming mushy.
- ✓ **Butter:** For a dairy-free version, substitute butter with olive oil.
- ✓ **Customization:** Add other ingredients like cherry tomatoes or spinach for extra flavor and nutrition.
- ✓ **Serving Suggestions:** Pair with a fresh green salad or a side of garlic bread (low carb) for a complete meal.

Shrimp and zoodle scampi is a delicious, low-carb version of the classic shrimp scampi, featuring tender shrimp and zucchini noodles in a buttery, garlicky sauce.

Recipe 17: Low-Carb BLT Salad

Prep Time: 10 minutes | Cooking Time: 10 minutes | Servings: 2

Ingredients

- 6 slices of bacon
- 4 cups romaine lettuce, chopped
- 1 cup cherry tomatoes, halved
- 1 avocado, diced
- 1/4 cup red onion, thinly sliced
- 1/4 cup ranch dressing (low carb)
- Salt and pepper to taste

Cooking Instructions

1. **Cook the Bacon:** In a large skillet, cook the bacon over medium heat until crispy, about 5-7 minutes. Remove and drain on paper towels. Once cooled, crumble or chop the bacon into bite-sized pieces.
2. **Prepare the Vegetables:** Chop the romaine lettuce, halve the cherry tomatoes, dice the avocado, and thinly slice the red onion.
3. **Assemble the Salad:** In a large bowl, combine the chopped romaine lettuce, cherry tomatoes, avocado, red onion, and bacon pieces.
4. **Dress the Salad:** Drizzle the low-carb ranch dressing over the salad. Toss gently to combine.
5. **Season and Serve:** Season with salt and pepper to taste. Serve immediately.

Nutritional Facts

- **Calories:** 400 kcal
- **Protein:** 12g
- **Fat:** 35g
- **Saturated Fat:** 10g
- **Cholesterol:** 50mg
- **Sodium:** 800mg
- **Potassium:** 700mg
- **Fiber:** 7g
- **Sugar:** 3g
- **Vitamin A:** 8000 IU

Cooking Tips

- ✓ **Bacon:** Cook bacon until crispy for the best texture. Use turkey bacon as a lower-fat alternative if desired.
- ✓ **Avocado:** Choose a ripe but firm avocado to avoid it becoming mushy in the salad.
- ✓ **Dressing:** Use your favorite low-carb dressing or make a homemade version to control the ingredients.
- ✓ **Customization:** Add a boiled egg, cheese, or cucumber slices for additional flavor and nutrients.
- ✓ **Serving Suggestions:** Serve with a side of low-carb bread or crackers for a more filling meal.

Low-carb BLT salad is a refreshing and satisfying meal that captures the classic flavors of a BLT sandwich without the bread, making it a perfect choice for a light lunch or dinner.

Recipe 18: Chicken and Spinach Stuffed Peppers
Prep Time: 15 minutes | Cooking Time: 30 minutes | Servings: 4

Ingredients

- 4 large bell peppers, tops cut off and seeds removed
- 1 lb. ground chicken
- 2 cups fresh spinach, chopped
- 1/2 cup onion, finely chopped
- 2 cloves garlic, minced
- 1 cup shredded mozzarella cheese
- 1/2 cup tomato sauce (low carb)
- 1 tablespoon olive oil
- 1 teaspoon Italian seasoning
- 1/2 teaspoon salt
- 1/4 teaspoon black pepper
- Fresh parsley, chopped (optional for garnish)

Cooking Instructions

1. **Preheat the Oven:** Preheat your oven to 375°F (190°C).
2. **Prepare the Peppers:** Cut the tops off the bell peppers and remove the seeds. Place them upright in a baking dish.
3. **Cook the Chicken:** In a large skillet, heat olive oil over medium heat. Add the finely chopped onion and garlic and cook for 2-3 minutes until softened.
4. **Add the Chicken:** Add the ground chicken to the skillet and cook until browned and cooked through about 5-7 minutes.
5. **Add Spinach and Seasoning:** Stir in the chopped spinach, tomato sauce, Italian seasoning, salt, and black pepper. Cook for an additional 2-3 minutes until the spinach is wilted.
6. **Stuff the Peppers:** Divide the chicken and spinach mixture evenly among the prepared bell peppers. Top each stuffed pepper with shredded mozzarella cheese.
7. **Bake:** Cover the baking dish with foil and bake in the preheated oven for 25 minutes. Remove the foil and bake for an additional 5 minutes until the cheese is melted and bubbly.
8. **Serve:** Garnish with fresh parsley if desired and serve hot.

Nutritional Facts

- **Calories:** 350 kcal
- **Protein:** 30g
- **Fat:** 18g
- **Saturated Fat:** 7g
- **Cholesterol:** 80mg
- **Sodium:** 600mg
- **Potassium:** 800mg
- **Fiber:** 5g
- **Sugar:** 6g
- **Vitamin C:** 150mg

Cooking Tips

- ✓ **Bell Peppers:** Use a variety of colored bell peppers for a visually appealing dish.
- ✓ **Chicken:** Ground turkey or beef can be used as an alternative to chicken.
- ✓ **Cheese:** Substitute mozzarella with another cheese like cheddar or pepper jack for different flavor profiles.
- ✓ **Tomato Sauce:** Ensure the tomato sauce is low in sugar to keep the recipe low carb.
- ✓ **Meal Prep:** These stuffed peppers can be made ahead of time and stored in the refrigerator for up to 3 days. Reheat before serving.

Chicken and spinach stuffed peppers are a delicious and nutritious meal that combines lean protein, fresh vegetables, and melted cheese, perfect for a healthy and satisfying dinner.

Recipe 19: Beef and Cabbage Stir-Fry

Prep Time: 10 minutes | Cooking Time: 15 minutes | Servings: 4

Ingredients

- 1 lb. ground beef
- 4 cups cabbage, shredded
- 1 large carrot, julienned
- 1 bell pepper, sliced
- 1/2 cup onion, sliced
- 3 cloves garlic, minced
- 2 tablespoons soy sauce (low sodium)
- 1 tablespoon sesame oil
- 1 tablespoon olive oil
- 1 teaspoon fresh ginger, minced
- 1/4 teaspoon red pepper flakes (optional)
- 2 tablespoons green onions, chopped (optional for garnish)
- Sesame seeds (optional for garnish)

Cooking Instructions

1. **Prepare the Ingredients:** Shred the cabbage, julienne the carrot, slice the bell pepper and onion, and mince the garlic and ginger.
2. **Cook the Ground Beef:** In a large skillet or wok, heat olive oil over medium-high heat. Add the ground beef and cook until browned, about 5-7 minutes. Remove from the skillet and set aside.
3. **Cook the Vegetables:** In the same skillet, add sesame oil. Add the onion, bell pepper, and carrot. Stir-fry for 3-4 minutes until the vegetables start to soften.
4. **Add Cabbage and Seasonings:** Add the shredded cabbage, minced garlic, and ginger to the skillet. Stir-fry for another 3-4 minutes until the cabbage is tender.
5. **Combine and Season:** Return the cooked ground beef to the skillet. Add soy sauce and red pepper flakes (if using). Stir well to combine all ingredients and heat through.
6. **Serve:** Garnish with chopped green onions and sesame seeds if desired. Serve hot.

Nutritional Facts

- **Calories:** 300 kcal
- **Protein:** 20g
- **Fat:** 20g
- **Saturated Fat:** 7g
- **Cholesterol:** 60mg
- **Sodium:** 600mg
- **Potassium:** 600mg
- **Fiber:** 4g
- **Sugar:** 5g
- **Vitamin A:** 4000 IU

Cooking Tips

- ✓ **Ground Beef:** Choose lean ground beef to reduce the fat content. Ground turkey or chicken can also be used as a substitute.
- ✓ **Vegetables:** Add other favorite vegetables like broccoli or snap peas for extra variety and nutrition.
- ✓ **Soy Sauce:** Use tamari or coconut aminos for a gluten-free option.
- ✓ **Customization:** Adjust the red pepper flakes to control the heat level according to your preference.
- ✓ **Serving Suggestions:** Serve over cauliflower rice for a complete low-carb meal.

Beef and cabbage stir-fry is a quick, flavorful, and healthy dish that combines ground beef with crisp vegetables, perfect for a nutritious and satisfying dinner.

Recipe 20: Grilled Salmon with Asparagus

Prep Time: 10 minutes | Cooking Time: 15 minutes | Servings: 2

Ingredients

- 2 salmon fillets (6 oz each)
- 1 lb. asparagus, trimmed
- 2 tablespoons olive oil
- 1 tablespoon lemon juice
- 2 cloves garlic, minced
- 1 teaspoon sea salt
- 1/2 teaspoon black pepper
- 1 teaspoon dried dill (optional)
- Lemon wedges for serving

Cooking Instructions

1. **Preheat the Grill:** Preheat your grill to medium-high heat.
2. **Season the Salmon:** Brush the salmon fillets with 1 tablespoon of olive oil and sprinkle with 1/2 teaspoon of sea salt, 1/4 teaspoon of black pepper, and dried dill (if using). Set it aside.
3. **Prepare the Asparagus:** In a bowl, toss the asparagus with the remaining 1 tablespoon of olive oil, lemon juice, minced garlic, 1/2 teaspoon of sea salt, and 1/4 teaspoon of black pepper.
4. **Grill the Salmon:** Place the salmon fillets on the grill, skin-side down. Grill for 4-6 minutes per side or until the salmon is cooked through and flakes easily with a fork.
5. **Grill the Asparagus:** While the salmon is cooking, place the asparagus on the grill and cook for 5-7 minutes, turning occasionally, until tender and slightly charred.

6. **Serve:** Serve the grilled salmon and asparagus immediately with lemon wedges on the side.

Nutritional Facts

- **Calories:** 400 kcal
- **Protein:** 35g
- **Fat:** 25g
- **Saturated Fat:** 4g
- **Cholesterol:** 80mg
- **Sodium:** 800mg
- **Potassium:** 1200mg
- **Fiber:** 4g
- **Sugar:** 3g
- **Vitamin A:** 900 IU

Cooking Tips

- ✓ **Salmon:** Ensure the salmon fillets are of similar thickness to cook evenly. Fresh or frozen salmon can be used; if using frozen, thaw completely before grilling.
- ✓ **Asparagus:** Choose fresh, firm asparagus stalks for the best texture. Thicker stalks may require a longer grilling time.
- ✓ **Grill:** Oil the grill grates well to prevent the salmon from sticking.
- ✓ **Lemon Juice:** Squeeze fresh lemon juice over the salmon and asparagus just before serving for an extra burst of flavor.
- ✓ **Serving Suggestions:** Pair with a side salad or cauliflower rice for a complete low-carb meal.

Grilled salmon with asparagus is a healthy, flavorful dish that combines tender salmon with crisp-tender asparagus, perfect for a quick and nutritious dinner.

Dinner Recipes

Recipe 21: Lemon Garlic Chicken Thighs

Prep Time: 10 minutes | Cooking Time: 35 minutes | Servings: 4

Ingredients

- 4 bone-in, skin-on chicken thighs
- 3 tablespoons olive oil
- 4 cloves garlic, minced
- 2 tablespoons lemon juice
- 1 tablespoon lemon zest
- 1 teaspoon dried oregano
- 1 teaspoon dried thyme
- 1/2 teaspoon sea salt
- 1/4 teaspoon black pepper
- Fresh parsley, chopped (optional for garnish)
- Lemon wedges (optional for serving)

Cooking Instructions

1. **Preheat the Oven:** Preheat your oven to 400°F (200°C).
2. **Prepare the Marinade:** In a small bowl, mix together the olive oil, minced garlic, lemon juice, lemon zest, dried oregano, dried thyme, sea salt, and black pepper.
3. **Marinate the Chicken:** Place the chicken thighs in a large bowl or zip-top bag. Pour the marinade over the chicken, ensuring each thigh is well coated. Marinate for at least 15 minutes or up to 1 hour for more flavor.
4. **Bake the Chicken:** Arrange the marinated chicken thighs in a single layer on a baking sheet or in an oven-safe skillet. Bake in the preheated oven for 35-40 minutes, or until the internal temperature reaches 165°F (74°C) and the skin is crispy and golden brown.

5. **Serve:** Garnish with fresh parsley and serve with lemon wedges if desired.

Nutritional Facts

- **Calories:** 320 kcal
- **Protein:** 25g
- **Fat:** 23g
- **Saturated Fat:** 5g
- **Cholesterol:** 110mg
- **Sodium:** 500mg
- **Potassium:** 350mg
- **Fiber:** 1g
- **Sugar:** 0g
- **Vitamin C:** 15mg

Cooking Tips

- ✓ **Chicken Thighs:** For even cooking, ensure the chicken thighs are similar in size. Boneless, skinless thighs can be used but will have a shorter cooking time.
- ✓ **Marinade:** Marinate the chicken for at least 15 minutes, but for more flavor, marinate for up to 1 hour in the refrigerator.
- ✓ **Crispy Skin:** To achieve extra crispy skin, place the chicken thighs under the broiler for the last 2-3 minutes of cooking.
- ✓ **Serving Suggestions:** Serve with a side of roasted vegetables or a fresh salad for a complete meal.
- ✓ **Leftovers:** Store any leftovers in the refrigerator for up to 3 days. Reheat in the oven to maintain crispiness.

Lemon garlic chicken thighs are a delicious and easy-to-make dish featuring tender and juicy chicken with a zesty, flavorful marinade, perfect for any weeknight dinner.

Recipe 22: Baked Cod with Herbed Cauliflower Rice

Prep Time: 15 minutes | Cooking Time: 20 minutes | Servings: 4

Ingredients

- 4 cod fillets (6 oz each)
- 2 tablespoons olive oil
- 1 tablespoon lemon juice
- 2 cloves garlic, minced
- 1 teaspoon dried thyme
- 1 teaspoon dried rosemary
- 1/2 teaspoon sea salt
- 1/4 teaspoon black pepper
- 4 cups cauliflower rice
- 1/4 cup fresh parsley, chopped
- 1/4 cup fresh dill, chopped
- Lemon wedges for serving

Cooking Instructions

1. **Preheat the Oven:** Preheat your oven to 375°F (190°C).
2. **Prepare the Cod Marinade:** In a small bowl, mix together the olive oil, lemon juice, minced garlic, dried thyme, dried rosemary, sea salt, and black pepper.
3. **Marinate the Cod:** Place the cod fillets on a baking sheet lined with parchment paper. Brush the marinade evenly over each fillet. Let marinate for 10 minutes.
4. **Bake the Cod:** Bake the marinated cod in the preheated oven for 15-20 minutes or until the fish is opaque and flakes easily with a fork.
5. **Prepare the Cauliflower Rice:** While the cod is baking, heat a large skillet over medium heat. Add the cauliflower rice and cook for 5-7 minutes, stirring occasionally, until tender. Stir in the fresh parsley and dill, and season with additional salt and pepper to taste.
6. **Serve:** Serve the baked cod over a bed of herbed cauliflower rice. Garnish with lemon wedges and additional fresh herbs if desired.

Nutritional Facts

- **Calories:** 250 kcal
- **Protein:** 30g
- **Fat:** 10g
- **Saturated Fat:** 2g
- **Cholesterol:** 70mg
- **Sodium:** 500mg
- **Potassium:** 900mg
- **Fiber:** 3g
- **Sugar:** 2g
- **Vitamin C:** 60mg

Cooking Tips

- ✓ **Cod:** Use fresh or frozen cod fillets. If using frozen, thaw completely before marinating and baking.
- ✓ **Marinade:** Allow the fish to marinate for at least 10 minutes to absorb the flavors.
- ✓ **Cauliflower Rice:** To make cauliflower rice, pulse cauliflower florets in a food processor until they resemble rice grains.
- ✓ **Serving Suggestions:** Pair with a side of steamed vegetables or a green salad for a balanced meal.
- ✓ **Leftovers:** Store any leftovers in the refrigerator for up to 2 days. Reheat gently to avoid drying out the fish.

Baked cod with herbed cauliflower rice is a light, flavorful, and healthy dish combining tender, flaky cod with fresh and aromatic cauliflower rice, perfect for a nutritious dinner.

Recipe 23: Zucchini Lasagna with Ground Beef

Prep Time: 20 minutes | Cooking Time: 45 minutes | Servings: 6

Ingredients

- 4 medium zucchinis, sliced lengthwise into thin strips
- 1 lb. ground beef
- 2 cups marinara sauce (low carb)
- 1 cup ricotta cheese
- 1 egg
- 1 cup shredded mozzarella cheese
- 1/2 cup grated Parmesan cheese
- 1 tablespoon olive oil
- 1 teaspoon dried oregano
- 1 teaspoon dried basil
- 1/2 teaspoon garlic powder
- 1/2 teaspoon salt
- 1/4 teaspoon black pepper
- Fresh basil for garnish (optional)

Cooking Instructions

1. **Preheat the Oven:** Preheat your oven to 375°F (190°C).
2. **Prepare the Zucchini:** Slice the zucchini lengthwise into thin strips using a mandoline or a sharp knife. Lay the zucchini strips on paper towels and sprinkle with salt to draw out excess moisture. Let sit for 10 minutes, then pat dry.
3. **Cook the Ground Beef:** In a large skillet, heat olive oil over medium heat. Add the ground beef and cook until browned, breaking it up with a spoon as it cooks. Drain any excess fat.
4. **Add Marinara Sauce:** Stir in the marinara sauce, dried oregano, dried basil, garlic powder, salt, and black pepper. Simmer for 5 minutes.
5. **Prepare the Ricotta Mixture:** In a small bowl, mix together the ricotta cheese, egg, and half of the grated Parmesan cheese.
6. **Assemble the Lasagna:** In a 9x13-inch baking dish, spread a thin layer of the meat sauce. Add a layer of zucchini strips, followed by a layer of the ricotta mixture. Repeat the layers until all ingredients are used, ending with a layer of meat sauce.
7. **Top with Cheese:** Sprinkle the shredded mozzarella cheese and the remaining Parmesan cheese over the top.
8. **Bake:** Cover with foil and bake in the preheated oven for 30 minutes. Remove the foil and bake for an additional 15 minutes or until the cheese is bubbly and golden brown.
9. **Rest and Serve:** Let the lasagna rest for 10 minutes before slicing. Garnish with fresh basil if desired and serve hot.

Nutritional Facts

- **Calories:** 350 kcal
- **Protein:** 25g
- **Fat:** 22g
- **Saturated Fat:** 10g
- **Cholesterol:** 110mg
- **Sodium:** 700mg
- **Potassium:** 900mg
- **Fiber:** 3g
- **Sugar:** 5g
- **Vitamin A:** 800 IU

Cooking Tips

- ✓ **Zucchini:** Salting the zucchini helps draw out excess moisture, preventing the lasagna from becoming watery.
- ✓ **Cheese:** Use whole-milk ricotta and mozzarella for a richer flavor, or substitute with part-skim versions to reduce calories.
- ✓ **Sauce:** Choose a low-carb marinara sauce or make your own to control the ingredients and sugar content.
- ✓ **Meal Prep:** This lasagna can be assembled ahead of time and stored in the refrigerator for up to 24 hours before baking.

Recipe 24: Spicy Shrimp and Zoodles

Prep Time: 15 minutes | Cooking Time: 10 minutes | Servings: 4

Ingredients

- 1-pound large shrimp, peeled and deveined
- 4 medium zucchinis, spiralized into noodles (zoodles)
- 2 tablespoons olive oil
- 4 cloves garlic, minced
- 1 red chili pepper, finely chopped (or 1 teaspoon red pepper flakes)
- 1 teaspoon paprika
- 1/2 teaspoon cayenne pepper (adjust to taste)
- 1/2 teaspoon ground cumin
- 1/4 cup chicken or vegetable broth
- 2 tablespoons lemon juice (about 1 lemon)
- 1 tablespoon soy sauce (or tamari for gluten-free)
- 2 tablespoons fresh parsley, chopped
- Sea salt and black pepper, to taste
- Lemon wedges (optional for serving)

Cooking Instructions

1. **Prepare the Shrimp:** In a medium bowl, toss the shrimp with paprika, cayenne pepper, cumin, sea salt, and black pepper until evenly coated.

2. **Cook the Shrimp:** Heat 1 tablespoon of olive oil in a large skillet over medium-high heat. Add the shrimp and cook for 2-3 minutes on each side, or until they turn pink and opaque. Remove the shrimp from the skillet and set aside.

3. **Sauté the Aromatics:** In the same skillet, add the remaining 1 tablespoon of olive oil. Add the minced garlic and chopped red chili pepper. Sauté for about 1-2 minutes until fragrant.

4. **Add the Zoodles:** Add the spiralized zucchini noodles to the skillet and toss to coat in the garlic-chili mixture. Sauté for 2-3 minutes until the zoodles are slightly tender but still firm.

5. **Prepare the Sauce:** Pour the chicken or vegetable broth, lemon juice, and soy sauce over the zoodles. Stir well to combine and let it simmer for 1-2 minutes until the sauce slightly thickens.

6. **Combine and Serve:** Return the cooked shrimp to the skillet and toss with the zoodles and sauce until everything is well mixed and heated through. Sprinkle with fresh parsley.

7. **Garnish:** Serve hot, garnished with lemon wedges for an extra burst of flavor if desired.

Nutritional Facts

- **Calories:** 230 kcal
- **Protein:** 25g
- **Fat:** 10g
- **Saturated Fat:** 2g
- **Cholesterol:** 180mg
- **Sodium:** 800mg
- **Potassium:** 700mg
- **Fiber:** 3g
- **Sugar:** 4g
- **Vitamin C:** 25mg

Cooking Tips

- ✓ **Zoodles:** Spiralize the zucchini just before cooking to keep them fresh and avoid them becoming too watery.

- ✓ **Spice Level:** Adjust the amount of chili pepper or cayenne to your preferred spice level. For a milder version, reduce or omit the cayenne pepper.

- ✓ **Shrimp:** Make sure not to overcook the shrimp to keep them tender and juicy. They should be pink and opaque when done.

Recipe 25: Balsamic Glazed Steak with Brussels Sprouts

Prep Time: 15 minutes | Cooking Time: 20 minutes | Servings: 4

Ingredients

- 4 (6 oz) sirloin steaks
- 1 lb. Brussels sprouts, halved
- 2 tablespoons olive oil
- 1/4 cup balsamic vinegar
- 2 tablespoons soy sauce (low sodium)
- 2 cloves garlic, minced
- 1 teaspoon dried thyme
- 1/2 teaspoon sea salt
- 1/4 teaspoon black pepper
- Fresh parsley, chopped (optional for garnish)

Cooking Instructions

1. **Prepare the Brussels Sprouts:** Preheat your oven to 400°F (200°C). Toss the halved Brussels sprouts with 1 tablespoon of olive oil, sea salt, and black pepper. Spread them in a single layer on a baking sheet and roast for 20 minutes, turning halfway through, until they are tender and slightly crispy.
2. **Prepare the Steaks:** While the Brussels sprouts are roasting, pat the steaks dry with paper towels. Season with salt and pepper on both sides.
3. **Cook the Steaks:** Heat the remaining 1 tablespoon of olive oil in a large skillet over medium-high heat. Add the steaks and cook for 4-5 minutes per side or until they reach your desired level of doneness. Remove the steaks from the skillet and let them rest for 5 minutes.
4. **Make the Glaze:** In the same skillet, add the minced garlic and cook for 1 minute until fragrant. Add the balsamic vinegar, soy sauce, and dried thyme. Cook for 2-3 minutes, stirring frequently, until the glaze thickens slightly.
5. **Glaze the Steaks:** Return the steaks to the skillet and spoon the glaze over them, coating each side evenly. Cook for an additional 1-2 minutes to heat through.
6. **Serve:** Serve the balsamic glazed steaks with the roasted Brussels sprouts on the side. Garnish with fresh parsley if desired.

Nutritional Facts

- **Calories:** 450 kcal
- **Protein:** 35g
- **Fat:** 25g
- **Saturated Fat:** 8g
- **Cholesterol:** 100mg
- **Sodium:** 600mg
- **Potassium:** 900mg
- **Fiber:** 4g
- **Sugar:** 6g
- **Vitamin C:** 80mg

Cooking Tips

- ✓ **Steak:** Choose high-quality sirloin steaks for the best flavor and tenderness. Allow the steaks to come to room temperature before cooking for even cooking.
- ✓ **Brussels Sprouts:** For extra crispiness, increase the oven temperature to 425°F (220°C) for the last 5 minutes of roasting.
- ✓ **Glaze:** Keep an eye on the balsamic glaze as it reduces to avoid burning. It should be thick enough to coat the back of a spoon.
- ✓ **Serving Suggestions:** Pair with a side of mashed cauliflower or a fresh green salad for a complete low-carb meal.

Balsamic glazed steak with Brussels sprouts is a savory and satisfying meal, combining tender, flavorful steak with roasted Brussels sprouts and a rich balsamic glaze, perfect for a special dinner.

Recipe 26: Spaghetti Squash Bolognese

Prep Time: 15 minutes | Cooking Time: 45 minutes | Servings: 4

Ingredients

- 1 large spaghetti squash
- 1 lb. ground beef
- 1 cup onion, finely chopped
- 2 cloves garlic, minced
- 1 (14.5 oz) can crushed tomatoes
- 1/4 cup tomato paste
- 1/4 cup beef broth
- 1 teaspoon dried oregano
- 1 teaspoon dried basil
- 1/2 teaspoon salt
- 1/4 teaspoon black pepper
- 2 tablespoons olive oil
- Fresh basil, chopped (optional for garnish)
- Parmesan cheese, grated (optional for serving)

Cooking Instructions

1. **Prepare the Spaghetti Squash:** Preheat your oven to 400°F (200°C). Cut the spaghetti squash in half lengthwise and scoop out the seeds. Drizzle with 1 tablespoon of olive oil and season with salt and pepper. Place cut-side down on a baking sheet and bake for 40-45 minutes or until tender.
2. **Cook the Beef:** While the squash is baking, heat the remaining 1 tablespoon of olive oil in a large skillet over medium heat. Add the chopped onion and minced garlic and cook for 2-3 minutes until softened. Add the ground beef and cook until browned, breaking it up with a spoon as it cooks.
3. **Make the Bolognese Sauce:** Stir in the crushed tomatoes, tomato paste, beef broth,

dried oregano, dried basil, salt, and black pepper. Simmer for 20 minutes, stirring occasionally, until the sauce thickens.
4. **Prepare the Spaghetti Squash:** Once the spaghetti squash is cooked, use a fork to scrape out the strands into a large bowl.
5. **Serve:** Divide the spaghetti squash among four plates. Top with the Bolognese sauce. Garnish with fresh basil and grated Parmesan cheese if desired. Serve hot.

Nutritional Facts

- **Calories:** 350 kcal
- **Protein:** 25g
- **Fat:** 20g
- **Saturated Fat:** 7g
- **Cholesterol:** 70mg
- **Sodium:** 600mg
- **Potassium:** 1000mg
- **Fiber:** 6g
- **Sugar:** 8g
- **Vitamin C:** 20mg

Cooking Tips

✓ **Spaghetti Squash:** Ensure the squash is tender by poking it with a fork. If it doesn't easily penetrate, bake for an additional 5-10 minutes.
✓ **Ground Beef:** Use lean ground beef to reduce the fat content. Ground turkey or chicken can also be substituted.
✓ **Sauce:** For a richer flavor, simmer the sauce longer to allow the flavors to meld together.
✓ **Customization:** Add chopped carrots, celery, or bell peppers to the Bolognese sauce for extra vegetables and flavor.

Spaghetti squash Bolognese is a healthy and delicious alternative to traditional pasta, offering a satisfying, low-carb meal that is perfect for dinner.

Recipe 27: Herb-Crusted Pork Chops with Green Beans

Prep Time: 10 minutes | Cooking Time: 20 minutes | Servings: 4

Ingredients

- 4 bone-in pork chops (about 1 inch thick)
- 1 tablespoon olive oil
- 2 tablespoons fresh rosemary, chopped
- 2 tablespoons fresh thyme, chopped
- 2 cloves garlic, minced
- 1 teaspoon sea salt
- 1/2 teaspoon black pepper
- 1 lb. green beans, trimmed
- 1 tablespoon butter
- Lemon wedges for serving (optional)

Cooking Instructions

1. **Preheat the Oven:** Preheat your oven to 375°F (190°C).
2. **Season the Pork Chops:** In a small bowl, mix together the olive oil, rosemary, thyme, minced garlic, sea salt, and black pepper. Rub the mixture evenly over both sides of the pork chops.
3. **Sear the Pork Chops:** Heat a large oven-safe skillet over medium-high heat. Add the pork chops and sear for 2-3 minutes on each side until golden brown.
4. **Roast the Pork Chops:** Transfer the skillet to the preheated oven and roast for 10-12 minutes, or until the internal temperature reaches 145°F (63°C). Remove the pork chops from the skillet and let rest for 5 minutes.
5. **Cook the Green Beans:** While the pork chops are resting, melt the butter in a large skillet over medium heat. Add the green beans and cook for 5-7 minutes, stirring occasionally, until tender and slightly crispy.
6. **Serve:** Serve the herb-crusted pork chops with the green beans on the side. Garnish with lemon wedges if desired.

Nutritional Facts

- **Calories:** 350 kcal
- **Protein:** 30g
- **Fat:** 20g
- **Saturated Fat:** 6g
- **Cholesterol:** 90mg
- **Sodium:** 500mg
- **Potassium:** 700mg
- **Fiber:** 4g
- **Sugar:** 3g
- **Vitamin A:** 800 IU

Cooking Tips

- ✓ **Pork Chops:** For the best flavor, use bone-in pork chops. Boneless pork chops can be substituted but may cook faster.
- ✓ **Herbs:** Fresh herbs provide the best flavor, but dried herbs can be used in a pinch. Adjust the quantities if using dried herbs (1 teaspoon dried for each tablespoon fresh).
- ✓ **Green Beans:** For extra flavor, add a squeeze of lemon juice and a sprinkle of sea salt to the green beans before serving.
- ✓ **Serving Suggestions:** Pair with a side of mashed cauliflower or a fresh salad for a complete low-carb meal.
- ✓ **Leftovers:** Store any leftovers in the refrigerator for up to 3 days. Reheat gently to avoid drying out the pork chops.

Herb-crusted pork chops with green beans are a flavorful and nutritious dinner option, combining tender, juicy pork with fresh, crisp green beans.

Recipe 28: Keto Beef Stroganoff

Prep Time: 10 minutes | Cooking Time: 20 minutes | Servings: 4

Ingredients

- 1 lb. beef sirloin, thinly sliced
- 1/2 cup onion, finely chopped
- 2 cloves garlic, minced
- 1 cup mushrooms, sliced
- 1 cup beef broth
- 1/2 cup sour cream
- 2 tablespoons cream cheese
- 1 tablespoon Dijon mustard
- 2 tablespoons olive oil
- 1 teaspoon paprika
- 1/2 teaspoon salt
- 1/4 teaspoon black pepper
- Fresh parsley, chopped (optional for garnish)

Cooking Instructions

1. **Prepare the Beef:** Thinly slice the beef sirloin against the grain for tenderness. Season with salt, pepper, and paprika.
2. **Cook the Beef:** In a large skillet, heat 1 tablespoon of olive oil over medium-high heat. Add the beef slices and cook until browned, about 3-4 minutes. Remove from the skillet and set aside.
3. **Cook the Vegetables:** In the same skillet, add the remaining 1 tablespoon of olive oil. Add the chopped onion and minced garlic and cook for 2-3 minutes until softened. Add the sliced mushrooms and cook for another 5 minutes until they are tender and browned.
4. **Make the Sauce:** Stir in the beef broth, sour cream, cream cheese, and Dijon mustard. Cook for 3-4 minutes, stirring frequently, until the sauce is smooth and thickened.
5. **Combine:** Return the cooked beef to the skillet and stir to combine with the sauce. Cook for an additional 2-3 minutes until the beef is heated through.
6. **Serve:** Serve the beef stroganoff hot, garnished with chopped fresh parsley if desired.

Nutritional Facts

- **Calories:** 350 kcal
- **Protein:** 30g
- **Fat:** 22g
- **Saturated Fat:** 9g
- **Cholesterol:** 100mg
- **Sodium:** 600mg
- **Potassium:** 700mg
- **Fiber:** 1g
- **Sugar:** 3g
- **Vitamin C:** 5mg

Cooking Tips

✓ **Beef:** Use a tender cut of beef like sirloin or tenderloin for the best results. Ensure it is thinly sliced against the grain.
✓ **Mushrooms:** Any variety of mushrooms can be used, such as cremini, white button, or portobello.
✓ **Sauce:** Stir continuously when adding the sour cream and cream cheese to avoid curdling.
✓ **Serving Suggestions:** Serve over cauliflower rice, zucchini noodles, or shirataki noodles as a low-carb option.
✓ **Customization:** Add a splash of Worcestershire sauce or a pinch of nutmeg for extra depth of flavor.

Keto beef stroganoff is a rich and creamy dish that combines tender beef with a savory mushroom sauce, perfect for a comforting and low-carb dinner.

Recipe 29: Garlic Butter Shrimp with Broccoli

Prep Time: 10 minutes | Cooking Time: 15 minutes | Servings: 4

Ingredients

- 1-pound large shrimp, peeled and deveined
- 4 cups broccoli florets
- 4 tablespoons unsalted butter
- 4 cloves garlic, minced
- 1/2 teaspoon red pepper flakes (optional for spice)
- 1 tablespoon lemon juice (about half a lemon)
- 1 tablespoon olive oil
- 1/4 cup chicken or vegetable broth
- 2 tablespoons fresh parsley, chopped
- Sea salt and black pepper, to taste
- Lemon wedges (optional for serving)

Cooking Instructions

1. **Steam the Broccoli:** In a medium pot with a steamer insert, bring about an inch of water to a boil. Add the broccoli florets, cover, and steam for about 5 minutes until tender but still crisp. Remove from heat and set aside.
2. **Prepare the Shrimp:** Season the shrimp with sea salt and black pepper. In a large skillet, heat the olive oil over medium-high heat. Add the shrimp and cook for 2-3 minutes on each side until they turn pink and opaque. Remove the shrimp from the skillet and set aside.
3. **Make the Garlic Butter Sauce:** In the same skillet, melt the unsalted butter over medium heat. Add the minced garlic and red pepper flakes (if using) and sauté for 1-2 minutes until fragrant.
4. **Add the Shrimp:** Return the shrimp to the skillet and toss to coat in the garlic butter sauce. Add the chicken or vegetable broth and lemon juice. Cook for another 2 minutes until the sauce has slightly reduced and the shrimp are well coated.
5. **Combine and Serve:** Place the steamed broccoli on a serving platter or individual plates. Spoon the garlic butter shrimp over the broccoli. Garnish with fresh parsley and serve immediately.
6. **Optional:** Serve with lemon wedges for an extra burst of flavor.

Nutritional Facts

- **Calories:** 300 kcal
- **Protein:** 24g
- **Fat:** 20g
- **Saturated Fat:** 10g
- **Cholesterol:** 210mg
- **Sodium:** 600mg
- **Potassium:** 600mg
- **Fiber:** 4g
- **Sugar:** 2g
- **Vitamin C:** 60mg

Cooking Tips

- ✓ **Shrimp:** Use large, fresh shrimp for the best flavor. If using frozen shrimp, ensure they are fully thawed and patted dry before cooking.
- ✓ **Butter:** Use unsalted butter to control the saltiness of the dish. Adjust the amount of salt according to taste.
- ✓ **Broccoli:** For added flavor, you can toss the steamed broccoli with a little of the garlic butter sauce before serving.
- ✓ **Spice Level:** Adjust the amount of red pepper flakes to your desired level of heat. For a milder dish, omit the red pepper flakes.
- ✓ **Serving Suggestions:** This dish pairs well with a side of cauliflower rice or a simple green salad for a complete low-carb meal.

Garlic butter shrimp with broccoli is a quick and healthy meal featuring succulent shrimp in a rich garlic butter sauce, served with tender steamed broccoli. This dish offers a delicious combination of flavors and textures, perfect for a nutritious and satisfying dinner.

Recipe 30: Chicken Fajita Bowls

Prep Time: 15 minutes | Cooking Time: 20 minutes | Servings: 4

Ingredients

- 1 lb. boneless, skinless chicken breasts sliced into thin strips
- 2 tablespoons olive oil
- 2 bell peppers (any color), sliced
- 1 large onion, sliced
- 2 cloves garlic, minced
- 1 tablespoon chili powder
- 1 teaspoon ground cumin
- 1 teaspoon paprika
- 1/2 teaspoon dried oregano
- 1/2 teaspoon sea salt
- 1/4 teaspoon black pepper
- 1/4 cup fresh cilantro, chopped (optional for garnish)
- 1 avocado, sliced (optional for serving)
- Lime wedges (optional for serving)

Cauliflower Rice Ingredients

- 4 cups cauliflower rice
- 1 tablespoon olive oil
- 1/2 teaspoon garlic powder
- 1/2 teaspoon sea salt
- 1/4 teaspoon black pepper

Cooking Instructions

1. **Prepare the Chicken:** In a large bowl, toss the chicken strips with chili powder, ground cumin, paprika, dried oregano, sea salt, and black pepper.
2. **Cook the Chicken:** In a large skillet, heat 1 tablespoon of olive oil over medium-high heat. Add the chicken and cook for 5-7 minutes until browned and cooked through. Remove from the skillet and set aside.
3. **Cook the Vegetables:** In the same skillet, heat the remaining 1 tablespoon of olive oil. Add the sliced bell peppers, onion, and minced garlic. Cook for 5-7 minutes until the vegetables are tender and slightly charred.

4. **Combine Chicken and Vegetables:** Return the cooked chicken to the skillet with the vegetables and toss to combine. Cook for an additional 2-3 minutes to heat through.
5. **Prepare the Cauliflower Rice:** In a separate skillet, heat 1 tablespoon of olive oil over medium heat. Add the cauliflower rice, garlic powder, sea salt, and black pepper. Cook for 5-7 minutes until the cauliflower is tender.
6. **Assemble the Bowls:** Divide the cauliflower rice among four bowls. Top with the chicken and vegetable mixture.
7. **Serve:** Garnish with fresh cilantro, avocado slices, and lime wedges if desired. Serve immediately.

Nutritional Facts

- **Calories:** 350 kcal
- **Protein:** 30g
- **Fat:** 20g
- **Saturated Fat:** 3g
- **Cholesterol:** 75mg
- **Sodium:** 600mg
- **Potassium:** 900mg
- **Fiber:** 6g
- **Sugar:** 5g
- **Vitamin C:** 100mg

Cooking Tips

- ✓ **Chicken:** Ensure the chicken strips are of similar thickness to cook evenly. Chicken thighs can be used as an alternative.
- ✓ **Vegetables:** Add other vegetables like zucchini or mushrooms for extra flavor and variety.
- ✓ **Cauliflower Rice:** To make your own cauliflower rice, pulse cauliflower florets in a food processor until they resemble rice grains.

Snack Recipes

Recipe 31: Greek Yogurt Dip with Veggie Sticks

Prep Time: 10 minutes | Cooking Time: 0 minutes | Servings: 4

Ingredients

- 1 cup Greek yogurt
- 1/2 cucumber, finely diced
- 1 clove garlic, minced
- 1 tablespoon fresh dill, chopped
- 1 tablespoon fresh lemon juice
- 1/2 teaspoon sea salt
- 1/4 teaspoon black pepper
- 1 tablespoon olive oil
- Assorted veggie sticks (carrots, celery, bell peppers, cucumbers, etc.)

Nutritional Facts

- **Calories:** 100 kcal
- **Protein:** 5g
- **Fat:** 5g
- **Saturated Fat:** 1.5g
- **Cholesterol:** 5mg
- **Sodium:** 300mg
- **Potassium:** 300mg
- **Fiber:** 2g
- **Sugar:** 4g
- **Vitamin C:** 15mg

Cooking Instructions

1. **Prepare the Dip:** In a medium bowl, combine the Greek yogurt, finely diced cucumber, minced garlic, chopped dill, fresh lemon juice, sea salt, and black pepper. Mix well until all ingredients are thoroughly combined.
2. **Chill the Dip:** Drizzle with olive oil. Cover and refrigerate for at least 30 minutes to allow the flavors to meld together.
3. **Prepare the Veggie Sticks:** While the dip is chilling, wash and cut your assortment of vegetables into sticks.
4. **Serve:** Serve the chilled Greek yogurt dip with the assorted veggie sticks.

Cooking Tips

- ✓ **Cucumber:** For a smoother dip, you can peel the cucumber and remove the seeds before dicing.
- ✓ **Yogurt:** Use full-fat Greek yogurt for a creamier texture and richer flavor.
- ✓ **Dill:** Fresh dill is recommended, but you can use dried dill in a pinch (use 1 teaspoon of dried dill).
- ✓ **Customization:** Add other fresh herbs like parsley or mint for additional flavor.
- ✓ **Serving Suggestions:** This dip pairs well with whole-grain crackers or can be used as a spread for wraps and sandwiches.

Greek yogurt dip with veggie sticks is a refreshing and healthy snack that's high in protein and perfect for dipping fresh vegetables.

Recipe 32: Low-Carb Energy Balls

Prep Time: 15 minutes | Cooking Time: 0 minutes | Servings: 12 balls

Ingredients

- 1 cup almond flour
- 1/2 cup unsweetened shredded coconut
- 1/4 cup flaxseed meal
- 1/4 cup sugar-free chocolate chips
- 1/4 cup almond butter
- 1/4 cup sugar-free maple syrup
- 1 teaspoon vanilla extract
- 1/4 teaspoon sea salt

Cooking Instructions

1. **Mix Dry Ingredients:** In a large bowl, combine the almond flour, unsweetened shredded coconut, flaxseed meal, sugar-free chocolate chips, and sea salt. Mix well.
2. **Add Wet Ingredients:** Add the almond butter, sugar-free maple syrup, and vanilla extract to the dry ingredients. Mix thoroughly until all ingredients are well combined, and the mixture holds together.
3. **Form the Balls:** Using a tablespoon or a small cookie scoop, portion out the mixture and roll into balls. You should get about 12 energy balls.
4. **Chill:** Place the energy balls on a baking sheet lined with parchment paper and refrigerate for at least 30 minutes to firm up.
5. **Serve:** Once chilled, transfer the energy balls to an airtight container and store them in the refrigerator until ready to eat.

Nutritional Facts

- **Calories:** 120 kcal
- **Protein:** 3g
- **Fat:** 10g
- **Saturated Fat:** 3g
- **Cholesterol:** 0mg
- **Sodium:** 50mg
- **Potassium:** 100mg
- **Fiber:** 3g
- **Sugar:** 1g
- **Vitamin E:** 3mg

Cooking Tips

- ✓ **Binding:** If the mixture is too dry and doesn't hold together, add a little more almond butter or sugar-free maple syrup until it reaches the right consistency.
- ✓ **Customizations:** Add other mix-ins like chopped nuts, seeds, or dried berries for extra flavor and texture.
- ✓ **Serving Suggestions:** These energy balls are perfect as a quick snack, or a post-workout treat. Pair with a cup of tea or coffee for an afternoon pick-me-up.
- ✓ **Storage:** These energy balls can be stored in the refrigerator for up to 1 week or in the freezer for up to 1 month.

Low-carb energy balls are a nutritious and convenient snack packed with healthy fats and fiber, perfect for on-the-go energy boosts.

Recipe 33: Almond and Cheese Crackers

Prep Time: 10 minutes | Cooking Time: 15 minutes | Servings: 4

Ingredients

- 1 cup almond flour
- 1/2 cup shredded cheddar cheese
- 1/4 cup grated Parmesan cheese
- 1 egg
- 1/2 teaspoon garlic powder
- 1/2 teaspoon onion powder
- 1/4 teaspoon sea salt
- 1/4 teaspoon black pepper

Cooking Instructions

1. **Preheat the Oven:** Preheat your oven to 350°F (175°C). Line a baking sheet with parchment paper.
2. **Mix Ingredients:** In a large bowl, combine the almond flour, shredded cheddar cheese, grated Parmesan cheese, garlic powder, onion powder, sea salt, and black pepper.
3. **Add the Egg:** Add the egg to the mixture and stir until a dough forms.
4. **Roll Out the Dough:** Place the dough between two sheets of parchment paper. Roll it out to about 1/8-inch thickness.
5. **Cut the Crackers:** Remove the top parchment paper and cut the dough into small squares or desired shapes using a knife or cookie cutter.
6. **Bake:** Transfer the cut dough to the prepared baking sheet. Bake in the preheated oven for 12-15 minutes or until the crackers are golden brown and crispy.
7. **Cool and Serve:** Allow the crackers to cool on the baking sheet for a few minutes before transferring them to a wire rack to cool completely. Serve immediately or store in an airtight container.

Nutritional Facts

- **Calories:** 150 kcal
- **Protein:** 7g
- **Fat:** 12g
- **Saturated Fat:** 3g
- **Cholesterol:** 40mg
- **Sodium:** 300mg
- **Potassium:** 100mg
- **Fiber:** 2g
- **Sugar:** 1g
- **Calcium:** 150mg

Cooking Tips

✓ **Dough Thickness:** Ensure the dough is rolled out evenly to ensure consistent baking and crispiness.
✓ **Cheese:** Feel free to use other types of cheese, such as mozzarella or Gouda, for different flavors.
✓ **Crispiness:** If the crackers are not crispy enough after baking, return them to the oven for an additional 2-3 minutes.
✓ **Serving Suggestions:** Pair with your favorite dip spreads or enjoy on their own as a snack.
✓ **Storage:** Store in an airtight container at room temperature for up to 5 days.

Almond and cheese crackers are a delicious low-carb snack that combines the nuttiness of almond flour with the savory flavors of cheddar and Parmesan cheese, perfect for a crunchy and satisfying treat.

Recipe 34: Deviled Eggs

Prep Time: 15 minutes | Cooking Time: 10 minutes | Servings: 12 halves

Ingredients

- 6 large eggs
- 1/4 cup mayonnaise
- 1 teaspoon Dijon mustard
- 1 teaspoon white vinegar
- 1/4 teaspoon sea salt
- 1/4 teaspoon black pepper
- Paprika for garnish
- Fresh chives, chopped (optional for garnish)

Cooking Instructions

1. **Boil the Eggs:** Place the eggs in a saucepan and cover with cold water. Bring to a boil over medium-high heat. Once boiling, cover, remove from heat, and let sit for 10 minutes.
2. **Cool and Peel:** Drain the hot water and transfer the eggs to a bowl of ice water to cool for 5 minutes. Peel the eggs under running water.
3. **Prepare the Filling:** Slice the eggs in half lengthwise and remove the yolks. Place the yolks in a bowl and mash with a fork. Add the mayonnaise, Dijon mustard, white vinegar, sea salt, and black pepper. Mix until smooth.
4. **Fill the Eggs:** Spoon or pipe the yolk mixture back into the egg white halves.
5. **Garnish and Serve:** Sprinkle with paprika and garnish with chopped chives if desired. Serve immediately or refrigerate until ready to serve.

Nutritional Facts

- **Calories:** 70 kcal
- **Protein:** 4g
- **Fat:** 6g
- **Saturated Fat:** 1.5g
- **Cholesterol:** 110mg
- **Sodium:** 150mg
- **Potassium:** 50mg
- **Fiber:** 0g
- **Sugar:** 0g
- **Vitamin A:** 200 IU

Cooking Tips

- ✓ **Boiling Eggs:** For easier peeling, use eggs that are at least a week old and cool them immediately after boiling.
- ✓ **Filling:** For a smoother filling, use a hand mixer or food processor to blend the yolk mixture.
- ✓ **Customization:** Add other ingredients like relish, hot sauce, or minced pickles for different flavor variations.
- ✓ **Serving Suggestions:** Deviled eggs make a great appetizer or snack for parties and gatherings.
- ✓ **Storage:** Store in an airtight container in the refrigerator for up to 2 days.

Deviled eggs are a classic and versatile dish, perfect for any occasion, combining creamy yolk filling with a hint of tanginess and spice, making them a delightful and satisfying treat.

Recipe 35: Low-Carb Guacamole with Bell Pepper Slices

Prep Time: 10 minutes | Cooking Time: 0 minutes | Servings: 4

Ingredients

- 3 ripe avocados
- 1 small tomato, diced
- 1/4 cup red onion, finely chopped
- 1 jalapeño, seeded and minced
- 2 cloves garlic, minced
- 2 tablespoons fresh lime juice
- 1/4 cup fresh cilantro, chopped
- 1/2 teaspoon sea salt
- 1/4 teaspoon black pepper
- 2 bell peppers, cut into strips

Cooking Instructions

1. **Prepare the Avocados:** Cut the avocados in half, remove the pits, and scoop the flesh into a bowl. Mash with a fork until smooth.
2. **Mix the Ingredients:** Add the diced tomato, chopped red onion, minced jalapeño, minced garlic, fresh lime juice, chopped cilantro, sea salt, and black pepper to the mashed avocado. Stir to combine.
3. **Adjust Seasoning:** Taste and adjust seasoning with additional salt, pepper, or lime juice as needed.
4. **Serve:** Serve the guacamole with bell pepper strips for dipping.

Nutritional Facts

- **Calories:** 200 kcal
- **Protein:** 2g
- **Fat:** 18g
- **Saturated Fat:** 2.5g
- **Cholesterol:** 0mg
- **Sodium:** 300mg
- **Potassium:** 600mg
- **Fiber:** 7g
- **Sugar:** 3g
- **Vitamin C:** 60mg

Cooking Tips

- ✓ **Avocados:** Use ripe avocados for the best texture and flavor. They should yield slightly when pressed.
- ✓ **Spice Level:** Adjust the amount of jalapeño to control the heat level. For a milder guacamole, omit the jalapeño.
- ✓ **Customization:** Add other ingredients like cumin, smoked paprika, or diced mango for unique flavor variations.
- ✓ **Serving Suggestions:** This guacamole pairs well with other low-carb vegetables like cucumber slices or celery sticks.
- ✓ **Storage:** Store in an airtight container in the refrigerator for up to 2 days. To prevent browning, press plastic wrap directly onto the surface of the guacamole.

Low-carb guacamole with bell pepper slices is a refreshing and healthy snack, combining the creamy richness of avocados with the crunch of fresh bell peppers, perfect for a nutritious and satisfying treat.

Recipe 36: Low-Carb Fruit and Nut Mix

Prep Time: 5 minutes | Cooking Time: None | Servings: 4

Ingredients

- 1/2 cup raw almonds
- 1/2 cup raw walnuts
- 1/2 cup raw pecans
- 1/4 cup raw pumpkin seeds
- 1/4 cup raw sunflower seeds
- 1/4 cup dried unsweetened cranberries
- 1/4 cup dried unsweetened blueberries
- 1/4 cup unsweetened coconut flakes
- 1 tablespoon chia seeds
- 1 tablespoon flax seeds
- 1 teaspoon ground cinnamon (optional for flavor)

Cooking Instructions

1. **Mix the Nuts and Seeds:** In a large bowl, combine the raw almonds, walnuts, pecans, pumpkin seeds, and sunflower seeds. Stir to mix the nuts and seeds evenly.
2. **Add the Dried Fruits:** Add the dried cranberries, dried blueberries, and unsweetened coconut flakes to the nut mixture. Stir well to combine.
3. **Incorporate the Seeds:** Sprinkle the chia seeds and flax seeds over the mixture. Stir thoroughly to ensure even distribution.
4. **Add Flavor (Optional):** For a hint of warmth and extra flavor, sprinkle the ground cinnamon over the mix and stir to combine.
5. **Portion and Serve:** Divide the fruit and nut mix into individual portions or store in an airtight container. Enjoy as a quick and satisfying snack on the go.

Nutritional Facts

- **Calories:** 250 kcal
- **Protein:** 7g
- **Fat:** 21g
- **Saturated Fat:** 3g
- **Cholesterol:** 0mg
- **Sodium:** 5mg
- **Potassium:** 300mg
- **Fiber:** 6g
- **Sugar:** 5g
- **Vitamin E:** 4mg

Cooking Tips

- ✓ **Dried Fruits:** Choose unsweetened dried fruits to keep the sugar content low. You can also substitute with other low-carb dried fruits like goji berries or mulberries.
- ✓ **Nuts:** Feel free to use your favorite nuts or seeds. Pecans, Brazil nuts, or hazelnuts can be great alternatives.
- ✓ **Flavor Variations:** Experiment with different spices like nutmeg or ginger for additional flavor variations.
- ✓ **Storage:** Store the mix in an airtight container at room temperature for up to two weeks, or in the refrigerator for up to a month to keep the nuts and seeds fresh.
- ✓ **Serving Suggestions:** Enjoy this mix as a snack on its own or sprinkle it over yogurt or salads for added crunch and nutrition.
- ✓ **Portion Control:** Use a small container or snack-sized bag to portion out servings for easy grab-and-go snacks.

Low-carb fruit and nut mix is a perfect blend of crunchy nuts and chewy dried fruits, providing a nutritious and satisfying snack that is ideal for busy days or as a quick pick-me-up. This mix is easy to prepare, portable, and packed with healthy fats, fiber, and protein to keep you fueled throughout the day.

Recipe 37: Beef Jerky

Prep Time: 20 minutes (plus marinating time) | Cooking Time: 4 hours | Servings: 8

Ingredients

- 2 lbs. lean beef (such as flank steak or sirloin)
- 1/4 cup soy sauce (low sodium)
- 2 tablespoons Worcestershire sauce
- 1 tablespoon liquid smoke (optional)
- 1 tablespoon honey or low-carb sweetener
- 1 teaspoon garlic powder
- 1 teaspoon onion powder
- 1 teaspoon black pepper
- 1/2 teaspoon sea salt
- 1/2 teaspoon smoked paprika
- 1/4 teaspoon red pepper flakes (optional)

Cooking Instructions

1. **Prepare the Beef:** Trim any excess fat from the beef. Freeze the beef for 1-2 hours until firm (this makes it easier to slice thinly). Slice the beef against the grain into 1/4-inch-thick strips.
2. **Make the Marinade:** In a large bowl, combine the soy sauce, Worcestershire sauce, liquid smoke (if using), honey or low-carb sweetener, garlic powder, onion powder, black pepper, sea salt, smoked paprika, and red pepper flakes. Mix well.
3. **Marinate the Beef:** Add the beef strips to the marinade, ensuring they are well coated. Cover and refrigerate for at least 4 hours, preferably overnight.
4. **Preheat the Oven:** Preheat your oven to 175°F (80°C). Line two baking sheets with aluminum foil and place a wire rack on top of each sheet.
5. **Arrange the Beef:** Remove the beef from the marinade and pat dry with paper towels. Arrange the strips in a single layer on the wire racks.
6. **Dry the Beef:** Place the baking sheets in the preheated oven and dry the beef for 4-5 hours, or until the jerky is dry and firm but still slightly pliable. Rotate the pans halfway through the drying time for even drying.
7. **Cool and Store:** Let the beef jerky cool completely before storing. Store in an airtight container or resealable plastic bags.

Nutritional Facts

- **Calories:** 150 kcal
- **Protein:** 25g
- **Fat:** 3g
- **Saturated Fat:** 1g
- **Cholesterol:** 50mg
- **Sodium:** 600mg
- **Potassium:** 300mg
- **Fiber:** 0g
- **Sugar:** 2g
- **Vitamin B12:** 2mcg

Cooking Tips

- ✓ **Beef Selection:** Choose lean cuts of beef to reduce fat content and improve shelf life.
- ✓ **Slicing:** Slice the beef against the grain for more tender jerky.
- ✓ **Marinating:** Ensure the beef is fully submerged in the marinade for maximum flavor absorption.
- ✓ **Drying Time:** Check the jerky periodically towards the end of the drying time to ensure it doesn't become too brittle.

Beef jerky is a high-protein, low-carb snack that's perfect for on-the-go, combining the savory flavors of beef with a blend of spices for a delicious and satisfying treat.

Recipe 38: Pumpkin Seed Protein Bars

Prep Time: 15 minutes | Cooking Time: 0 minutes | Servings: 12 bars

Ingredients

- 1 cup raw pumpkin seeds
- 1/2 cup almond flour
- 1/2 cup protein powder (vanilla or unflavored)
- 1/4 cup flaxseed meal
- 1/4 cup unsweetened shredded coconut
- 1/2 cup almond butter
- 1/4 cup coconut oil, melted
- 1/4 cup sugar-free maple syrup or liquid stevia to taste
- 1 teaspoon vanilla extract
- 1/2 teaspoon sea salt
- 1/4 cup dark chocolate chips (optional)

Cooking Instructions

1. **Prepare the Dry Ingredients:** In a large bowl, combine the pumpkin seeds, almond flour, protein powder, flaxseed meal, and unsweetened shredded coconut. Mix well.
2. **Combine the Wet Ingredients:** In a separate bowl, mix together the almond butter, melted coconut oil, sugar-free maple syrup, vanilla extract, and sea salt until smooth.
3. **Mix the Ingredients:** Pour the wet ingredients into the bowl with the dry ingredients. Stir until the mixture is well combined and forms a thick dough.
4. **Add Chocolate Chips:** If using, fold in the dark chocolate chips.
5. **Press into a Pan:** Line an 8x8-inch baking dish with parchment paper. Press the mixture evenly into the dish, using a spatula or your hands to flatten the top.

6. **Chill:** Place the dish in the refrigerator and chill for at least 1 hour or until the bars are firm.
7. **Cut into Bars:** Once firm, remove from the refrigerator and lift the mixture out of the dish using the parchment paper. Cut into 12 bars.
8. **Store and Serve:** Store the pumpkin seed protein bars in an airtight container in the refrigerator for up to 1 week. Serve chilled or at room temperature.

Nutritional Facts

- **Calories:** 210 kcal
- **Protein:** 8g
- **Fat:** 16g
- **Saturated Fat:** 6g
- **Cholesterol:** 0mg
- **Sodium:** 85mg
- **Potassium:** 150mg
- **Fiber:** 4g
- **Sugar:** 1g
- **Vitamin E:** 2mg

Cooking Tips

- ✓ **Seeds and Nuts:** You can substitute or add other seeds and nuts, such as sunflower seeds or chopped almonds, for variety.
- ✓ **Sweetness:** Adjust the sweetness to your taste by adding more or less sugar-free maple syrup or stevia.
- ✓ **Binding:** If the mixture is too dry, add a little more almond butter or coconut oil to help bind the ingredients together.

Pumpkin seed protein bars are a nutritious and delicious homemade snack packed with protein and healthy fats, perfect for a quick energy boost or a post-workout treat.

Recipe 39: Edamame with Sea Salt

Prep Time: 5 minutes | Cooking Time: 10 minutes | Servings: 4

Ingredients

- 1 lb. edamame in pods (fresh or frozen)
- 1 tablespoon sea salt, or to taste
- 1 lemon, cut into wedges (optional)

Cooking Instructions

1. **Prepare the Edamame:** If using fresh edamame, rinse under cold water. If using frozen edamame, there's no need to thaw.
2. **Boil the Water:** Bring a large pot of water to a boil. Add a pinch of sea salt to the boiling water.
3. **Cook the Edamame:** Add the edamame pods to the boiling water and cook for 5-7 minutes, or until the pods are bright green and tender. For frozen edamame, follow the cooking time indicated on the package.
4. **Drain and Season:** Drain the edamame in a colander and transfer to a large bowl. While still hot, sprinkle generously with sea salt.
5. **Serve:** Serve the edamame warm or at room temperature. Optionally, serve with lemon wedges for an added burst of flavor.

Nutritional Facts

- **Calories:** 120 kcal
- **Protein:** 11g
- **Fat:** 5g
- **Saturated Fat:** 0.5g
- **Cholesterol:** 0mg
- **Sodium:** 600mg
- **Potassium:** 250mg
- **Fiber:** 4g
- **Sugar:** 1g
- **Vitamin C:** 10mg

Cooking Tips

- ✓ **Seasoning:** Adjust the amount of sea salt to taste. You can also add other seasonings like garlic powder, chili flakes, or sesame seeds for extra flavor.
- ✓ **Lemon:** Squeeze fresh lemon juice over the edamame for a tangy twist.
- ✓ **Serving Suggestions:** Edamame makes a great appetizer, snack, or side dish. Pair with sushi, salads, or grilled dishes.
- ✓ **Storage:** Store any leftover edamame in an airtight container in the refrigerator for up to 3 days. Reheat in the microwave or enjoy the cold.

Edamame with sea salt is a simple, healthy, and delicious snack or side dish, rich in protein and fiber, perfect for a quick and satisfying treat.

Recipe 40: Low-Carb Protein Muffins

Prep Time: 10 minutes | Cooking Time: 20 minutes | Servings: 12 muffins

Ingredients

- 1 1/2 cups almond flour
- 1/2 cup protein powder (vanilla or unflavored)
- 1/4 cup coconut flour
- 1/4 cup erythritol or your preferred low-carb sweetener
- 1 teaspoon baking powder
- 1/2 teaspoon baking soda
- 1/4 teaspoon sea salt
- 3 large eggs
- 1/2 cup unsweetened almond milk
- 1/4 cup coconut oil, melted
- 1 teaspoon vanilla extract
- 1/2 cup blueberries or chocolate chips (optional)

Cooking Instructions

1. **Preheat the Oven:** Preheat your oven to 350°F (175°C). Line a 12-cup muffin tin with paper liners or grease with coconut oil.
2. **Mix Dry Ingredients:** In a large bowl, combine the almond flour, protein powder, coconut flour, erythritol, baking powder, baking soda, and sea salt. Mix well.
3. **Mix Wet Ingredients:** In another bowl, whisk together the eggs, unsweetened almond milk, melted coconut oil, and vanilla extract until well combined.
4. **Combine Ingredients:** Pour the wet ingredients into the dry ingredients and stir until just combined. If using, fold in the blueberries or chocolate chips.
5. **Fill Muffin Tin:** Divide the batter evenly among the 12 muffin cups, filling each about 3/4 full.
6. **Bake:** Bake in the preheated oven for 18-20 minutes or until a toothpick inserted into the center of a muffin comes out clean.
7. **Cool:** Allow the muffins to cool in the tin for 5 minutes, then transfer to a wire rack to cool completely.
8. **Serve:** Enjoy the muffins warm or at room temperature.

Nutritional Facts

- **Calories:** 150 kcal
- **Protein:** 8g
- **Fat:** 12g
- **Saturated Fat:** 5g
- **Cholesterol:** 40mg
- **Sodium:** 150mg
- **Potassium:** 50mg
- **Fiber:** 3g
- **Sugar:** 1g
- **Vitamin A:** 60 IU

Cooking Tips

- ✓ **Protein Powder:** Choose a protein powder with a flavor you enjoy. Vanilla works well with most recipes.
- ✓ **Sweetener:** Adjust the amount of sweetener to your taste. You can use other low-carb sweeteners like stevia or monk fruit.
- ✓ **Add-ins:** Customize your muffins with your favorite low-carb add-ins, such as nuts, seeds, or different berries.
- ✓ **Storage:** Store muffins in an airtight container at room temperature for up to 3 days or in the refrigerator for up to a week. They can also be frozen for up to 3 months.

Low-carb protein muffins are a delicious and healthy treat, perfect for a quick breakfast or snack; they are packed with protein and low in carbs to keep you energized and satisfied.

Dessert Recipes

Recipe 41: Low-Carb Chocolate Mousse

Prep Time: 10 minutes | Cooking Time: 0 minutes | Servings: 4

Ingredients

- 1 cup heavy cream
- 2 tablespoons unsweetened cocoa powder
- 2 tablespoons powdered erythritol (or another low-carb sweetener)
- 1 teaspoon vanilla extract
- Fresh berries and mint leaves for garnish (optional)

Cooking Instructions

1. **Whip the Cream:** In a large mixing bowl, beat the heavy cream with an electric mixer on medium-high speed until it begins to thicken.
2. **Add Cocoa and Sweetener:** Sift the unsweetened cocoa powder and powdered erythritol into the whipped cream. Add the vanilla extract. Continue to beat until stiff peaks form and the mixture is smooth and creamy.
3. **Serve:** Spoon the chocolate mousse into serving dishes. Garnish with fresh berries and mint leaves if desired. Serve immediately or refrigerate until ready to serve.

Nutritional Facts

- **Calories:** 200 kcal
- **Protein:** 2g
- **Fat:** 20g
- **Saturated Fat:** 12g
- **Cholesterol:** 75mg
- **Sodium:** 20mg
- **Potassium:** 100mg
- **Fiber:** 1g
- **Sugar:** 1g
- **Vitamin A:** 800 IU

Cooking Tips

- ✓ **Cream:** Ensure the heavy cream is very cold before whipping to achieve the best texture.
- ✓ **Sweetener:** Adjust the amount of sweetener to taste. If you prefer a sweeter mousse, add more powdered erythritol.
- ✓ **Cocoa Powder:** Use high-quality unsweetened cocoa powder for a richer chocolate flavor.
- ✓ **Serving Suggestions:** Pair with fresh berries or a dollop of whipped cream for an extra indulgence.
- ✓ **Storage:** Store any leftovers in an airtight container in the refrigerator for up to 3 days. Re-whip before serving if needed.

Low-carb chocolate mousse is a rich, creamy, and satisfying dessert that is low in carbs and high in flavor, perfect for indulging your sweet tooth while staying on track with your dietary goals.

Recipe 42: Almond Flour Brownies

Prep Time: 10 minutes | Cooking Time: 25 minutes | Servings: 12 brownies

Ingredients

- 1 cup almond flour
- 1/2 cup unsweetened cocoa powder
- 1/2 cup powdered erythritol (or another low-carb sweetener)
- 1/2 teaspoon baking powder
- 1/4 teaspoon sea salt
- 3 large eggs
- 1/2 cup butter, melted
- 1 teaspoon vanilla extract
- 1/4 cup dark chocolate chips (optional)

Cooking Instructions

1. **Preheat the Oven:** Preheat your oven to 350°F (175°C). Line an 8x8-inch baking dish with parchment paper.
2. **Mix Dry Ingredients:** In a large bowl, whisk together the almond flour, cocoa powder, powdered erythritol, baking powder, and sea salt.
3. **Add Wet Ingredients:** In another bowl, whisk the eggs, melted butter, and vanilla extract until well combined. Pour the wet ingredients into the dry ingredients and stir until just combined. Fold in the dark chocolate chips if using.
4. **Bake:** Pour the batter into the prepared baking dish and spread it out evenly. Bake in the preheated oven for 20-25 minutes or until a toothpick inserted into the center comes out clean.
5. **Cool:** Allow the brownies to cool completely in the dish before lifting them out using the parchment paper. Cut into 12 squares.
6. **Serve:** Enjoy the brownies at room temperature or slightly warmed.

Nutritional Facts

- **Calories:** 180 kcal
- **Protein:** 4g
- **Fat:** 16g
- **Saturated Fat:** 7g
- **Cholesterol:** 60mg
- **Sodium:** 100mg
- **Potassium:** 100mg
- **Fiber:** 3g
- **Sugar:** 1g
- **Vitamin A:** 350 IU

Cooking Tips

- ✓ **Cocoa Powder:** Use high-quality unsweetened cocoa powder for a richer chocolate flavor.
- ✓ **Sweetener:** Adjust the amount of sweetener to your taste. You can use other low-carb sweeteners like stevia or monk fruit.
- ✓ **Mix-ins:** Add nuts, seeds, or more chocolate chips for additional texture and flavor.
- ✓ **Storage:** Store any leftovers in an airtight container at room temperature for up to 3 days or in the refrigerator for up to a week. They can also be frozen for up to 3 months.

Almond flour brownies are fudgy, rich, and delicious, making them a perfect low-carb dessert option that doesn't compromise on flavor or texture.

Recipe 43: Keto Cheesecake Bites

Prep Time: 15 minutes | Cooking Time: 0 minutes | Servings: 16 bites

Ingredients

- 1 cup almond flour
- 1/4 cup powdered erythritol (or another low-carb sweetener)
- 1/4 cup melted butter
- 8 oz cream cheese, softened
- 1/4 cup heavy cream
- 1/4 cup powdered erythritol (for filling)
- 1 teaspoon vanilla extract
- Fresh berries for topping (optional)

Cooking Instructions

1. **Prepare the Crust:** In a medium bowl, combine the almond flour, 1/4 cup powdered erythritol, and melted butter. Mix until well combined. Press the mixture into the bottom of a mini muffin tin or silicone mold to form the crust.
2. **Prepare the Filling:** In a large bowl, beat the softened cream cheese with an electric mixer until smooth. Add the heavy cream, 1/4 cup powdered erythritol, and vanilla extract. Continue to beat until the mixture is creamy and well combined.
3. **Assemble the Cheesecake Bites:** Spoon the cream cheese mixture over the crust in the mini muffin tin or silicone mold. Smooth the tops with a spatula.
4. **Chill:** Refrigerate for at least 2 hours or until the cheesecake bites are firm.
5. **Serve:** Carefully remove the cheesecake bites from the tin or mold. Top with fresh berries if desired and serve chilled.

Nutritional Facts

- **Calories:** 130 kcal
- **Protein:** 3g
- **Fat:** 12g
- **Saturated Fat:** 6g
- **Cholesterol:** 30mg
- **Sodium:** 70mg
- **Potassium:** 40mg
- **Fiber:** 1g
- **Sugar:** 1g
- **Vitamin A:** 300 IU

Cooking Tips

- ✓ **Cream Cheese:** Ensure the cream cheese is fully softened for a smooth filling.
- ✓ **Sweetener:** Adjust the sweetness to your taste preference. You can use other low-carb sweeteners like stevia or monk fruit.
- ✓ **Mold:** Using a silicone mold makes it easier to remove the cheesecake bites without sticking.
- ✓ **Storage:** Store any leftovers in an airtight container in the refrigerator for up to 5 days. They can also be frozen for up to 1 month. Thaw in the refrigerator before serving.

Keto cheesecake bites are a creamy and delicious low-carb dessert that satisfies your sweet tooth without the extra carbs, perfect for a quick and easy treat.

Recipe 44: Protein-Packed Peanut Butter Cookies

Prep Time: 10 minutes | Cooking Time: 10 minutes | Servings: 12 cookies

Ingredients

- 1 cup natural peanut butter (no added sugar)
- 1/2 cup powdered erythritol (or another low-carb sweetener)
- 1/2 cup vanilla protein powder
- 1 large egg
- 1 teaspoon vanilla extract
- 1/2 teaspoon baking soda
- 1/4 teaspoon sea salt

Cooking Instructions

1. **Preheat the Oven:** Preheat your oven to 350°F (175°C). Line a baking sheet with parchment paper.
2. **Mix Ingredients:** In a large bowl, combine the peanut butter, powdered erythritol, protein powder, egg, vanilla extract, baking soda, and sea salt. Mix until well combined and a dough forms.
3. **Shape the Cookies:** Scoop tablespoon-sized balls of dough and place them on the prepared baking sheet. Flatten each ball with a fork, creating a crisscross pattern.
4. **Bake:** Bake in the preheated oven for 8-10 minutes or until the edges are golden brown. Be careful not to overbake.
5. **Cool:** Allow the cookies to cool on the baking sheet for 5 minutes before transferring them to a wire rack to cool completely.
6. **Serve:** Enjoy the cookies at room temperature.

Nutritional Facts

- **Calories:** 150 kcal
- **Protein:** 8g
- **Fat:** 11g
- **Saturated Fat:** 2g
- **Cholesterol:** 15mg
- **Sodium:** 150mg
- **Potassium:** 100mg
- **Fiber:** 2g
- **Sugar:** 1g
- **Vitamin E:** 2mg

Cooking Tips

- ✓ **Peanut Butter:** Use natural peanut butter without added sugars or oils for the best results.
- ✓ **Protein Powder:** Choose a protein powder with a flavor you enjoy. Vanilla works well with peanut butter.
- ✓ **Sweetener:** Adjust the amount of sweetener to your taste. You can use other low-carb sweeteners like stevia or monk fruit.
- ✓ **Storage:** Store any leftovers in an airtight container at room temperature for up to 3 days or in the refrigerator for up to a week. They can also be frozen for up to 3 months.

Protein-packed peanut butter cookies are a delicious and nutritious treat, perfect for a quick snack or dessert that satisfies your sweet tooth while providing a good source of protein.

Recipe 45: Berry and Cream Parfait

Prep Time: 10 minutes | Cooking Time: 0 minutes | Servings: 4

Ingredients

- 1 cup fresh strawberries, sliced
- 1 cup fresh blueberries
- 1 cup fresh raspberries
- 1 cup heavy cream
- 2 tablespoons powdered erythritol (or another low-carb sweetener)
- 1 teaspoon vanilla extract
- Fresh mint leaves for garnish (optional)

Cooking Instructions

1. **Prepare the Berries:** Wash and prepare the strawberries, blueberries, and raspberries. Slice the strawberries.
2. **Whip the Cream:** In a large mixing bowl, beat the heavy cream with an electric mixer on medium-high speed until it begins to thicken. Add the powdered erythritol and vanilla extract. Continue to beat until stiff peaks form.
3. **Assemble the Parfaits:** In 4 serving glasses, layer the berries and whipped cream, starting with a layer of berries, then a layer of whipped cream, and repeat until the glasses are filled. End with a layer of whipped cream.
4. **Garnish and Serve:** Garnish each parfait with fresh mint leaves if desired. Serve immediately.

Nutritional Facts

- **Calories:** 200 kcal
- **Protein:** 2g
- **Fat:** 18g
- **Saturated Fat:** 11g
- **Cholesterol:** 65mg
- **Sodium:** 20mg
- **Potassium:** 200mg
- **Fiber:** 4g
- **Sugar:** 5g
- **Vitamin C:** 45mg

Cooking Tips

- ✓ **Berries:** Use a variety of fresh berries for the best flavor and presentation. Frozen berries can be used if fresh berries are not available; thaw them before using.
- ✓ **Cream:** Ensure the heavy cream is very cold before whipping to achieve the best texture.
- ✓ **Sweetener:** Adjust the sweetness to your taste preference. You can use other low-carb sweeteners like stevia or monk fruit.
- ✓ **Serving Suggestions:** This parfait makes a great breakfast, dessert, or snack. Pair with a low-carb granola for added texture.
- ✓ **Storage:** Parfaits are best enjoyed immediately. If you need to prepare them in advance, store the whipped cream and berries separately in the refrigerator and assemble them just before serving.

Berry and cream parfaits are a delightful and refreshing dessert, combining the natural sweetness of fresh berries with rich, creamy whipped cream, perfect for a light and satisfying treat.

Recipe 46: Coconut Flour Cupcakes

Prep Time: 15 minutes | Cooking Time: 20 minutes | Servings: 12 cupcakes

Ingredients

For the Cupcakes:

- 1/2 cup coconut flour
- 1/4 cup powdered erythritol (or another low-carb sweetener)
- 1/2 teaspoon baking powder
- 1/4 teaspoon sea salt
- 6 large eggs
- 1/2 cup melted coconut oil
- 1/2 cup unsweetened almond milk
- 1 teaspoon vanilla extract

For the Frosting:

- 1/2 cup heavy cream
- 2 tablespoons powdered erythritol (or another low-carb sweetener)
- 1/2 teaspoon vanilla extract

Cooking Instructions

1. **Preheat the Oven:** Preheat your oven to 350°F (175°C). Line a 12-cup muffin tin with paper liners.
2. **Mix Dry Ingredients:** In a large bowl, whisk together the coconut flour, powdered erythritol, baking powder, and sea salt.
3. **Mix Wet Ingredients:** In another bowl, whisk together the eggs, melted coconut oil, unsweetened almond milk, and vanilla extract until well combined.
4. **Combine Ingredients:** Pour the wet ingredients into the dry ingredients and stir until just combined. Let the batter sit for a few minutes to allow the coconut flour to absorb the liquid.
5. **Fill Muffin Tin:** Divide the batter evenly among the 12 muffin cups, filling each about 3/4 full.
6. **Bake:** Bake in the preheated oven for 18-20 minutes or until a toothpick inserted into the center of a cupcake comes out clean.
7. **Cool:** Allow the cupcakes to cool in the tin for 5 minutes, then transfer to a wire rack to cool completely.
8. **Prepare the Frosting:** In a large mixing bowl, beat the heavy cream, powdered erythritol, and vanilla extract with an electric mixer on medium-high speed until stiff peaks form.
9. **Frost the Cupcakes:** Once the cupcakes are completely cool, frost them with the whipped cream frosting using a piping bag or a spatula.
10. **Serve:** Enjoy the cupcakes immediately or refrigerate until ready to serve.

Nutritional Facts

- **Calories:** 150 kcal
- **Protein:** 4g
- **Fat:** 13g
- **Saturated Fat:** 9g
- **Cholesterol:** 80mg
- **Sodium:** 100mg
- **Potassium:** 50mg
- **Fiber:** 3g
- **Sugar:** 1g
- **Vitamin A:** 200 IU

Cooking Tips

✓ **Coconut Flour:** Measure the coconut flour carefully as it is very absorbent, and a small change in quantity can affect the texture.
✓ **Sweetener:** Adjust the sweetness to your taste. You can use other low-carb sweeteners like stevia or monk fruit.
✓ **Frosting:** Ensure the heavy cream is very cold before whipping to achieve the best texture.
✓ **Add-ins:** Add a handful of sugar-free chocolate chips or unsweetened shredded coconut to the batter for extra flavor.

Recipe 47: Low-Carb Lemon Bars

Prep Time: 20 minutes | Cooking Time: 25 minutes | Servings: 16 bars

Ingredients

For the Crust:

- 1 1/2 cups almond flour
- 1/4 cup powdered erythritol (or another low-carb sweetener)
- 1/4 cup melted butter
- 1/4 teaspoon sea salt

For the Lemon Filling:

- 1/2 cup fresh lemon juice (about 2-3 lemons)
- 2 tablespoons lemon zest
- 1/2 cup powdered erythritol (or another low-carb sweetener)
- 4 large eggs
- 1/4 cup coconut flour
- 1/2 teaspoon baking powder

Cooking Instructions

1. **Preheat the Oven:** Preheat your oven to 350°F (175°C). Line an 8x8-inch baking dish with parchment paper.
2. **Prepare the Crust:** In a medium bowl, combine the almond flour, powdered erythritol, melted butter, and sea salt. Mix until well combined. Press the mixture evenly into the bottom of the prepared baking dish.
3. **Bake the Crust:** Bake in the preheated oven for 10-12 minutes or until the edges are lightly golden. Remove from the oven and let cool slightly.
4. **Prepare the Lemon Filling:** In a large bowl, whisk together the fresh lemon juice, lemon zest, powdered erythritol, and eggs until well combined. Sift in the coconut flour and baking powder, and whisk until smooth.
5. **Bake the Lemon Bars:** Pour the lemon filling over the pre-baked crust. Return the dish to the oven and bake for an additional 15-20 minutes, or until the filling is set and the top is slightly golden.
6. **Cool:** Allow the lemon bars to cool completely in the dish. Once cool, refrigerate for at least 1 hour before cutting into 16 squares.
7. **Serve:** Dust with additional powdered erythritol if desired and serve chilled.

Nutritional Facts

- **Calories:** 110 kcal
- **Protein:** 4g
- **Fat:** 9g
- **Saturated Fat:** 3g
- **Cholesterol:** 45mg
- **Sodium:** 100mg
- **Potassium:** 30mg
- **Fiber:** 2g
- **Sugar:** 1g
- **Vitamin C:** 6mg

Cooking Tips

- ✓ **Lemon Juice:** Use fresh lemon juice for the best flavor. Bottled lemon juice can be used in a pinch, but it may alter the taste.
- ✓ **Sweetener:** Adjust the sweetness to your taste. You can use other low-carb sweeteners like stevia or monk fruit.
- ✓ **Coconut Flour:** Sift the coconut flour to avoid lumps in the filling.
- ✓ **Storage:** Store any leftovers in an airtight container in the refrigerator for up to 5 days. They can also be frozen for up to 1 month.
- ✓ **Serving Suggestions:** Serve with a dollop of whipped cream or a sprinkle of unsweetened shredded coconut for extra flavor.

Low-carb lemon bars are a tangy and sweet treat with a delicious almond flour crust, perfect for satisfying your sweet tooth without the extra carbs.

Recipe 48: Keto-Friendly Chocolate Chip Cookies

Prep Time: 10 minutes | Cooking Time: 15 minutes | Servings: 18 cookies

Ingredients

- 2 cups almond flour
- 1/2 cup powdered erythritol (or another low-carb sweetener)
- 1/4 cup melted butter
- 1 large egg
- 1 teaspoon vanilla extract
- 1/2 teaspoon baking soda
- 1/4 teaspoon sea salt
- 1/2 cup sugar-free chocolate chips

Cooking Instructions

1. **Preheat the Oven:** Preheat your oven to 350°F (175°C). Line a baking sheet with parchment paper.
2. **Mix Dry Ingredients:** In a large bowl, whisk together the almond flour, powdered erythritol, baking soda, and sea salt.
3. **Mix Wet Ingredients:** In another bowl, whisk together the melted butter, egg, and vanilla extract until well combined.
4. **Combine Ingredients:** Pour the wet ingredients into the dry ingredients and stir until just combined. Fold in the sugar-free chocolate chips.
5. **Shape the Cookies:** Scoop tablespoon-sized balls of dough and place them on the prepared baking sheet. Flatten each ball slightly with your hand or a spatula.
6. **Bake:** Bake in the preheated oven for 12-15 minutes or until the edges are golden brown.
7. **Cool:** Allow the cookies to cool on the baking sheet for 5 minutes before transferring them to a wire rack to cool completely.
8. **Serve:** Enjoy the cookies at room temperature.

Nutritional Facts

- **Calories:** 120 kcal
- **Protein:** 3g
- **Fat:** 10g
- **Saturated Fat:** 3g
- **Cholesterol:** 15mg
- **Sodium:** 80mg
- **Potassium:** 20mg
- **Fiber:** 2g
- **Sugar:** 1g
- **Vitamin E:** 1mg

Cooking Tips

- ✓ **Almond Flour:** Use finely ground almond flour for the best texture. Almond meal can be used but will result in a coarser texture.
- ✓ **Sweetener:** Adjust the sweetness to your taste. You can use other low-carb sweeteners like stevia or monk fruit.
- ✓ **Chocolate Chips:** Ensure the chocolate chips are sugar-free to keep the recipe low-carb.
- ✓ **Storage:** Store any leftovers in an airtight container at room temperature for up to 3 days or in the refrigerator for up to a week. They can also be frozen for up to 3 months.
- ✓ **Add-ins:** Add a handful of chopped nuts or unsweetened coconut flakes for extra texture and flavor.

Keto-friendly chocolate chip cookies are a delicious and satisfying treat, perfect for indulging your sweet tooth while staying on track with your low-carb diet.

Recipe 49: Vanilla Protein Ice Cream

Prep Time: 10 minutes | Cooking Time: 0 minutes (plus freezing time) | Servings: 4

Ingredients

- 2 cups heavy cream
- 1 cup unsweetened almond milk
- 1/2 cup vanilla protein powder
- 1/4 cup powdered erythritol (or another low-carb sweetener)
- 2 teaspoons vanilla extract

Cooking Instructions

1. **Combine Ingredients:** In a large mixing bowl, whisk together the heavy cream, unsweetened almond milk, vanilla protein powder, powdered erythritol, and vanilla extract until well combined and smooth.
2. **Chill Mixture:** Cover the bowl and refrigerate for at least 1 hour to chill the mixture thoroughly.
3. **Churn the Ice Cream:** Pour the chilled mixture into an ice cream maker and churn according to the manufacturer's instructions until it reaches a soft-serve consistency.
4. **Freeze:** Transfer the ice cream to an airtight container and freeze for at least 2 hours or until firm.
5. **Serve:** Scoop the ice cream into bowls or cones and enjoy immediately.

Nutritional Facts

- **Calories:** 300 kcal
- **Protein:** 12g
- **Fat:** 25g
- **Saturated Fat:** 15g
- **Cholesterol:** 90mg
- **Sodium:** 100mg
- **Potassium:** 150mg
- **Fiber:** 1g
- **Sugar:** 1g
- **Vitamin A:** 800 IU

Cooking Tips

- ✓ **Protein Powder:** Use a high-quality vanilla protein powder that you enjoy. Different brands may vary in sweetness, so adjust the sweetener accordingly.
- ✓ **Chill Thoroughly:** Ensure the mixture is thoroughly chilled before churning for the best texture.
- ✓ **Add-ins:** Add your favorite low-carb mix-ins like chopped nuts, sugar-free chocolate chips, or berries during the last few minutes of churning.
- ✓ **Storage:** Store any leftovers in an airtight container in the freezer for up to 1 month. Let the ice cream sit at room temperature for a few minutes before scooping if it becomes too hard.
- ✓ **Serving Suggestions:** Serve with a drizzle of sugar-free chocolate syrup or a sprinkle of chopped nuts for extra flavor.

Vanilla protein ice cream is a creamy and delicious treat, perfect for a high-protein, low-carb dessert that satisfies your sweet tooth while supporting your dietary goals.

Recipe 50: Low-Carb Matcha Green Tea Pudding

Prep Time: 5 minutes (plus overnight chilling) | Cooking Time: None | Servings: 4

Ingredients

- 1 1/2 cups full-fat coconut milk (or any preferred milk alternative)
- 1/4 cup chia seeds
- 1 tablespoon matcha green tea powder
- 1 teaspoon vanilla extract
- 2 tablespoons erythritol or your favorite low-carb sweetener (adjust to taste)
- Fresh berries or coconut flakes (optional for topping)
- Mint leaves (optional for garnish)

Cooking Instructions

1. **Mix the Pudding Base:** In a medium-sized mixing bowl, combine the coconut milk, chia seeds, matcha green tea powder, vanilla extract, and erythritol. Whisk thoroughly to ensure the matcha and sweetener are fully dissolved, and the chia seeds are evenly distributed.
2. **Chill the Pudding:** Cover the bowl with plastic wrap or a lid and refrigerate for at least 2 hours, or preferably overnight, to allow the chia seeds to absorb the liquid and form a thick, creamy pudding.
3. **Stir the Pudding:** After chilling, give the pudding a good stir to break up any clumps and to ensure a smooth consistency.
4. **Serve:** Divide the pudding into four serving bowls or jars. Top with fresh berries or coconut flakes, if desired, and garnish with mint leaves.

5. **Enjoy:** Serve immediately or store in the refrigerator until ready to enjoy.

Nutritional Facts

- **Calories:** 190 kcal
- **Protein:** 3g
- **Fat:** 15g
- **Saturated Fat:** 11g
- **Cholesterol:** 0mg
- **Sodium:** 25mg
- **Potassium:** 200mg
- **Fiber:** 5g
- **Sugar:** 1g
- **Vitamin C:** 3mg

Cooking Tips

- ✓ **Matcha:** Use high-quality matcha green tea powder for the best flavor and vibrant green color. Adjust the amount of matcha to taste if you prefer a stronger or milder flavor.
- ✓ **Sweetener:** Choose a low-carb sweetener that you like. Stevia or monk fruit sweetener are good alternatives to erythritol.
- ✓ **Milk Alternatives:** Almond milk, soy milk, or any other preferred milk can be used instead of coconut milk, though it may alter the pudding's creaminess.
- ✓ **Toppings:** Customize your pudding with your favorite low-carb toppings such as nuts, seeds, or even a sprinkle of cinnamon for added flavor and texture.

Low-carb matcha green tea pudding is a creamy and delicious treat that combines the earthy flavor of matcha with the rich texture of coconut milk. It's an easy-to-make, healthy dessert or snack that's low in carbs and packed with antioxidants, perfect for those who love a good balance of flavor and nutrition.

Vegetarian Recipes

Recipe 51: Eggplant Parmesan

Prep Time: 20 minutes | Cooking Time: 40 minutes | Servings: 6

Ingredients

- 2 large eggplants, sliced into 1/4-inch rounds
- 1 teaspoon sea salt
- 1/2 cup almond flour
- 1/2 cup grated Parmesan cheese
- 1 teaspoon Italian seasoning
- 1/2 teaspoon garlic powder
- 2 large eggs, beaten
- 2 cups marinara sauce (low carb)
- 2 cups shredded mozzarella cheese
- Fresh basil leaves for garnish (optional)

Cooking Instructions

1. **Preheat the Oven:** Preheat your oven to 375°F (190°C). Line a baking sheet with parchment paper.
2. **Prepare the Eggplant:** Place the eggplant slices on paper towels and sprinkle both sides with sea salt. Let them sit for 15 minutes to draw out excess moisture. Pat dry with paper towels.
3. **Prepare the Breading:** In a shallow bowl, combine the almond flour, grated Parmesan cheese, Italian seasoning, and garlic powder. In another shallow bowl, beat the eggs.
4. **Bread the Eggplant:** Dip each eggplant slice into the beaten eggs, then coat with the almond flour mixture. Place the coated slices on the prepared baking sheet.
5. **Bake the Eggplant:** Bake in the preheated oven for 20 minutes, flipping halfway through, until the eggplant is golden and tender.
6. **Assemble the Dish:** Spread 1/2 cup of marinara sauce on the bottom of a 9x13-inch baking dish. Layer half of the baked eggplant slices over the sauce. Spread another 1/2 cup of marinara sauce over the eggplant and sprinkle with 1 cup of shredded mozzarella cheese. Repeat the layers with the remaining eggplant, sauce, and cheese.
7. **Bake:** Bake in the preheated oven for 20 minutes or until the cheese is melted and bubbly.
8. **Serve:** Garnish with fresh basil leaves if desired. Serve hot.

Nutritional Facts

- **Calories:** 250 kcal
- **Protein:** 12g
- **Fat:** 18g
- **Saturated Fat:** 6g
- **Cholesterol:** 75mg
- **Sodium:** 600mg
- **Potassium:** 400mg
- **Fiber:** 4g
- **Sugar:** 6g
- **Vitamin A:** 400 IU

Cooking Tips

- ✓ **Eggplant:** Salting the eggplant helps remove bitterness and excess moisture, resulting in a better texture.
- ✓ **Sauce:** Use a low-carb marinara sauce to keep the dish keto-friendly. You can make your own or find a store-bought option.
- ✓ **Cheese:** Freshly grated Parmesan cheese and mozzarella will melt better and provide a better texture.
- ✓ **Storage:** Store any leftovers in an airtight container in the refrigerator for up to 3 days. Reheat in the oven or microwave before serving.

Eggplant Parmesan is a classic Italian dish made low-carb, featuring layers of tender baked eggplant, marinara sauce, and melted mozzarella cheese, perfect for a comforting and satisfying meal.

Recipe 52: Zucchini Pizza Bites

Prep Time: 10 minutes | Cooking Time: 10 minutes | Servings: 4

Ingredients

- 2 large zucchinis, sliced into 1/4-inch-thick rounds
- 1 tablespoon olive oil
- 1/2 teaspoon sea salt
- 1/4 teaspoon black pepper
- 1/2 teaspoon garlic powder
- 1 cup marinara sauce (preferably low-carb)
- 1 1/2 cups shredded mozzarella cheese
- 1/4 cup grated Parmesan cheese
- 1 teaspoon dried oregano
- Fresh basil leaves, chopped (for garnish)
- Crushed red pepper flakes (optional for a spicy kick)

Cooking Instructions

1. **Preheat the Oven:** Preheat your oven to 400°F (200°C). Line a large baking sheet with parchment paper or lightly grease it with cooking spray.
2. **Prepare the Zucchini:** Place the zucchini rounds in a single layer on the prepared baking sheet. Drizzle with olive oil and sprinkle with sea salt, black pepper, and garlic powder. Use your hands to toss and coat the zucchini slices evenly.
3. **Bake the Zucchini:** Bake in the preheated oven for 5 minutes to soften the zucchini slightly.
4. **Add the Toppings:** Remove the baking sheet from the oven. Spread a small spoonful of marinara sauce onto each zucchini round. Top with a generous sprinkle of shredded mozzarella cheese and a small amount of grated Parmesan cheese. Sprinkle dried oregano over the top.

5. **Bake Until Golden:** Return the baking sheet to the oven and bake for an additional 5-7 minutes, or until the cheese is melted and bubbly, and the edges of the zucchini are lightly browned.
6. **Garnish and Serve:** Remove the zucchini pizza bites from the oven and let them cool for a few minutes. Garnish with fresh basil leaves and, if desired, a sprinkle of crushed red pepper flakes. Serve warm and enjoy.

Nutritional Facts

- **Calories:** 150 kcal
- **Protein:** 9g
- **Fat:** 11g
- **Saturated Fat:** 5g
- **Cholesterol:** 25mg
- **Sodium:** 400mg
- **Potassium:** 350mg
- **Fiber:** 2g
- **Sugar:** 4g
- **Vitamin A:** 500 IU

Cooking Tips

- ✓ **Zucchini:** Choose zucchinis that are firm and medium-sized for the best texture. Slicing them evenly ensures they cook uniformly.
- ✓ **Marinara Sauce:** Opt for a low-carb marinara sauce or make your own to control the sugar content. You can also use a pesto sauce for a different flavor profile.
- ✓ **Cheese:** For a more indulgent bite, add a sprinkle of feta or goat cheese along with the mozzarella. If you prefer a dairy-free option, use vegan cheese.
- ✓ **Spice Level:** Adjust the amount of crushed red pepper flakes according to your heat preference. For a mild version, you can omit them entirely.

Zucchini pizza bites are a delightful and healthy alternative to traditional pizza, offering all the delicious flavors of pizza without the carbs. These bite-sized treats are perfect for a quick snack, a party appetizer, or a light meal that's both nutritious and satisfying.

Recipe 53: Low-Carb Veggie Stir-Fry

Prep Time: 15 minutes | Cooking Time: 15 minutes | Servings: 4

Ingredients

- 1 tablespoon olive oil
- 1 red bell pepper, sliced
- 1 yellow bell pepper, sliced
- 1 medium zucchini, sliced into half-moons
- 1 cup broccoli florets
- 1 cup snow peas
- 1 cup mushrooms, sliced
- 3 cloves garlic, minced
- 1 tablespoon ginger, minced
- 3 tablespoons soy sauce (or tamari for gluten-free)
- 1 tablespoon rice vinegar
- 1 teaspoon sesame oil
- 1/4 teaspoon red pepper flakes (optional)
- 1/4 cup green onions, sliced
- Sesame seeds for garnish (optional)

Cooking Instructions

1. **Prepare the Vegetables:** Wash and slice the bell peppers, zucchini, broccoli, snow peas, and mushrooms. Mince the garlic and ginger.
2. **Heat the Oil:** In a large skillet or wok, heat the olive oil over medium-high heat.
3. **Cook the Vegetables:** Add the bell peppers, zucchini, broccoli, and snow peas to the skillet. Stir-fry for 5-7 minutes or until the vegetables are tender-crisp.
4. **Add Garlic and Ginger:** Add the sliced mushrooms, minced garlic, and ginger to the skillet. Stir-fry for an additional 3-4 minutes until the mushrooms are cooked.
5. **Add Sauce:** In a small bowl, mix together the soy sauce, rice vinegar, sesame oil, and red pepper flakes (if using). Pour the sauce over the vegetables and stir to combine. Cook for 2 more minutes to heat through.
6. **Serve:** Garnish with sliced green onions and sesame seeds if desired. Serve hot.

Nutritional Facts

- **Calories:** 100 kcal
- **Protein:** 3g
- **Fat:** 5g
- **Saturated Fat:** 1g
- **Cholesterol:** 0mg
- **Sodium:** 500mg
- **Potassium:** 450mg
- **Fiber:** 4g
- **Sugar:** 6g
- **Vitamin C:** 120mg

Cooking Tips

- ✓ **Vegetables:** Use a variety of colorful vegetables for the best flavor and nutritional value. Feel free to add or substitute other vegetables based on your preference.
- ✓ **Heat:** Adjust the heat level by adding more or less red pepper flakes.
- ✓ **Soy Sauce:** Use low-sodium soy sauce to reduce the salt content, or tamari for a gluten-free option.
- ✓ **Serving Suggestions:** Serve over cauliflower rice or shirataki noodles for a complete low-carb meal.

Low-carb veggie stir-fry is a quick, easy, and nutritious dish packed with a variety of colorful vegetables and a savory sauce, perfect for a healthy and satisfying meal.

Recipe 54: Spinach and Mushroom Stuffed Peppers

Prep Time: 20 minutes | Cooking Time: 30 minutes | Servings: 4

Ingredients

- 4 large bell peppers (any color), tops cut off and seeds removed
- 1 tablespoon olive oil
- 1 small onion, finely chopped
- 2 cloves garlic, minced
- 2 cups fresh spinach, chopped
- 1 cup mushrooms, finely chopped
- 1/2 cup ricotta cheese
- 1/2 cup shredded mozzarella cheese
- 1/4 cup grated Parmesan cheese
- 1 teaspoon dried oregano
- 1/2 teaspoon sea salt
- 1/4 teaspoon black pepper
- Fresh basil leaves for garnish (optional)

Cooking Instructions

1. **Preheat the Oven:** Preheat your oven to 375°F (190°C). Lightly grease a baking dish with olive oil.
2. **Prepare the Peppers:** Cut the tops off the bell peppers and remove the seeds and membranes. Please place them in the prepared baking dish.
3. **Cook the Vegetables:** In a large skillet, heat the olive oil over medium heat. Add the chopped onion and minced garlic and cook for 2-3 minutes until softened.
4. **Add Spinach and Mushrooms:** Add the chopped spinach and mushrooms to the skillet. Cook for 5-7 minutes until the vegetables are tender and any liquid has evaporated. Remove from heat and let cool slightly.
5. **Mix the Filling:** In a large bowl, combine the cooked vegetables, ricotta cheese, shredded mozzarella, grated Parmesan, dried oregano, sea salt, and black pepper. Mix until well combined.
6. **Stuff the Peppers:** Spoon the filling mixture evenly into each bell pepper. Top with additional shredded mozzarella if desired.
7. **Bake:** Bake in the preheated oven for 25-30 minutes or until the peppers are tender and the cheese is melted and bubbly.
8. **Serve:** Garnish with fresh basil leaves if desired. Serve hot.

Nutritional Facts

- **Calories:** 200 kcal
- **Protein:** 10g
- **Fat:** 12g
- **Saturated Fat:** 6g
- **Cholesterol:** 35mg
- **Sodium:** 500mg
- **Potassium:** 600mg
- **Fiber:** 4g
- **Sugar:** 6g
- **Vitamin A:** 2500 IU

Cooking Tips

- ✓ **Peppers:** Use a variety of colored bell peppers for a vibrant presentation and varied flavor.
- ✓ **Vegetables:** Ensure the spinach and mushrooms are well cooked to remove excess moisture, preventing the filling from becoming too watery.
- ✓ **Cheese:** Use freshly grated cheeses for the best melting quality and flavor.
- ✓ **Storage:** Store any leftovers in an airtight container in the refrigerator for up to 3 days. Reheat in the oven or microwave before serving.

Spinach and mushroom stuffed peppers are a delicious and nutritious vegetarian dish filled with a savory mixture of fresh vegetables and cheese, perfect for a satisfying and healthy meal.

Recipe 55: Zoodle Alfredo with Sun-Dried Tomatoes

Prep Time: 15 minutes | Cooking Time: 10 minutes | Servings: 4

Ingredients

- 4 medium zucchinis, spiralized into noodles (zoodles)
- 1 tablespoon olive oil
- 2 cloves garlic, minced
- 1 cup heavy cream
- 1/2 cup grated Parmesan cheese
- 1/4 cup sun-dried tomatoes, chopped
- 1/4 teaspoon sea salt
- 1/4 teaspoon black pepper
- Fresh basil leaves for garnish (optional)

Cooking Instructions

1. **Prepare the Zoodles:** Spiralize the zucchini into noodles using a spiralizer. Set it aside.
2. **Heat the Oil:** In a large skillet, heat the olive oil over medium heat. Add the minced garlic and cook for 1-2 minutes until fragrant.
3. **Make the Alfredo Sauce:** Pour the heavy cream into the skillet with the garlic. Bring to a gentle simmer and cook for 2-3 minutes, stirring frequently. Add the grated Parmesan cheese, sun-dried tomatoes, sea salt, and black pepper. Stir until the cheese is melted and the sauce is smooth.
4. **Add the Zoodles:** Add the spiralized zucchini noodles to the skillet. Toss gently to coat the zoodles with the Alfredo sauce. Cook for 2-3 minutes or until the zoodles are just tender but still firm (al dente).
5. **Serve:** Divide the zoodle Alfredo among four plates. Garnish with fresh basil leaves if desired. Serve immediately.

Nutritional Facts

- **Calories:** 300 kcal
- **Protein:** 6g
- **Fat:** 28g
- **Saturated Fat:** 16g
- **Cholesterol:** 90mg
- **Sodium:** 400mg
- **Potassium:** 600mg
- **Fiber:** 3g
- **Sugar:** 6g
- **Vitamin A:** 1000 IU

Cooking Tips

- ✓ **Zoodles:** For the best texture, do not overcook the zoodles. They should be tender but still slightly firm (al dente).
- ✓ **Sun-Dried Tomatoes:** Use sun-dried tomatoes packed in oil for extra flavor. Drain and chop them before adding to the sauce.
- ✓ **Cheese:** Use freshly grated Parmesan cheese for the best melting quality and flavor.
- ✓ **Storage:** Store any leftovers in an airtight container in the refrigerator for up to 2 days. Reheat gently in a skillet over low heat.

Zoodle Alfredo with sun-dried tomatoes is a creamy and delicious low-carb dish, combining tender zucchini noodles with a rich Alfredo sauce and tangy sun-dried tomatoes, perfect for a light and satisfying meal.

Recipe 56: Keto Vegetable Curry

Prep Time: 15 minutes | Cooking Time: 25 minutes | Servings: 4

Ingredients

- 1 tablespoon coconut oil
- 1 small onion, finely chopped
- 3 cloves garlic, minced
- 1 tablespoon fresh ginger, minced
- 1 tablespoon curry powder
- 1 teaspoon ground cumin
- 1/2 teaspoon ground turmeric
- 1/4 teaspoon cayenne pepper (optional)
- 1 cup coconut milk (full fat)
- 1 cup vegetable broth
- 1 medium zucchini, diced
- 1 red bell pepper, diced
- 1 cup cauliflower florets
- 1 cup broccoli florets
- 1/2 cup snow peas
- 1/4 cup fresh cilantro, chopped (optional)
- Sea salt and black pepper to taste
- Lime wedges for serving (optional)

Cooking Instructions

1. **Heat the Oil:** In a large skillet or pot, heat the coconut oil over medium heat. Add the chopped onion and cook for 3-4 minutes until softened.
2. **Add Garlic and Ginger:** Add the minced garlic and ginger to the skillet. Cook for 1-2 minutes until fragrant.
3. **Add Spices:** Stir in the curry powder, ground cumin, ground turmeric, and cayenne pepper (if using). Cook for 1 minute to toast the spices.
4. **Add Liquids:** Pour in the coconut milk and vegetable broth. Stir well to combine.
5. **Cook Vegetables:** Add the diced zucchini, red bell pepper, cauliflower florets, and broccoli florets to the skillet. Bring the mixture to a simmer and cook for 10-15 minutes until the vegetables are tender.
6. **Add Snow Peas:** Stir in the snow peas and cook for an additional 3-4 minutes until they are tender-crisp.
7. **Season:** Season the curry with sea salt and black pepper to taste. Stir in the chopped cilantro if desired.
8. **Serve:** Serve the vegetable curry hot with lime wedges on the side for squeezing over the top.

Nutritional Facts

- **Calories:** 250 kcal
- **Protein:** 5g
- **Fat:** 20g
- **Saturated Fat:** 15g
- **Cholesterol:** 0mg
- **Sodium:** 350mg
- **Potassium:** 800mg
- **Fiber:** 6g
- **Sugar:** 7g
- **Vitamin C:** 150mg

Cooking Tips

- ✓ **Vegetables:** Use a variety of colorful vegetables for the best flavor and nutritional value. Feel free to add or substitute other vegetables based on your preference.
- ✓ **Spice Level:** Adjust the amount of cayenne pepper to control the heat level according to your taste.
- ✓ **Coconut Milk:** Use full-fat coconut milk for a richer, creamier curry. Light coconut milk can be used but will result in a thinner sauce.

Keto vegetable curry is a rich and flavorful dish packed with a variety of nutritious vegetables and aromatic spices, perfect for a satisfying and healthy low-carb meal.

Recipe 57: Portobello Mushroom Burgers

Prep Time: 10 minutes | Cooking Time: 10 minutes | Servings: 4

Ingredients

- 4 large portobello mushroom caps
- 2 tablespoons olive oil
- 2 tablespoons balsamic vinegar
- 2 cloves garlic, minced
- 1 teaspoon dried oregano
- 1/2 teaspoon sea salt
- 1/4 teaspoon black pepper
- 4 slices of tomato
- 4 slices of red onion
- 4 lettuce leaves
- 4 slices of cheese (optional)
- Low-carb burger buns or lettuce wraps for serving

Cooking Instructions

1. **Prepare the Marinade:** In a small bowl, whisk together the olive oil, balsamic vinegar, minced garlic, dried oregano, sea salt, and black pepper.
2. **Marinate the Mushrooms:** Place the portobello mushroom caps in a shallow dish and pour the marinade over them. Let them marinate for at least 15 minutes, flipping occasionally.
3. **Preheat the Grill:** Preheat your grill to medium-high heat.
4. **Grill the Mushrooms:** Place the marinated mushroom caps on the grill, gill side up. Grill for 5-7 minutes on each side or until the mushrooms are tender and have nice grill marks. If using cheese, add a slice to each mushroom cap during the last 2 minutes of cooking to melt.
5. **Assemble the Burgers:** Place each grilled mushroom cap on a low-carb burger bun or lettuce wrap. Top with a slice of tomato, red onion, and a lettuce leaf.
6. **Serve:** Serve the portobello mushroom burgers immediately with your favorite low-carb condiments.

Nutritional Facts

- **Calories:** 120 kcal
- **Protein:** 3g
- **Fat:** 10g
- **Saturated Fat:** 2g
- **Cholesterol:** 0mg
- **Sodium:** 400mg
- **Potassium:** 400mg
- **Fiber:** 2g
- **Sugar:** 3g
- **Vitamin C:** 15mg

Cooking Tips

- ✓ **Mushrooms:** Choose large, firm portobello mushrooms for the best results. Remove the stems and scrape out the gills if you prefer a less earthy flavor.
- ✓ **Marinating:** Marinate the mushrooms for at least 15 minutes, but for the best results, marinate for up to 1 hour.
- ✓ **Grilling:** Ensure the grill is properly preheated to avoid sticking. Use a grill mat or foil if needed.

Portobello mushroom burgers are a hearty and flavorful vegetarian option, perfect for a healthy and satisfying low-carb meal that even meat lovers will enjoy.

Recipe 58: Roasted Beet and Feta Salad

Prep Time: 10 minutes | Cooking Time: 40 minutes (plus cooling time) | Servings: 4

Ingredients

- 4 medium beets, scrubbed and trimmed
- 2 tablespoons olive oil
- Sea salt and black pepper, to taste
- 4 cups fresh arugula (or mixed greens)
- 1/2 cup crumbled feta cheese
- 1/4 cup red onion, thinly sliced
- 1/4 cup walnuts, toasted and roughly chopped
- 1/4 cup fresh mint leaves, chopped (optional for garnish)

For the Balsamic Vinaigrette:

- 1/4 cup balsamic vinegar
- 2 tablespoons olive oil
- 1 teaspoon Dijon mustard
- 1 teaspoon honey (optional)
- Sea salt and black pepper, to taste

Cooking Instructions

1. **Preheat the Oven:** Preheat your oven to 400°F (200°C). Line a baking sheet with aluminum foil.
2. **Prepare the Beets:** Rub the beets with 1 tablespoon of olive oil and season with sea salt and black pepper. Wrap each beet individually in aluminum foil and place them on the prepared baking sheet.
3. **Roast the Beets:** Roast the beets in the preheated oven for 35-45 minutes, or until they are tender when pierced with a fork. Remove them from the oven and let them cool completely.
4. **Peel and Slice the Beets:** Once the beets are cool enough to handle, use your fingers or a knife to peel off the skins. Slice the beets into thin wedges or rounds.
5. **Prepare the Vinaigrette:** In a small bowl, whisk together the balsamic vinegar, olive oil, Dijon mustard, honey (if using), sea salt, and black pepper until well combined.
6. **Assemble the Salad:** In a large salad bowl or on individual plates, arrange the arugula. Top with the roasted beet slices, crumbled feta cheese, thinly sliced red onion, and toasted walnuts.
7. **Dress the Salad:** Drizzle the balsamic vinaigrette over the salad and toss gently to combine.
8. **Garnish and Serve:** Garnish with fresh mint leaves if desired. Serve immediately and enjoy.

Nutritional Facts

- **Calories:** 200 kcal
- **Protein:** 5g
- **Fat:** 14g
- **Saturated Fat:** 4g
- **Cholesterol:** 15mg
- **Sodium:** 300mg
- **Potassium:** 500mg
- **Fiber:** 4g
- **Sugar:** 9g
- **Vitamin C:** 10mg

Cooking Tips

- ✓ **Beets:** Choose firm, unblemished beets for the best flavor. You can also use a mix of red and golden beets for a colorful presentation.
- ✓ **Roasting Beets:** Wrapping the beets in foil helps them retain moisture and makes peeling easier. For extra flavor, you can add a splash of vinegar or a sprig of herbs inside the foil.
- ✓ **Cheese Alternatives:** If you prefer, substitute the feta cheese with goat cheese or blue cheese for a different flavor profile.
- ✓ **Nuts:** To toast the walnuts, spread them on a baking sheet and bake at 350°F (175°C) for 5-7 minutes, or until fragrant and golden.
- ✓ **Vinaigrette:** Adjust the sweetness of the vinaigrette by adding more or less honey. You can also add a clove of minced garlic for extra depth of flavor.

Roasted beet and feta salad is a vibrant and flavorful dish that combines the earthy sweetness of roasted beets with the tangy creaminess of feta cheese, complemented by the peppery bite of arugula and the crunch of toasted walnuts.

Recipe 59: Cauliflower Tacos

Prep Time: 15 minutes | Cooking Time: 25 minutes | Servings: 4

Ingredients

For the Cauliflower Filling:

- 1 large head of cauliflower, cut into small florets
- 2 tablespoons olive oil
- 1 teaspoon ground cumin
- 1 teaspoon smoked paprika
- 1/2 teaspoon chili powder
- 1/2 teaspoon garlic powder
- 1/2 teaspoon onion powder
- 1/2 teaspoon sea salt
- 1/4 teaspoon black pepper

For the Tacos:

- 8 small low-carb tortillas or lettuce wraps
- 1 cup shredded lettuce
- 1/2 cup diced tomatoes
- 1/4 cup diced red onion
- 1/4 cup chopped fresh cilantro
- 1/2 cup guacamole
- 1/2 cup sour cream (optional)
- Lime wedges for serving

Cooking Instructions

1. **Preheat the Oven:** Preheat your oven to 400°F (200°C). Line a baking sheet with parchment paper.
2. **Prepare the Cauliflower:** In a large bowl, toss the cauliflower florets with olive oil, ground cumin, smoked paprika, chili powder, garlic powder, onion powder, sea salt, and black pepper until well coated.
3. **Roast the Cauliflower:** Spread the seasoned cauliflower florets in a single layer on the prepared baking sheet. Roast in the preheated oven for 20-25 minutes or until the cauliflower is tender and golden brown, stirring halfway through.
4. **Assemble the Tacos:** Warm the low-carb tortillas or lettuce wraps. Fill each tortilla with a portion of roasted cauliflower, shredded lettuce, diced tomatoes, red onion, and cilantro. Top with guacamole and sour cream if desired.
5. **Serve:** Serve the cauliflower tacos immediately with lime wedges on the side.

Nutritional Facts

- **Calories:** 180 kcal
- **Protein:** 3g
- **Fat:** 13g
- **Saturated Fat:** 2g
- **Cholesterol:** 0mg
- **Sodium:** 400mg
- **Potassium:** 450mg
- **Fiber:** 6g
- **Sugar:** 4g
- **Vitamin C:** 60mg

Cooking Tips

- ✓ **Cauliflower:** Cut the cauliflower into small, even-sized florets to ensure they roast evenly.
- ✓ **Spices:** Adjust the spices to your taste. Add more chili powder or a pinch of cayenne pepper for extra heat.
- ✓ **Tortillas:** Use your favorite low-carb tortillas or opt for lettuce wraps for an even lower-carb option.

Cauliflower tacos are a delicious and healthy vegetarian option featuring roasted cauliflower with a blend of spices, perfect for a light and satisfying low-carb meal.

Recipe 60: Low-Carb Mushroom Barley Soup

Prep Time: 10 minutes | Cooking Time: 45 minutes | Servings: 6

Ingredients

- 2 tablespoons olive oil
- 1 large onion, finely chopped
- 2 cloves garlic, minced
- 2 cups mushrooms, sliced (such as cremini, shiitake, or button)
- 1 cup celery, chopped
- 1 cup carrots, chopped
- 1 cup cauliflower rice
- 1/2 cup barley (or a low-carb grain substitute like hemp hearts)
- 6 cups vegetable broth (or beef broth for a richer flavor)
- 2 teaspoons fresh thyme leaves (or 1 teaspoon dried thyme)
- 1 teaspoon fresh rosemary, chopped (or 1/2 teaspoon dried rosemary)
- 1 bay leaf
- Sea salt and black pepper, to taste
- 1/4 cup fresh parsley, chopped (for garnish)

Cooking Instructions

1. **Heat the Oil:** In a large pot, heat the olive oil over medium heat. Add the finely chopped onion and sauté for 3-4 minutes until it becomes translucent.
2. **Sauté the Garlic and Mushrooms:** Add the minced garlic and sliced mushrooms to the pot. Sauté for another 5 minutes, stirring occasionally, until the mushrooms are browned and fragrant.
3. **Add the Vegetables:** Stir in the chopped celery, carrots, and cauliflower rice. Cook for 2-3 minutes until the vegetables begin to soften.
4. **Add the Barley and Broth:** Add the barley (or low-carb substitute), vegetable broth, thyme, rosemary, and bay leaf. Stir to combine.
5. **Simmer the Soup:** Bring the soup to a boil, then reduce the heat to low. Cover and simmer for 30-35 minutes, or until the barley is tender and the flavors have melted together.
6. **Season and Serve:** Remove the bay leaf and season the soup with sea salt and black pepper to taste. Ladle the soup into bowls and garnish with fresh parsley. Serve hot.

Nutritional Facts

- **Calories:** 150 kcal
- **Protein:** 5g
- **Fat:** 5g
- **Saturated Fat:** 1g
- **Cholesterol:** 0mg
- **Sodium:** 400mg
- **Potassium:** 400mg
- **Fiber:** 5g
- **Sugar:** 4g
- **Vitamin A:** 3000 IU

Cooking Tips

- ✓ **Mushrooms:** Use a variety of mushrooms for a more complex flavor. Portobello mushrooms can add a meatier texture.
- ✓ **Low-Carb Substitutes:** If you're strictly following a low-carb diet, substitute the barley with a lower-carb option like hemp hearts or cauliflower rice. Adjust cooking times as necessary.
- ✓ **Broth:** For a richer, more savory soup, use beef broth instead of vegetable broth. You can also add a splash of soy sauce or tamari for extra umami.
- ✓ **Herbs:** Fresh herbs provide the best flavor, but dried herbs can be used if fresh are not available. Adjust quantities to taste.
- ✓ **Storage:** Store any leftovers in an airtight container in the refrigerator for up to 4 days. The soup's flavors will deepen as it sits.

Low-carb mushroom barley soup is a comforting and nourishing dish, featuring the earthy flavors of mushrooms and the hearty texture of barley, complemented by a medley of fresh vegetables and herbs.

Vegan Recipes

Recipe 61: Tofu Scramble with Veggies

Prep Time: 10 minutes | Cooking Time: 10 minutes | Servings: 4

Ingredients

- 1 tablespoon olive oil
- 1 small onion, finely chopped
- 1 red bell pepper, diced
- 1 zucchini, diced
- 2 cups fresh spinach, chopped
- 14 oz firm tofu, drained and crumbled
- 1 teaspoon turmeric powder
- 1/2 teaspoon ground cumin
- 1/2 teaspoon garlic powder
- 1/2 teaspoon sea salt
- 1/4 teaspoon black pepper
- 1/4 teaspoon red pepper flakes (optional)
- Fresh cilantro, chopped (optional for garnish)
- Avocado slices for serving (optional)

Cooking Instructions

1. **Heat the Oil:** In a large skillet, heat the olive oil over medium heat. Add the chopped onion and cook for 2-3 minutes until softened.
2. **Cook the Vegetables:** Add the diced red bell pepper and zucchini to the skillet. Cook for another 3-4 minutes until the vegetables are tender.
3. **Add the Spinach:** Stir in the chopped spinach and cook for 1-2 minutes until wilted.
4. **Add the Tofu:** Add the crumbled tofu to the skillet. Sprinkle with turmeric powder, ground cumin, garlic powder, sea salt, black pepper, and red pepper flakes (if using). Stir well to combine and cook for another 2-3 minutes until the tofu is heated through.
5. **Serve:** Garnish with fresh cilantro if desired. Serve hot with avocado slices on the side.

Nutritional Facts

- **Calories:** 150 kcal
- **Protein:** 12g
- **Fat:** 9g
- **Saturated Fat:** 1g
- **Cholesterol:** 0mg
- **Sodium:** 400mg
- **Potassium:** 450mg
- **Fiber:** 3g
- **Sugar:** 3g
- **Vitamin C:** 60mg

Cooking Tips

- ✓ **Tofu:** Use firm or extra-firm tofu for the best texture. Press the tofu before crumbling to remove excess moisture.
- ✓ **Spices:** Adjust the spices to your taste. Add more turmeric or cumin for a stronger flavor.
- ✓ **Vegetables:** Feel free to add other vegetables like mushrooms, tomatoes, or kale for variety.

Tofu scrambled with veggies is a flavorful and nutritious vegan dish packed with protein and fresh vegetables, perfect for a healthy and satisfying breakfast or brunch.

Recipe 62: Low-Carb Vegan Buddha Bowl

Prep Time: 15 minutes | Cooking Time: 20 minutes | Servings: 4

Ingredients

- 1 cup quinoa (optional for higher carb content)
- 1 large head of cauliflower, cut into florets
- 2 tablespoons olive oil
- 1 teaspoon ground cumin
- 1 teaspoon paprika
- 1/2 teaspoon sea salt
- 1/4 teaspoon black pepper
- 1 avocado, sliced
- 1 cup cherry tomatoes, halved
- 1 cup shredded red cabbage
- 1 cup baby spinach
- 1/4 cup sunflower seeds
- Fresh parsley, chopped (optional for garnish)

For the Tahini Dressing:

- 1/4 cup tahini
- 2 tablespoons lemon juice
- 1 tablespoon olive oil
- 1 clove garlic, minced
- 2-3 tablespoons water (to thin the dressing)
- Sea salt and black pepper to taste

Cooking Instructions

1. **Optional Quinoa:** If using quinoa, cook according to package instructions and set aside.
2. **Preheat the Oven:** Preheat your oven to 400°F (200°C). Line a baking sheet with parchment paper.
3. **Roast the Cauliflower:** In a large bowl, toss the cauliflower florets with olive oil, ground cumin, paprika, sea salt, and black pepper. Spread the cauliflower in a single layer on the prepared baking sheet. Roast in the preheated oven for 20 minutes or until tender and golden brown.
4. **Prepare the Dressing:** In a small bowl, whisk together the tahini, lemon juice, olive oil, minced garlic, water, sea salt, and black pepper until smooth. Adjust the consistency with more water if needed.
5. **Assemble the Bowls:** Divide the roasted cauliflower, avocado slices, cherry tomatoes, shredded red cabbage, baby spinach, and sunflower seeds evenly among the four bowls. Add the cooked quinoa if using.
6. **Add Dressing:** Drizzle the tahini dressing over the bowls.
7. **Serve:** Garnish with fresh parsley if desired. Serve immediately.

Nutritional Facts

- **Calories:** 300 kcal
- **Protein:** 6g
- **Fat:** 25g
- **Saturated Fat:** 3.5g
- **Cholesterol:** 0mg
- **Sodium:** 400mg
- **Potassium:** 900mg
- **Fiber:** 9g
- **Sugar:** 5g
- **Vitamin C:** 70mg

Cooking Tips

- ✓ **Cauliflower:** Cut the cauliflower into even-sized florets to ensure they roast evenly.
- ✓ **Tahini Dressing:** Adjust the thickness of the dressing by adding more or less water to achieve the desired consistency.
- ✓ **Add-Ins:** Customize your Buddha bowl with additional low-carb vegetables, nuts, or seeds.

Low-carb vegan Buddha bowls are a nutritious and colorful dish featuring roasted cauliflower, fresh vegetables, and a creamy tahini dressing, perfect for a healthy and satisfying meal.

Recipe 63: Cauliflower Fried Rice with Tofu

Prep Time: 15 minutes | Cooking Time: 15 minutes | Servings: 4

Ingredients

- 1 large head of cauliflower, riced
- 14 oz firm tofu, drained and crumbled
- 2 tablespoons coconut oil, divided
- 1 small onion, finely chopped
- 2 cloves garlic, minced
- 1 cup frozen peas and carrots
- 1 red bell pepper, diced
- 3 green onions, sliced
- 3 tablespoons soy sauce (or tamari for gluten-free)
- 1 teaspoon sesame oil
- 1/2 teaspoon ground ginger
- 1/4 teaspoon black pepper
- Fresh cilantro, chopped (optional for garnish)
- Lime wedges for serving (optional)

Cooking Instructions

1. **Prepare the Cauliflower:** Cut the cauliflower into florets and pulse in a food processor until it resembles rice. Set aside.
2. **Cook the Tofu:** Heat 1 tablespoon of coconut oil in a large skillet or wok over medium-high heat. Add the crumbled tofu and cook for 5-7 minutes until golden brown and slightly crispy. Remove from the skillet and set aside.
3. **Cook the Vegetables:** In the same skillet, add the remaining tablespoon of coconut oil. Add the chopped onion and cook for 2-3 minutes until softened. Add the minced garlic, frozen peas and carrots, and diced red bell pepper. Cook for another 3-4 minutes until the vegetables are tender.

4. **Add the Cauliflower Rice:** Stir in the riced cauliflower and cook for 5-7 minutes until the cauliflower is tender but still slightly firm.
5. **Add the Tofu and Seasoning:** Return the cooked tofu to the skillet. Stir in the soy sauce, sesame oil, ground ginger, and black pepper. Cook for another 2 minutes until everything is well combined and heated through.
6. **Finish:** Stir in the sliced green onions.
7. **Serve:** Garnish with fresh cilantro if desired. Serve hot with lime wedges on the side.

Nutritional Facts

- **Calories:** 200 kcal
- **Protein:** 10g
- **Fat:** 12g
- **Saturated Fat:** 5g
- **Cholesterol:** 0mg
- **Sodium:** 600mg
- **Potassium:** 500mg
- **Fiber:** 5g
- **Sugar:** 4g
- **Vitamin C:** 70mg

Cooking Tips

- ✓ **Tofu:** Press the tofu before crumbling to remove excess moisture and achieve a better texture.
- ✓ **Cauliflower Rice:** Ensure the cauliflower is riced evenly for consistent cooking.
- ✓ **Vegetables:** Use your favorite vegetables or whatever you have on hand. Bell peppers, snap peas, and broccoli all work well.

Cauliflower fried rice with tofu is a healthy and delicious vegan dish packed with protein and vegetables, perfect for a satisfying and low-carb meal.

Recipe 64: Vegan Stuffed Zucchini Boats

Prep Time: 15 minutes | Cooking Time: 30 minutes | Servings: 4

Ingredients

- 4 medium zucchinis, halved lengthwise
- 1 tablespoon olive oil
- 1 small onion, finely chopped
- 2 cloves garlic, minced
- 1 red bell pepper, diced
- 1 cup cooked quinoa
- 1 (15 oz) can black beans, drained and rinsed
- 1 cup corn kernels (fresh or frozen)
- 1 teaspoon ground cumin
- 1 teaspoon chili powder
- 1/2 teaspoon sea salt
- 1/4 teaspoon black pepper
- 1/4 cup fresh cilantro, chopped
- 1/2 cup salsa
- 1/4 cup nutritional yeast (optional, for a cheesy flavor)
- Lime wedges for serving (optional)

Cooking Instructions

1. **Preheat the Oven:** Preheat your oven to 375°F (190°C). Line a baking sheet with parchment paper.
2. **Prepare the Zucchinis:** Using a spoon, scoop out the center of each zucchini half, creating a boat shape. Reserve the scooped-out flesh and chop it finely.
3. **Cook the Vegetables:** In a large skillet, heat the olive oil over medium heat. Add the chopped onion and cook for 3-4 minutes until softened. Add the minced garlic and cook for another minute.
4. **Add the Fillings:** Stir in the diced red bell pepper, reserved zucchini flesh, cooked quinoa, black beans, corn, ground cumin, chili powder, sea salt, and black pepper.

Cook for 5-7 minutes until the vegetables are tender and the mixture is well combined.

5. **Stuff the Zucchini Boats:** Place the zucchini halves on the prepared baking sheet. Spoon the filling mixture into each zucchini boat, pressing down gently to pack the filling.
6. **Bake:** Top each stuffed zucchini with salsa and nutritional yeast if using. Bake in the preheated oven for 20-25 minutes or until the zucchinis are tender.
7. **Serve:** Garnish with fresh cilantro and serve with lime wedges if desired.

Nutritional Facts

- **Calories:** 200 kcal
- **Protein:** 6g
- **Fat:** 6g
- **Saturated Fat:** 1g
- **Cholesterol:** 0mg
- **Sodium:** 500mg
- **Potassium:** 700mg
- **Fiber:** 8g
- **Sugar:** 6g
- **Vitamin C:** 70mg

Cooking Tips

- ✓ **Zucchinis:** Choose medium-sized zucchinis for the best texture and ease of handling.
- ✓ **Quinoa:** Make sure the quinoa is fully cooked before adding it to the vegetable mixture.
- ✓ **Seasoning:** Adjust the spices to your taste. Add more chili powder for extra heat or more cumin for a deeper flavor.

Vegan stuffed zucchini boats are a flavorful and nutritious dish filled with a hearty mixture of quinoa, black beans, and vegetables, perfect for a satisfying and healthy meal.

Recipe 65: Spaghetti Squash Pad Thai

Prep Time: 20 minutes | Cooking Time: 40 minutes | Servings: 4

Ingredients

- 1 large spaghetti squash
- 2 tablespoons olive oil, divided
- 1 small onion, thinly sliced
- 3 cloves garlic, minced
- 2 cups shredded carrots
- 1 red bell pepper, thinly sliced
- 1 cup bean sprouts
- 3 green onions, sliced
- 1/4 cup chopped fresh cilantro
- 1/4 cup crushed peanuts (optional for garnish)
- Lime wedges for serving

For the Sauce:

- 1/4 cup soy sauce (or tamari for gluten-free)
- 2 tablespoons peanut butter
- 2 tablespoons rice vinegar
- 1 tablespoon lime juice
- 1 tablespoon erythritol or your preferred sweetener
- 1 teaspoon chili paste (optional for heat)

Cooking Instructions

1. **Prepare the Spaghetti Squash:** Preheat your oven to 400°F (200°C). Cut the spaghetti squash in half lengthwise and scoop out the seeds. Drizzle with 1 tablespoon of olive oil and place cut-side down on a baking sheet. Roast for 35-40 minutes or until tender. Let cool slightly, then use a fork to scrape out the strands into a large bowl.
2. **Make the Sauce:** In a small bowl, whisk together the soy sauce, peanut butter, rice vinegar, lime juice, erythritol, and chili paste until smooth. Set aside.

3. **Cook the Vegetables:** In a large skillet, heat the remaining tablespoon of olive oil over medium heat. Add the sliced onion and cook for 2-3 minutes until softened. Add the minced garlic, shredded carrots, and sliced red bell pepper. Cook for another 5-7 minutes until the vegetables are tender.
4. **Combine Ingredients:** Add the spaghetti squash strands, bean sprouts, and the prepared sauce to the skillet. Toss well to combine and heat through, about 2-3 minutes.
5. **Serve:** Divide the spaghetti squash Pad Thai among four plates. Garnish with sliced green onions, fresh cilantro, crushed peanuts (if using), and lime wedges. Serve hot.

Nutritional Facts

- **Calories:** 250 kcal
- **Protein:** 6g
- **Fat:** 14g
- **Saturated Fat:** 2g
- **Cholesterol:** 0mg
- **Sodium:** 800mg
- **Potassium:** 700mg
- **Fiber:** 6g
- **Sugar:** 8g
- **Vitamin A:** 12000 IU

Cooking Tips

- ✓ **Spaghetti Squash:** To make cutting the squash easier, microwave it for 3-4 minutes to soften the skin slightly.
- ✓ **Sauce:** Adjust the sweetness and spiciness of the sauce to your taste. Add more chilies paste for a spicier dish or more erythritol for a sweeter flavor.

Spaghetti squash Pad Thai is a delicious and healthy low-carb version of the classic Thai dish, featuring tender spaghetti squash noodles and a flavorful peanut sauce, perfect for a light and satisfying meal.

Recipe 66: Vegan Protein Smoothie with Hemp Seeds

Prep Time: 5 minutes | Cooking Time: 0 minutes | Servings: 2

Ingredients

- 1 banana, frozen
- 1 cup unsweetened almond milk
- 1/2 cup frozen berries (strawberries, blueberries, or mixed)
- 1/4 cup plain or vanilla vegan protein powder
- 2 tablespoons hemp seeds
- 1 tablespoon chia seeds
- 1 tablespoon almond butter
- 1 teaspoon vanilla extract
- Ice cubes (optional for a thicker smoothie)

Cooking Instructions

1. **Combine Ingredients:** In a blender, combine the frozen banana, unsweetened almond milk, frozen berries, vegan protein powder, hemp seeds, chia seeds, almond butter, and vanilla extract.
2. **Blend:** Blend on high speed until smooth and creamy. If the smoothie is too thick, add a bit more almond milk. If you prefer a thicker consistency, add a few ice cubes and blend again.
3. **Serve:** Pour the smoothie into two glasses. Enjoy immediately.

Nutritional Facts

- **Calories:** 250 kcal
- **Protein:** 15g
- **Fat:** 12g
- **Saturated Fat:** 1g
- **Cholesterol:** 0mg
- **Sodium:** 150mg
- **Potassium:** 500mg
- **Fiber:** 6g
- **Sugar:** 10g
- **Vitamin C:** 15mg

Cooking Tips

- ✓ **Frozen Banana:** Using a frozen banana helps to create a thicker, creamier smoothie. If you don't have a frozen banana, you can use a fresh one and add more ice.
- ✓ **Sweetness:** Adjust the sweetness by adding a touch of maple syrup or agave if desired.
- ✓ **Protein Powder:** Use your favorite vegan protein powder. The vanilla flavor works well, but chocolate or berry-flavored protein powder can also be used.

A vegan protein smoothie with hemp seeds is a nutritious and delicious way to start your day, providing a good source of plant-based protein, healthy fats, and essential nutrients, perfect for a quick and satisfying breakfast or snack.

Recipe 67: Low-Carb Vegetable Soup

Prep Time: 15 minutes | Cooking Time: 30 minutes | Servings: 4

Ingredients

- 2 tablespoons olive oil
- 1 small onion, finely chopped
- 2 cloves garlic, minced
- 2 medium carrots, diced
- 2 celery stalks, diced
- 1 zucchini, diced
- 1 yellow squash, diced
- 1 cup green beans, trimmed and cut into 1-inch pieces
- 1 (14.5 oz) can diced tomatoes
- 4 cups vegetable broth
- 1 teaspoon dried basil
- 1 teaspoon dried oregano
- 1/2 teaspoon dried thyme
- 1/2 teaspoon sea salt
- 1/4 teaspoon black pepper
- 2 cups fresh spinach, chopped
- 1/4 cup fresh parsley, chopped (optional for garnish)

Cooking Instructions

1. **Heat the Oil:** In a large pot, heat the olive oil over medium heat. Add the chopped onion and cook for 3-4 minutes until softened.
2. **Add Garlic and Vegetables:** Add the minced garlic, diced carrots, and diced celery to the pot. Cook for another 5 minutes, stirring occasionally.
3. **Add Remaining Vegetables:** Stir in the diced zucchini, yellow squash, and green beans. Cook for another 3-4 minutes.
4. **Add Broth and Tomatoes:** Pour in the vegetable broth and add the diced tomatoes with their juice. Stir in the dried basil, dried oregano, dried thyme, sea salt, and black pepper. Bring the mixture to a boil.
5. **Simmer:** Reduce the heat to low and let the soup simmer for 20-25 minutes or until the vegetables are tender.
6. **Add Spinach:** Stir in the chopped spinach and cook for another 2-3 minutes until wilted.
7. **Serve:** Ladle the soup into bowls and garnish with fresh parsley if desired. Serve hot.

Nutritional Facts

- **Calories:** 120 kcal
- **Protein:** 3g
- **Fat:** 6g
- **Saturated Fat:** 1g
- **Cholesterol:** 0mg
- **Sodium:** 600mg
- **Potassium:** 700mg
- **Fiber:** 4g
- **Sugar:** 6g
- **Vitamin A:** 8000 IU

Cooking Tips

- ✓ **Vegetables:** Use fresh, seasonal vegetables for the best flavor and nutritional value. Feel free to add or substitute other low-carb vegetables like bell peppers, cauliflower, or mushrooms.
- ✓ **Herbs:** Adjust the herbs to your taste. Fresh herbs can also be used instead of dried ones.
- ✓ **Broth:** Use a low-sodium vegetable broth to control the salt content. You can also use chicken broth if not strictly vegan.

Low-carb vegetable soup is a healthy and delicious dish packed with a variety of fresh vegetables and flavorful herbs, perfect for a light and satisfying meal.

Recipe 68: Vegan Collard Wraps with Hummus

Prep Time: 15 minutes | Cooking Time: 0 minutes | Servings: 4

Ingredients

- 8 large collard green leaves, stems removed
- 1 cup hummus (store-bought or homemade)
- 1 cup shredded carrots
- 1 red bell pepper, thinly sliced
- 1 cucumber, thinly sliced
- 1 avocado, sliced
- 1/4 cup red onion, thinly sliced
- 1/4 cup fresh cilantro, chopped
- 1/4 cup sunflower seeds (optional)
- Lemon wedges for serving

Cooking Instructions

1. **Prepare the Collard Leaves:** Carefully remove the thick stems from the collard green leaves. If the leaves are large, you can cut them in half along the stem to create smaller wraps.
2. **Spread the Hummus:** Lay each collard leaf flat and spread a generous tablespoon of hummus down the center.
3. **Add the Vegetables:** Top the hummus with shredded carrots, red bell pepper slices, cucumber slices, avocado slices, red onion, fresh cilantro, and sunflower seeds if using.
4. **Wrap the Collard Leaves:** Fold the sides of the collard leaf over the filling, then roll it up tightly from the bottom to the top, like a burrito.
5. **Serve:** Serve the collard wraps with lemon wedges on the side for squeezing over the top.

Nutritional Facts

- **Calories:** 200 kcal
- **Protein:** 6g
- **Fat:** 14g
- **Saturated Fat:** 2g
- **Cholesterol:** 0mg
- **Sodium:** 300mg
- **Potassium:** 700mg
- **Fiber:** 8g
- **Sugar:** 4g
- **Vitamin A:** 8000 IU

Cooking Tips

- ✓ **Collard Leaves:** To make the collard leaves more pliable, blanch them in boiling water for 30 seconds and then plunge them into ice water before using.
- ✓ **Hummus:** Use your favorite flavor of hummus to add variety. Roasted red pepper or garlic hummus works well.
- ✓ **Vegetables:** Customize the fillings with your favorite vegetables or whatever you have on hand. Bell peppers, shredded cabbage, and sprouts all work well.

Vegan collard wraps with hummus are a nutritious and refreshing dish featuring crisp collard leaves filled with creamy hummus and fresh vegetables, perfect for a healthy and satisfying meal.

Recipe 69: Cauliflower Tabbouleh

Prep Time: 20 minutes | Cooking Time: 5 minutes | Servings: 4

Ingredients

- 1 large head of cauliflower, riced
- 1 cup cherry tomatoes, quartered
- 1 cucumber, finely diced
- 1/2 red onion, finely diced
- 1/4 cup fresh mint, chopped
- 1/2 cup fresh parsley, chopped
- 1/4 cup olive oil
- 2 tablespoons lemon juice
- 1 teaspoon sea salt
- 1/4 teaspoon black pepper

Cooking Instructions

1. **Prepare the Cauliflower:** Cut the cauliflower into florets and pulse in a food processor until it resembles rice. Transfer to a large bowl.
2. **Lightly Cook the Cauliflower:** In a large skillet, lightly toast the cauliflower rice over medium heat for 3-5 minutes until slightly tender but not mushy. Let cool.
3. **Combine Ingredients:** In a large bowl, combine the cooled cauliflower rice, cherry tomatoes, cucumber, red onion, fresh mint, and fresh parsley.
4. **Make the Dressing:** In a small bowl, whisk together the olive oil, lemon juice, sea salt, and black pepper.
5. **Dress the Salad:** Pour the dressing over the cauliflower mixture and toss to combine.
6. **Serve:** Serve the cauliflower tabbouleh chilled or at room temperature.

Nutritional Facts

- **Calories:** 150 kcal
- **Protein:** 3g
- **Fat:** 11g
- **Saturated Fat:** 1.5g
- **Cholesterol:** 0mg
- **Sodium:** 600mg
- **Potassium:** 500mg
- **Fiber:** 4g
- **Sugar:** 4g
- **Vitamin C:** 40mg

Cooking Tips

- ✓ **Cauliflower:** Ensure the cauliflower is pulsed to a fine consistency, similar to traditional tabbouleh.
- ✓ **Herbs:** Use fresh mint and parsley for the best flavor. Adjust the amount of herbs to your taste.
- ✓ **Dressing:** Adjust the lemon juice and olive oil to your preference for a more tangy or rich flavor.

Cauliflower tabbouleh is a light and refreshing low-carb twist on the classic Middle Eastern salad, featuring fresh herbs, vegetables, and a zesty lemon dressing, perfect for a healthy and flavorful side dish.

Recipe 70: Grilled Portobello Mushrooms with Avocado Salsa

Prep Time: 15 minutes | Cooking Time: 10 minutes | Servings: 4

Ingredients

For the Mushrooms:

- 4 large portobello mushroom caps, stems removed
- 2 tablespoons olive oil
- 1 tablespoon balsamic vinegar
- 2 cloves garlic, minced
- 1/2 teaspoon sea salt
- 1/4 teaspoon black pepper

For the Avocado Salsa:

- 2 ripe avocados, diced
- 1 cup cherry tomatoes, quartered
- 1/4 cup red onion, finely diced
- 1/4 cup fresh cilantro, chopped
- 1 tablespoon lime juice
- 1/2 teaspoon sea salt
- 1/4 teaspoon black pepper

Cooking Instructions

1. **Prepare the Marinade:** In a small bowl, whisk together the olive oil, balsamic vinegar, minced garlic, sea salt, and black pepper.
2. **Marinate the Mushrooms:** Place the portobello mushroom caps in a shallow dish and brush both sides with the marinade. Let them marinate for at least 15 minutes.
3. **Preheat the Grill:** Preheat your grill to medium-high heat.
4. **Grill the Mushrooms:** Place the marinated mushroom caps on the grill, gill side up. Grill for 5-7 minutes on each side or until tender and slightly charred.

5. **Prepare the Avocado Salsa:** In a medium bowl, combine the diced avocados, cherry tomatoes, red onion, fresh cilantro, lime juice, sea salt, and black pepper. Gently toss to combine.
6. **Serve:** Place the grilled portobello mushrooms on a serving platter and top with avocado salsa. Serve immediately.

Nutritional Facts

- **Calories:** 200 kcal
- **Protein:** 3g
- **Fat:** 18g
- **Saturated Fat:** 3g
- **Cholesterol:** 0mg
- **Sodium:** 600mg
- **Potassium:** 700mg
- **Fiber:** 6g
- **Sugar:** 3g
- **Vitamin C:** 20mg

Cooking Tips

- ✓ **Mushrooms:** Ensure the mushrooms are well-coated with the marinade for the best flavor.
- ✓ **Grill:** If you don't have a grill, you can use a grill pan or broil the mushrooms in the oven.
- ✓ **Salsa:** Adjust the lime juice and salt to your taste. Add a diced jalapeño for extra heat if desired.
- ✓ **Serving Suggestions:** Serve as a main dish with a side of quinoa or as a topping for a salad.

Grilled portobello mushrooms with avocado salsa is a flavorful and satisfying vegan dish featuring tender, marinated mushrooms topped with fresh and zesty avocado salsa, perfect for a healthy and delicious meal.

International
Cuisine Recipes

Recipe 71: Chicken Shawarma Lettuce Wraps

Prep Time: 20 minutes | Cooking Time: 15 minutes | Servings: 4

Ingredients

For the Chicken:

- 1 lb boneless, skinless chicken thighs cut into strips
- 2 tablespoons olive oil
- 1 tablespoon lemon juice
- 3 cloves garlic, minced
- 2 teaspoons ground cumin
- 2 teaspoons ground paprika
- 1 teaspoon ground turmeric
- 1/2 teaspoon ground cinnamon
- 1/2 teaspoon ground black pepper
- 1/2 teaspoon sea salt

For the Wraps:

- 8 large lettuce leaves (Romaine or Butter lettuce work well)
- 1 cup cherry tomatoes, halved
- 1/2 red onion, thinly sliced
- 1/4 cup fresh parsley, chopped
- 1/4 cup tahini sauce or Greek yogurt
- Lemon wedges for serving

Cooking Instructions

1. **Marinate the Chicken:** In a large bowl, combine the olive oil, lemon juice, minced garlic, ground cumin, paprika, turmeric, cinnamon, black pepper, and sea salt. Add the chicken strips and toss to coat evenly. Cover and marinate in the refrigerator for at least 1 hour or overnight for the best flavor.
2. **Cook the Chicken:** Heat a large skillet over medium-high heat. Add the marinated chicken strips and cook for 10-15 minutes, or until the chicken is cooked through and slightly crispy on the edges.
3. **Prepare the Lettuce Wraps:** Lay out the lettuce leaves on a large serving platter. Divide the cooked chicken evenly among the lettuce leaves.
4. **Add Toppings:** Top each lettuce wrap with cherry tomatoes, red onion, fresh parsley, and a drizzle of tahini sauce or Greek yogurt.
5. **Serve:** Serve the chicken shawarma lettuce wraps immediately with lemon wedges on the side.

Nutritional Facts

- **Calories:** 300 kcal
- **Protein:** 25g
- **Fat:** 18g
- **Saturated Fat:** 3g
- **Cholesterol:** 100mg
- **Sodium:** 500mg
- **Potassium:** 600mg
- **Fiber:** 3g
- **Sugar:** 2g
- **Vitamin C:** 20mg

Cooking Tips

- ✓ **Chicken:** For a more authentic flavor, marinate the chicken for at least a few hours or overnight.
- ✓ **Lettuce:** Use large, sturdy lettuce leaves that can hold the filling without tearing.
- ✓ **Sauce:** Adjust the amount of tahini sauce or Greek yogurt according to your taste. You can also add a bit of hot sauce for extra heat.

Chicken shawarma lettuce wraps are a flavorful and healthy low-carb meal featuring spiced chicken served in crisp lettuce leaves with fresh vegetables and a creamy sauce, perfect for a light and satisfying dish.

Recipe 72: Low-Carb Beef Tacos with Cauliflower Tortillas

Prep Time: 20 minutes | Cooking Time: 25 minutes | Servings: 4

Ingredients

For the Cauliflower Tortillas:

- 1 large head of cauliflower, riced
- 2 large eggs
- 1/2 cup shredded cheddar cheese
- 1/4 teaspoon sea salt
- 1/4 teaspoon black pepper

For the Beef Filling:

- 1 lb. ground beef
- 1 small onion, finely chopped
- 2 cloves garlic, minced
- 1 tablespoon chili powder
- 1 teaspoon ground cumin
- 1 teaspoon paprika
- 1/2 teaspoon dried oregano
- 1/2 teaspoon sea salt
- 1/4 teaspoon black pepper
- 1/4 cup water

Toppings:

- Shredded lettuce
- Diced tomatoes
- Sliced avocado
- Shredded cheddar cheese
- Sour cream
- Fresh cilantro, chopped
- Lime wedges

Cooking Instructions

1. **Preheat the Oven:** Preheat your oven to 375°F (190°C). Line a baking sheet with parchment paper.
2. **Prepare the Cauliflower Tortillas:**
   Cut the cauliflower into florets and pulse in a food processor until it resembles rice. Place the cauliflower rice in a microwave-safe bowl and microwave on high for 5 minutes. Let cool slightly. Transfer the cauliflower rice to a clean kitchen towel or cheesecloth and squeeze out as much moisture as possible. In a large bowl, combine the cauliflower rice, eggs, shredded cheddar cheese, sea salt, and black pepper. Mix well.

Divide the mixture into 8 portions and shape each portion into a thin, round tortilla on the prepared baking sheet.
Bake in the preheated oven for 15-20 minutes or until the tortillas are golden brown and firm.

3. **Prepare the Beef Filling:**
   In a large skillet over medium-high heat, cook the ground beef and break it up with a spoon until browned. Add the chopped onion and minced garlic and cook for 2-3 minutes until softened.
   Stir in the chili powder, ground cumin, paprika, dried oregano, sea salt, black pepper, and water. Simmer for 5-7 minutes until the beef is cooked through, and the flavors are well combined.
4. **Assemble the Tacos:**
   Place a portion of the beef filling onto each cauliflower tortilla. Top with shredded lettuce, diced tomatoes, sliced avocado, shredded cheddar cheese, sour cream, fresh cilantro, and a squeeze of lime juice.
5. **Serve:** Serve the beef tacos immediately while the tortillas are still warm.

Nutritional Facts

- **Calories:** 350 kcal
- **Protein:** 25g
- **Fat:** 20g
- **Saturated Fat:** 8g
- **Cholesterol:** 120mg
- **Sodium:** 650mg
- **Potassium:** 700mg
- **Fiber:** 4g
- **Sugar:** 3g
- **Vitamin A:** 800 IU

Cooking Tips

- ✓ **Cauliflower Rice:** Ensure you squeeze out as much moisture as possible from the cauliflower to achieve firm tortillas.
- ✓ **Tortilla Shape:** Use a silicone baking mat for easier shaping and removal of the tortillas.

Recipe 73: Keto-Friendly Chicken Tikka Masala

Prep Time: 15 minutes | Cooking Time: 30 minutes | Servings: 4

Ingredients

For the Chicken Marinade:

- 1 lb. boneless, skinless chicken breasts cut into bite-sized pieces
- 1/2 cup Greek yogurt (full fat)
- 1 tablespoon lemon juice
- 2 cloves garlic, minced
- 1 teaspoon fresh ginger, grated
- 1 teaspoon ground cumin
- 1 teaspoon ground coriander
- 1 teaspoon paprika
- 1/2 teaspoon turmeric
- 1/2 teaspoon sea salt

For the Tikka Masala Sauce:

- 2 tablespoons ghee or butter
- 1 small onion, finely chopped
- 3 cloves garlic, minced
- 1 tablespoon fresh ginger, grated
- 1 tablespoon garam masala
- 1 teaspoon ground cumin
- 1 teaspoon ground coriander
- 1 teaspoon smoked paprika
- 1/2 teaspoon turmeric
- 1/2 teaspoon chili powder (optional for heat)
- 1 (14 oz) can crushed tomatoes
- 1 cup heavy cream
- 1/2 teaspoon sea salt
- 1/4 teaspoon black pepper
- Fresh cilantro, chopped (optional for garnish)
- Lime wedges for serving (optional)

Cooking Instructions

1. **Marinate the Chicken:** In a large bowl, combine the Greek yogurt, lemon juice, minced garlic, grated ginger, ground cumin, ground coriander, paprika, turmeric, and sea salt. Add the chicken pieces and toss to coat evenly. Cover and refrigerate for at least 1 hour or overnight for the best results.

2. **Cook the Chicken:** Preheat your oven to 400°F (200°C). Line a baking sheet with parchment paper. Place the marinated chicken pieces on the prepared baking sheet and bake for 15-20 minutes, or until the chicken is cooked through and slightly charred on the edges.

3. **Prepare the Sauce:** In a large skillet, heat the ghee or butter over medium heat. Add the chopped onion and cook for 3-4 minutes until softened. Add the minced garlic and grated ginger and cook for another 1-2 minutes until fragrant.

4. **Add the Spices:** Stir in the garam masala, ground cumin, ground coriander, smoked paprika, turmeric, and chili powder (if using). Cook for 1 minute to toast the spices.

5. **Add the Tomatoes:** Pour in the crushed tomatoes and bring to a simmer. Cook for 5-7 minutes until the sauce thickens slightly.

6. **Add the Cream:** Stir in the heavy cream, sea salt, and black pepper. Simmer for another 5 minutes until the sauce is rich and creamy.

7. **Combine Chicken and Sauce:** Add the cooked chicken to the skillet with the sauce. Stir to coat the chicken evenly with the sauce and simmer for an additional 5 minutes to meld the flavors.

8. **Serve:** Garnish with fresh cilantro and serve with lime wedges if desired.

Nutritional Facts

- **Calories:** 400 kcal
- **Protein:** 28g
- **Fat:** 28g
- **Saturated Fat:** 16g
- **Cholesterol:** 140mg
- **Sodium:** 700mg
- **Potassium:** 600mg
- **Fiber:** 2g
- **Sugar:** 4g
- **Vitamin A:** 1200 IU

Recipe 74: Greek Chicken Souvlaki

Prep Time: 20 minutes (plus marinating time) | Cooking Time: 15 minutes | Servings: 4

Ingredients

- 1 1/2 lbs. boneless, skinless chicken breasts cut into bite-sized pieces
- 1/4 cup olive oil
- 2 tablespoons lemon juice
- 1 tablespoon red wine vinegar
- 3 cloves garlic, minced
- 1 tablespoon dried oregano
- 1 teaspoon dried thyme
- 1 teaspoon sea salt
- 1/2 teaspoon black pepper
- 1/4 teaspoon ground cumin
- Wooden or metal skewers
- Fresh parsley, chopped (optional for garnish)
- Lemon wedges for serving (optional)

Cooking Instructions

1. **Prepare the Marinade:** In a large bowl, whisk together the olive oil, lemon juice, red wine vinegar, minced garlic, dried oregano, dried thyme, sea salt, black pepper, and ground cumin.
2. **Marinate the Chicken:** Add the chicken pieces to the bowl and toss to coat them evenly with the marinade. Cover and refrigerate for at least 1 hour or up to 4 hours for best results.
3. **Preheat the Grill:** Preheat your grill to medium-high heat. If using wooden skewers, soak them in water for 30 minutes to prevent burning.
4. **Skewer the Chicken:** Thread the marinated chicken pieces onto the skewers, leaving a small gap between each piece to ensure even cooking.
5. **Grill the Chicken:** Grill the chicken skewers for 10-15 minutes, turning occasionally, until the chicken is cooked through and has a nice char. The internal temperature should reach 165°F (74°C).
6. **Serve:** Garnish with fresh parsley and serve with lemon wedges if desired. Enjoy with a side of tzatziki sauce, Greek salad, or cauliflower rice for a complete meal.

Nutritional Facts

- **Calories:** 300 kcal
- **Protein:** 28g
- **Fat:** 18g
- **Saturated Fat:** 3g
- **Cholesterol:** 90mg
- **Sodium:** 600mg
- **Potassium:** 500mg
- **Fiber:** 1g
- **Sugar:** 0g
- **Vitamin C:** 10mg

Cooking Tips

- ✓ **Chicken:** Cut the chicken into uniform pieces to ensure even cooking.
- ✓ **Marinating:** Marinate the chicken for at least 1 hour, but for the best flavor, marinate for up to 4 hours.
- ✓ **Grill:** If you don't have a grill, you can cook the skewers under the broiler in your oven or on a stovetop grill pan.

Greek chicken souvlaki is a flavorful and healthy dish featuring marinated chicken skewers grilled to perfection, perfect for a light and satisfying meal with a taste of the Mediterranean.

Recipe 75: Low-Carb Sushi Rolls with Cauliflower Rice

Prep Time: 30 minutes | Cooking Time: 10 minutes | Servings: 4

Ingredients

- 1 large head of cauliflower, riced
- 2 tablespoons rice vinegar
- 1 tablespoon erythritol
- 1 teaspoon sea salt
- 4 sheets nori (seaweed)
- 1 cucumber, julienned
- 1 carrot, julienned
- 1 avocado, sliced
- 1/2-pound cooked shrimp, sliced
- Soy sauce or tamari for dipping
- Pickled ginger and wasabi for serving (optional)

Cooking Instructions

1. **Prepare the Cauliflower Rice:** Cut the cauliflower into florets and pulse in a food processor until it resembles rice. Transfer to a microwave-safe bowl and microwave on high for 5-7 minutes until tender. Let cool slightly.
2. **Season the Cauliflower Rice:** Stir in the rice vinegar, erythritol, and sea salt until well combined.
3. **Prepare the Filling:** Julienne the cucumber and carrot and slice the avocado and cooked shrimp.
4. **Assemble the Sushi Rolls:** Place a sheet of nori on a bamboo sushi mat. Spread a thin layer of cauliflower rice over the nori, leaving a 1-inch border at the top. Arrange the cucumber, carrot, avocado, and shrimp in a line across the center of the rice.
5. **Roll the Sushi:** Using the bamboo mat, roll the sushi tightly from the bottom, pressing firmly to seal. Moisten the

border with a little water to help it stick. Repeat with the remaining nori sheets and fillings.
6. **Slice the Rolls:** Use a sharp knife to cut each roll into 8 pieces.
7. **Serve:** Serve the sushi rolls with soy sauce or tamari for dipping. Add pickled ginger and wasabi if desired.

Nutritional Facts

- **Calories:** 150 kcal
- **Protein:** 12g
- **Fat:** 7g
- **Saturated Fat:** 1g
- **Cholesterol:** 70mg
- **Sodium:** 600mg
- **Potassium:** 500mg
- **Fiber:** 5g
- **Sugar:** 3g
- **Vitamin C:** 30mg

Cooking Tips

- ✓ **Cauliflower Rice:** Ensure the cauliflower rice is not too wet to prevent the sushi from becoming soggy. Squeeze out excess moisture if needed.
- ✓ **Rolling:** Use a bamboo sushi mat for the best results when rolling the sushi. If you don't have one, use a clean kitchen towel.
- ✓ **Fillings:** Customize your sushi rolls with your favorite low-carb fillings like smoked salmon, crab, or cream cheese.
- ✓ **Storage:** Sushi is best enjoyed fresh. Store any leftovers in an airtight container in the refrigerator for up to 1 day.

Low-carb sushi rolls with cauliflower rice are a delicious and healthy alternative to traditional sushi, featuring fresh vegetables and shrimp wrapped in nori, perfect for a light and satisfying meal.

Recipe 76: Thai Coconut Curry Chicken

Prep Time: 15 minutes | Cooking Time: 25 minutes | Servings: 4

Ingredients

- 1 tablespoon coconut oil
- 1 small onion, finely chopped
- 3 cloves garlic, minced
- 1 tablespoon fresh ginger, minced
- 1-pound boneless, skinless chicken thighs cut into bite-sized pieces
- 1 red bell pepper, sliced
- 1 yellow bell pepper, sliced
- 1 zucchini, sliced
- 1 cup broccoli florets
- 1 (14 oz) can full-fat coconut milk
- 2 tablespoons red curry paste
- 1 tablespoon fish sauce (optional)
- 1 tablespoon lime juice
- 1 teaspoon erythritol (optional)
- Fresh basil leaves for garnish
- Fresh cilantro for garnish
- Lime wedges for serving

Cooking Instructions

1. **Heat the Oil:** In a large skillet or wok, heat the coconut oil over medium heat. Add the chopped onion and cook for 3-4 minutes until softened.
2. **Add Garlic and Ginger:** Add the minced garlic and fresh ginger to the skillet. Cook for 1-2 minutes until fragrant.
3. **Cook the Chicken:** Add the chicken pieces to the skillet and cook for 5-7 minutes until browned and cooked through.
4. **Add Vegetables:** Stir in the red bell pepper, yellow bell pepper, zucchini, and broccoli florets. Cook for 3-4 minutes until the vegetables are tender-crisp.
5. **Add Coconut Milk and Curry Paste:** Pour in the coconut milk and stir in the red curry paste. Bring to a simmer and cook for 5 minutes, allowing the flavors to meld.
6. **Season the Curry:** Stir in the fish sauce (if using), lime juice, and erythritol (if using). Adjust seasoning to taste.
7. **Serve:** Serve the curry hot, garnished with fresh basil leaves and cilantro. Serve with lime wedges on the side.

Nutritional Facts

- **Calories:** 350 kcal
- **Protein:** 25g
- **Fat:** 25g
- **Saturated Fat:** 18g
- **Cholesterol:** 100mg
- **Sodium:** 600mg
- **Potassium:** 800mg
- **Fiber:** 4g
- **Sugar:** 6g
- **Vitamin A:** 3000 IU

Cooking Tips

- ✓ **Chicken:** Use boneless, skinless chicken thighs for the best flavor and texture. Chicken breasts can be substituted if preferred.
- ✓ **Vegetables:** Customize the curry with your favorite vegetables or whatever you have on hand. Snap peas, carrots, and mushrooms all work well.
- ✓ **Curry Paste:** Adjust the amount of red curry paste to your preferred spice level.

Thai coconut curry chicken is a flavorful and aromatic dish featuring tender chicken, and fresh vegetables simmered in a rich coconut curry sauce, perfect for a satisfying and healthy low-carb meal.

Recipe 77: Italian Meatballs with Zoodles

Prep Time: 20 minutes | Cooking Time: 25 minutes | Servings: 4

Ingredients

For the Meatballs:
- 1 pound ground beef
- 1/2 cup grated Parmesan cheese
- 1/4 cup almond flour
- 1 large egg
- 2 cloves garlic, minced
- 1 teaspoon dried oregano
- 1 teaspoon dried basil
- 1/2 teaspoon sea salt
- 1/4 teaspoon black pepper

For the Sauce:
- 1 tablespoon olive oil
- 1 small onion, finely chopped
- 3 cloves garlic, minced
- 1 (28 oz) can crushed tomatoes
- 1 teaspoon dried basil
- 1 teaspoon dried oregano
- 1/2 teaspoon sea salt
- 1/4 teaspoon black pepper
- 1/4 teaspoon red pepper flakes (optional)

For the Zoodles:
- 4 medium zucchinis, spiralized into noodles
- 1 tablespoon olive oil
- Fresh basil for garnish
- Grated Parmesan cheese for garnish

Cooking Instructions

1. **Prepare the Meatballs:** In a large bowl, combine the ground beef, grated Parmesan cheese, almond flour, egg, minced garlic, dried oregano, dried basil, sea salt, and black pepper. Mix until well combined. Form into 16 meatballs.
2. **Cook the Meatballs:** Heat a large skillet over medium heat. Add the meatballs and cook, turning occasionally, for 8-10 minutes until browned on all sides and cooked through. Remove from the skillet and set aside.
3. **Make the Sauce:** In the same skillet, heat the olive oil over medium heat. Add the chopped onion and cook for 3-4 minutes until softened. Add the minced garlic and cook for another minute. Stir in the crushed tomatoes, dried basil, dried oregano, sea salt, black pepper, and red pepper flakes if using. Simmer for 10 minutes.
4. **Add the Meatballs to the Sauce:** Return the meatballs to the skillet with the sauce. Simmer for an additional 5 minutes to heat through.
5. **Prepare the Zoodles:** In a separate large skillet, heat the olive oil over medium heat. Add the spiralized zucchini noodles and cook for 2-3 minutes until just tender but still firm (al dente).
6. **Serve:** Divide the zoodles among four plates. Top with the meatballs and sauce. Garnish with fresh basil and grated Parmesan cheese.

Nutritional Facts

- **Calories:** 350 kcal
- **Protein:** 25g
- **Fat:** 22g
- **Saturated Fat:** 8g
- **Cholesterol:** 100mg
- **Sodium:** 800mg
- **Potassium:** 1000mg
- **Fiber:** 4g
- **Sugar:** 8g
- **Vitamin A:** 1500 IU

Cooking Tips

✓ **Meatballs:** Ensure the meatballs are evenly sized for consistent cooking. Use a cookie scoop to make it easier.
✓ **Zoodles:** Cook the zoodles just until tender to avoid them becoming mushy. Drain any excess water before serving.

Recipe 78: Keto-Friendly Chicken Pho

Prep Time: 20 minutes | Cooking Time: 45 minutes | Servings: 4

Ingredients

For the Broth:

- 8 cups chicken broth
- 1 small onion, halved
- 1 2-inch piece of ginger, sliced
- 3-star anise pods
- 3 whole cloves
- 1 cinnamon stick
- 1 tablespoon fish sauce
- 1 tablespoon soy sauce (or tamari for gluten-free)
- 1 teaspoon sea salt
- 1/2 teaspoon black peppercorns

For the Chicken:

- 2 boneless, skinless chicken breasts

For the Toppings:

- 2 medium zucchinis, spiralized into noodles (zoodles)
- 1 cup bean sprouts
- 1/2 cup fresh cilantro, chopped
- 1/2 cup fresh basil leaves
- 1/2 cup fresh mint leaves
- 1 jalapeño, sliced
- 1 lime, cut into wedges
- Sriracha or hoisin sauce (optional)

Cooking Instructions

1. **Prepare the Broth:** In a large pot, bring the chicken broth to a boil. Add the halved onion, sliced ginger, star anise, cloves, cinnamon stick, fish sauce, soy sauce, sea salt, and black peppercorns. Reduce heat and simmer for 30 minutes to allow the flavors to meld.
2. **Cook the Chicken:** Add the chicken breasts to the simmering broth. Poach for 15-20 minutes or until the chicken is cooked through. Remove the chicken from the broth and set aside to cool slightly. Shred the chicken using two forks.
3. **Strain the Broth:** Strain the broth through a fine-mesh sieve into another pot to remove the solids. Discard the solids and return the clear broth to the pot.
4. **Prepare the Zoodles:** While the broth is simmering, spiralize the zucchini into noodles and set aside.
5. **Assemble the Pho:** Divide the zoodles among four bowls. Top with shredded chicken.
6. **Ladle the Broth:** Pour the hot broth over the zoodles and chicken in each bowl.
7. **Add Toppings:** Top each bowl with bean sprouts, cilantro, basil leaves, mint leaves, sliced jalapeño, and lime wedges. Add Sriracha or hoisin sauce if desired.
8. **Serve:** Serve the pho immediately, allowing each person to customize their bowl with the fresh herbs and sauces.

Nutritional Facts

- **Calories:** 200 kcal
- **Protein:** 25g
- **Fat:** 6g
- **Saturated Fat:** 1.5g
- **Cholesterol:** 60mg
- **Sodium:** 1200mg
- **Potassium:** 800mg
- **Fiber:** 3g
- **Sugar:** 4g
- **Vitamin C:** 30mg

Cooking Tips

- ✓ **Broth:** For the most flavorful broth, use high-quality chicken broth and simmer with the spices for the full 30 minutes.
- ✓ **Chicken:** Ensure the chicken is fully cooked by checking for an internal temperature of 165°F (75°C).

Recipe 79: Low-Carb Shepherd's Pie

Prep Time: 20 minutes | Cooking Time: 30 minutes | Servings: 4

Ingredients

For the Meat Filling:

- 1 pound ground beef or lamb
- 1 small onion, finely chopped
- 2 cloves garlic, minced
- 1 cup carrots, diced
- 1 cup celery, diced
- 1 cup green beans, chopped
- 1/2 cup beef broth
- 1 tablespoon tomato paste
- 1 teaspoon Worcestershire sauce
- 1 teaspoon dried thyme
- 1/2 teaspoon sea salt
- 1/4 teaspoon black pepper

For the Cauliflower Mash Topping:

- 1 large head of cauliflower, cut into florets
- 2 tablespoons butter
- 1/4 cup heavy cream
- 1/4 cup grated Parmesan cheese
- 1/2 teaspoon sea salt
- 1/4 teaspoon black pepper

Cooking Instructions

1. **Preheat the Oven:** Preheat your oven to 400°F (200°C).
2. **Prepare the Meat Filling:** In a large skillet, cook the ground beef or lamb over medium heat until browned and cooked through. Remove the meat from the skillet and set aside. In the same skillet, add the chopped onion and garlic. Cook for 3-4 minutes until softened. Add the diced carrots, celery, and green beans, and cook for another 5 minutes.
3. **Combine Ingredients:** Return the cooked meat to the skillet with the vegetables. Stir in the beef broth, tomato paste, Worcestershire sauce, dried thyme, sea salt, and black pepper. Simmer for 5 minutes until the mixture thickens slightly. Transfer the meat mixture to a baking dish.
4. **Prepare the Cauliflower Mash:** While the meat mixture is cooking, steam the cauliflower florets until tender, about 10 minutes. Drain and transfer to a food processor. Add the butter, heavy cream, grated Parmesan cheese, sea salt, and black pepper. Blend until smooth and creamy.
5. **Assemble the Shepherd's Pie:** Spread the cauliflower mash evenly over the meat mixture in the baking dish.
6. **Bake:** Bake in the preheated oven for 20 minutes or until the top is golden brown and the filling is bubbly.
7. **Serve:** Let the shepherd's pie cool for a few minutes before serving.

Nutritional Facts

- **Calories:** 350 kcal
- **Protein:** 20g
- **Fat:** 24g
- **Saturated Fat:** 12g
- **Cholesterol:** 90mg
- **Sodium:** 900mg
- **Potassium:** 1000mg
- **Fiber:** 5g
- **Sugar:** 6g
- **Vitamin A:** 5000 IU

Cooking Tips

- ✓ **Meat:** Ground beef or lamb can be used for the meat filling. Choose lean cuts for a healthier option.
- ✓ **Vegetables:** Customize the vegetable mixture with your favorite low-carb vegetables like mushrooms or zucchini.

Recipe 80: Moroccan Spiced Lamb with Cauliflower Couscous

Prep Time: 20 minutes | Cooking Time: 30 minutes | Servings: 4

Ingredients

For the Lamb:

- 1 pound lamb shoulder or lamb leg, cut into bite-sized pieces
- 2 tablespoons olive oil
- 1 teaspoon ground cumin
- 1 teaspoon ground coriander
- 1 teaspoon ground cinnamon
- 1/2 teaspoon ground turmeric
- 1/2 teaspoon ground paprika
- 1/4 teaspoon cayenne pepper
- 1/2 teaspoon sea salt
- 1/4 teaspoon black pepper
- 3 cloves garlic, minced
- 1 small onion, finely chopped
- 1 cup beef or lamb broth
- 1/2 cup canned diced tomatoes
- 1/4 cup dried apricots, chopped (optional)
- 1/4 cup chopped fresh parsley (optional for garnish)

For the Cauliflower Couscous:

- 1 large head of cauliflower, riced
- 2 tablespoons olive oil
- 1/4 cup slivered almonds
- 1/4 cup raisins (optional)
- 1/4 teaspoon sea salt
- 1/4 teaspoon black pepper
- 1 tablespoon lemon juice
- 1/4 cup fresh parsley, chopped

Cooking Instructions

1. **Prepare the Lamb:** In a large bowl, combine the olive oil, ground cumin, ground coriander, ground cinnamon, ground turmeric, ground paprika, cayenne pepper, sea salt, and black pepper. Add the lamb pieces and toss to coat evenly.
2. **Cook the Lamb:** In a large skillet or Dutch oven, heat a bit of olive oil over medium-high heat. Add the lamb pieces and cook until browned on all sides, about 5-7 minutes. Remove the lamb from the skillet and set aside.
3. **Cook the Aromatics:** In the same skillet, add the minced garlic and chopped onion. Cook for 3-4 minutes until softened.
4. **Simmer the Lamb:** Return the lamb to the skillet. Add the beef or lamb broth, diced tomatoes, and chopped dried apricots if using. Bring to a simmer, cover, and cook for 20-25 minutes until the lamb is tender and the sauce has thickened.
5. **Prepare the Cauliflower Couscous:** While the lamb is cooking, cut the cauliflower into florets and pulse in a food processor until it resembles rice. In a large skillet, heat the olive oil over medium heat. Add the rice cauliflower and cook for 5-7 minutes until tender. Stir in the slivered almonds raisins, if using sea salt, black pepper, lemon juice, and chopped parsley.
6. **Serve:** Divide the cauliflower couscous among four plates. Top with the Moroccan spiced lamb and garnish with fresh parsley if desired. Serve hot.

Nutritional Facts

- **Calories:** 400 kcal
- **Protein:** 25g
- **Fat:** 28g
- **Saturated Fat:** 8g
- **Cholesterol:** 80mg
- **Sodium:** 700mg
- **Potassium:** 800mg
- **Fiber:** 6g
- **Sugar:** 8g
- **Vitamin C:** 70mg

Cooking Tips

✓ **Lamb:** Use tender cuts of lamb, such as shoulder or leg, for the best results. Ensure the pieces are evenly sized for even cooking.
✓ **Spices:** Adjust the spices to your taste. Add more cayenne pepper for extra heat or more cinnamon for a sweeter flavor.

Meal Prep Recipes

Recipe 81: Grilled Chicken with Roasted Veggies

Prep Time: 15 minutes | Cooking Time: 30 minutes | Servings: 4

Ingredients

For the Chicken:

- 4 boneless, skinless chicken breasts
- 2 tablespoons olive oil
- 1 tablespoon lemon juice
- 2 cloves garlic, minced
- 1 teaspoon dried thyme
- 1 teaspoon dried rosemary
- 1/2 teaspoon sea salt
- 1/4 teaspoon black pepper

For the Roasted Veggies:

- 1 red bell pepper, chopped
- 1 yellow bell pepper, chopped
- 1 zucchini, sliced into half-moons
- 1 cup cherry tomatoes
- 1 small red onion, chopped
- 2 tablespoons olive oil
- 1 teaspoon dried oregano
- 1/2 teaspoon sea salt
- 1/4 teaspoon black pepper

Cooking Instructions

1. **Marinate the Chicken:** In a large bowl, combine the olive oil, lemon juice, minced garlic, dried thyme, dried rosemary, sea salt, and black pepper. Add the chicken breasts and toss to coat evenly. Cover and marinate in the refrigerator for at least 30 minutes or up to 2 hours.
2. **Preheat the Oven:** Preheat your oven to 400°F (200°C).
3. **Prepare the Veggies:** In a large bowl, combine the chopped red bell pepper, yellow bell pepper, zucchini, cherry tomatoes, and red onion. Drizzle with olive oil and sprinkle with dried oregano, sea salt, and black pepper. Toss to coat.
4. **Roast the Veggies:** Spread the vegetables in a single layer on a baking sheet. Roast in the preheated oven for 20-25 minutes or until the vegetables are tender and slightly charred.
5. **Grill the Chicken:** While the vegetables are roasting, preheat your grill to medium-high heat. Grill the marinated chicken breasts for 6-8 minutes per side or until fully cooked, and the internal temperature reaches 165°F (75°C).
6. **Serve:** Divide the grilled chicken breasts among four plates. Serve with a generous portion of roasted veggies on the side.

Nutritional Facts

- **Calories:** 350 kcal
- **Protein:** 35g
- **Fat:** 18g
- **Saturated Fat:** 3g
- **Cholesterol:** 90mg
- **Sodium:** 600mg
- **Potassium:** 900mg
- **Fiber:** 4g
- **Sugar:** 6g
- **Vitamin A:** 2000 IU

Cooking Tips

- ✓ **Chicken:** For the juiciest chicken, avoid overcooking. Use a meat thermometer to ensure it reaches 165°F (75°C).
- ✓ **Veggies:** Cut the vegetables into similar sizes to ensure even roasting.
- ✓ **Marinating:** The longer you marinate the chicken, the more flavorful it will be. If you're short on time, marinate for at least 30 minutes.

Recipe 82: Turkey and Spinach Meatballs

Prep Time: 15 minutes | Cooking Time: 25 minutes | Servings: 4

Ingredients

- 1 pound ground turkey
- 1 cup fresh spinach, finely chopped
- 1/2 cup grated Parmesan cheese
- 1/4 cup almond flour
- 1 large egg
- 2 cloves garlic, minced
- 1 teaspoon dried oregano
- 1 teaspoon dried basil
- 1/2 teaspoon sea salt
- 1/4 teaspoon black pepper
- 2 tablespoons olive oil

Cooking Instructions

1. **Preheat the Oven:** Preheat your oven to 400°F (200°C). Line a baking sheet with parchment paper.
2. **Prepare the Meatballs:** In a large bowl, combine the ground turkey, chopped spinach, grated Parmesan cheese, almond flour, egg, minced garlic, dried oregano, dried basil, sea salt, and black pepper. Mix until well combined.
3. **Form the Meatballs:** Using your hands, shape the mixture into 16 meatballs, about 1 inch in diameter. Place the meatballs on the prepared baking sheet.
4. **Bake the Meatballs:** Drizzle the meatballs with olive oil. Bake in the preheated oven for 20-25 minutes or until the meatballs are cooked through and golden brown.

5. **Serve:** Serve the meatballs hot with your favorite low-carb marinara sauce, zucchini noodles, or a side salad.

Nutritional Facts

- **Calories:** 280 kcal
- **Protein:** 25g
- **Fat:** 18g
- **Saturated Fat:** 5g
- **Cholesterol:** 120mg
- **Sodium:** 600mg
- **Potassium:** 500mg
- **Fiber:** 2g
- **Sugar:** 1g
- **Vitamin A:** 1000 IU

Cooking Tips

- ✓ **Turkey:** Use ground turkey with a bit of fat for more flavorful and moist meatballs. Ground turkey breast can be used as a leaner option.
- ✓ **Spinach:** Finely chop the spinach to evenly distribute it throughout the meatballs.
- ✓ **Serving Suggestions:** Pair with a low-carb marinara sauce and zucchini noodles or serve as an appetizer with toothpicks.
- ✓ **Storage:** Store any leftovers in an airtight container in the refrigerator for up to 3 days. Reheat in the oven or microwave before serving.

Turkey and spinach meatballs are a healthy and delicious option, featuring tender turkey combined with fresh spinach and savory herbs, perfect for a nutritious and satisfying meal.

Recipe 83: Mediterranean Chicken Salad

Prep Time: 15 minutes | Cooking Time: 10 minutes | Servings: 4

Ingredients

- 2 boneless, skinless chicken breasts
- 1 tablespoon olive oil
- 1 teaspoon dried oregano
- 1 teaspoon garlic powder
- Sea salt and black pepper, to taste
- 4 cups mixed greens (such as romaine, spinach, or arugula)
- 1 cup cherry tomatoes, halved
- 1 large cucumber, sliced
- 1/2 cup Kalamata olives, pitted and halved
- 1/4 cup red onion, thinly sliced
- 1/2 cup crumbled feta cheese

For the Lemon-Oregano Vinaigrette:

- 1/4 cup olive oil
- 2 tablespoons fresh lemon juice
- 1 teaspoon Dijon mustard
- 1 teaspoon dried oregano
- 1 clove garlic, minced
- Sea salt and black pepper, to taste

Cooking Instructions

1. **Prepare the Chicken:** Rub the chicken breasts with olive oil, dried oregano, garlic powder, sea salt, and black pepper. Ensure they are well-coated with the seasoning.
2. **Grill the Chicken:** Preheat a grill or grill pan over medium-high heat. Grill the chicken for about 5-7 minutes on each side, or until the internal temperature reaches 165°F (74°C) and the chicken is cooked through. Let the chicken rest for a few minutes, then slice it into thin strips.
3. **Prepare the Salad:** In a large salad bowl, combine the mixed greens, halved cherry tomatoes, sliced cucumber, Kalamata olives, and thinly sliced red onion.
4. **Make the Vinaigrette:** In a small bowl or a jar with a lid, combine the olive oil, fresh lemon juice, Dijon mustard, dried oregano, minced garlic, sea salt, and black pepper. Whisk or shake well to combine.
5. **Assemble the Salad:** Add the grilled chicken slices to the salad bowl. Drizzle the lemon-oregano vinaigrette over the salad and toss gently to combine.
6. **Garnish and Serve:** Sprinkle the crumbled feta cheese on top of the salad. Serve immediately and enjoy a refreshing and flavorful Mediterranean chicken salad.

Nutritional Facts

- **Calories:** 320 kcal
- **Protein:** 26g
- **Fat:** 20g
- **Saturated Fat:** 5g
- **Cholesterol:** 70mg
- **Sodium:** 600mg
- **Potassium:** 800mg
- **Fiber:** 3g
- **Sugar:** 3g
- **Vitamin C:** 20mg

Cooking Tips

- ✓ **Chicken:** For extra flavor, marinate the chicken in the seasoning for at least 30 minutes before grilling. You can also use pre-cooked or rotisserie chicken for convenience.
- ✓ **Vinaigrette:** Adjust the amount of lemon juice and Dijon mustard to your taste preference. You can also add a touch of honey for a hint of sweetness.
- ✓ **Toppings:** Customize your salad with additional toppings like roasted red peppers, artichoke hearts, or toasted pine nuts for added texture and flavor.

Recipe 84: Beef and Veggie Stir-Fry

Prep Time: 15 minutes | Cooking Time: 15 minutes | Servings: 4

Ingredients

- 1 pound beef sirloin, thinly sliced
- 2 tablespoons soy sauce (or tamari for gluten-free)
- 1 tablespoon rice vinegar
- 1 tablespoon sesame oil
- 1 tablespoon olive oil
- 2 cloves garlic, minced
- 1 tablespoon fresh ginger, minced
- 1 red bell pepper, sliced
- 1 yellow bell pepper, sliced
- 1 medium zucchini, sliced into half-moons
- 1 cup broccoli florets
- 1 cup snow peas
- 1/4 cup sliced green onions
- 1/4 cup chopped fresh cilantro (optional)
- 1/4 teaspoon red pepper flakes (optional)

Cooking Instructions

1. **Marinate the Beef:** In a large bowl, combine the soy sauce, rice vinegar, and sesame oil. Add the sliced beef and toss to coat. Marinate for at least 15 minutes.
2. **Prepare the Vegetables:** While the beef is marinating, prepare the vegetables by slicing the bell peppers, zucchini, and broccoli.
3. **Cook the Beef:** In a large skillet or wok, heat the olive oil over medium-high heat. Add the minced garlic and fresh ginger and cook for 1-2 minutes until fragrant. Add the marinated beef and stir-fry for 4-5 minutes until browned and cooked through. Remove the beef from the skillet and set aside.
4. **Cook the Vegetables:** In the same skillet, add the sliced bell peppers, zucchini, broccoli, and snow peas. Stir-fry for 5-7 minutes until the vegetables are tender-crisp.
5. **Combine and Serve:** Return the cooked beef to the skillet and toss to combine with the vegetables. Cook for an additional 2 minutes to heat through. Garnish with sliced green onions, chopped fresh cilantro, and red pepper flakes if using. Serve hot.

Nutritional Facts

- **Calories:** 300 kcal
- **Protein:** 25g
- **Fat:** 15g
- **Saturated Fat:** 4g
- **Cholesterol:** 70mg
- **Sodium:** 600mg
- **Potassium:** 800mg
- **Fiber:** 4g
- **Sugar:** 5g
- **Vitamin C:** 100mg

Cooking Tips

- ✓ **Beef:** Choose a tender cut of beef like sirloin or flank steak for the best results. Slice the beef thinly for quicker cooking.
- ✓ **Vegetables:** Customize the stir-fry with your favorite vegetables or whatever you have on hand. Snap peas, carrots, and mushrooms all work well.

Beef and veggie stir-fry is a quick and healthy dish featuring tender beef and colorful vegetables in a flavorful sauce, perfect for a satisfying and low-carb meal.

Recipe 85: Lemon Herb Shrimp with Asparagus

Prep Time: 10 minutes | Cooking Time: 10 minutes | Servings: 4

Ingredients

- 1-pound large shrimp, peeled and deveined
- 1 bunch asparagus, trimmed and cut into 2-inch pieces
- 2 tablespoons olive oil
- 2 cloves garlic, minced
- 1 teaspoon lemon zest
- 2 tablespoons lemon juice
- 1 teaspoon dried oregano
- 1 teaspoon dried thyme
- 1/2 teaspoon sea salt
- 1/4 teaspoon black pepper
- Fresh parsley, chopped (optional for garnish)

Cooking Instructions

1. **Prepare the Shrimp and Asparagus:** Pat the shrimp dry with paper towels. Trim the asparagus and cut into 2-inch pieces.
2. **Heat the Oil:** In a large skillet, heat the olive oil over medium-high heat. Add the minced garlic and cook for 1 minute until fragrant.
3. **Cook the Shrimp:** Add the shrimp to the skillet and cook for 2-3 minutes on each side until pink and opaque. Remove the shrimp from the skillet and set aside.
4. **Cook the Asparagus:** In the same skillet, add the asparagus pieces. Cook for 3-4 minutes until tender but still crisp.
5. **Combine and Season:** Return the shrimp to the skillet with the asparagus. Add the lemon zest, lemon juice, dried oregano, dried thyme, sea salt, and black pepper. Toss to combine and cook for an additional 1-2 minutes until heated through.
6. **Serve:** Transfer the shrimp and asparagus to a serving platter. Garnish with fresh parsley if desired. Serve hot.

Nutritional Facts

- **Calories:** 180 kcal
- **Protein:** 20g
- **Fat:** 8g
- **Saturated Fat:** 1g
- **Cholesterol:** 190mg
- **Sodium:** 600mg
- **Potassium:** 300mg
- **Fiber:** 2g
- **Sugar:** 2g
- **Vitamin C:** 20mg

Cooking Tips

- ✓ **Shrimp:** Use fresh or frozen shrimp that have been peeled and deveined. If using frozen shrimp, thaw them completely and pat dry before cooking.
- ✓ **Asparagus:** Choose fresh, firm asparagus spears. Avoid overcooking to keep them tender-crisp.
- ✓ **Lemon:** Fresh lemon juice and zest give the best flavor. Adjust the amount of lemon juice to your taste preference.
- ✓ **Serving Suggestions:** Serve with cauliflower rice, a side salad, or zucchini noodles for a complete low-carb meal.
- ✓ **Storage:** Store any leftovers in an airtight container in the refrigerator for up to 2 days. Reheat gently in a skillet before serving.

Lemon herb shrimp with asparagus is a light and flavorful dish featuring tender shrimp and crisp asparagus tossed in a lemony herb sauce, perfect for a healthy and delicious low-carb meal.

Recipe 86: Spicy Tuna Patties

Prep Time: 15 minutes | Cooking Time: 10 minutes | Servings: 4

Ingredients

- 2 (5 oz) cans tuna, drained
- 1/2 cup almond flour
- 1/4 cup mayonnaise
- 1 large egg
- 2 green onions, finely chopped
- 1 small red bell pepper, finely chopped
- 1 tablespoon Dijon mustard
- 1 tablespoon hot sauce (or to taste)
- 1 teaspoon lemon juice
- 1/2 teaspoon sea salt
- 1/4 teaspoon black pepper
- 2 tablespoons olive oil (for frying)

Cooking Instructions

1. **Prepare the Mixture:** In a large bowl, combine the drained tuna, almond flour, mayonnaise, egg, green onions, red bell pepper, Dijon mustard, hot sauce, lemon juice, sea salt, and black pepper. Mix until well combined.
2. **Form the Patties:** Divide the mixture into 8 equal portions and shape into patties.
3. **Heat the Oil:** In a large skillet, heat the olive oil over medium-high heat.
4. **Cook the Patties:** Add the tuna patties to the skillet and cook for 3-4 minutes on each side until golden brown and crispy.
5. **Serve:** Transfer the cooked patties to a serving plate. Serve hot with a side of salad or low-carb dipping sauce.

Nutritional Facts

- **Calories:** 250 kcal
- **Protein:** 20g
- **Fat:** 18g
- **Saturated Fat:** 3g
- **Cholesterol:** 70mg
- **Sodium:** 600mg
- **Potassium:** 200mg
- **Fiber:** 2g
- **Sugar:** 1g
- **Vitamin C:** 15mg

Cooking Tips

- ✓ **Tuna:** Use high-quality canned tuna in water or oil, well-drained. Freshly cooked and flaked tuna can also be used.
- ✓ **Binding:** Ensure the mixture is well-combined and holds together when shaping into patties. If it's too dry, add a bit more mayonnaise.
- ✓ **Heat:** Adjust the amount of hot sauce to your taste preference for a spicier or milder patty.

Spicy tuna patties are a flavorful and protein-packed dish featuring tender tuna combined with fresh vegetables and a kick of heat, perfect for a healthy and satisfying low-carb meal.

Recipe 87: BBQ Chicken Drumsticks

Prep Time: 10 minutes | Cooking Time: 40 minutes | Servings: 4

Ingredients

- 8 chicken drumsticks
- 1/2 cup sugar-free BBQ sauce
- 1 tablespoon olive oil
- 1 teaspoon smoked paprika
- 1 teaspoon garlic powder
- 1 teaspoon onion powder
- 1/2 teaspoon sea salt
- 1/4 teaspoon black pepper

Cooking Instructions

1. **Preheat the Oven:** Preheat your oven to 400°F (200°C). Line a baking sheet with parchment paper.
2. **Prepare the Drumsticks:** Pat the chicken drumsticks dry with paper towels. In a large bowl, combine the olive oil, smoked paprika, garlic powder, onion powder, sea salt, and black pepper. Add the drumsticks and toss to coat evenly.
3. **Arrange the Drumsticks:** Place the drumsticks in a single layer on the prepared baking sheet.
4. **Bake the Drumsticks:** Bake in the preheated oven for 30 minutes, flipping halfway through.
5. **Add the BBQ Sauce:** Remove the drumsticks from the oven and brush them generously with sugar-free BBQ sauce. Return to the oven and bake for an additional 10 minutes, or until the internal temperature reaches 165°F (75°C) and the sauce is caramelized.
6. **Serve:** Serve the BBQ chicken drumsticks hot, with extra BBQ sauce on the side if desired.

Nutritional Facts

- **Calories:** 250 kcal
- **Protein:** 25g
- **Fat:** 15g
- **Saturated Fat:** 4g
- **Cholesterol:** 100mg
- **Sodium:** 600mg
- **Potassium:** 300mg
- **Fiber:** 1g
- **Sugar:** 2g
- **Vitamin A:** 500 IU

Cooking Tips

- ✓ **Chicken:** Pat the drumsticks dry to ensure the seasoning sticks and the skin gets crispy.
- ✓ **BBQ Sauce:** Use your favorite sugar-free BBQ sauce for the best flavor. Brush on additional sauce after baking for a more intense BBQ flavor.
- ✓ **Crispy Skin:** For extra crispy skin, broil the drumsticks for the last 2-3 minutes of baking, watching closely to prevent burning.
- ✓ **Serving Suggestions:** Serve with a side of coleslaw, roasted vegetables, or a fresh green salad for a complete meal.
- ✓ **Storage:** Store any leftovers in an airtight container in the refrigerator for up to 3 days. Reheat in the oven or microwave before serving.

BBQ chicken drumsticks are a delicious and easy dish featuring tender chicken with a smoky, flavorful seasoning and a tangy BBQ glaze, perfect for a healthy and satisfying low-carb meal.

Recipe 88: Cauliflower and Chicken Fried Rice

Prep Time: 15 minutes | Cooking Time: 15 minutes | Servings: 4

Ingredients

- 1 large head of cauliflower, riced
- 1-pound boneless, skinless chicken breasts, diced
- 2 tablespoons olive oil, divided
- 1 small onion, finely chopped
- 2 cloves garlic, minced
- 1 cup frozen peas and carrots
- 3 green onions, sliced
- 2 large eggs, lightly beaten
- 3 tablespoons soy sauce (or tamari for gluten-free)
- 1 tablespoon sesame oil
- 1/4 teaspoon black pepper
- Fresh cilantro, chopped (optional for garnish)

Cooking Instructions

1. **Prepare the Cauliflower Rice:** Cut the cauliflower into florets and pulse in a food processor until it resembles rice. Set it aside.
2. **Cook the Chicken:** In a large skillet or wok, heat 1 tablespoon of olive oil over medium-high heat. Add the diced chicken and cook for 5-7 minutes until browned and cooked through. Remove the chicken from the skillet and set aside.
3. **Cook the Vegetables:** In the same skillet, add the remaining tablespoon of olive oil. Add the chopped onion and cook for 2-3 minutes until softened. Add the minced garlic and cook for another minute. Stir in the frozen peas and carrots and cook for 3-4 minutes until heated through.
4. **Add the Cauliflower Rice:** Add the cauliflower rice to the skillet with the vegetables. Cook for 5-7 minutes until the cauliflower is tender.
5. **Add the Eggs:** Push the cauliflower rice mixture to the side of the skillet and pour the beaten eggs into the empty space. Scramble the eggs until fully cooked, then mix them into the cauliflower rice.
6. **Combine and Season:** Return the cooked chicken to the skillet. Stir in the soy sauce, sesame oil, and black pepper. Cook for an additional 2 minutes until everything is well combined and heated through.
7. **Serve:** Garnish with sliced green onions and fresh cilantro if desired. Serve hot.

Nutritional Facts

- **Calories:** 300 kcal
- **Protein:** 25g
- **Fat:** 15g
- **Saturated Fat:** 3g
- **Cholesterol:** 150mg
- **Sodium:** 800mg
- **Potassium:** 700mg
- **Fiber:** 5g
- **Sugar:** 5g
- **Vitamin C:** 60mg

Cooking Tips

- ✓ **Cauliflower Rice:** Ensure the cauliflower is pulsed to a rice-like consistency. Avoid over-processing to prevent it from becoming mushy.
- ✓ **Chicken:** Use boneless, skinless chicken thighs for a juicier option if preferred.
- ✓ **Seasoning:** Adjust the amount of soy sauce and sesame oil to your taste. Add a pinch of red pepper flakes for a spicy kick.

Cauliflower and chicken fried rice is a healthy and delicious low-carb version of the classic dish, featuring tender chicken, fresh vegetables, and savory cauliflower rice, perfect for a satisfying meal.

Recipe 89: Greek Chicken Bowl

Prep Time: 20 minutes | Cooking Time: 15 minutes | Servings: 4

Ingredients

- 1-pound boneless, skinless chicken breasts, diced
- 2 tablespoons olive oil
- 1 tablespoon lemon juice
- 2 cloves garlic, minced
- 1 teaspoon dried oregano
- 1/2 teaspoon sea salt
- 1/4 teaspoon black pepper
- 1 cup cherry tomatoes, halved
- 1 cucumber, diced
- 1/4 red onion, thinly sliced
- 1/2 cup Kalamata olives, pitted and halved
- 1/2 cup feta cheese, crumbled
- 2 cups mixed greens (such as spinach, arugula, and romaine)
- Fresh parsley, chopped (optional for garnish)

For the Tzatziki Sauce:

- 1 cup Greek yogurt
- 1/2 cucumber, grated, and excess water squeezed out
- 1 tablespoon lemon juice
- 1 clove garlic, minced
- 1 tablespoon fresh dill, chopped
- 1/2 teaspoon sea salt
- 1/4 teaspoon black pepper

Cooking Instructions

1. **Marinate the Chicken:** In a large bowl, combine the olive oil, lemon juice, minced garlic, dried oregano, sea salt, and black pepper. Add the diced chicken and toss to coat evenly. Marinate for at least 15 minutes.
2. **Prepare the Tzatziki Sauce:** In a small bowl, combine the Greek yogurt, grated cucumber, lemon juice, minced garlic, fresh dill, sea salt, and black pepper. Mix well and refrigerate until ready to use.
3. **Cook the Chicken:** In a large skillet over medium-high heat, cook the marinated chicken for 5-7 minutes on each side or until fully cooked and golden brown.
4. **Assemble the Bowls:** Divide the mixed greens among four bowls. Top each bowl with cooked chicken, cherry tomatoes, diced cucumber, sliced red onion, Kalamata olives, and crumbled feta cheese.
5. **Add the Tzatziki:** Spoon the prepared tzatziki sauce over each bowl.
6. **Serve:** Garnish with fresh parsley if desired. Serve immediately.

Nutritional Facts

- **Calories:** 350 kcal
- **Protein:** 30g
- **Fat:** 20g
- **Saturated Fat:** 6g
- **Cholesterol:** 80mg
- **Sodium:** 800mg
- **Potassium:** 700mg
- **Fiber:** 4g
- **Sugar:** 5g
- **Vitamin C:** 25mg

Cooking Tips

✓ **Chicken:** Ensure the chicken is diced into even pieces for uniform cooking. Use chicken thighs for a juicier option.

✓ **Tzatziki Sauce:** Squeeze out as much water as possible from the grated cucumber to prevent the sauce from becoming watery.

✓ **Greens:** Use a mix of your favorite greens for added texture and flavor.

Recipe 90: Low-Carb Burrito Bowl

Prep Time: 20 minutes | Cooking Time: 20 minutes | Servings: 4

Ingredients

For the Cauliflower Rice:
- 1 large head of cauliflower, riced
- 2 tablespoons olive oil
- 1/2 teaspoon sea salt
- 1/4 teaspoon black pepper

For the Chicken:
- 1-pound boneless, skinless chicken breasts, diced
- 2 tablespoons olive oil
- 1 tablespoon lime juice
- 2 cloves garlic, minced
- 1 teaspoon ground cumin
- 1 teaspoon chili powder
- 1/2 teaspoon smoked paprika
- 1/2 teaspoon sea salt
- 1/4 teaspoon black pepper

For the Toppings:
- 1 cup romaine lettuce, shredded
- 1 cup cherry tomatoes, halved
- 1 avocado, diced
- 1/4 red onion, finely chopped
- 1/4 cup fresh cilantro, chopped
- 1/2 cup shredded cheese (optional)
- 1/4 cup sour cream (optional)
- Lime wedges for serving

Cooking Instructions

1. **Prepare the Cauliflower Rice:** Cut the cauliflower into florets and pulse in a food processor until it resembles rice. Heat the olive oil in a large skillet over medium heat. Add the cauliflower rice, sea salt, and black pepper. Cook for 5-7 minutes until tender. Set aside.
2. **Marinate the Chicken:** In a large bowl, combine the olive oil, lime juice, minced garlic, ground cumin, chili powder, smoked paprika, sea salt, and black pepper. Add the diced chicken and toss to coat. Marinate for at least 15 minutes.
3. **Cook the Chicken:** In a large skillet over medium-high heat, cook the marinated chicken for 5-7 minutes on each side or until fully cooked and slightly charred. Remove from heat.
4. **Assemble the Bowls:** Divide the cauliflower rice among four bowls. Top with cooked chicken, shredded romaine lettuce, cherry tomatoes, diced avocado, chopped red onion, fresh cilantro, shredded cheese, and sour cream if used.
5. **Serve:** Garnish with lime wedges and serve immediately.

Nutritional Facts

- **Calories:** 350 kcal
- **Protein:** 30g
- **Fat:** 20g
- **Saturated Fat:** 4g
- **Cholesterol:** 80mg
- **Sodium:** 700mg
- **Potassium:** 800mg
- **Fiber:** 7g
- **Sugar:** 5g
- **Vitamin C:** 35mg

Cooking Tips

- ✓ **Cauliflower Rice:** Ensure the cauliflower is pulsed to a rice-like consistency. Avoid over-processing to prevent it from becoming mushy.
- ✓ **Chicken:** Use boneless, skinless chicken thighs for a juicier option. Ensure the chicken is fully cooked to an internal temperature of 165°F (75°C).
- ✓ **Toppings:** Customize your burrito bowl with your favorite low-carb toppings like jalapeños, salsa, or guacamole.

Soup Recipes

Recipe 91: Chicken and Cauliflower Rice Soup

Prep Time: 15 minutes | Cooking Time: 30 minutes | Servings: 4

Ingredients

- 1 tablespoon olive oil
- 1 small onion, finely chopped
- 2 cloves garlic, minced
- 2 medium carrots, diced
- 2 celery stalks, diced
- 1-pound boneless, skinless chicken breasts, diced
- 6 cups chicken broth
- 1 large head of cauliflower, riced
- 1 teaspoon dried thyme
- 1 teaspoon dried parsley
- 1/2 teaspoon sea salt
- 1/4 teaspoon black pepper
- 1/4 cup fresh parsley, chopped (optional for garnish)

Cooking Instructions

1. **Heat the Oil:** In a large pot, heat the olive oil over medium heat. Add the chopped onion and cook for 3-4 minutes until softened.
2. **Add Garlic and Vegetables:** Add the minced garlic, diced carrots, and diced celery. Cook for an additional 5 minutes, stirring occasionally.
3. **Cook the Chicken:** Add the diced chicken to the pot. Cook for 5-7 minutes until the chicken is browned and cooked through.
4. **Add the Broth and Cauliflower Rice:** Pour in the chicken broth and bring to a boil. Add the rice cauliflower, dried thyme, dried parsley, sea salt, and black pepper.
5. **Simmer:** Reduce the heat to low and let the soup simmer for 20 minutes or until the vegetables are tender and the flavors are well combined.
6. **Serve:** Ladle the soup into bowls and garnish with fresh parsley if desired. Serve hot.

Nutritional Facts

- **Calories:** 250 kcal
- **Protein:** 30g
- **Fat:** 10g
- **Saturated Fat:** 2g
- **Cholesterol:** 80mg
- **Sodium:** 800mg
- **Potassium:** 900mg
- **Fiber:** 4g
- **Sugar:** 5g
- **Vitamin C:** 40mg

Cooking Tips

- ✓ **Cauliflower Rice:** To make your own cauliflower rice, pulse cauliflower florets in a food processor until they resemble rice grains. You can also use store-bought cauliflower rice for convenience.
- ✓ **Chicken:** Use boneless, skinless chicken thighs for a juicier option if preferred.
- ✓ **Seasoning:** Adjust the amount of herbs and seasoning to your taste. Add more garlic or fresh herbs for additional flavor.

Chicken and cauliflower rice soup is a hearty and nutritious dish featuring tender chicken and vegetables in a flavorful broth, perfect for a comforting and healthy low-carb meal.

Recipe 92: Low-Carb Broccoli Cheddar Soup

Prep Time: 10 minutes | Cooking Time: 20 minutes | Servings: 4

Ingredients

- 2 tablespoons butter
- 1 small onion, finely chopped
- 2 cloves garlic, minced
- 4 cups broccoli florets
- 4 cups chicken or vegetable broth
- 1 cup heavy cream
- 2 cups shredded sharp cheddar cheese
- 1/2 teaspoon sea salt
- 1/4 teaspoon black pepper
- 1/4 teaspoon ground nutmeg (optional)
- Fresh parsley, chopped (optional for garnish)

Cooking Instructions

1. **Heat the Butter:** In a large pot, melt the butter over medium heat. Add the chopped onion and cook for 3-4 minutes until softened.
2. **Add the Garlic and Broccoli:** Add the minced garlic and broccoli florets. Cook for another 2-3 minutes until the garlic is fragrant.
3. **Add the Broth:** Pour in the chicken or vegetable broth and bring to a boil. Reduce the heat and let it simmer for 10-12 minutes until the broccoli is tender.
4. **Blend the Soup:** Use an immersion blender to puree the soup until smooth. Alternatively, transfer the soup to a blender in batches and blend until smooth, then return it to the pot.
5. **Add the Cream and Cheese:** Stir in the heavy cream, shredded cheddar cheese, sea salt, black pepper, and ground nutmeg (if using). Cook for another 5 minutes, stirring frequently, until the cheese is melted, and the soup is heated through.
6. **Serve:** Ladle the soup into bowls and garnish with fresh parsley if desired. Serve hot.

Nutritional Facts

- **Calories:** 350 kcal
- **Protein:** 15g
- **Fat:** 30g
- **Saturated Fat:** 18g
- **Cholesterol:** 90mg
- **Sodium:** 900mg
- **Potassium:** 600mg
- **Fiber:** 3g
- **Sugar:** 3g
- **Vitamin A:** 1500 IU

Cooking Tips

- ✓ **Broccoli:** For a chunkier soup, reserve some broccoli florets, chop them finely, and add them back into the soup after blending.
- ✓ **Cheese:** Use sharp cheddar cheese for a more pronounced flavor. Feel free to experiment with other cheeses like Gouda or Swiss.
- ✓ **Blending:** Be cautious when blending hot soup. If using a countertop blender, blend in batches and cover the lid with a kitchen towel to prevent spills.

Low-carb broccoli cheddar soup is a rich and creamy dish featuring tender broccoli blended with sharp cheddar cheese, perfect for a comforting and satisfying low-carb meal.

Recipe 93: Keto Tomato Basil Soup

Prep Time: 10 minutes | Cooking Time: 25 minutes | Servings: 4

Ingredients

- 2 tablespoons olive oil
- 1 small onion, finely chopped
- 2 cloves garlic, minced
- 2 (14.5 oz) cans diced tomatoes
- 2 cups chicken or vegetable broth
- 1/2 cup heavy cream
- 1/4 cup fresh basil leaves, chopped
- 1 teaspoon sea salt
- 1/2 teaspoon black pepper
- 1/4 teaspoon red pepper flakes (optional)
- Fresh basil leaves for garnish (optional)

Cooking Instructions

1. **Heat the Oil:** In a large pot, heat the olive oil over medium heat. Add the chopped onion and cook for 3-4 minutes until softened.
2. **Add the Garlic and Tomatoes:** Add the minced garlic and cook for another minute. Stir in the diced tomatoes and cook for 5 minutes until they begin to break down.
3. **Add the Broth:** Pour in the chicken or vegetable broth and bring to a boil. Reduce the heat and let it simmer for 15 minutes.
4. **Blend the Soup:** Use an immersion blender to puree the soup until smooth. Alternatively, transfer the soup to a blender in batches and blend until smooth, then return it to the pot.
5. **Add the Cream and Basil:** Stir in the heavy cream, chopped fresh basil, sea salt, black pepper, and red pepper flakes

(if using). Cook for another 5 minutes until heated through.

6. **Serve:** Ladle the soup into bowls and garnish with fresh basil leaves if desired. Serve hot.

Nutritional Facts

- **Calories:** 220 kcal
- **Protein:** 3g
- **Fat:** 18g
- **Saturated Fat:** 9g
- **Cholesterol:** 50mg
- **Sodium:** 900mg
- **Potassium:** 600mg
- **Fiber:** 3g
- **Sugar:** 6g
- **Vitamin C:** 30mg

Cooking Tips

- ✓ **Tomatoes:** Use high-quality canned tomatoes for the best flavor. Fresh tomatoes can also be used if desired.
- ✓ **Blending:** Be cautious when blending hot soup. If using a countertop blender, blend in batches and cover the lid with a kitchen towel to prevent spills.
- ✓ **Cream:** For a dairy-free option, substitute heavy cream with coconut milk.
- ✓ **Serving Suggestions:** Serve with a side of low-carb bread or a fresh green salad for a complete meal.
- ✓ **Storage:** Store any leftovers in an airtight container in the refrigerator for up to 3 days. Reheat gently on the stovetop or in the microwave before serving.

Keto tomato basil soup is a rich and flavorful dish featuring fresh tomatoes and basil blended with creamy broth, perfect for a comforting and low-carb meal.

Recipe 94: Beef and Cabbage Soup

Prep Time: 15 minutes | Cooking Time: 40 minutes | Servings: 4

Ingredients

- 1 tablespoon olive oil
- 1 pound ground beef
- 1 small onion, finely chopped
- 2 cloves garlic, minced
- 2 medium carrots, diced
- 2 celery stalks, diced
- 1 small head of cabbage, chopped
- 4 cups beef broth
- 1 (14.5 oz) can diced tomatoes
- 1 teaspoon dried thyme
- 1 teaspoon dried oregano
- 1/2 teaspoon sea salt
- 1/4 teaspoon black pepper
- 1/4 teaspoon red pepper flakes (optional)
- Fresh parsley, chopped (optional for garnish)

Cooking Instructions

1. **Heat the Oil:** In a large pot, heat the olive oil over medium-high heat. Add the ground beef and cook, breaking it up with a spoon, until browned and cooked through about 5-7 minutes. Drain any excess fat.
2. **Cook the Vegetables:** Add the chopped onion, minced garlic, diced carrots, and diced celery to the pot. Cook for 5-7 minutes until the vegetables are softened.
3. **Add the Cabbage:** Stir in the chopped cabbage and cook for another 5 minutes until it begins to wilt.
4. **Add the Broth and Tomatoes:** Pour in the beef broth and diced tomatoes. Add the dried thyme, dried oregano, sea salt, black pepper, and red pepper flakes if using. Bring to a boil, then reduce the heat and let it simmer for 20-25 minutes until the vegetables are tender.
5. **Serve:** Ladle the soup into bowls and garnish with fresh parsley if desired. Serve hot.

Nutritional Facts

- **Calories:** 250 kcal
- **Protein:** 20g
- **Fat:** 15g
- **Saturated Fat:** 6g
- **Cholesterol:** 60mg
- **Sodium:** 700mg
- **Potassium:** 800mg
- **Fiber:** 4g
- **Sugar:** 6g
- **Vitamin A:** 5000 IU

Cooking Tips

- ✓ **Beef:** Use lean ground beef for a healthier option. Ground turkey or chicken can also be used.
- ✓ **Vegetables:** Feel free to add other vegetables like zucchini, bell peppers, or green beans.
- ✓ **Seasoning:** Adjust the seasoning to your taste. Add more herbs or spices if desired.
- ✓ **Serving Suggestions:** Serve with a side of low-carb bread or a fresh green salad for a complete meal.
- ✓ **Storage:** Store any leftovers in an airtight container in the refrigerator for up to 3 days. Reheat gently on the stovetop or in the microwave before serving.

Beef and cabbage soup is a hearty and comforting dish featuring tender ground beef and fresh vegetables in a flavorful broth, perfect for a nutritious and satisfying low-carb meal.

Recipe 95: Spicy Chicken and Avocado Soup

Prep Time: 15 minutes | Cooking Time: 30 minutes | Servings: 4

Ingredients

- 1 tablespoon olive oil
- 1 small onion, finely chopped
- 2 cloves garlic, minced
- 1 jalapeño, finely chopped (seeds removed for less heat)
- 1-pound boneless, skinless chicken breasts, diced
- 4 cups chicken broth
- 1 (14.5 oz) can diced tomatoes
- 1 teaspoon ground cumin
- 1 teaspoon chili powder
- 1/2 teaspoon sea salt
- 1/4 teaspoon black pepper
- 2 avocados, diced
- 1/4 cup fresh cilantro, chopped
- 1 lime, cut into wedges

Cooking Instructions

1. **Heat the Oil:** In a large pot, heat the olive oil over medium heat. Add the chopped onion and cook for 3-4 minutes until softened.
2. **Add Garlic and Jalapeño:** Add the minced garlic and chopped jalapeño to the pot. Cook for another 1-2 minutes until fragrant.
3. **Cook the Chicken:** Add the diced chicken to the pot and cook for 5-7 minutes until browned and cooked through.
4. **Add Broth and Tomatoes:** Pour in the chicken broth and add the diced tomatoes. Stir in the ground cumin, chili powder, sea salt, and black pepper. Bring to a boil, then reduce the heat and let it simmer for 15-20 minutes.
5. **Add Avocado:** Stir in the diced avocados and cook for another 2-3 minutes until heated through.
6. **Serve:** Ladle the soup into bowls and garnish with fresh cilantro. Serve with lime wedges on the side.

Nutritional Facts

- **Calories:** 300 kcal
- **Protein:** 25g
- **Fat:** 18g
- **Saturated Fat:** 3g
- **Cholesterol:** 50mg
- **Sodium:** 700mg
- **Potassium:** 900mg
- **Fiber:** 7g
- **Sugar:** 3g
- **Vitamin C:** 30mg

Cooking Tips

- ✓ **Chicken:** Use boneless, skinless chicken thighs for a juicier option if preferred.
- ✓ **Heat Level:** Adjust the amount of jalapeño to your taste preference. Remove the seeds for a milder heat.
- ✓ **Avocado:** Add the avocado just before serving to prevent it from becoming too mushy.
- ✓ **Serving Suggestions:** Serve with a side of low-carb tortilla chips or a fresh green salad for a complete meal.
- ✓ **Storage:** Store any leftovers in an airtight container in the refrigerator for up to 2 days. Reheat gently on the stovetop or in the microwave before serving.

Spicy chicken and avocado soup is a flavorful and nutritious dish featuring tender chicken, creamy avocado, and a kick of heat from jalapeños, perfect for a warming and satisfying low-carb meal.

Recipe 96: Cauliflower and Leek Soup

Prep Time: 15 minutes | Cooking Time: 30 minutes | Servings: 4

Ingredients

- 2 tablespoons butter
- 2 leeks, white and light green parts only, cleaned and sliced
- 2 cloves garlic, minced
- 1 large head of cauliflower, cut into florets
- 4 cups chicken or vegetable broth
- 1/2 cup heavy cream
- 1/2 teaspoon sea salt
- 1/4 teaspoon black pepper
- Fresh chives, chopped (optional for garnish)

Cooking Instructions

1. **Heat the Butter:** In a large pot, melt the butter over medium heat. Add the sliced leeks and cook for 5-7 minutes until softened.
2. **Add Garlic and Cauliflower:** Add the minced garlic and cauliflower florets to the pot. Cook for another 3-4 minutes.
3. **Add the Broth:** Pour in the chicken or vegetable broth and bring to a boil. Reduce the heat and let it simmer for 20 minutes until the cauliflower is tender.
4. **Blend the Soup:** Use an immersion blender to puree the soup until smooth. Alternatively, transfer the soup to a blender in batches and blend until smooth, then return it to the pot.
5. **Add Cream and Seasoning:** Stir in the heavy cream, sea salt, and black pepper. Cook for an additional 5 minutes until heated through.

6. **Serve:** Ladle the soup into bowls and garnish with fresh chives if desired. Serve hot.

Nutritional Facts

- **Calories:** 250 kcal
- **Protein:** 4g
- **Fat:** 20g
- **Saturated Fat:** 12g
- **Cholesterol:** 60mg
- **Sodium:** 700mg
- **Potassium:** 600mg
- **Fiber:** 3g
- **Sugar:** 4g
- **Vitamin C:** 40mg

Cooking Tips

- ✓ **Leeks:** Make sure to clean the leeks thoroughly to remove any dirt or sand.
- ✓ **Cauliflower:** Cut the cauliflower into small, even-sized florets for quicker cooking.
- ✓ **Blending:** Be cautious when blending hot soup. If using a countertop blender, blend in batches and cover the lid with a kitchen towel to prevent spills.
- ✓ **Serving Suggestions:** Serve with a side of low-carb bread or a fresh green salad for a complete meal.
- ✓ **Storage:** Store any leftovers in an airtight container in the refrigerator for up to 3 days. Reheat gently on the stovetop or in the microwave before serving.

Cauliflower and leek soup is a smooth and creamy dish featuring tender cauliflower and leeks blended to perfection, perfect for a comforting and healthy low-carb meal.

Recipe 97: Low-Carb Minestrone Soup

Prep Time: 15 minutes | Cooking Time: 30 minutes | Servings: 4

Ingredients

- 2 tablespoons olive oil
- 1 small onion, finely chopped
- 2 cloves garlic, minced
- 2 medium carrots, diced
- 2 celery stalks, diced
- 1 small zucchini, diced
- 1 (14.5 oz) can diced tomatoes
- 4 cups vegetable broth
- 1 teaspoon dried basil
- 1 teaspoon dried oregano
- 1/2 teaspoon sea salt
- 1/4 teaspoon black pepper
- 1 cup green beans, trimmed and cut into 1-inch pieces
- 2 cups fresh spinach, chopped
- 1/4 cup grated Parmesan cheese (optional for garnish)

Cooking Instructions

1. **Heat the Oil:** In a large pot, heat the olive oil over medium heat. Add the chopped onion and cook for 3-4 minutes until softened.
2. **Add Garlic and Vegetables:** Add the minced garlic, diced carrots, and diced celery. Cook for another 5 minutes, stirring occasionally.
3. **Add Zucchini and Tomatoes:** Stir in the diced zucchini and canned diced tomatoes with their juice. Cook for 3-4 minutes until the zucchini begins to soften.
4. **Add Broth and Seasoning:** Pour in the vegetable broth and stir in the dried basil, dried oregano, sea salt, and black pepper.

Bring to a boil, then reduce the heat and let it simmer for 15 minutes.

5. **Add Green Beans and Spinach:** Stir in the green beans and chopped spinach. Cook for another 5 minutes until the vegetables are tender.
6. **Serve:** Ladle the soup into bowls and garnish with grated Parmesan cheese if desired. Serve hot.

Nutritional Facts

- **Calories:** 200 kcal
- **Protein:** 5g
- **Fat:** 10g
- **Saturated Fat:** 2g
- **Cholesterol:** 5mg
- **Sodium:** 700mg
- **Potassium:** 800mg
- **Fiber:** 6g
- **Sugar:** 8g
- **Vitamin C:** 30mg

Cooking Tips

- ✓ **Vegetables:** Feel free to add other low-carb vegetables like bell peppers, mushrooms, or cauliflower for more variety.
- ✓ **Seasoning:** Adjust the herbs and seasoning to your taste. Add a pinch of red pepper flakes for a bit of heat.
- ✓ **Serving Suggestions:** Serve with a side of low-carb bread or a fresh green salad for a complete meal.
- ✓ **Storage:** Store any leftovers in an airtight container in the refrigerator for up to 3 days. Reheat gently on the stovetop or in the microwave before serving.

Low-carb minestrone soup is a hearty and nutritious dish featuring a medley of fresh vegetables in a flavorful broth, perfect for a comforting and healthy low-carb meal.

Recipe 98: Creamy Mushroom Soup

Prep Time: 10 minutes | Cooking Time: 25 minutes | Servings: 4

Ingredients

- 2 tablespoons butter
- 1 small onion, finely chopped
- 2 cloves garlic, minced
- 1-pound mushrooms, sliced (button, cremini, or a mix)
- 4 cups chicken or vegetable broth
- 1 cup heavy cream
- 1 teaspoon dried thyme
- 1/2 teaspoon sea salt
- 1/4 teaspoon black pepper
- 1 tablespoon fresh parsley, chopped (optional for garnish)

Cooking Instructions

1. **Heat the Butter:** In a large pot, melt the butter over medium heat. Add the chopped onion and cook for 3-4 minutes until softened.
2. **Add Garlic and Mushrooms:** Add the minced garlic and sliced mushrooms. Cook for 8-10 minutes until the mushrooms are tender and browned.
3. **Add the Broth:** Pour in the chicken or vegetable broth. Bring to a boil, then reduce the heat and let it simmer for 10 minutes.
4. **Blend the Soup:** Use an immersion blender to puree the soup until smooth. Alternatively, transfer the soup to a blender in batches and blend until smooth, then return it to the pot.
5. **Add the Cream and Seasoning:** Stir in the heavy cream, dried thyme, sea salt, and black pepper. Cook for an additional 5 minutes until heated through.
6. **Serve:** Ladle the soup into bowls and garnish with fresh parsley if desired. Serve hot.

Nutritional Facts

- **Calories:** 300 kcal
- **Protein:** 5g
- **Fat:** 28g
- **Saturated Fat:** 18g
- **Cholesterol:** 90mg
- **Sodium:** 700mg
- **Potassium:** 600mg
- **Fiber:** 2g
- **Sugar:** 4g
- **Vitamin C:** 10mg

Cooking Tips

- ✓ **Mushrooms:** Use a variety of mushrooms for a richer flavor. Button, cremini, and shiitake all work well.
- ✓ **Blending:** Be cautious when blending hot soup. If using a countertop blender, blend in batches and cover the lid with a kitchen towel to prevent spills.
- ✓ **Cream:** For a dairy-free option, substitute heavy cream with coconut milk or almond milk.
- ✓ **Serving Suggestions:** Serve with a side of low-carb bread or a fresh green salad for a complete meal.
- ✓ **Storage:** Store any leftovers in an airtight container in the refrigerator for up to 3 days. Reheat gently on the stovetop or in the microwave before serving.

Creamy mushroom soup is a rich and velvety dish featuring tender mushrooms blended with a creamy broth, perfect for a comforting and delicious low-carb meal.

Recipe 99: Zucchini and Basil Soup

Prep Time: 10 minutes | Cooking Time: 20 minutes | Servings: 4

Ingredients

- 2 tablespoons olive oil
- 1 small onion, finely chopped
- 2 cloves garlic, minced
- 4 medium zucchinis, chopped
- 4 cups chicken or vegetable broth
- 1/2 cup fresh basil leaves
- 1/2 cup heavy cream
- 1/2 teaspoon sea salt
- 1/4 teaspoon black pepper
- Fresh basil leaves for garnish (optional)

Cooking Instructions

1. **Heat the Oil:** In a large pot, heat the olive oil over medium heat. Add the chopped onion and cook for 3-4 minutes until softened.
2. **Add Garlic and Zucchini:** Add the minced garlic and chopped zucchini. Cook for another 5 minutes, stirring occasionally.
3. **Add the Broth:** Pour in the chicken or vegetable broth. Bring to a boil, then reduce the heat and let it simmer for 10-15 minutes until the zucchinis are tender.
4. **Blend the Soup:** Use an immersion blender to puree the soup until smooth. Alternatively, transfer the soup to a blender in batches and blend until smooth, then return it to the pot.
5. **Add the Basil and Cream:** Stir in the fresh basil leaves, heavy cream, sea salt, and black pepper. Cook for an additional 5 minutes until heated through.

6. **Serve:** Ladle the soup into bowls and garnish with fresh basil leaves if desired. Serve hot.

Nutritional Facts

- **Calories:** 250 kcal
- **Protein:** 4g
- **Fat:** 22g
- **Saturated Fat:** 10g
- **Cholesterol:** 50mg
- **Sodium:** 700mg
- **Potassium:** 800mg
- **Fiber:** 3g
- **Sugar:** 5g
- **Vitamin C:** 30mg

Cooking Tips

- ✓ **Zucchini:** Use fresh, firm zucchini for the best flavor and texture. Ensure they are evenly chopped for consistent cooking.
- ✓ **Blending:** Be cautious when blending hot soup. If using a countertop blender, blend in batches and cover the lid with a kitchen towel to prevent spills.
- ✓ **Basil:** Fresh basil adds a vibrant flavor to the soup. Add more or less to suit your taste.
- ✓ **Serving Suggestions:** Serve with a side of low-carb bread or a fresh green salad for a complete meal.
- ✓ **Storage:** Store any leftovers in an airtight container in the refrigerator for up to 3 days. Reheat gently on the stovetop or in the microwave before serving.

Zucchini and basil soup is a light and refreshing dish featuring fresh zucchini blended with fragrant basil, perfect for a healthy and delicious low-carb meal.

Recipe 100: Shrimp and Coconut Milk Soup

Prep Time: 10 minutes | Cooking Time: 20 minutes | Servings: 4

Ingredients

- 1 tablespoon coconut oil
- 1 small onion, finely chopped
- 2 cloves garlic, minced
- 1 tablespoon fresh ginger, minced
- 1 red bell pepper, thinly sliced
- 1-pound large shrimp, peeled and deveined
- 3 cups chicken or vegetable broth
- 1 (14 oz) can full-fat coconut milk
- 1 tablespoon fish sauce
- 1 tablespoon lime juice
- 1 teaspoon red curry paste
- 1/2 teaspoon sea salt
- 1/4 teaspoon black pepper
- 1/4 cup fresh cilantro, chopped (optional for garnish)
- Lime wedges for serving

Cooking Instructions

1. **Heat the Oil:** In a large pot, heat the coconut oil over medium heat. Add the chopped onion and cook for 3-4 minutes until softened.
2. **Add Garlic and Ginger:** Add the minced garlic and fresh ginger to the pot. Cook for another 1-2 minutes until fragrant.
3. **Add Bell Pepper and Shrimp:** Stir in the sliced red bell pepper and shrimp. Cook for 2-3 minutes until the shrimp starts to turn pink.
4. **Add Broth and Coconut Milk:** Pour in the chicken or vegetable broth and coconut milk. Stir in the fish sauce, lime juice, red curry paste, sea salt, and black pepper. Bring to a simmer and cook for 5-7 minutes until the shrimp are fully cooked.

5. **Serve:** Ladle the soup into bowls and garnish with fresh cilantro. Serve with lime wedges on the side.

Nutritional Facts

- **Calories:** 300 kcal
- **Protein:** 20g
- **Fat:** 22g
- **Saturated Fat:** 15g
- **Cholesterol:** 150mg
- **Sodium:** 900mg
- **Potassium:** 500mg
- **Fiber:** 2g
- **Sugar:** 4g
- **Vitamin C:** 30mg

Cooking Tips

- ✓ **Shrimp:** Use fresh or frozen shrimp that have been peeled and deveined. If using frozen shrimp, thaw them completely and pat dry before cooking.
- ✓ **Curry Paste:** Adjust the amount of red curry paste to your taste preference for a spicier or milder soup.
- ✓ **Coconut Milk:** Use full-fat coconut milk for a richer and creamier soup. Light coconut milk can be used as a lower-fat option.
- ✓ **Serving Suggestions:** Serve with a side of cauliflower rice or a fresh green salad for a complete meal.
- ✓ **Storage:** Store any leftovers in an airtight container in the refrigerator for up to 2 days. Reheat gently on the stovetop or in the microwave before serving.

Shrimp and coconut milk soup is a fragrant and flavorful dish featuring tender shrimp simmered in a rich coconut milk broth with vibrant spices, perfect for a comforting and delicious low-carb meal.

Salad Recipes

Recipe 101: Spinach and Strawberry Salad

Prep Time: 10 minutes | Cooking Time: 0 minutes | Servings: 4

Ingredients

- 6 cups fresh spinach leaves
- 1 cup strawberries, sliced
- 1/4 cup red onion, thinly sliced
- 1/4 cup crumbled feta cheese
- 1/4 cup sliced almonds, toasted
- 2 tablespoons balsamic vinegar
- 2 tablespoons olive oil
- 1 teaspoon honey (optional)
- 1/2 teaspoon sea salt
- 1/4 teaspoon black pepper

Nutritional Facts

- **Calories:** 150 kcal
- **Protein:** 4g
- **Fat:** 11g
- **Saturated Fat:** 2g
- **Cholesterol:** 10mg
- **Sodium:** 300mg
- **Potassium:** 500mg
- **Fiber:** 3g
- **Sugar:** 5g
- **Vitamin C:** 45mg

Cooking Instructions

1. **Prepare the Dressing:** In a small bowl, whisk together the balsamic vinegar, olive oil, honey (if using), sea salt, and black pepper.
2. **Combine Salad Ingredients:** In a large bowl, combine the fresh spinach leaves, sliced strawberries, thinly sliced red onion, crumbled feta cheese, and toasted sliced almonds.
3. **Toss the Salad:** Drizzle the dressing over the salad and toss gently to combine.
4. **Serve:** Serve the salad immediately.

Cooking Tips

- ✓ **Spinach:** Use fresh, crisp spinach leaves for the best texture and flavor.
- ✓ **Strawberries:** Choose ripe, sweet strawberries for a natural sweetness.
- ✓ **Nuts:** Toast the sliced almonds in a dry skillet over medium heat for 2-3 minutes until golden and fragrant.
- ✓ **Serving Suggestions:** Serve with grilled chicken or salmon for a complete meal.
- ✓ **Storage:** If making ahead, store the salad ingredients and dressing separately. Toss together just before serving to keep the spinach from wilting.

Spinach and strawberry salad is a fresh and vibrant dish featuring sweet strawberries, tangy feta, and crunchy almonds tossed with a light balsamic vinaigrette, perfect for a healthy and delicious meal.

Recipe 102: Low-Carb Greek Salad

Prep Time: 15 minutes | Cooking Time: 0 minutes | Servings: 4

Ingredients

- 1 large cucumber, diced
- 1 cup cherry tomatoes, halved
- 1/2 red onion, thinly sliced
- 1 green bell pepper, diced
- 1/4 cup Kalamata olives, pitted and halved
- 1/2 cup feta cheese, crumbled
- 2 tablespoons red wine vinegar
- 2 tablespoons olive oil
- 1 teaspoon dried oregano
- 1/2 teaspoon sea salt
- 1/4 teaspoon black pepper

Cooking Instructions

1. **Prepare the Dressing:** In a small bowl, whisk together the red wine vinegar, olive oil, dried oregano, sea salt, and black pepper.
2. **Combine Salad Ingredients:** In a large bowl, combine the diced cucumber, halved cherry tomatoes, thinly sliced red onion, diced green bell pepper, Kalamata olives, and crumbled feta cheese.
3. **Toss the Salad:** Drizzle the dressing over the salad and toss gently to combine.
4. **Serve:** Serve the salad immediately.

Nutritional Facts

- **Calories:** 150 kcal
- **Protein:** 4g
- **Fat:** 12g
- **Saturated Fat:** 4g
- **Cholesterol:** 15mg
- **Sodium:** 500mg
- **Potassium:** 400mg
- **Fiber:** 2g
- **Sugar:** 3g
- **Vitamin C:** 35mg

Cooking Tips

- ✓ **Cucumber:** Use a firm, fresh cucumber for the best texture. Seedless cucumbers work well.
- ✓ **Feta:** Use high-quality feta cheese for a richer flavor. You can use blocks of feta and crumble it yourself for better texture.
- ✓ **Dressing:** Adjust the amount of red wine vinegar and olive oil to taste. Add more oregano if you prefer a stronger herb flavor.
- ✓ **Serving Suggestions:** Serve with grilled chicken, lamb, or fish for a complete meal.
- ✓ **Storage:** If making ahead, store the salad ingredients and dressing separately. Toss together just before serving to keep the vegetables crisp.

Low-carb Greek salad is a refreshing and flavorful dish featuring crunchy vegetables, tangy feta, and briny olives tossed with a simple vinaigrette, perfect for a healthy and satisfying meal.

Recipe 103: Tuna and Avocado Salad

Prep Time: 10 minutes | Cooking Time: 0 minutes | Servings: 4

Ingredients

- 2 (5 oz) cans tuna, drained
- 2 ripe avocados, diced
- 1 cup cherry tomatoes, halved
- 1/4 cup red onion, finely chopped
- 1/4 cup fresh cilantro, chopped
- 2 tablespoons lime juice
- 2 tablespoons olive oil
- 1/2 teaspoon sea salt
- 1/4 teaspoon black pepper

Cooking Instructions

1. **Combine Salad Ingredients:** In a large bowl, combine the drained tuna, diced avocados, halved cherry tomatoes, finely chopped red onion, and fresh cilantro.
2. **Prepare the Dressing:** In a small bowl, whisk together the lime juice, olive oil, sea salt, and black pepper.
3. **Toss the Salad:** Drizzle the dressing over the salad and toss gently to combine.
4. **Serve:** Serve the salad immediately.

Nutritional Facts

- **Calories:** 300 kcal
- **Protein:** 20g
- **Fat:** 22g
- **Saturated Fat:** 3g
- **Cholesterol:** 30mg
- **Sodium:** 500mg
- **Potassium:** 800mg
- **Fiber:** 7g
- **Sugar:** 2g
- **Vitamin C:** 20mg

Cooking Tips

- ✓ **Tuna:** Use high-quality canned tuna in water or oil. Freshly cooked and flaked tuna can also be used.
- ✓ **Avocado:** Choose ripe avocados for a creamy texture. Add them just before serving to prevent browning.
- ✓ **Dressing:** Adjust the amount of lime juice and olive oil to taste. Add more lime juice for extra tanginess.
- ✓ **Serving Suggestions:** Serve with a side of low-carb crackers or on a bed of mixed greens for a complete meal.
- ✓ **Storage:** Store any leftovers in an airtight container in the refrigerator for up to 1 day. The avocado may brown slightly but will still be delicious.

Tuna and avocado salad is a light and nutritious dish featuring protein-rich tuna and creamy avocado tossed with fresh vegetables and a zesty lime dressing, perfect for a healthy and satisfying meal.

Recipe 104: Avocado Chicken Salad with Lime

Prep Time: 15 minutes | Cooking Time: None (use pre-cooked chicken) | Servings: 4

Ingredients

For the Chicken Salad:

- 2 cups cooked chicken breast, shredded or diced (use rotisserie or pre-cooked chicken)
- 2 large avocados, diced
- 1/2 cup red bell pepper, diced
- 1/4 cup red onion, finely chopped
- 1/4 cup fresh cilantro, chopped
- 2 tablespoons green onions, thinly sliced
- 1 cup cherry tomatoes, halved
- Mixed greens or lettuce leaves, for serving

For the Lime Dressing:

- 3 tablespoons fresh lime juice (about 1-2 limes)
- 2 tablespoons olive oil
- 1 teaspoon lime zest
- 1 clove garlic, minced
- 1 tablespoon honey or agave nectar (optional for sweetness)
- Sea salt and black pepper, to taste

Cooking Instructions

1. **Prepare the Chicken Salad:**
   In a large bowl, combine the shredded or diced cooked chicken, diced avocados, diced red bell pepper, finely chopped red onion, chopped cilantro, sliced green onions, and halved cherry tomatoes. Toss gently to combine the ingredients.
2. **Make the Lime Dressing:**
   In a small bowl, whisk together the fresh lime juice, olive oil, lime zest, minced garlic, honey or agave nectar (if using), sea salt, and black pepper until well combined.
   Taste and adjust the seasoning as needed.
3. **Assemble the Salad:**

Pour the lime dressing over the chicken and avocado mixture. Toss gently to coat the ingredients evenly with the dressing.
Serve the salad immediately over a bed of mixed greens or in lettuce leaves for a fresh and light meal.

4. **Serve:**
Divide the salad among four plates or bowls. Serve with extra lime wedges for a burst of fresh lime juice, if desired.
Enjoy a creamy and refreshing chicken salad that's perfect for a healthy lunch or dinner.

Nutritional Facts

- **Calories:** 350 kcal
- **Protein:** 20g
- **Fat:** 26g
- **Saturated Fat:** 4g
- **Cholesterol:** 60mg
- **Sodium:** 250mg
- **Potassium:** 900mg
- **Fiber:** 8g
- **Sugar:** 5g
- **Vitamin C:** 60mg

Cooking Tips

- ✓ **Chicken:** Use rotisserie chicken or leftover cooked chicken for convenience. You can also poach or grill chicken breasts specifically for this recipe.
- ✓ **Avocado:** Choose ripe but firm avocados to ensure they hold their shape in the salad. Add them just before serving to prevent browning.
- ✓ **Dressing:** Adjust the lime juice and honey to your taste. For a spicier version, add a pinch of cayenne pepper or a dash of hot sauce.

Avocado chicken salad with lime is a fresh and creamy dish, featuring tender chicken, ripe avocados, and a zesty lime dressing. This salad is perfect for a light and healthy meal, offering a delicious combination of flavors and textures that's both satisfying and nutritious.

Recipe 105: Blackened Shrimp Salad

Prep Time: 15 minutes | Cooking Time: 10 minutes | Servings: 4

Ingredients

For the Blackened Shrimp:
- 1-pound large shrimp, peeled and deveined
- 2 tablespoons olive oil
- 1 tablespoon smoked paprika
- 1 teaspoon garlic powder
- 1 teaspoon onion powder
- 1 teaspoon dried thyme
- 1 teaspoon dried oregano
- 1/2 teaspoon cayenne pepper (adjust to taste)
- 1/2 teaspoon sea salt
- 1/4 teaspoon black pepper

For the Salad:
- 6 cups mixed greens (such as spinach, arugula, or romaine)
- 1 cup cherry tomatoes, halved
- 1/2 cup cucumber, diced
- 1/4 cup red onion, thinly sliced
- 1/4 cup red bell pepper, diced
- 1 avocado, sliced
- 1/4 cup fresh cilantro, chopped

For the Tangy Avocado Dressing:
- 1 large avocado, peeled and pitted
- 1/4 cup olive oil
- 2 tablespoons fresh lime juice
- 2 tablespoons water
- 1 clove garlic, minced
- 1/2 teaspoon ground cumin
- Sea salt and black pepper, to taste

Cooking Instructions

1. **Prepare the Blackened Shrimp:**
   In a medium bowl, combine the smoked paprika, garlic powder, onion powder, dried thyme, dried oregano, cayenne pepper, sea salt, and black pepper.
   Toss the shrimp in the seasoning mixture until they are evenly coated.

2. **Cook the Shrimp:**
   Heat the olive oil in a large skillet over medium-high heat.
   Add the seasoned shrimp in a single layer and cook for 2-3 minutes per side, or until they are opaque and cooked through. Remove from heat and set aside.

3. **Make the Tangy Avocado Dressing:**
   In a blender or food processor, combine the avocado, olive oil, fresh lime juice, water, minced garlic, ground cumin, sea salt, and black pepper.
   Blend until smooth and creamy. Adjust the seasoning to taste and add more water if needed to achieve your desired consistency.

4. **Assemble the Salad:**
   In a large salad bowl, combine the mixed greens, halved cherry tomatoes, diced cucumber, thinly sliced red onion, diced red bell pepper, and avocado slices.
   Toss gently to mix the ingredients.

5. **Serve:**
   Divide the salad among four plates. Top each salad with a portion of the blackened shrimp. Drizzle with the tangy avocado dressing and garnish with chopped fresh cilantro.
   Serve immediately and enjoy a flavorful and healthy meal.

Nutritional Facts

- **Calories**: 320 kcal
- **Protein**: 18g
- **Fat**: 24g
- **Saturated Fat**: 4g
- **Cholesterol**: 170mg
- **Sodium**: 500mg
- **Potassium**: 900mg
- **Fiber**: 8g
- **Sugar**: 4g
- **Vitamin C**: 50mg

Cooking Tips

✓ **Shrimp**: Use fresh or thawed shrimp for the best flavor and texture. If using frozen shrimp, thaw them completely and pat them dry before seasoning to ensure they cook evenly.

✓ **Seasoning**: Adjust the cayenne pepper in the shrimp seasoning to your preferred level of heat. For a milder flavor, reduce the amount of cayenne or omit it altogether.

Recipe 106: Turkey Cobb Salad

Prep Time: 15 minutes | Cooking Time: 10 minutes | Servings: 4

Ingredients

- 1 pound turkey breast, cooked and diced
- 4 slices bacon, cooked and crumbled
- 4 cups mixed greens (such as spinach, arugula, and romaine)
- 1 avocado, diced
- 1 cup cherry tomatoes, halved
- 2 hard-boiled eggs, chopped
- 1/4 cup blue cheese crumbles (optional)
- 2 tablespoons red wine vinegar
- 2 tablespoons olive oil
- 1 teaspoon Dijon mustard
- 1/2 teaspoon sea salt
- 1/4 teaspoon black pepper

Cooking Instructions

1. **Prepare the Dressing:** In a small bowl, whisk together the red wine vinegar, olive oil, Dijon mustard, sea salt, and black pepper.
2. **Combine Salad Ingredients:** In a large bowl, combine the mixed greens, diced turkey breast, crumbled bacon, diced avocado, halved cherry tomatoes, chopped hard-boiled eggs, and blue cheese crumbles if using.
3. **Toss the Salad:** Drizzle the dressing over the salad and toss gently to combine.
4. **Serve:** Serve the salad immediately.

Nutritional Facts

- **Calories:** 350 kcal
- **Protein:** 25g
- **Fat:** 25g
- **Saturated Fat:** 7g
- **Cholesterol:** 250mg
- **Sodium:** 800mg
- **Potassium:** 700mg
- **Fiber:** 4g
- **Sugar:** 3g
- **Vitamin A:** 1500 IU

Cooking Tips

- ✓ **Turkey:** Use leftover cooked turkey breast or turkey tenderloin. Rotisserie chicken can be used as a substitute.
- ✓ **Bacon:** Cook the bacon until crispy for the best texture. Blot excess grease with a paper towel.
- ✓ **Dressing:** Adjust the amount of red wine vinegar and Dijon mustard to your taste. Add a pinch of sweetener if you prefer a slightly sweeter dressing.
- ✓ **Serving Suggestions:** Serve with a side of low-carb bread or a fresh green smoothie for a complete meal.
- ✓ **Storage:** Store any leftovers in an airtight container in the refrigerator for up to 2 days. Keep the dressing separate and toss just before serving to keep the salad fresh.

Turkey Cobb salad is a hearty and satisfying dish featuring tender turkey, crispy bacon, and fresh vegetables tossed with a tangy Dijon vinaigrette, perfect for a healthy and delicious low-carb meal.

Recipe 107: Cauliflower Potato Salad

Prep Time: 15 minutes | Cooking Time: 10 minutes | Servings: 4

Ingredients

- 1 large head of cauliflower, cut into florets
- 3 hard-boiled eggs, chopped
- 1/2 cup celery, diced
- 1/4 cup red onion, finely chopped
- 1/4 cup dill pickles, diced
- 1/2 cup mayonnaise
- 2 tablespoons Dijon mustard
- 1 tablespoon apple cider vinegar
- 1 teaspoon sea salt
- 1/2 teaspoon black pepper
- 1/4 teaspoon paprika
- Fresh parsley, chopped (optional for garnish)

Cooking Instructions

1. **Cook the Cauliflower:** Bring a large pot of water to a boil. Add the cauliflower florets and cook for 5-7 minutes until tender but still firm. Drain and let cool slightly.
2. **Prepare the Salad:** In a large bowl, combine the cooked cauliflower, chopped hard-boiled eggs, diced celery, finely chopped red onion, and diced dill pickles.
3. **Make the Dressing:** In a small bowl, whisk together the mayonnaise, Dijon mustard, apple cider vinegar, sea salt, black pepper, and paprika.
4. **Combine and Toss:** Pour the dressing over the cauliflower mixture and toss gently to combine.

5. **Serve:** Garnish with fresh parsley if desired. Serve the salad immediately or chill in the refrigerator for 1-2 hours for the flavors to meld.

Nutritional Facts

- **Calories:** 250 kcal
- **Protein:** 5g
- **Fat:** 22g
- **Saturated Fat:** 4g
- **Cholesterol:** 120mg
- **Sodium:** 900mg
- **Potassium:** 400mg
- **Fiber:** 3g
- **Sugar:** 3g
- **Vitamin C:** 45mg

Cooking Tips

- ✓ **Cauliflower:** Cook the cauliflower until tender but not mushy to maintain a potato-like texture.
- ✓ **Eggs:** Use fresh, hard-boiled eggs for the best flavor and texture.
- ✓ **Dressing:** Adjust the amount of mayonnaise and Dijon mustard to your taste. Add more vinegar for extra tanginess.
- ✓ **Serving Suggestions:** Serve as a side dish with grilled meats or as part of a picnic spread.
- ✓ **Storage:** Store any leftovers in an airtight container in the refrigerator for up to 2 days. The flavors will continue to develop as it chills.

Cauliflower potato salad is a delicious low-carb alternative to traditional potato salad, featuring tender cauliflower and fresh vegetables tossed in a creamy dressing, perfect for a healthy and satisfying side dish.

Recipe 108: Egg and Cucumber Salad

Prep Time: 10 minutes | Cooking Time: 10 minutes | Servings: 4

Ingredients

- 6 hard-boiled eggs, chopped
- 1 large cucumber, diced
- 1/4 cup red onion, finely chopped
- 1/4 cup fresh dill, chopped
- 1/2 cup Greek yogurt
- 1 tablespoon Dijon mustard
- 1 tablespoon lemon juice
- 1/2 teaspoon sea salt
- 1/4 teaspoon black pepper

Cooking Instructions

1. **Prepare the Salad Ingredients:** In a large bowl, combine the chopped hard-boiled eggs, diced cucumber, finely chopped red onion, and chopped fresh dill.
2. **Make the Dressing:** In a small bowl, whisk together the Greek yogurt, Dijon mustard, lemon juice, sea salt, and black pepper.
3. **Combine and Toss:** Pour the dressing over the salad ingredients and toss gently to combine.
4. **Serve:** Serve the salad immediately or chill in the refrigerator for 1-2 hours for the flavors to meld.

Nutritional Facts

- **Calories:** 150 kcal
- **Protein:** 10g
- **Fat:** 10g
- **Saturated Fat:** 3g
- **Cholesterol:** 220mg
- **Sodium:** 450mg
- **Potassium:** 300mg
- **Fiber:** 1g
- **Sugar:** 3g
- **Vitamin C:** 8mg

Cooking Tips

- ✓ **Eggs:** Use fresh, hard-boiled eggs for the best flavor and texture.
- ✓ **Cucumber:** Choose a firm, fresh cucumber for a crisp texture. Seedless cucumbers work well.
- ✓ **Dressing:** Adjust the amount of Greek yogurt and Dijon mustard to your taste. Add more lemon juice for extra tanginess.
- ✓ **Serving Suggestions:** Serve as a side dish with grilled meats or as a light lunch on its own.
- ✓ **Storage:** Store any leftovers in an airtight container in the refrigerator for up to 2 days. The flavors will continue to develop as it chills.

Egg and cucumber salad is a light and refreshing dish featuring protein-rich eggs and crisp cucumber tossed in a tangy Greek yogurt dressing, perfect for a healthy and satisfying low-carb meal.

Recipe 109: Asian Chicken Salad

Prep Time: 20 minutes | Cooking Time: 10 minutes | Servings: 4

Ingredients

- 1-pound boneless, skinless chicken breasts
- 4 cups mixed greens (such as spinach, arugula, and romaine)
- 1 cup shredded red cabbage
- 1 cup shredded carrots
- 1 red bell pepper, thinly sliced
- 1/4 cup fresh cilantro, chopped
- 1/4 cup green onions, sliced
- 1/4 cup slivered almonds, toasted
- 1 tablespoon olive oil
- 1/2 teaspoon sea salt
- 1/4 teaspoon black pepper

For the Dressing:

- 3 tablespoons soy sauce (or tamari for gluten-free)
- 2 tablespoons rice vinegar
- 1 tablespoon sesame oil
- 1 tablespoon olive oil
- 1 tablespoon lime juice
- 1 teaspoon honey (optional)
- 1 teaspoon fresh ginger, minced
- 1 clove garlic, minced

Cooking Instructions

1. **Cook the Chicken:** Season the chicken breasts with sea salt and black pepper. In a skillet, heat 1 tablespoon of olive oil over medium-high heat. Cook the chicken for 6-7 minutes on each side until fully cooked. Remove from the skillet and let it rest for a few minutes before slicing.
2. **Prepare the Dressing:** In a small bowl, whisk together the soy sauce, rice vinegar, sesame oil, olive oil, lime juice, honey (if using), minced ginger, and minced garlic.
3. **Combine Salad Ingredients:** In a large bowl, combine the mixed greens, shredded red cabbage, shredded carrots, thinly sliced red bell pepper, chopped cilantro, and sliced green onions.
4. **Add the Chicken:** Slice the cooked chicken breasts and add them to the salad.
5. **Toss the Salad:** Drizzle the dressing over the salad and toss gently to combine.
6. **Serve:** Sprinkle the toasted slivered almonds on top and serve the salad immediately.

Nutritional Facts

- **Calories:** 350 kcal
- **Protein:** 30g
- **Fat:** 20g
- **Saturated Fat:** 3g
- **Cholesterol:** 75mg
- **Sodium:** 800mg
- **Potassium:** 900mg
- **Fiber:** 5g
- **Sugar:** 6g
- **Vitamin C:** 45mg

Cooking Tips

- ✓ **Chicken:** Ensure the chicken is fully cooked by checking for an internal temperature of 165°F (75°C).
- ✓ **Vegetables:** Use fresh, crisp vegetables for the best texture and flavor. Feel free to add other vegetables like cucumber or snap peas.
- ✓ **Dressing:** Adjust the amount of soy sauce and rice vinegar to taste. Add more honey for a sweeter dressing.
- ✓ **Serving Suggestions:** Serve with a side of low-carb noodles or a fresh green smoothie for a complete meal.

Asian chicken salad is a vibrant and flavorful dish featuring tender chicken and fresh vegetables tossed with a zesty sesame-ginger dressing, perfect for a healthy and satisfying low-carb meal.

Recipe 110: Avocado and Tomato Salad

Prep Time: 10 minutes | Cooking Time: 0 minutes | Servings: 4

Ingredients

- 2 large avocados, diced
- 1-pint cherry tomatoes, halved
- 1/4 red onion, thinly sliced
- 1/4 cup fresh basil leaves, chopped
- 2 tablespoons olive oil
- 1 tablespoon balsamic vinegar
- 1/2 teaspoon sea salt
- 1/4 teaspoon black pepper

Cooking Instructions

1. **Combine Salad Ingredients:** In a large bowl, combine the diced avocados, halved cherry tomatoes, thinly sliced red onion, and chopped fresh basil leaves.
2. **Prepare the Dressing:** In a small bowl, whisk together the olive oil, balsamic vinegar, sea salt, and black pepper.
3. **Toss the Salad:** Drizzle the dressing over the salad and toss gently to combine.
4. **Serve:** Serve the salad immediately.

Nutritional Facts

- **Calories:** 200 kcal
- **Protein:** 2g
- **Fat:** 18g
- **Saturated Fat:** 2.5g
- **Cholesterol:** 0mg
- **Sodium:** 300mg
- **Potassium:** 600mg
- **Fiber:** 6g
- **Sugar:** 3g
- **Vitamin C:** 20mg

Cooking Tips

- ✓ **Avocado:** Use ripe avocados for the best texture and flavor. Add them just before serving to prevent browning.
- ✓ **Tomatoes:** Use fresh, ripe cherry tomatoes for a sweet and juicy flavor.
- ✓ **Dressing:** Adjust the amount of balsamic vinegar and olive oil to taste. Add a pinch of sweetener if you prefer a slightly sweeter dressing.
- ✓ **Serving Suggestions:** Serve as a side dish with grilled chicken or fish or enjoy on your own as a light meal.
- ✓ **Storage:** Store any leftovers in an airtight container in the refrigerator for up to 1 day. The avocado may brown slightly but will still be delicious.

Avocado and tomato salad is a fresh and flavorful dish featuring creamy avocado and juicy tomatoes tossed with a simple balsamic vinaigrette, perfect for a healthy and satisfying low-carb meal.

High Protein Recipes

Recipe 111: Grilled Chicken Breast with Quinoa

Prep Time: 15 minutes | Cooking Time: 20 minutes | Servings: 4

Ingredients

For the Chicken:

- 4 boneless, skinless chicken breasts
- 2 tablespoons olive oil
- 1 tablespoon lemon juice
- 2 cloves garlic, minced
- 1 teaspoon dried thyme
- 1 teaspoon dried oregano
- 1/2 teaspoon sea salt
- 1/4 teaspoon black pepper

For the Quinoa:

- 1 cup quinoa, rinsed
- 2 cups chicken broth or water
- 1/2 teaspoon sea salt

For the Garnish:

- 1/4 cup fresh parsley, chopped
- Lemon wedges (optional)

Cooking Instructions

1. **Marinate the Chicken:** In a large bowl, combine the olive oil, lemon juice, minced garlic, dried thyme, dried oregano, sea salt, and black pepper. Add the chicken breasts and toss to coat. Marinate for at least 15 minutes.
2. **Cook the Quinoa:** In a medium saucepan, bring the chicken broth or water and sea salt to a boil. Add the rinsed quinoa, reduce the heat to low, cover, and simmer for 15-20 minutes until the quinoa is tender and the liquid is absorbed. Fluff with a fork and set aside.
3. **Grill the Chicken:** Preheat your grill to medium-high heat. Grill the marinated chicken breasts for 6-7 minutes on each side or until the internal temperature reaches 165°F (75°C). Remove from the grill and let rest for a few minutes before slicing.
4. **Serve:** Divide the quinoa among four plates. Top with sliced grilled chicken. Garnish with fresh parsley and lemon wedges if desired. Serve hot.

Nutritional Facts

- **Calories:** 350 kcal
- **Protein:** 35g
- **Fat:** 12g
- **Saturated Fat:** 2g
- **Cholesterol:** 75mg
- **Sodium:** 700mg
- **Potassium:** 700mg
- **Fiber:** 3g
- **Sugar:** 1g
- **Vitamin C:** 10mg

Cooking Tips

- ✓ **Chicken:** Ensure the chicken is fully cooked by checking for an internal temperature of 165°F (75°C).
- ✓ **Quinoa:** Rinse the quinoa thoroughly before cooking to remove the natural coating that can make it taste not very pleasant.
- ✓ **Marinating:** The longer you marinate the chicken, the more flavorful it will be. Marinate for up to 2 hours if time allows.

Grilled chicken breast with quinoa is a healthy and balanced meal featuring juicy marinated chicken served over fluffy quinoa, perfect for a nutritious and satisfying low-carb dish.

Recipe 112: Baked Tofu with Broccoli

Prep Time: 10 minutes | Cooking Time: 30 minutes | Servings: 4

Ingredients

- 1 (14 oz) block of firm tofu, drained and pressed
- 2 tablespoons soy sauce (or tamari for gluten-free)
- 1 tablespoon olive oil
- 1 tablespoon rice vinegar
- 2 cloves garlic, minced
- 1 teaspoon fresh ginger, minced
- 1/2 teaspoon sea salt
- 1/4 teaspoon black pepper
- 1 large head of broccoli, cut into florets
- 2 tablespoons sesame seeds (optional for garnish)

Cooking Instructions

1. **Preheat the Oven:** Preheat your oven to 400°F (200°C). Line a baking sheet with parchment paper.
2. **Prepare the Tofu:** Cut the pressed tofu into 1-inch cubes. In a large bowl, combine the soy sauce, olive oil, rice vinegar, minced garlic, minced ginger, sea salt, and black pepper. Add the tofu cubes and toss to coat evenly. Let it marinate for at least 10 minutes.
3. **Bake the Tofu:** Spread the marinated tofu cubes in a single layer on one-half of the prepared baking sheet. Bake in the preheated oven for 10 minutes.
4. **Add the Broccoli:** After 10 minutes, remove the baking sheet from the oven and add the broccoli florets to the other half of the baking sheet. Drizzle with a bit of olive oil and sprinkle with sea salt and black pepper. Return to the oven and bake for an additional 20 minutes or until the tofu is golden and the broccoli is tender.
5. **Serve:** Divide the baked tofu and broccoli among four plates. Garnish with sesame seeds if desired. Serve hot.

Nutritional Facts

- **Calories:** 200 kcal
- **Protein:** 12g
- **Fat:** 12g
- **Saturated Fat:** 2g
- **Cholesterol:** 0mg
- **Sodium:** 700mg
- **Potassium:** 600mg
- **Fiber:** 5g
- **Sugar:** 2g
- **Vitamin C:** 90mg

Cooking Tips

- ✓ **Tofu:** Press the tofu well to remove excess moisture, which helps it absorb the marinade better and achieve a firmer texture.
- ✓ **Broccoli:** Cut the broccoli into even-sized florets to ensure they cook evenly.
- ✓ **Marinating:** For more flavorful tofu, marinate for up to 30 minutes if time allows.
- ✓ **Serving Suggestions:** Serve with a side of cauliflower rice or a fresh salad for a complete meal.
- ✓ **Storage:** Store any leftovers in an airtight container in the refrigerator for up to 3 days. Reheat gently in the microwave or oven before serving.

Baked tofu with broccoli is a simple and nutritious dish featuring marinated tofu cubes and tender broccoli florets baked to perfection, perfect for a healthy and satisfying low-carb meal.

Recipe 113: Steak and Asparagus

Prep Time: 10 minutes | Cooking Time: 15 minutes | Servings: 4

Ingredients

- 4 (6 oz) sirloin steaks
- 2 tablespoons olive oil
- 2 cloves garlic, minced
- 1 tablespoon fresh rosemary, chopped
- 1 tablespoon fresh thyme, chopped
- 1 teaspoon sea salt
- 1/2 teaspoon black pepper
- 1 pound asparagus, trimmed
- 1 lemon, cut into wedges (optional for serving)

Cooking Instructions

1. **Prepare the Steaks:** Pat the steaks dry with paper towels. In a small bowl, combine the olive oil, minced garlic, chopped rosemary, chopped thyme, sea salt, and black pepper. Rub the mixture all over the steaks.
2. **Preheat the Grill:** Preheat your grill to medium-high heat. If using a stovetop, heat a grill pan over medium-high heat.
3. **Cook the Steaks:** Grill the steaks for 4-5 minutes per side or until they reach your desired level of doneness. Remove from the grill and let them rest for a few minutes before slicing.
4. **Cook the Asparagus:** While the steaks are resting, toss the asparagus with a little olive oil, sea salt, and black pepper. Grill the asparagus for 3-4 minutes, turning occasionally, until tender and slightly charred.
5. **Serve:** Slice the steaks against the grain and serve with the grilled asparagus. Garnish with lemon wedges if desired.

Nutritional Facts

- **Calories:** 350 kcal
- **Protein:** 30g
- **Fat:** 20g
- **Saturated Fat:** 5g
- **Cholesterol:** 90mg
- **Sodium:** 600mg
- **Potassium:** 800mg
- **Fiber:** 3g
- **Sugar:** 2g
- **Vitamin C:** 20mg

Cooking Tips

- ✓ **Steak:** For the best flavor, allow the steaks to come to room temperature before grilling. Use a meat thermometer to check for doneness: 130°F (54°C) for medium-rare, 140°F (60°C) for medium, and 150°F (66°C) for medium-well.
- ✓ **Asparagus:** Choose fresh, thin asparagus spears for the best texture. Thicker spears may need a bit more cooking time.
- ✓ **Serving Suggestions:** Serve with a side of cauliflower mash or a fresh green salad for a complete meal.
- ✓ **Storage:** Store any leftovers in an airtight container in the refrigerator for up to 2 days. Reheat gently in the microwave or on the stovetop before serving.

Steak and asparagus is a simple and elegant dish featuring juicy grilled sirloin steaks paired with tender asparagus, perfect for a healthy and satisfying low-carb meal.

Recipe 114: Turkey and Spinach Meatloaf

Prep Time: 15 minutes | Cooking Time: 45 minutes | Servings: 4

Ingredients

- 1 pound ground turkey
- 1 cup fresh spinach, finely chopped
- 1/2 cup almond flour
- 1/4 cup grated Parmesan cheese
- 1 small onion, finely chopped
- 2 cloves garlic, minced
- 1 large egg
- 2 tablespoons tomato paste
- 1 tablespoon Worcestershire sauce
- 1 teaspoon dried oregano
- 1 teaspoon dried basil
- 1/2 teaspoon sea salt
- 1/4 teaspoon black pepper

Cooking Instructions

1. **Preheat the Oven:** Preheat your oven to 375°F (190°C). Line a loaf pan with parchment paper or lightly grease it.
2. **Prepare the Meatloaf Mixture:** In a large bowl, combine the ground turkey, chopped spinach, almond flour, grated Parmesan cheese, chopped onion, minced garlic, egg, tomato paste, Worcestershire sauce, dried oregano, dried basil, sea salt, and black pepper. Mix until well combined.
3. **Shape the Meatloaf:** Transfer the mixture to the prepared loaf pan and shape it into a loaf.
4. **Bake:** Bake in the preheated oven for 45-50 minutes, or until the internal temperature reaches 165°F (75°C) and the meatloaf is cooked through.

5. **Rest and Serve:** Let the meatloaf rest for 10 minutes before slicing. Serve hot.

Nutritional Facts

- **Calories:** 300 kcal
- **Protein:** 28g
- **Fat:** 15g
- **Saturated Fat:** 3g
- **Cholesterol:** 120mg
- **Sodium:** 600mg
- **Potassium:** 700mg
- **Fiber:** 2g
- **Sugar:** 3g
- **Vitamin A:** 1500 IU

Cooking Tips

- ✓ **Turkey:** Use lean ground turkey for a healthier option or a mix of lean and regular ground turkey for a juicier meatloaf.
- ✓ **Spinach:** Ensure the spinach is finely chopped to distribute evenly throughout the meatloaf.
- ✓ **Resting:** Allow the meatloaf to rest before slicing to help it hold together better.
- ✓ **Serving Suggestions:** Serve with a side of mashed cauliflower or roasted vegetables for a complete meal.
- ✓ **Storage:** Store any leftovers in an airtight container in the refrigerator for up to 3 days. Reheat gently in the microwave or oven before serving.

Turkey and spinach meatloaf is a healthy and flavorful dish featuring lean ground turkey and fresh spinach combined with savory herbs and Parmesan cheese, perfect for a nutritious and satisfying low-carb meal.

Recipe 115: Shrimp and Avocado Salad

Prep Time: 15 minutes | Cooking Time: 5 minutes | Servings: 4

Ingredients

- 1-pound large shrimp, peeled and deveined
- 1 tablespoon olive oil
- 1/2 teaspoon sea salt
- 1/4 teaspoon black pepper
- 2 avocados, diced
- 1 cup cherry tomatoes, halved
- 1/4 red onion, thinly sliced
- 1/4 cup fresh cilantro, chopped
- 1 tablespoon lime juice
- 1 tablespoon olive oil
- 1/2 teaspoon sea salt
- 1/4 teaspoon black pepper

Cooking Instructions

1. **Cook the Shrimp:** In a large skillet, heat 1 tablespoon of olive oil over medium-high heat. Season the shrimp with 1/2 teaspoon sea salt and 1/4 teaspoon black pepper. Cook the shrimp for 2-3 minutes on each side until pink and opaque. Remove from heat and let cool slightly.
2. **Prepare the Salad:** In a large bowl, combine the diced avocados, halved cherry tomatoes, thinly sliced red onion, and chopped fresh cilantro.
3. **Make the Dressing:** In a small bowl, whisk together the lime juice, 1 tablespoon olive oil, 1/2 teaspoon sea salt, and 1/4 teaspoon black pepper.
4. **Combine and Toss:** Add the cooked shrimp to the salad bowl. Drizzle the dressing over the salad and toss gently to combine.
5. **Serve:** Serve the salad immediately.

Nutritional Facts

- **Calories:** 300 kcal
- **Protein:** 20g
- **Fat:** 22g
- **Saturated Fat:** 3g
- **Cholesterol:** 150mg
- **Sodium:** 700mg
- **Potassium:** 800mg
- **Fiber:** 7g
- **Sugar:** 3g
- **Vitamin C:** 20mg

Cooking Tips

- ✓ **Shrimp:** Use fresh or frozen shrimp that have been peeled and deveined. If using frozen shrimp, thaw them completely and pat dry before cooking.
- ✓ **Avocado:** Choose ripe avocados for a creamy texture. Add them just before serving to prevent browning.
- ✓ **Dressing:** Adjust the amount of lime juice and olive oil to taste. Add a pinch of cayenne pepper for a spicy kick.
- ✓ **Serving Suggestions:** Serve with a side of low-carb tortilla chips or on a bed of mixed greens for a complete meal.
- ✓ **Storage:** Store any leftovers in an airtight container in the refrigerator for up to 1 day. The avocado may brown slightly but will still be delicious.

Shrimp and avocado salad is a fresh and nutritious dish featuring tender shrimp and creamy avocado tossed with cherry tomatoes and red onion in a zesty lime dressing, perfect for a healthy and satisfying low-carb meal.

Recipe 116: Chicken and Veggie Skewers

Prep Time: 20 minutes | Cooking Time: 10 minutes | Servings: 4

Ingredients

- 1-pound boneless, skinless chicken breasts cut into 1-inch cubes
- 1 red bell pepper, cut into 1-inch pieces
- 1 yellow bell pepper, cut into 1-inch pieces
- 1 zucchini, sliced into 1/2-inch rounds
- 1 red onion, cut into 1-inch pieces
- 1/4 cup olive oil
- 2 tablespoons lemon juice
- 2 cloves garlic, minced
- 1 teaspoon dried oregano
- 1 teaspoon dried thyme
- 1/2 teaspoon sea salt
- 1/4 teaspoon black pepper
- Wooden or metal skewers

Cooking Instructions

1. **Marinate the Chicken:** In a large bowl, combine the olive oil, lemon juice, minced garlic, dried oregano, dried thyme, sea salt, and black pepper. Add the chicken cubes and toss to coat. Marinate for at least 15 minutes.
2. **Prepare the Skewers:** If using wooden skewers, soak them in water for at least 30 minutes to prevent burning. Thread the marinated chicken, red bell pepper pieces, yellow bell pepper pieces, zucchini slices, and red onion pieces onto the skewers, alternating as you go.
3. **Preheat the Grill:** Preheat your grill to medium-high heat. If using a stovetop, heat a grill pan over medium-high heat.
4. **Cook the Skewers:** Grill the skewers for 4-5 minutes on each side or until the chicken is cooked through and the vegetables are tender and slightly charred. Ensure the internal temperature of the chicken reaches 165°F (75°C).
5. **Serve:** Transfer the skewers to a serving platter. Serve hot with lemon wedges if desired.

Nutritional Facts

- **Calories:** 300 kcal
- **Protein:** 25g
- **Fat:** 18g
- **Saturated Fat:** 3g
- **Cholesterol:** 75mg
- **Sodium:** 500mg
- **Potassium:** 700mg
- **Fiber:** 3g
- **Sugar:** 5g
- **Vitamin C:** 80mg

Cooking Tips

- ✓ **Chicken:** Ensure the chicken cubes are cut into even-sized pieces for uniform cooking.
- ✓ **Vegetables:** Feel free to add other vegetables like cherry tomatoes or mushrooms to the skewers.
- ✓ **Marinating:** For more flavorful chicken, marinate for up to 2 hours if time allows.
- ✓ **Serving Suggestions:** Serve with a side of cauliflower rice or a fresh green salad for a complete meal.
- ✓ **Storage:** Store any leftovers in an airtight container in the refrigerator for up to 2 days. Reheat gently on the grill or in the microwave before serving.

Chicken and veggie skewers are a flavorful and colorful dish featuring marinated chicken and fresh vegetables grilled to perfection, perfect for a healthy and satisfying low-carb meal.

Recipe 117: Low-Carb Protein Smoothie

Prep Time: 5 minutes | Cooking Time: 0 minutes | Servings: 2

Ingredients

- 1 cup unsweetened almond milk
- 1/2 cup Greek yogurt
- 1 scoop vanilla protein powder
- 1/2 avocado
- 1/2 cup frozen berries (such as strawberries, blueberries, or raspberries)
- 1 tablespoon chia seeds
- 1 tablespoon almond butter
- 1/2 teaspoon vanilla extract
- Ice cubes (optional for thicker consistency)

Cooking Instructions

1. **Blend Ingredients:** In a blender, combine the unsweetened almond milk, Greek yogurt, vanilla protein powder, avocado, frozen berries, chia seeds, almond butter, and vanilla extract. Add a few ice cubes if you prefer a thicker smoothie.
2. **Blend Until Smooth:** Blend on high speed until smooth and creamy.
3. **Serve:** Pour the smoothie into two glasses and serve immediately.

Nutritional Facts

- **Calories:** 250 kcal
- **Protein:** 20g
- **Fat:** 15g
- **Saturated Fat:** 2g
- **Cholesterol:** 15mg
- **Sodium:** 150mg
- **Potassium:** 500mg
- **Fiber:** 7g
- **Sugar:** 5g
- **Vitamin C:** 10mg

Cooking Tips

- ✓ **Protein Powder:** Choose a high-quality vanilla protein powder that suits your dietary preferences (whey, plant-based, etc.).
- ✓ **Avocado:** Use a ripe avocado for a creamy texture and add healthy fats.
- ✓ **Sweetness:** Adjust the sweetness by adding a natural sweetener like stevia or a little more fruit if desired.
- ✓ **Serving Suggestions:** Enjoy as a quick breakfast or post-workout snack. Top with extra chia seeds or fresh berries for added texture.
- ✓ **Storage:** Smoothies are best enjoyed fresh, but you can store any leftovers in an airtight container in the refrigerator for up to 1 day. Shake or blend again before drinking.

Low-carb protein smoothies are a quick and nutritious option featuring a blend of healthy fats, protein, and fiber, perfect for a satisfying and refreshing low-carb meal or snack.

Recipe 118: Almond-Crusted Salmon

Prep Time: 10 minutes | Cooking Time: 20 minutes | Servings: 4

Ingredients

- 4 salmon fillets (about 6 oz each)
- 1/2 cup almond flour
- 1/4 cup grated Parmesan cheese
- 2 tablespoons fresh parsley, chopped
- 1 teaspoon lemon zest
- 1/2 teaspoon sea salt
- 1/4 teaspoon black pepper
- 1 tablespoon Dijon mustard
- 1 tablespoon olive oil
- Lemon wedges (optional for serving)

Cooking Instructions

1. **Preheat the Oven:** Preheat your oven to 400°F (200°C). Line a baking sheet with parchment paper.

2. **Prepare the Crust:** In a small bowl, combine the almond flour, grated Parmesan cheese, chopped fresh parsley, lemon zest, sea salt, and black pepper.

3. **Coat the Salmon:** Brush each salmon fillet with Dijon mustard, then press the almond flour mixture onto the top of each fillet to form a crust.

4. **Bake:** Place the coated salmon fillets on the prepared baking sheet. Drizzle with olive oil and bake in the preheated oven for 15-20 minutes, or until the salmon is cooked through and the crust is golden brown.

5. **Serve:** Serve the almond-crusted salmon with lemon wedges if desired.

Nutritional Facts

- **Calories:** 350 kcal
- **Protein:** 30g
- **Fat:** 22g
- **Saturated Fat:** 4g
- **Cholesterol:** 70mg
- **Sodium:** 500mg
- **Potassium:** 800mg
- **Fiber:** 3g
- **Sugar:** 1g
- **Vitamin C:** 8mg

Cooking Tips

✓ **Salmon:** Use fresh, high-quality salmon fillets for the best flavor. You can also use other types of fishlike cod or tilapia.

✓ **Almond Flour:** Ensure the almond flour is finely ground for a smoother crust. You can also use crushed almonds for a chunkier texture.

✓ **Lemon Zest:** Fresh lemon zest adds a bright flavor to the crust. Use a microplane to finely grate the zest.

✓ **Serving Suggestions:** Serve with a side of roasted vegetables or a fresh green salad for a complete meal.

Almond-crusted salmon is a delicious and healthy dish featuring tender salmon fillets with a crunchy almond and Parmesan crust, perfect for a nutritious and satisfying low-carb meal.

Recipe 119: Beef and Cauliflower Stir-Fry

Prep Time: 15 minutes | Cooking Time: 15 minutes | Servings: 4

Ingredients

- 1 pound flank steak, thinly sliced
- 1 large head of cauliflower, riced
- 2 tablespoons olive oil, divided
- 1 small onion, thinly sliced
- 2 cloves garlic, minced
- 1 red bell pepper, thinly sliced
- 1 cup snap peas, trimmed
- 3 tablespoons soy sauce (or tamari for gluten-free)
- 1 tablespoon oyster sauce
- 1 tablespoon rice vinegar
- 1 teaspoon sesame oil
- 1/4 teaspoon red pepper flakes (optional)
- 1/4 cup green onions, sliced
- 1 tablespoon sesame seeds (optional for garnish)

Cooking Instructions

1. **Prepare the Cauliflower Rice:** Cut the cauliflower into florets and pulse in a food processor until it resembles rice. Set it aside.

2. **Cook the Beef:** In a large skillet or wok, heat 1 tablespoon of olive oil over medium-high heat. Add the thinly sliced flank steak and cook for 3-4 minutes until browned and cooked through. Remove the beef from the skillet and set aside.

3. **Cook the Vegetables:** In the same skillet, add the remaining tablespoon of olive oil. Add the sliced onion, minced garlic, red bell pepper, and snap peas. Cook for 5-6 minutes until the vegetables are tender-crisp.

4. **Add the Cauliflower Rice:** Stir in the riced cauliflower and cook for another 3-4 minutes until tender.

5. **Combine and Season:** Return the cooked beef to the skillet. Add the soy sauce, oyster sauce, rice vinegar, sesame oil, and red pepper flakes if using. Toss everything together and cook for another 2 minutes until heated through.

6. **Serve:** Garnish with sliced green onions and sesame seeds if desired. Serve hot.

Nutritional Facts

- **Calories:** 350 kcal
- **Protein:** 25g
- **Fat:** 18g
- **Saturated Fat:** 4g
- **Cholesterol:** 70mg
- **Sodium:** 800mg
- **Potassium:** 800mg
- **Fiber:** 5g
- **Sugar:** 5g
- **Vitamin C:** 70mg

Cooking Tips

- ✓ **Beef:** Ensure the flank steak is thinly sliced against the grain for a tender texture. Partially freeze the steak for easier slicing.

- ✓ **Vegetables:** Use fresh, crisp vegetables for the best texture and flavor. Feel free to add or substitute other low-carb vegetables like broccoli or zucchini.

- ✓ **Sauces:** Adjust the amount of soy sauce and oyster sauce to taste. For a gluten-free option, use tamari and gluten-free oyster sauce.

Beef and cauliflower stir-fry is a flavorful and nutritious dish featuring tender beef and fresh vegetables tossed with cauliflower rice and a savory sauce, perfect for a healthy and satisfying low-carb meal.

Recipe 120: Spicy Tuna Steaks

Prep Time: 10 minutes | Cooking Time: 10 minutes | Servings: 4

Ingredients

- 4 (6 oz) tuna steaks
- 2 tablespoons olive oil
- 2 tablespoons soy sauce (or tamari for gluten-free)
- 1 tablespoon lime juice
- 1 tablespoon Sriracha sauce
- 2 cloves garlic, minced
- 1 teaspoon fresh ginger, minced
- 1/2 teaspoon sea salt
- 1/4 teaspoon black pepper
- 1/4 cup green onions, sliced (optional for garnish)
- Lime wedges (optional for serving)

Cooking Instructions

1. **Marinate the Tuna:** In a small bowl, combine the olive oil, soy sauce, lime juice, Sriracha sauce, minced garlic, minced ginger, sea salt, and black pepper. Place the tuna steaks in a shallow dish and pour the marinade over them, turning to coat. Marinate for at least 10 minutes.

2. **Preheat the Grill or Pan:** Preheat your grill to medium-high heat. If using a stovetop, heat a grill pan or skillet over medium-high heat.

3. **Cook the Tuna Steaks:** Remove the tuna steaks from the marinade, shaking off any excess. Grill the tuna steaks for 2-3 minutes on each side for medium-rare, or longer if desired. The outside should be seared, and the inside should remain pink.

4. **Serve:** Transfer the tuna steaks to a serving platter. Garnish with sliced green onions and lime wedges if desired. Serve hot.

Nutritional Facts

- **Calories:** 300 kcal
- **Protein:** 40g
- **Fat:** 15g
- **Saturated Fat:** 2g
- **Cholesterol:** 70mg
- **Sodium:** 600mg
- **Potassium:** 800mg
- **Fiber:** 1g
- **Sugar:** 1g
- **Vitamin C:** 10mg

Cooking Tips

- ✓ **Tuna:** Choose high-quality, sushi-grade tuna for the best flavor and texture. Adjust the cooking time based on your preferred doneness.

- ✓ **Marinating:** Marinate the tuna for up to 30 minutes for a more intense flavor. Avoid marinating for too long, as the acid in the lime juice can start to "cook" the fish.

Spicy tuna steaks are a quick and flavorful dish featuring tender tuna marinated in a spicy sauce and grilled to perfection, perfect for a healthy and satisfying low-carb meal.

Low-Carb Recipes

Recipe 121: Cauliflower Rice Pilaf

Prep Time: 10 minutes | Cooking Time: 15 minutes | Servings: 4

Ingredients

- 1 large head of cauliflower, riced
- 2 tablespoons olive oil
- 1 small onion, finely chopped
- 2 cloves garlic, minced
- 1/2 cup carrots, finely diced
- 1/2 cup peas (fresh or frozen)
- 1/4 cup slivered almonds, toasted
- 1/4 cup fresh parsley, chopped
- 1/2 teaspoon sea salt
- 1/4 teaspoon black pepper
- 1/4 teaspoon turmeric
- 1/4 teaspoon cumin
- 1/4 teaspoon paprika
- 1/2 lemon, juiced

Cooking Instructions

1. **Prepare the Cauliflower Rice:** Cut the cauliflower into florets and pulse in a food processor until it resembles rice. Set it aside.

2. **Cook the Aromatics:** In a large skillet, heat the olive oil over medium heat. Add the chopped onion and cook for 3-4 minutes until softened. Add the minced garlic and cook for another minute.

3. **Add the Vegetables:** Stir in the diced carrots and cook for 5 minutes until they begin to soften. Add the peas and cook for another 2 minutes.

4. **Add the Cauliflower Rice:** Stir in the cauliflower rice, sea salt, black pepper, turmeric, cumin, and paprika. Cook for 5-7 minutes until the cauliflower is tender.

5. **Finish the Pilaf:** Stir in the toasted slivered almonds, chopped fresh parsley, and lemon juice. Cook for another minute until everything is well combined and heated through.

6. **Serve:** Transfer the cauliflower rice pilaf to a serving dish and serve hot.

Nutritional Facts

- **Calories:** 150 kcal
- **Protein:** 4g
- **Fat:** 10g
- **Saturated Fat:** 1g
- **Cholesterol:** 0mg
- **Sodium:** 300mg
- **Potassium:** 500mg
- **Fiber:** 4g
- **Sugar:** 4g
- **Vitamin C:** 45mg

Cooking Tips

- ✓ **Cauliflower Rice:** Ensure the cauliflower is pulsed to a rice-like consistency. Avoid over-processing to prevent it from becoming mushy.

- ✓ **Vegetables:** Use fresh or frozen peas and finely dice the carrots for even cooking.

- ✓ **Flavor:** Adjust the amount of spices to your taste. Add more turmeric for color or cumin for a deeper flavor.

Cauliflower rice pilaf is a delicious and nutritious low-carb dish featuring tender cauliflower rice mixed with vegetables and spices, perfect for a healthy and satisfying meal.

Recipe 122: Zoodle Carbonara

Prep Time: 15 minutes | Cooking Time: 10 minutes | Servings: 4

Ingredients

- 4 medium zucchinis, spiralized into noodles
- 4 slices bacon, chopped
- 2 cloves garlic, minced
- 1/2 cup grated Parmesan cheese
- 2 large eggs
- 1/4 cup heavy cream
- 1/2 teaspoon sea salt
- 1/4 teaspoon black pepper
- 1/4 teaspoon red pepper flakes (optional)
- Fresh parsley, chopped (optional for garnish)

Cooking Instructions

1. **Prepare the Zoodles:** Spiralize the zucchini into noodles and set aside.
2. **Cook the Bacon:** In a large skillet, cook the chopped bacon over medium heat until crispy. Remove the bacon with a slotted spoon and set aside, leaving the bacon fat in the skillet.
3. **Cook the Garlic:** Add the minced garlic to the skillet and cook for 1-2 minutes until fragrant.
4. **Prepare the Sauce:** In a small bowl, whisk together the grated Parmesan cheese, eggs, heavy cream, sea salt, black pepper, and red pepper flakes if using.
5. **Cook the Zoodles:** Add the spiralized zucchini to the skillet and toss to coat in the bacon fat and garlic. Cook for 2-3 minutes until the zoodles are tender but still slightly firm.
6. **Combine and Serve:** Remove the skillet from the heat and quickly pour the sauce over the zoodles, tossing to coat. The residual heat will cook the eggs, creating a creamy sauce. Stir in the cooked bacon. Serve immediately, garnished with fresh parsley if desired.

Nutritional Facts

- **Calories:** 250 kcal
- **Protein:** 15g
- **Fat:** 20g
- **Saturated Fat:** 7g
- **Cholesterol:** 150mg
- **Sodium:** 700mg
- **Potassium:** 700mg
- **Fiber:** 2g
- **Sugar:** 4g
- **Vitamin C:** 20mg

Cooking Tips

- ✓ **Zoodles:** Spiralize the zucchini just before cooking to keep them fresh. Pat them dry with paper towels to remove excess moisture.
- ✓ **Bacon:** Use high-quality bacon for the best flavor. Turkey bacon can be used as a leaner alternative.
- ✓ **Sauce:** Work quickly to mix the sauce into the hot zoodles to avoid scrambling the eggs.
- ✓ **Serving Suggestions:** Serve with a side of grilled chicken or shrimp for added protein or enjoy as a light main course.
- ✓ **Storage:** Zoodle carbonara is best enjoyed fresh, but you can store any leftovers in an airtight container in the refrigerator for up to 1 day. Reheat gently in a skillet before serving.

Zoodle carbonara is a light and flavorful low-carb dish featuring spiralized zucchini noodles tossed in a creamy Parmesan sauce with crispy bacon, perfect for a healthy and satisfying meal.

Recipe 123: Grilled Pork Chops with Veggies

Prep Time: 15 minutes | Cooking Time: 20 minutes | Servings: 4

Ingredients

- 4 bone-in pork chops (about 1 inch thick)
- 2 tablespoons olive oil
- 1 tablespoon lemon juice
- 2 cloves garlic, minced
- 1 teaspoon dried rosemary
- 1 teaspoon dried thyme
- 1/2 teaspoon sea salt
- 1/4 teaspoon black pepper
- 1 red bell pepper, cut into strips
- 1 yellow bell pepper, cut into strips
- 1 zucchini, sliced
- 1 red onion, cut into wedges

Cooking Instructions

1. **Marinate the Pork Chops:** In a large bowl, combine 1 tablespoon of olive oil, lemon juice, minced garlic, dried rosemary, dried thyme, sea salt, and black pepper. Add the pork chops and toss to coat. Marinate for at least 15 minutes.

2. **Prepare the Vegetables:** In another bowl, combine the red and yellow bell pepper strips, zucchini slices, and red onion wedges with the remaining tablespoon of olive oil. Season with a pinch of sea salt and black pepper.

3. **Preheat the Grill:** Preheat your grill to medium-high heat.

4. **Grill the Pork Chops:** Place the pork chops on the grill and cook for 4-5 minutes per side or until the internal temperature reaches 145°F (63°C). Please remove it from the grill and let it rest for a few minutes.

5. **Grill the Vegetables:** While the pork chops are resting, grill the vegetables for 3-4 minutes on each side until tender and slightly charred.

6. **Serve:** Arrange the grilled pork chops and vegetables on a serving platter. Serve hot.

Nutritional Facts

- **Calories:** 350 kcal
- **Protein:** 30g
- **Fat:** 20g
- **Saturated Fat:** 6g
- **Cholesterol:** 80mg
- **Sodium:** 600mg
- **Potassium:** 800mg
- **Fiber:** 3g
- **Sugar:** 5g
- **Vitamin C:** 50mg

Cooking Tips

- ✓ **Pork Chops:** Choose bone-in pork chops for a juicier and more flavorful result. Ensure they are cooked to the correct internal temperature to avoid dryness.

- ✓ **Vegetables:** Use a mix of your favorite vegetables. Asparagus, cherry tomatoes, and mushrooms also work well.

- ✓ **Marinating:** For more flavor, marinate the pork chops for up to 2 hours.

- ✓ **Serving Suggestions:** Serve with a side of cauliflower mash or a fresh green salad for a complete meal.

Grilled pork chops with veggies is a simple and delicious dish featuring tender marinated pork chops and fresh vegetables grilled to perfection, perfect for a healthy and satisfying low-carb meal.

Recipe 124: Baked Chicken Wings

Prep Time: 10 minutes | Cooking Time: 45 minutes | Servings: 4

Ingredients

- 2 pounds of chicken wings
- 2 tablespoons olive oil
- 1 teaspoon sea salt
- 1/2 teaspoon black pepper
- 1 teaspoon garlic powder
- 1 teaspoon onion powder
- 1 teaspoon smoked paprika
- 1/2 teaspoon cayenne pepper (optional for extra heat)
- Fresh parsley, chopped (optional for garnish)

Cooking Instructions

1. **Preheat the Oven:** Preheat your oven to 400°F (200°C). Line a baking sheet with parchment paper or lightly grease it.

2. **Prepare the Chicken Wings:** In a large bowl, combine the olive oil, sea salt, black pepper, garlic powder, onion powder, smoked paprika, and cayenne pepper if using. Add the chicken wings and toss to coat evenly.

3. **Arrange on Baking Sheet:** Place the seasoned chicken wings in a single layer on the prepared baking sheet.

4. **Bake:** Bake in the preheated oven for 40-45 minutes, flipping halfway through, until the wings are crispy and cooked through. The internal temperature should reach 165°F (75°C).

5. **Serve:** Transfer the baked chicken wings to a serving platter. Garnish with fresh parsley if desired and serve hot.

Nutritional Facts

- **Calories:** 350 kcal
- **Protein:** 25g
- **Fat:** 25g
- **Saturated Fat:** 7g
- **Cholesterol:** 120mg
- **Sodium:** 700mg
- **Potassium:** 300mg
- **Fiber:** 1g
- **Sugar:** 0g
- **Vitamin A:** 10% DV

Cooking Tips

- ✓ **Wings:** Pat the chicken wings dry with paper towels before seasoning to ensure they get crispy in the oven.

- ✓ **Seasoning:** Adjust the spices to your taste. For a milder flavor, reduce the amount of cayenne pepper or omit it altogether.

- ✓ **Crisping:** For extra crispy wings, bake on a wire rack set over the baking sheet to allow air to circulate around the wings.

- ✓ **Serving Suggestions:** Serve with a side of celery sticks and low-carb ranch or blue cheese dressing.

- ✓ **Storage:** Store any leftovers in an airtight container in the refrigerator for up to 3 days. Reheat in the oven to retain crispiness.

Baked chicken wings are a flavorful and easy-to-make dish featuring crispy seasoned wings baked to perfection, perfect for a healthy and satisfying low-carb meal or snack.

Recipe 125: Low-Carb Pizza with Cauliflower Crust

Prep Time: 20 minutes | Cooking Time: 25 minutes | Servings: 4

Ingredients

For the Cauliflower Crust:
- 1 large head of cauliflower, riced
- 1/2 cup shredded mozzarella cheese
- 1/4 cup grated Parmesan cheese
- 1 large egg
- 1 teaspoon dried oregano
- 1 teaspoon dried basil
- 1/2 teaspoon garlic powder
- 1/2 teaspoon sea salt

For the Toppings:
- 1/2 cup sugar-free pizza sauce
- 1 cup shredded mozzarella cheese
- 1/2 cup sliced pepperoni
- 1/4 cup sliced black olives
- 1/4 cup sliced green bell pepper
- 1/4 cup sliced red onion
- Fresh basil leaves (optional for garnish)

Cooking Instructions

1. **Preheat the Oven:** Preheat your oven to 425°F (220°C). Line a baking sheet with parchment paper or a silicone baking mat.
2. **Prepare the Cauliflower Rice:** Cut the cauliflower into florets and pulse in a food processor until it resembles rice. Transfer to a microwave-safe bowl and microwave for 4-5 minutes until tender. Let it cool, then place the cauliflower rice in a clean kitchen towel and squeeze out as much moisture as possible.
3. **Make the Crust:** In a large bowl, combine the cauliflower rice, shredded mozzarella cheese, grated Parmesan cheese, egg, dried oregano, dried basil, garlic powder, and sea salt. Mix until well combined.
4. **Form the Crust:** Transfer the cauliflower mixture to the prepared baking sheet and press it into a 12-inch circle, about 1/4 inch thick.
5. **Bake the Crust:** Bake in the preheated oven for 12-15 minutes or until the crust is golden brown and firm.
6. **Add the Toppings:** Remove the crust from the oven and spread the sugar-free pizza sauce over it. Sprinkle with shredded mozzarella cheese and add your desired toppings.
7. **Bake the Pizza:** Return the pizza to the oven and bake for an additional 8-10 minutes, or until the cheese is melted and bubbly.
8. **Serve:** Garnish with fresh basil leaves if desired. Slice and serve hot.

Nutritional Facts

- **Calories:** 300 kcal
- **Protein:** 20g
- **Fat:** 18g
- **Saturated Fat:** 8g
- **Cholesterol:** 80mg
- **Sodium:** 700mg
- **Potassium:** 500mg
- **Fiber:** 4g
- **Sugar:** 3g
- **Vitamin C:** 30mg

Cooking Tips

- ✓ **Cauliflower:** Ensure you squeeze out as much moisture as possible from the cauliflower rice to achieve a crispy crust.
- ✓ **Cheese:** Use a combination of cheeses for extra flavor. You can also experiment with different toppings.
- ✓ **Crisping:** For an even crispier crust, bake the cauliflower crust on a pizza stone if you have one.

Recipe 126: Spaghetti Squash with Pesto

Prep Time: 10 minutes | Cooking Time: 40 minutes | Servings: 4

Ingredients

- 1 large spaghetti squash
- 2 tablespoons olive oil
- 1/2 teaspoon sea salt
- 1/4 teaspoon black pepper
- 1 cup fresh basil leaves
- 1/4 cup pine nuts
- 1/4 cup grated Parmesan cheese
- 2 cloves garlic, minced
- 1/2 cup olive oil
- 1/2 teaspoon sea salt
- 1/4 teaspoon black pepper
- Cherry tomatoes, halved (optional for garnish)
- Fresh basil leaves (optional for garnish)

Cooking Instructions

1. **Preheat the Oven:** Preheat your oven to 400°F (200°C). Line a baking sheet with parchment paper.
2. **Prepare the Squash:** Cut the spaghetti squash in half lengthwise and scoop out the seeds. Drizzle the cut sides with 2 tablespoons of olive oil and season with sea salt and black pepper. Place the squash halves cut side down on the prepared baking sheet.
3. **Bake the Squash:** Bake in the preheated oven for 35-40 minutes or until the squash is tender and easily pierced with a fork. Let it cool slightly.
4. **Make the Pesto:** In a food processor, combine the fresh basil leaves, pine nuts, grated Parmesan cheese, and minced garlic. Pulse until finely chopped. With the food processor running, slowly drizzle in 1/2 cup of olive oil until the pesto is smooth. Season with sea salt and black pepper.
5. **Prepare the Spaghetti Squash:** Use a fork to scrape the flesh of the squash into strands. Transfer the strands to a large bowl.
6. **Combine and Serve:** Add the pesto to the spaghetti squash strands and toss to combine. Garnish with halved cherry tomatoes and fresh basil leaves if desired. Serve hot.

Nutritional Facts

- **Calories:** 300 kcal
- **Protein:** 6g
- **Fat:** 28g
- **Saturated Fat:** 4g
- **Cholesterol:** 5mg
- **Sodium:** 400mg
- **Potassium:** 600mg
- **Fiber:** 4g
- **Sugar:** 5g
- **Vitamin C:** 20mg

Cooking Tips

- ✓ **Spaghetti Squash:** For easier cutting, microwave the squash for a few minutes to soften the skin.
- ✓ **Pesto:** Use high-quality olive oil and fresh basil for the best flavor. You can also substitute walnuts or almonds for pine nuts.
- ✓ **Serving Suggestions:** Serve with grilled chicken or shrimp for added protein.
- ✓ **Storage:** Store any leftovers in an airtight container in the refrigerator for up to 2 days. Reheat gently in the microwave before serving.

Spaghetti squash with pesto is a light and flavorful dish featuring tender spaghetti squash strands tossed with a fresh and vibrant pesto sauce, perfect for a healthy and satisfying low-carb meal.

Recipe 127: Cauliflower Rice Stuffed Peppers

Prep Time: 20 minutes | Cooking Time: 35 minutes | Servings: 4

Ingredients

For the Stuffed Peppers:

- 4 large bell peppers (any color), tops cut off and seeds removed
- 1 pound ground beef (or ground turkey for a leaner option)
- 2 tablespoons olive oil
- 1 medium onion, finely chopped
- 2 cloves garlic, minced
- 2 cups cauliflower rice (store-bought or homemade)
- 1 can (15 oz) diced tomatoes, drained
- 1 teaspoon smoked paprika
- 1 teaspoon ground cumin
- 1/2 teaspoon dried oregano
- 1/2 teaspoon sea salt
- 1/4 teaspoon black pepper
- 1/4 cup chopped fresh parsley or cilantro
- 1/2 cup shredded cheddar or mozzarella cheese (optional for topping)

For Garnish:

- Fresh parsley or cilantro, chopped
- Sour cream or Greek yogurt (optional)
- Hot sauce (optional)

Cooking Instructions

1. **Prepare the Bell Peppers:** Preheat your oven to 375°F (190°C). Lightly grease a baking dish large enough to hold the peppers upright. Cut the tops off the bell peppers and remove the seeds and membranes. Set the peppers aside.
2. **Cook the Ground Beef:** In a large skillet, heat the olive oil over medium heat. Add the finely chopped onion and sauté for 2-3 minutes until it becomes translucent. Add the minced garlic and cook for another minute until fragrant. Add the ground beef to the skillet and cook for 5-7 minutes, breaking it up with a spoon, until it is browned and cooked through. Drain any excess fat if necessary.
3. **Prepare the Stuffing Mixture:** Add the cauliflower rice to the skillet with the cooked beef and stir well to combine. Stir in the drained diced tomatoes, smoked paprika, ground cumin, dried oregano, sea salt, and black pepper. Cook for 5 minutes, stirring occasionally, until the cauliflower rice is tender, and the flavors are well combined. Stir in the chopped fresh parsley or cilantro.
4. **Stuff the Peppers:** Place the bell peppers upright in the prepared baking dish. Spoon the cauliflower rice and beef mixture into each pepper, packing it down slightly. Fill each pepper generously. If desired, sprinkle the tops with shredded cheese.
5. **Bake the Stuffed Peppers:** Cover the baking dish with aluminum foil and bake in the preheated oven for 25 minutes. Remove the foil and bake for an additional 10 minutes, or until the peppers are tender and the tops are slightly browned. If using cheese, bake until it is melted and bubbly.
6. **Serve:** Remove the stuffed peppers from the oven and let them cool slightly. Garnish with chopped fresh parsley or cilantro. Serve hot with a dollop of sour cream or Greek yogurt and a drizzle of hot sauce if desired.

Nutritional Fact

- **Calories:** 300 kcal
- **Protein:** 20g
- **Fat:** 18g
- **Saturated Fat:** 6g
- **Cholesterol:** 60mg
- **Sodium:** 500mg
- **Potassium:** 900mg
- **Fiber:** 6g
- **Sugar:** 8g
- **Vitamin C:** 120mg

Cooking Tips

- ✓ **Bell Peppers:** Choose peppers that can stand upright and have a wide opening for easier stuffing. Any color of bell pepper can be used, but red and yellow are sweeter.
- ✓ **Cauliflower Rice:** To make your own cauliflower rice, pulse cauliflower florets in a food processor until they resemble rice grains. You can also use store-bought cauliflower rice for convenience.
- ✓ **Ground Meat:** Ground turkey or chicken can be used as a leaner alternative to ground beef.

Recipe 128: Low-Carb Nachos

Prep Time: 10 minutes | Cooking Time: 15 minutes | Servings: 4

Ingredients

- 1 large zucchini, thinly sliced
- 1 large yellow squash, thinly sliced
- 1 tablespoon olive oil
- 1/2 teaspoon sea salt
- 1/4 teaspoon black pepper
- 1/2 teaspoon chili powder
- 1/2 teaspoon cumin
- 1 cup shredded cheddar cheese
- 1/2 cup cooked ground beef or turkey (optional)
- 1/4 cup sliced black olives
- 1/4 cup diced tomatoes
- 1/4 cup sliced jalapeños
- 1/4 cup chopped green onions
- 1/4 cup fresh cilantro, chopped
- 1/2 avocado, diced
- 1/4 cup sour cream (optional)
- 1/4 cup salsa (optional)

Cooking Instructions

1. **Preheat the Oven:** Preheat your oven to 400°F (200°C). Line a baking sheet with parchment paper or a silicone baking mat.
2. **Prepare the Veggie Chips:** In a large bowl, toss the thinly sliced zucchini and yellow squash with olive oil, sea salt, black pepper, chili powder, and cumin. Arrange the slices in a single layer on the prepared baking sheet.
3. **Bake the Veggie Chips:** Bake in the preheated oven for 10-12 minutes or until the slices are crisp and golden brown. Keep an eye on them to prevent burning. Remove from the oven and let cool slightly.

4. **Assemble the Nachos:** Transfer the baked veggie chips to an oven-safe serving platter. Sprinkle with shredded cheddar cheese and cooked ground beef or turkey if using. Add sliced black olives, diced tomatoes, and sliced jalapeños.
5. **Melt the Cheese:** Return the platter to the oven and bake for an additional 3-5 minutes, or until the cheese is melted and bubbly.
6. **Garnish and Serve:** Remove from the oven and top with chopped green onions, fresh cilantro, diced avocado, sour cream, and salsa if desired. Serve hot.

Nutritional Facts

- **Calories:** 250 kcal
- **Protein:** 12g
- **Fat:** 18g
- **Saturated Fat:** 6g
- **Cholesterol:** 30mg
- **Sodium:** 600mg
- **Potassium:** 500mg
- **Fiber:** 4g
- **Sugar:** 3g
- **Vitamin C:** 30mg

Cooking Tips

- ✓ **Veggie Chips:** Slice the zucchini and yellow squash thinly and evenly to ensure they crisp up nicely in the oven.
- ✓ **Cheese:** Use your favorite type of shredded cheese. Cheddar, Monterey Jack, or a blend work well.
- ✓ **Toppings:** Customize the nachos with your favorite low-carb toppings such as guacamole, pico de gallo, or diced bell peppers.

Low-carb nachos are a fun and tasty dish featuring baked zucchini and yellow squash chips topped with melted cheese and a variety of fresh toppings, perfect for a healthy and satisfying snack or appetizer.

Recipe 129: Eggplant Rollatini

Prep Time: 20 minutes | Cooking Time: 30 minutes | Servings: 4

Ingredients

- 2 large eggplants, sliced lengthwise into 1/4-inch-thick slices
- 1 tablespoon olive oil
- 1 teaspoon sea salt, divided
- 1/2 teaspoon black pepper, divided
- 1 cup ricotta cheese
- 1 cup shredded mozzarella cheese, divided
- 1/4 cup grated Parmesan cheese
- 1 egg
- 2 tablespoons fresh basil, chopped
- 2 tablespoons fresh parsley, chopped
- 2 cups marinara sauce (sugar-free)
- Fresh basil leaves (optional for garnish)

Cooking Instructions

1. **Preheat the Oven:** Preheat your oven to 375°F (190°C). Line a baking sheet with parchment paper.
2. **Prepare the Eggplant:** Arrange the eggplant slices on the prepared baking sheet. Brush both sides with olive oil and season with 1/2 teaspoon sea salt and 1/4 teaspoon black pepper. Bake in the preheated oven for 10-15 minutes until the eggplant is tender and slightly golden. Remove from the oven and let cool slightly.
3. **Prepare the Filling:** In a medium bowl, combine the ricotta cheese, 1/2 cup shredded mozzarella cheese, grated Parmesan cheese, egg, chopped basil, chopped parsley, and the remaining 1/2 teaspoon sea salt and 1/4 teaspoon black pepper. Mix well.
4. **Assemble the Rollatini:** Spread a thin layer of marinara sauce on the bottom of a baking dish. Place a spoonful of the ricotta mixture at the wider end of each eggplant slice and roll it up. Arrange the rolls seam-side down in the baking dish.
5. **Top with Sauce and Cheese:** Pour the remaining marinara sauce over the eggplant rolls and sprinkle with the remaining 1/2 cup of shredded mozzarella cheese.
6. **Bake:** Bake in the preheated oven for 20 minutes or until the cheese is melted and bubbly.
7. **Serve:** Garnish with fresh basil leaves if desired. Serve hot.

Nutritional Facts

- **Calories:** 300 kcal
- **Protein:** 15g
- **Fat:** 20g
- **Saturated Fat:** 8g
- **Cholesterol:** 70mg
- **Sodium:** 800mg
- **Potassium:** 700mg
- **Fiber:** 5g
- **Sugar:** 7g
- **Vitamin C:** 10mg

Cooking Tips

- ✓ **Eggplant:** Use a mandoline slicer for even, thin slices of eggplant. This helps ensure they cook evenly.
- ✓ **Cheese:** Choose high-quality cheeses for the best flavor. You can also add other herbs like oregano or thyme for extra flavor.
- ✓ **Marinara Sauce:** Use a sugar-free marinara sauce to keep the dish low-carb. Homemade marinara sauce is also a great option.

Eggplant rollatini is a delicious and elegant dish featuring tender eggplant slices rolled with a rich ricotta filling and baked in marinara sauce, perfect for a healthy and satisfying low-carb meal.

Recipe 130: Lemon Butter Shrimp

Prep Time: 10 minutes | Cooking Time: 10 minutes | Servings: 4

Ingredients

- 1-pound large shrimp, peeled and deveined
- 2 tablespoons olive oil
- 2 tablespoons butter
- 3 cloves garlic, minced
- 1/4 cup fresh lemon juice (about 2 lemons)
- 1 teaspoon lemon zest
- 1/4 teaspoon red pepper flakes (optional)
- 1/2 teaspoon sea salt
- 1/4 teaspoon black pepper
- 2 tablespoons fresh parsley, chopped
- Lemon wedges (optional for serving)

Cooking Instructions

1. **Heat the Oil and Butter:** In a large skillet, heat the olive oil and butter over medium-high heat until the butter is melted and bubbly.
2. **Cook the Shrimp:** Add the minced garlic and cook for 1 minute until fragrant. Add the shrimp in a single layer and cook for 2-3 minutes on each side until pink and opaque.
3. **Add the Lemon Juice:** Pour in the fresh lemon juice and add the lemon zest, red pepper flakes (if using), sea salt, and black pepper. Cook for an additional 1-2 minutes, stirring to coat the shrimp in the lemon butter sauce.
4. **Garnish and Serve:** Remove from heat and sprinkle with fresh parsley. Serve immediately with lemon wedges if desired.

Nutritional Facts

- **Calories:** 200 kcal
- **Protein:** 20g
- **Fat:** 12g
- **Saturated Fat:** 5g
- **Cholesterol:** 180mg
- **Sodium:** 600mg
- **Potassium:** 200mg
- **Fiber:** 1g
- **Sugar:** 1g
- **Vitamin C:** 20mg

Cooking Tips

- ✓ **Shrimp:** Use fresh or frozen shrimp that have been peeled and deveined. Thaw frozen shrimp completely and pat dry before cooking.
- ✓ **Lemon:** Fresh lemon juice is key for the best flavor. Avoid bottled lemon juice if possible.
- ✓ **Garlic:** Adjust the amount of garlic to your taste. You can also add other herbs like thyme or rosemary for extra flavor.
- ✓ **Serving Suggestions:** Serve over cauliflower rice, zoodles, or with a side of steamed vegetables for a complete meal.
- ✓ **Storage:** Store any leftovers in an airtight container in the refrigerator for up to 2 days. Reheat gently in a skillet before serving.

Lemon butter shrimp is a quick and flavorful dish featuring succulent shrimp cooked in a zesty lemon butter sauce, perfect for a healthy and satisfying low-carb meal.

Quick & Easy Recipes

Recipe 131: Chicken and Avocado Salad

Prep Time: 15 minutes | Cooking Time: 10 minutes | Servings: 4

Ingredients

- 1-pound boneless, skinless chicken breasts
- 2 tablespoons olive oil, divided
- 1/2 teaspoon sea salt, divided
- 1/4 teaspoon black pepper, divided
- 1 teaspoon garlic powder
- 1 teaspoon paprika
- 2 ripe avocados, diced
- 1 cup cherry tomatoes, halved
- 1/4 red onion, thinly sliced
- 4 cups mixed greens
- 1/4 cup fresh cilantro, chopped

For the Dressing:

- 2 tablespoons olive oil
- 2 tablespoons lime juice
- 1 tablespoon apple cider vinegar
- 1 teaspoon honey (optional)
- 1/2 teaspoon sea salt
- 1/4 teaspoon black pepper

Cooking Instructions

1. **Prepare the Chicken:** Season the chicken breasts with 1 tablespoon olive oil, 1/4 teaspoon sea salt, black pepper, garlic powder, and paprika.
2. **Cook the Chicken:** Heat a skillet over medium-high heat. Add the seasoned chicken breasts and cook for 5-7 minutes on each side until fully cooked. Remove from the skillet and let cool slightly, then slice.
3. **Prepare the Dressing:** In a small bowl, whisk together the olive oil, lime juice, apple cider vinegar, honey (if using), sea salt, and black pepper.

4. **Assemble the Salad:** In a large bowl, combine the diced avocados, halved cherry tomatoes, thinly sliced red onion, and mixed greens. Add the sliced chicken and chopped cilantro.
5. **Toss and Serve:** Drizzle the dressing over the salad and toss gently to combine. Serve immediately.

Nutritional Facts

- **Calories:** 350 kcal
- **Protein:** 25g
- **Fat:** 25g
- **Saturated Fat:** 4g
- **Cholesterol:** 60mg
- **Sodium:** 600mg
- **Potassium:** 800mg
- **Fiber:** 7g
- **Sugar:** 3g
- **Vitamin C:** 20mg

Cooking Tips

- ✓ **Chicken:** Ensure the chicken is fully cooked by checking for an internal temperature of 165°F (75°C).
- ✓ **Avocado:** Use ripe avocados for a creamy texture. Add them just before serving to prevent browning.
- ✓ **Dressing:** Adjust the amount of lime juice and apple cider vinegar to taste. Add more honey for a sweeter dressing.
- ✓ **Serving Suggestions:** Serve with a side of low-carb crackers or a fresh green smoothie for a complete meal.

Chicken and avocado salad is a fresh and nutritious dish featuring tender chicken and creamy avocado tossed with cherry tomatoes, red onion, and a zesty lime dressing, perfect for a healthy and satisfying low-carb meal.

Recipe 132: Low-Carb Breakfast Smoothie

Prep Time: 5 minutes | Cooking Time: 0 minutes | Servings: 2

Ingredients

- 1 cup unsweetened almond milk
- 1/2 cup Greek yogurt
- 1 scoop vanilla protein powder
- 1/2 avocado
- 1/2 cup frozen berries (such as strawberries, blueberries, or raspberries)
- 1 tablespoon chia seeds
- 1 tablespoon almond butter
- 1/2 teaspoon vanilla extract
- Ice cubes (optional for a thicker consistency)

Cooking Instructions

1. **Blend Ingredients:** In a blender, combine the unsweetened almond milk, Greek yogurt, vanilla protein powder, avocado, frozen berries, chia seeds, almond butter, and vanilla extract. Add a few ice cubes if you prefer a thicker smoothie.
2. **Blend Until Smooth:** Blend on high speed until smooth and creamy.
3. **Serve:** Pour the smoothie into two glasses and serve immediately.

Nutritional Facts

- **Calories:** 250 kcal
- **Protein:** 20g
- **Fat:** 15g
- **Saturated Fat:** 2g
- **Cholesterol:** 10mg
- **Sodium:** 150mg
- **Potassium:** 500mg
- **Fiber:** 7g
- **Sugar:** 5g
- **Vitamin C:** 10mg

Cooking Tips

- ✓ **Protein Powder:** Choose a high-quality vanilla protein powder that suits your dietary preferences (whey, plant-based, etc.).
- ✓ **Avocado:** Use a ripe avocado for a creamy texture and add healthy fats.
- ✓ **Sweetness:** Adjust the sweetness by adding a natural sweetener like stevia or a little more fruit if desired.
- ✓ **Serving Suggestions:** Enjoy as a quick breakfast or post-workout snack. Top with extra chia seeds or fresh berries for added texture.
- ✓ **Storage:** Smoothies are best enjoyed fresh, but you can store any leftovers in an airtight container in the refrigerator for up to 1 day. Shake or blend again before drinking.

Low-carb breakfast smoothies are a quick and nutritious option, featuring a blend of healthy fats, protein, and fiber, perfect for a satisfying and refreshing low-carb meal or snack.

Recipe 133: Grilled Salmon with Lemon

Prep Time: 10 minutes | Cooking Time: 15 minutes | Servings: 4

Ingredients

- 4 salmon fillets (about 6 oz each)
- 2 tablespoons olive oil
- 2 cloves garlic, minced
- 1 teaspoon lemon zest
- 2 tablespoons fresh lemon juice
- 1 teaspoon sea salt
- 1/2 teaspoon black pepper
- Fresh dill, chopped (optional for garnish)
- Lemon wedges (optional for serving)

Cooking Instructions

1. **Prepare the Marinade:** In a small bowl, combine the olive oil, minced garlic, lemon zest, fresh lemon juice, sea salt, and black pepper.
2. **Marinate the Salmon:** Place the salmon fillets in a shallow dish and pour the marinade over them, turning to coat. Let the salmon marinate for at least 10 minutes.
3. **Preheat the Grill:** Preheat your grill to medium-high heat. If using a stovetop, heat a grill pan over medium-high heat.
4. **Grill the Salmon:** Remove the salmon from the marinade and place it on the grill. Cook for 4-5 minutes on each side, or until the salmon is cooked through and has grill marks. The internal temperature should reach 145°F (63°C).

5. **Serve:** Transfer the grilled salmon to a serving platter. Garnish with fresh dill and lemon wedges if desired. Serve hot.

Nutritional Facts

- **Calories:** 300 kcal
- **Protein:** 25g
- **Fat:** 20g
- **Saturated Fat:** 3g
- **Cholesterol:** 70mg
- **Sodium:** 600mg
- **Potassium:** 800mg
- **Fiber:** 1g
- **Sugar:** 0g
- **Vitamin C:** 10mg

Cooking Tips

- ✓ **Salmon:** Use fresh, high-quality salmon fillets for the best flavor. You can also use other types of fishlike cod or halibut.
- ✓ **Grilling:** Make sure the grill or grill pan is preheated to prevent the salmon from sticking. Oil the grates lightly if necessary.
- ✓ **Serving Suggestions:** Serve with a side of grilled vegetables, cauliflower rice, or a fresh green salad for a complete meal.
- ✓ **Storage:** Store any leftovers in an airtight container in the refrigerator for up to 2 days. Reheat gently in the microwave or enjoy cold.

Grilled salmon with lemon is a simple and elegant dish, featuring tender salmon fillets marinated in a zesty lemon garlic mixture and grilled to perfection, perfect for a healthy and satisfying low-carb meal.

Recipe 134: Cauliflower Fried Rice

Prep Time: 10 minutes | Cooking Time: 15 minutes | Servings: 4

Ingredients

- 1 large head of cauliflower, riced
- 2 tablespoons olive oil
- 2 cloves garlic, minced
- 1 small onion, finely chopped
- 1 cup frozen peas and carrots, thawed
- 2 eggs, beaten
- 3 tablespoons soy sauce (or tamari for gluten-free)
- 1 tablespoon sesame oil
- 1/4 teaspoon black pepper
- 1/4 cup green onions, sliced
- 1/4 cup fresh cilantro, chopped (optional for garnish)

Cooking Instructions

1. **Prepare the Cauliflower Rice:** Cut the cauliflower into florets and pulse in a food processor until it resembles rice. Set it aside.
2. **Cook the Aromatics:** In a large skillet or wok, heat the olive oil over medium-high heat. Add the minced garlic and finely chopped onion and cook for 3-4 minutes until softened.
3. **Add the Vegetables:** Stir in the thawed peas and carrots and cook for another 2 minutes until heated through.
4. **Cook the Eggs:** Push the vegetables to one side of the skillet and pour the beaten eggs into the empty space. Scramble the eggs until fully cooked, then mix them with the vegetables.
5. **Add the Cauliflower Rice:** Stir in the cauliflower rice, soy sauce, sesame oil, and black pepper. Cook for 5-7 minutes until the cauliflower is tender.
6. **Finish and Serve:** Remove from heat and stir in the sliced green onions. Garnish with fresh cilantro if desired. Serve hot.

Nutritional Facts

- **Calories:** 200 kcal
- **Protein:** 7g
- **Fat:** 12g
- **Saturated Fat:** 2g
- **Cholesterol:** 70mg
- **Sodium:** 600mg
- **Potassium:** 600mg
- **Fiber:** 4g
- **Sugar:** 4g
- **Vitamin C:** 45mg

Cooking Tips

- ✓ **Cauliflower:** Ensure the cauliflower is pulsed to a rice-like consistency. Avoid over-processing to prevent it from becoming mushy.
- ✓ **Eggs:** Scramble the eggs separately in the skillet to ensure they cook evenly and integrate well with the other ingredients.
- ✓ **Vegetables:** Use fresh or frozen vegetables, and feel free to add more veggies like bell peppers or mushrooms.
- ✓ **Serving Suggestions:** Serve with a side of grilled chicken, shrimp, or tofu for added protein.
- ✓ **Storage:** Store any leftovers in an airtight container in the refrigerator for up to 3 days. Reheat gently in a skillet or microwave before serving.

Cauliflower fried rice is a delicious and healthy low-carb alternative to traditional fried rice, featuring tender cauliflower rice stir-fried with vegetables, eggs, and savory seasonings, perfect for a satisfying meal.

Recipe 135: Zoodle and Chicken Stir-Fry

Prep Time: 15 minutes | Cooking Time: 10 minutes | Servings: 4

Ingredients

- 1-pound boneless, skinless chicken breasts, thinly sliced
- 4 medium zucchinis, spiralized into noodles
- 2 tablespoons olive oil
- 2 cloves garlic, minced
- 1 small onion, thinly sliced
- 1 red bell pepper, thinly sliced
- 1 cup snap peas, trimmed
- 1/4 cup soy sauce (or tamari for gluten-free)
- 1 tablespoon rice vinegar
- 1 tablespoon sesame oil
- 1 teaspoon fresh ginger, minced
- 1/2 teaspoon red pepper flakes (optional)
- 1/4 cup green onions, sliced
- 1 tablespoon sesame seeds (optional for garnish)

Cooking Instructions

1. **Prepare the Chicken:** In a large skillet or wok, heat 1 tablespoon of olive oil over medium-high heat. Add the thinly sliced chicken and cook for 4-5 minutes until browned and cooked through. Remove from the skillet and set aside.
2. **Cook the Vegetables:** In the same skillet, add the remaining tablespoon of olive oil. Add the minced garlic and thinly sliced onion and cook for 2-3 minutes until fragrant. Add the red bell pepper and snap peas and cook for another 3-4 minutes until tender crisp.
3. **Add the Zoodles:** Stir in the spiralized zucchini noodles and cook for 2 minutes until just tender.
4. **Prepare the Sauce:** In a small bowl, whisk together the soy sauce, rice vinegar, sesame oil, minced ginger, and red pepper flakes (if using).
5. **Combine and Serve:** Return the cooked chicken to the skillet and pour the sauce over the stir-fry. Toss to coat evenly and cook for another minute until everything is heated through. Garnish with sliced green onions and sesame seeds if desired. Serve hot.

Nutritional Facts

- **Calories:** 250 kcal
- **Protein:** 30g
- **Fat:** 10g
- **Saturated Fat:** 2g
- **Cholesterol:** 70mg
- **Sodium:** 800mg
- **Potassium:** 900mg
- **Fiber:** 4g
- **Sugar:** 5g
- **Vitamin C:** 70mg

Cooking Tips

- ✓ **Chicken:** Ensure the chicken is thinly sliced for quick and even cooking. You can also use shrimp or tofu as a protein alternative.
- ✓ **Zoodles:** Spiralize the zucchini just before cooking to keep them fresh. Pat them dry with paper towels to remove excess moisture.
- ✓ **Vegetables:** Use fresh, crisp vegetables for the best texture and flavor. Feel free to add other veggies like broccoli or mushrooms.

Zoodle and chicken stir-fry is a quick and healthy low-carb dish, featuring tender chicken and fresh vegetables stir-fried with spiralized zucchini noodles and a savory sauce, perfect for a satisfying meal.

Recipe 136: Keto Egg Salad

Prep Time: 15 minutes | Cooking Time: 0 minutes | Servings: 4

Ingredients

- 8 hard-boiled eggs, chopped
- 1/2 cup mayonnaise
- 1 tablespoon Dijon mustard
- 1 teaspoon apple cider vinegar
- 1/2 teaspoon sea salt
- 1/4 teaspoon black pepper
- 1/4 teaspoon paprika
- 1/4 cup celery, finely chopped
- 1/4 cup red onion, finely chopped
- 1 tablespoon fresh chives, chopped (optional for garnish)
- Lettuce leaves (optional for serving)

Cooking Instructions

1. **Prepare the Eggs:** Peel and chop the hard-boiled eggs. Please place them in a large bowl.
2. **Make the Dressing:** In a small bowl, combine the mayonnaise, Dijon mustard, apple cider vinegar, sea salt, black pepper, and paprika. Mix well.
3. **Combine and Toss:** Add the finely chopped celery and red onion to the bowl with the eggs. Pour the dressing over the egg mixture and gently toss to combine until everything is evenly coated.
4. **Serve:** Garnish with fresh chives if desired. Serve on a bed of lettuce leaves or in a lettuce wrap for a low-carb option.

Nutritional Facts

- **Calories:** 250 kcal
- **Protein:** 12g
- **Fat:** 22g
- **Saturated Fat:** 4g
- **Cholesterol:** 375mg
- **Sodium:** 600mg
- **Potassium:** 200mg
- **Fiber:** 1g
- **Sugar:** 1g
- **Vitamin A:** 300 IU

Cooking Tips

- ✓ **Eggs:** Use fresh, hard-boiled eggs for the best flavor and texture. To make peeling easier, cool the eggs in an ice water bath after boiling.
- ✓ **Dressing:** Adjust the amount of mayonnaise and mustard to your taste. You can also add a pinch of cayenne pepper for a spicy kick.
- ✓ **Serving Suggestions:** Serve with low-carb crackers or on top of a fresh green salad. You can also add avocado slices for extra creaminess.
- ✓ **Storage:** Store any leftovers in an airtight container in the refrigerator for up to 3 days. The flavors will continue to develop as it chills.

Keto egg salad is a classic and satisfying dish, featuring hard-boiled eggs mixed with a creamy and tangy dressing, perfect for a quick and healthy low-carb meal or snack.

Recipe 137: Beef and Broccoli Skillet

Prep Time: 10 minutes | Cooking Time: 15 minutes | Servings: 4

Ingredients

- 1 pound flank steak, thinly sliced against the grain
- 4 cups broccoli florets
- 2 tablespoons olive oil, divided
- 2 cloves garlic, minced
- 1 tablespoon fresh ginger, minced
- 1/4 cup soy sauce (or tamari for gluten-free)
- 2 tablespoons oyster sauce
- 1 tablespoon rice vinegar
- 1 teaspoon sesame oil
- 1/2 teaspoon red pepper flakes (optional)
- 1/4 cup water
- 1 tablespoon sesame seeds (optional for garnish)
- 2 green onions, sliced (optional for garnish)

Cooking Instructions

1. **Prepare the Beef:** In a large skillet or wok, heat 1 tablespoon of olive oil over medium-high heat. Add the thinly sliced beef and cook for 3-4 minutes until browned. Remove from the skillet and set aside.
2. **Cook the Broccoli:** In the same skillet, add the remaining tablespoon of olive oil. Add the broccoli florets and cook for 3-4 minutes until they start to soften. Add the minced garlic and ginger and cook for another minute.
3. **Make the Sauce:** In a small bowl, whisk together the soy sauce, oyster sauce, rice vinegar, sesame oil, and red pepper flakes if using.
4. **Combine and Cook:** Return the beef to the skillet and pour the sauce over the beef and broccoli. Add the water and stir to combine. Cook for an additional 3-4 minutes until the broccoli is tender and the sauce has thickened slightly.
5. **Serve:** Garnish with sesame seeds and sliced green onions if desired. Serve hot.

Nutritional Facts

- **Calories:** 300 kcal
- **Protein:** 25g
- **Fat:** 15g
- **Saturated Fat:** 3g
- **Cholesterol:** 60mg
- **Sodium:** 1000mg
- **Potassium:** 700mg
- **Fiber:** 3g
- **Sugar:** 3g
- **Vitamin C:** 80mg

Cooking Tips

- ✓ **Beef:** Slice the beef thinly against the grain for a tender texture. Partially freezing the beef before slicing can make this easier.
- ✓ **Broccoli:** Use fresh broccoli for the best texture. If using frozen broccoli, thaw and pat dry before cooking.
- ✓ **Sauce:** Adjust the amount of soy sauce and oyster sauce to taste. For a thicker sauce, mix in 1 teaspoon of cornstarch dissolved in water before adding to the skillet.
- ✓ **Serving Suggestions:** Serve with cauliflower rice or a fresh green salad for a complete meal.
- ✓ **Storage:** Store any leftovers in an airtight container in the refrigerator for up to 2 days. Reheat gently in a skillet before serving.

Beef and broccoli skillet is a quick and delicious low-carb dish, featuring tender beef and fresh broccoli cooked in a savory sauce, perfect for a healthy and satisfying meal.

Recipe 138: Chia Seed Breakfast Bowl

Prep Time: 5 minutes (plus overnight soaking) | Cooking Time: None | Servings: 4

Ingredients

- 1 cup chia seeds
- 2 cups coconut milk (or any preferred milk alternative)
- 1 teaspoon vanilla extract
- 2 tablespoons maple syrup (optional for sweetness)
- 1 cup fresh mixed berries (such as strawberries, blueberries, and raspberries)
- 1 banana, sliced
- 1/4 cup unsweetened shredded coconut
- 1/4 cup chopped nuts (such as almonds, walnuts, or pecans)
- 2 tablespoons pumpkin seeds
- 2 tablespoons flax seeds
- Honey or additional maple syrup (optional for drizzling)

Cooking Instructions

1. **Prepare the Chia Pudding Base:** In a medium-sized bowl, combine the chia seeds, coconut milk, vanilla extract, and maple syrup (if using). Stir well to ensure the chia seeds are evenly distributed in the liquid.

2. **Refrigerate:** Cover the bowl with plastic wrap or a lid and refrigerate for at least 2 hours, or overnight. The chia seeds will absorb the liquid and expand to form a gel-like consistency.

3. **Assemble the Breakfast Bowl:** Once the chia pudding has set, give it a good stir to break up any clumps. Divide the chia pudding into four bowls.

4. **Add the Toppings:** Top each bowl with fresh mixed berries, banana slices, shredded coconut, chopped nuts, pumpkin seeds, and flax seeds. Drizzle with honey or additional maple syrup if desired.

5. **Serve:** Serve immediately and enjoy a nutritious and satisfying breakfast.

Nutritional Facts

- **Calories:** 250 kcal
- **Protein:** 6g
- **Fat:** 16g
- **Saturated Fat:** 8g
- **Cholesterol:** 0mg
- **Sodium:** 30mg
- **Potassium:** 400mg
- **Fiber:** 10g
- **Sugar:** 10g
- **Vitamin C:** 20mg

Cooking Tips

- ✓ **Chia Seeds:** Use high-quality chia seeds for the best texture and nutritional benefits. Ensure they are well mixed with the liquid to avoid clumping.

- ✓ **Milk Alternatives:** You can use almond milk, soy milk, or any other preferred milk alternative instead of coconut milk.

- ✓ **Sweetness:** Adjust the sweetness to your liking by adding more or less maple syrup or honey.

- ✓ **Toppings:** Get creative with your toppings! You can add any fruits, nuts, or seeds you like. Try adding dried fruits or a dollop of nut butter for extra flavor.

- ✓ **Storage:** Store any leftover chia pudding in an airtight container in the refrigerator for up to 3 days. Add fresh toppings just before serving.

Chia seed breakfast bowls are a healthy and versatile option for a quick and easy breakfast, packed with fiber, healthy fats, and a variety of delicious toppings to keep you satisfied throughout the morning.

Recipe 139: Tuna Salad Lettuce Wraps

Prep Time: 10 minutes | Cooking Time: 0 minutes | Servings: 4

Ingredients

- 2 (5 oz) cans tuna, drained
- 1/4 cup mayonnaise
- 1 tablespoon Dijon mustard
- 1 tablespoon lemon juice
- 1/4 cup celery, finely chopped
- 1/4 cup red onion, finely chopped
- 1 tablespoon fresh dill, chopped
- 1/2 teaspoon sea salt
- 1/4 teaspoon black pepper
- 8 large lettuce leaves (such as romaine or butter lettuce)
- 1 avocado, sliced (optional)
- Cherry tomatoes, halved (optional)

Cooking Instructions

1. **Prepare the Tuna Salad:** In a large bowl, combine the drained tuna, mayonnaise, Dijon mustard, lemon juice, celery, red onion, fresh dill, sea salt, and black pepper. Mix well until everything is evenly combined.
2. **Assemble the Lettuce Wraps:** Place a generous spoonful of the tuna salad onto each lettuce leaf.
3. **Add Optional Toppings:** Top with avocado slices and cherry tomato halves if desired.
4. **Serve:** Serve immediately as a light lunch or snack.

Nutritional Facts

- **Calories:** 200 kcal
- **Protein:** 18g
- **Fat:** 12g
- **Saturated Fat:** 2g
- **Cholesterol:** 35mg
- **Sodium:** 450mg
- **Potassium:** 400mg
- **Fiber:** 3g
- **Sugar:** 2g
- **Vitamin C:** 8mg

Cooking Tips

- ✓ **Tuna:** Use high-quality canned tuna in water for a lighter option or tuna in oil for a richer flavor. Make sure to drain the tuna well.
- ✓ **Lettuce:** Use sturdy lettuce leaves that can hold the tuna salad without tearing. Romaine, butter lettuce, or iceberg lettuce works well.
- ✓ **Customization:** Feel free to add other ingredients like chopped pickles, capers, or olives for additional flavor.
- ✓ **Serving Suggestions:** Serve with a side of low-carb crackers or vegetable sticks for a complete meal.
- ✓ **Storage:** Store any leftover tuna salad in an airtight container in the refrigerator for up to 2 days. Assemble the lettuce wraps just before serving to keep them fresh.

Tuna salad lettuce wraps are a quick and healthy low-carb dish featuring creamy tuna salad served in crisp lettuce leaves, perfect for a light and satisfying meal or snack.

Recipe 140: Asian Chicken Lettuce Wraps

Prep Time: 15 minutes | Cooking Time: 15 minutes | Servings: 4

Ingredients

- 1 tablespoon olive oil
- 1 pound ground chicken
- 1 small onion, finely chopped
- 2 cloves garlic, minced
- 1 tablespoon ginger, minced
- 1 cup shredded carrots
- 1 cup bell pepper, finely diced
- 1/2 cup water chestnuts, chopped
- 1/4 cup soy sauce (or tamari for gluten-free)
- 1 tablespoon rice vinegar
- 1 tablespoon hoisin sauce
- 1 teaspoon sesame oil
- 1/2 teaspoon red pepper flakes (optional for spice)
- 1 head of butter lettuce or romaine lettuce, leaves separated and washed
- 1/4 cup green onions, thinly sliced
- 1/4 cup fresh cilantro, chopped
- 1/4 cup crushed peanuts or cashews (optional for garnish)
- Lime wedges (optional for serving)

Cooking Instructions

1. **Cook the Chicken:** Heat the olive oil in a large skillet over medium heat. Add the ground chicken and cook until browned, breaking it up with a spoon, about 5-7 minutes.

2. **Add Aromatics:** Add the chopped onion, minced garlic, and minced ginger to the skillet. Cook for 2-3 minutes until the onions are translucent and fragrant.

3. **Add Vegetables:** Stir in the shredded carrots, diced bell pepper, and chopped water chestnuts. Cook for another 2-3 minutes until the vegetables are slightly tender.

4. **Add Seasonings:** In a small bowl, combine the soy sauce, rice vinegar, hoisin sauce, sesame oil, and red pepper flakes (if using). Pour the mixture over the chicken and vegetables. Stir well to coat and cook for another 2 minutes until heated through.

5. **Assemble the Wraps:** Lay out the lettuce leaves on a serving platter. Spoon a generous amount of the chicken mixture into the center of each leaf.

6. **Garnish and Serve:** Top the lettuce wraps with sliced green onions, chopped cilantro, and crushed peanuts or cashews if desired. Serve with lime wedges for an extra burst of flavor.

Nutritional Facts

- **Calories:** 220 kcal
- **Protein:** 20g
- **Fat:** 10g
- **Saturated Fat:** 2g
- **Cholesterol:** 70mg
- **Sodium:** 750mg
- **Potassium:** 500mg
- **Fiber:** 2g
- **Sugar:** 3g
- **Vitamin C:** 35mg

Cooking Tips

✓ **Ground Chicken:** You can substitute ground turkey or beef for the chicken if you prefer. Adjust the seasoning accordingly.

✓ **Lettuce:** Butter lettuce is ideal for wrapping due to its soft texture and wide leaves. Romaine or iceberg lettuce also works well for a crispier wrap.

✓ **Spice Level:** Adjust the red pepper flakes to your taste preference for a mild or spicy kick.

Asian chicken lettuce wraps are a light and flavorful dish, perfect for a healthy lunch or appetizer. These wraps offer a satisfying crunch and a delicious combination of seasoned chicken and fresh vegetables, all wrapped up in crisp lettuce leaves.

Advanced Recipes

Recipe 141: Beef Wellington with Cauliflower Mash

Prep Time: 30 minutes | Cooking Time: 1 hour | Servings: 4

Ingredients

For the Beef Wellington:
- 1 pound beef tenderloin
- 2 tablespoons olive oil
- 1/2 teaspoon sea salt
- 1/4 teaspoon black pepper
- 1 tablespoon Dijon mustard
- 1 cup mushrooms, finely chopped
- 1 small shallot, finely chopped
- 2 cloves garlic, minced
- 1 tablespoon fresh thyme, chopped
- 1 tablespoon fresh parsley, chopped
- 8 slices prosciutto
- 1 sheet puff pastry (low-carb or regular, depending on dietary preference)
- 1 egg, beaten

For the Cauliflower Mash:
- 1 large head of cauliflower, cut into florets
- 2 tablespoons butter
- 1/4 cup heavy cream
- 1/2 teaspoon sea salt
- 1/4 teaspoon black pepper
- 1/4 cup grated Parmesan cheese

Cooking Instructions

1. **Prepare the Beef Wellington:** Preheat your oven to 400°F (200°C). Season the beef tenderloin with sea salt and black pepper. In a large skillet, heat the olive oil over medium-high heat. Sear the beef on all sides until browned, about 2 minutes per side. Remove from the skillet and brush with Dijon mustard. Let cool.

2. **Make the Mushroom Duxelles:** In the same skillet, add the chopped mushrooms, shallot, and garlic. Cook over medium heat until the moisture has evaporated, about 10 minutes. Stir in the thyme and parsley and let cool.

3. **Assemble the Beef Wellington:** On a sheet of plastic wrap, lay out the prosciutto slices, overlapping slightly. Spread the mushroom mixture evenly over the prosciutto. Place the beef on top and roll tightly using the plastic wrap. Chill in the refrigerator for 15 minutes.

4. **Wrap in Puff Pastry:** Roll out the puff pastry on a floured surface. Remove the plastic wrap from the beef and place it on the pastry. Wrap the beef tightly in the pastry, sealing the edges. Brush with beaten egg.

5. **Bake:** Place the wrapped beef on a baking sheet and bake in the preheated oven for 25-30 minutes, or until the pastry is golden brown and the internal temperature reaches 130°F (54°C) for medium-rare. Let rest for 10 minutes before slicing.

6. **Prepare the Cauliflower Mash:** While the beef is baking, steam the cauliflower florets until tender, about 10 minutes. Drain and transfer to a food processor. Add the butter, heavy cream, sea salt, black pepper, and grated Parmesan cheese. Blend until smooth.

7. **Serve:** Slice the beef in Wellington and serve with the cauliflower mash.

Nutritional Facts

- **Calories**: 600 kcal
- **Protein**: 40g
- **Fat**: 40g
- **Saturated Fat**: 15g
- **Cholesterol**: 160mg
- **Sodium**: 1200mg
- **Potassium**: 800mg
- **Fiber**: 5g
- **Sugar**: 4g
- **Vitamin C**: 50mg

Cooking Tips

✓ **Beef:** Use a meat thermometer to ensure the beef is cooked to your preferred doneness. Adjust cooking time as needed.

✓ **Mushroom Duxelles:** Make sure to cook the mushroom mixture until all the moisture is gone to avoid a soggy pastry.

Recipe 142: Keto Sushi Rolls with Cauliflower Rice

Prep Time: 30 minutes | Cooking Time: 5 minutes | Servings: 4

Ingredients

For the Cauliflower Rice:

- 1 large head of cauliflower, riced
- 2 tablespoons rice vinegar
- 1 tablespoon sesame oil
- 1 teaspoon sea salt

For the Sushi Rolls:

- 4 sheets nori (seaweed)
- 1/2-pound sashimi-grade salmon or tuna, thinly sliced
- 1/2 avocado, thinly sliced
- 1/2 cucumber, julienned
- 1 carrot, julienned
- 1/4 cup pickled ginger
- Soy sauce or tamari (for dipping)
- Wasabi (optional)

Cooking Instructions

1. **Prepare the Cauliflower Rice:** Cut the cauliflower into florets and pulse in a food processor until it resembles rice. In a large skillet, cook the riced cauliflower over medium heat for 5-7 minutes until tender. Remove from heat and stir in the rice vinegar, sesame oil, and sea salt. Let cool completely.
2. **Assemble the Sushi Rolls:** Place a sheet of nori on a bamboo sushi mat or a clean kitchen towel. Spread a thin layer of cauliflower rice over the nori, leaving a 1-inch border at the top.
3. **Add Fillings:** Arrange thin slices of salmon or tuna, avocado, cucumber, and carrot in a line across the center of the rice.
4. **Roll the Sushi:** Use the bamboo mat or towel to tightly roll the nori around the fillings, starting from the bottom edge. Wet the top border of the nori with a little water to seal the roll.
5. **Slice and Serve:** Using a sharp knife, slice the sushi roll into 6-8 pieces. Repeat with the remaining ingredients. Serve with pickled ginger, soy sauce or tamari, and wasabi if desired.

Nutritional Facts

- **Calories:** 200 kcal
- **Protein:** 18g
- **Fat:** 10g
- **Saturated Fat:** 2g
- **Cholesterol:** 30mg
- **Sodium:** 600mg
- **Potassium:** 400mg
- **Fiber:** 5g
- **Sugar:** 3g
- **Vitamin C:** 20mg

Cooking Tips

- ✓ **Cauliflower Rice:** Make sure to cook the cauliflower rice until it's tender but not mushy. Let it cool completely before using it in the sushi rolls.
- ✓ **Fish:** Use sashimi-grade fish for the best flavor and safety. You can also use cooked shrimp or crab if preferred.
- ✓ **Rolling:** Be sure to roll the sushi tightly to keep the fillings in place. A bamboo sushi mat makes this easier.

Keto sushi rolls with cauliflower rice are a delicious and healthy alternative to traditional sushi, featuring fresh fish and vegetables wrapped in nori and served with flavorful condiments, perfect for a satisfying low-carb meal or appetizer.

Recipe 143: Chicken Cordon Bleu

Prep Time: 20 minutes | Cooking Time: 30 minutes | Servings: 4

Ingredients

- 4 boneless, skinless chicken breasts
- 4 slices Swiss cheese
- 4 slices deli ham
- 1/4 cup almond flour
- 1/4 cup grated Parmesan cheese
- 1 teaspoon garlic powder
- 1 teaspoon onion powder
- 1/2 teaspoon sea salt
- 1/4 teaspoon black pepper
- 2 tablespoons Dijon mustard
- 1 tablespoon olive oil
- Fresh parsley, chopped (optional for garnish)

Cooking Instructions

1. **Preheat the Oven:** Preheat your oven to 375°F (190°C). Lightly grease a baking dish.
2. **Prepare the Chicken:** Place each chicken breast between two sheets of plastic wrap and pound to an even 1/2-inch thickness.
3. **Assemble the Cordon Bleu:** Lay a slice of Swiss cheese and a slice of ham on each chicken breast. Roll up the chicken breasts and secure them with toothpicks.
4. **Make the Coating:** In a shallow dish, combine the almond flour, grated Parmesan cheese, garlic powder, onion powder, sea salt, and black pepper.
5. **Coat the Chicken:** Brush each chicken roll with Dijon mustard, then roll in the almond flour mixture to coat evenly.
6. **Bake:** Place the coated chicken rolls in the prepared baking dish and drizzle with olive oil. Bake in the preheated oven for 25-30 minutes or until the chicken is cooked through and the coating is golden brown.
7. **Serve:** Remove the toothpicks, garnish with chopped parsley if desired, and serve hot.

Nutritional Facts

- **Calories:** 400 kcal
- **Protein:** 40g
- **Fat:** 20g
- **Saturated Fat:** 6g
- **Cholesterol:** 110mg
- **Sodium:** 900mg
- **Potassium:** 600mg
- **Fiber:** 2g
- **Sugar:** 1g
- **Vitamin C:** 4mg

Cooking Tips

- ✓ **Chicken:** Ensure the chicken breasts are pounded evenly for consistent cooking. Use a meat thermometer to check for an internal temperature of 165°F (75°C).
- ✓ **Coating:** For a crispier coating, you can lightly spray the chicken with cooking spray before baking.
- ✓ **Cheese and Ham:** Use high-quality Swiss cheese and deli ham for the best flavor.
- ✓ **Serving Suggestions:** Serve with a side of steamed green beans or cauliflower mash for a complete meal.
- ✓ **Storage:** Store any leftovers in an airtight container in the refrigerator for up to 2 days. Reheat in the oven to retain crispiness.

Chicken Cordon Bleu is a classic and flavorful dish featuring tender chicken breasts stuffed with Swiss cheese and ham, coated in a crispy almond flour mixture, perfect for a gourmet low-carb meal.

Recipe 144: Low-Carb Lobster Bisque

Prep Time: 15 minutes | Cooking Time: 30 minutes | Servings: 4

Ingredients

- 1 pound lobster meat, chopped
- 2 tablespoons butter
- 1 small onion, finely chopped
- 2 cloves garlic, minced
- 1/2 cup celery, finely chopped
- 1/2 cup carrots, finely chopped
- 1/4 cup tomato paste
- 4 cups seafood stock or chicken broth
- 1 cup heavy cream
- 1/4 cup dry white wine (optional)
- 1 teaspoon paprika
- 1/2 teaspoon sea salt
- 1/4 teaspoon black pepper
- 1/4 teaspoon cayenne pepper (optional)
- 1 tablespoon fresh parsley, chopped (optional for garnish)

Cooking Instructions

1. **Prepare the Vegetables:** In a large pot, melt the butter over medium heat. Add the finely chopped onion, garlic, celery, and carrots. Cook for 5-7 minutes until the vegetables are soft and fragrant.
2. **Add the Tomato Paste:** Stir in the tomato paste and cook for another 2 minutes.
3. **Add the Stock:** Pour in the seafood stock or chicken broth and add the dry white wine if using. Bring to a simmer and cook for 10 minutes.
4. **Blend the Soup:** Use an immersion blender to puree the soup until smooth. Alternatively, transfer the soup in batches to a blender and blend until smooth, then return to the pot.
5. **Add the Lobster:** Stir in the heavy cream, chopped lobster meat, paprika, sea salt, black pepper, and cayenne pepper if using. Simmer for another 5-10 minutes until the lobster is heated through, and the bisque is creamy.
6. **Serve:** Ladle the bisque into bowls and garnish with fresh parsley if desired. Serve hot.

Nutritional Facts

- **Calories:** 350 kcal
- **Protein:** 20g
- **Fat:** 25g
- **Saturated Fat:** 15g
- **Cholesterol:** 150mg
- **Sodium:** 800mg
- **Potassium:** 600mg
- **Fiber:** 2g
- **Sugar:** 4g
- **Vitamin C:** 10mg

Cooking Tips

- ✓ **Lobster:** Use fresh or high-quality frozen lobster meat for the best flavor. You can also substitute shrimp or crab if preferred.
- ✓ **Stock:** Seafood stock gives the best flavor, but chicken broth can be used if necessary.
- ✓ **Blending:** Be cautious when blending hot liquids. If using a traditional blender, blend in batches and leave the lid slightly ajar to allow steam to escape.
- ✓ **Serving Suggestions:** Serve with a side of low-carb bread or a fresh green salad for a complete meal.
- ✓ **Storage:** Store any leftovers in an airtight container in the refrigerator for up to 2 days. Reheat gently on the stovetop before serving.

Low-carb lobster bisque is a rich and creamy soup featuring tender lobster meat in a velvety broth, perfect for a luxurious and satisfying low-carb meal.

Recipe 145: Pork Belly with Cabbage Slaw

Prep Time: 20 minutes | Cooking Time: 1 hour | Servings: 4

Ingredients

For the Pork Belly:
- 2 pounds pork belly, skin scored
- 1 tablespoon olive oil
- 1 teaspoon sea salt
- 1/2 teaspoon black pepper
- 1 teaspoon smoked paprika
- 1 teaspoon garlic powder
- 1 teaspoon onion powder

For the Cabbage Slaw:
- 2 cups green cabbage, thinly sliced
- 1 cup red cabbage, thinly sliced
- 1 carrot, julienned
- 1/4 cup mayonnaise
- 1 tablespoon apple cider vinegar
- 1 tablespoon Dijon mustard
- 1 teaspoon sea salt
- 1/4 teaspoon black pepper
- 1/4 teaspoon celery seed
- 2 tablespoons fresh parsley, chopped

Cooking Instructions

1. **Preheat the Oven:** Preheat your oven to 425°F (220°C). Line a baking sheet with aluminum foil.
2. **Prepare the Pork Belly:** Rub the pork belly with olive oil, sea salt, black pepper, smoked paprika, garlic powder, and onion powder. Place the pork belly on the prepared baking sheet, skin side up.
3. **Roast the Pork Belly:** Roast in the preheated oven for 30 minutes. Reduce the oven temperature to 325°F (165°C) and continue to roast for an additional 30 minutes, or until the pork belly is tender and the skin is crispy.
4. **Prepare the Cabbage Slaw:** While the pork belly is roasting, combine the green cabbage, red cabbage, and julienned carrot in a large bowl. In a small bowl, whisk together the mayonnaise, apple cider vinegar, Dijon mustard, sea salt, black pepper, and celery seed. Pour the dressing over the cabbage mixture and toss to coat. Garnish with fresh parsley.
5. **Serve:** Slice the pork belly into bite-sized pieces. Serve hot with the cabbage slaw on the side.

Nutritional Facts

- **Calories:** 600 kcal
- **Protein:** 20g
- **Fat:** 50g
- **Saturated Fat:** 18g
- **Cholesterol:** 100mg
- **Sodium:** 1200mg
- **Potassium:** 400mg
- **Fiber:** 3g
- **Sugar:** 3g
- **Vitamin C:** 30mg

Cooking Tips

- ✓ **Pork Belly:** Score the skin of the pork belly to help it crisp up during roasting. Use a sharp knife and be careful not to cut too deeply.
- ✓ **Cabbage Slaw:** For a creamier slaw, increase the amount of mayonnaise. Adjust the seasoning to taste.
- ✓ **Serving Suggestions:** Serve with a side of cauliflower rice or roasted vegetables for a complete meal.

Pork belly with cabbage slaw is a rich and flavorful dish featuring tender, and crispy pork belly served with fresh and tangy cabbage slaw, perfect for a satisfying low-carb meal.

Recipe 146: Cauliflower Gnocchi with Pesto

Prep Time: 20 minutes | Cooking Time: 15 minutes | Servings: 4

Ingredients

For the Cauliflower Gnocchi:
- 1 large head of cauliflower, riced
- 1/2 cup almond flour
- 1/4 cup grated Parmesan cheese
- 1 egg, beaten
- 1/2 teaspoon sea salt
- 1/4 teaspoon black pepper

For the Pesto:
- 2 cups fresh basil leaves
- 1/4 cup pine nuts
- 1/4 cup grated Parmesan cheese
- 2 cloves garlic, minced
- 1/2 cup olive oil
- 1/2 teaspoon sea salt
- 1/4 teaspoon black pepper

Cooking Instructions

1. **Prepare the Cauliflower Rice:** Cut the cauliflower into florets and pulse in a food processor until it resembles rice. Steam the cauliflower rice for 5-7 minutes until tender. Let cool slightly, then squeeze out as much moisture as possible using a clean kitchen towel.
2. **Make the Gnocchi Dough:** In a large bowl, combine the cauliflower rice, almond flour, grated Parmesan cheese, beaten egg, sea salt, and black pepper. Mix until the dough forms.
3. **Shape the Gnocchi:** On a floured surface, roll the dough into long ropes about 1/2 inch in diameter. Cut the ropes into 1-inch pieces and shape each piece into small gnocchi.
4. **Cook the Gnocchi:** Bring a large pot of salted water to a boil. Add the gnocchi and cook for 2-3 minutes or until they float to the surface. Remove with a slotted spoon and set aside.

5. **Prepare the Pesto:** In a food processor, combine the fresh basil leaves, pine nuts, grated Parmesan cheese, and minced garlic. Pulse until finely chopped. With the food processor running, slowly drizzle in the olive oil until the pesto is smooth. Season with sea salt and black pepper.
6. **Combine and Serve:** In a large skillet, heat the pesto over low heat. Add the cooked gnocchi and toss to coat evenly. Serve hot, garnished with extra Parmesan cheese if desired.

Nutritional Facts

- **Calories**: 350 kcal
- **Protein:** 10g
- **Fat:** 30g
- **Saturated Fat:** 6g
- **Cholesterol:** 50mg
- **Sodium:** 500mg
- **Potassium:** 400mg
- **Fiber:** 5g
- **Sugar:** 3g
- **Vitamin C:** 40mg

Cooking Tips

- ✓ **Cauliflower:** Ensure the cauliflower rice is well-drained to prevent the dough from becoming too wet.
- ✓ **Shaping:** Use extra almond flour to prevent the gnocchi dough from sticking while shaping.
- ✓ **Pesto:** For a nuttier flavor, toast the pine nuts before adding them to the food processor.
- ✓ **Serving Suggestions:** Serve with a side of grilled chicken or a fresh green salad for a complete meal.
- ✓ **Storage:** Store any leftovers in an airtight container in the refrigerator for up to 2 days. Reheat gently in a skillet before serving.

Recipe 147: Stuffed Chicken Breast with Spinach and Cheese

Prep Time: 15 minutes | Cooking Time: 25 minutes | Servings: 4

Ingredients

- 4 boneless, skinless chicken breasts
- 1 tablespoon olive oil
- 2 cloves garlic, minced
- 2 cups fresh spinach, chopped
- 1/2 cup ricotta cheese
- 1/2 cup shredded mozzarella cheese
- 1/4 cup grated Parmesan cheese
- 1 teaspoon Italian seasoning
- 1/2 teaspoon sea salt
- 1/4 teaspoon black pepper
- 1/4 teaspoon red pepper flakes (optional)

Cooking Instructions

1. **Preheat the Oven:** Preheat your oven to 375°F (190°C). Lightly grease a baking dish.

2. **Prepare the Chicken:** Using a sharp knife, make a deep pocket in each chicken breast by cutting horizontally through the thickest part of the breast, being careful not to cut all the way through.

3. **Prepare the Filling:** In a medium skillet, heat the olive oil over medium heat. Add the minced garlic and cook for 1-2 minutes until fragrant. Add the chopped spinach and cook until wilted, about 2-3 minutes. Remove from heat and let cool slightly. In a medium bowl, combine the cooked spinach, ricotta cheese, shredded mozzarella cheese, grated Parmesan cheese, Italian seasoning, sea salt, black pepper, and red pepper flakes if using. Mix well.

4. **Stuff the Chicken:** Spoon the spinach and cheese mixture into the pocket of each chicken breast, dividing it evenly. Secure the opening with toothpicks if needed.

5. **Bake:** Place the stuffed chicken breasts in the prepared baking dish and bake in the preheated oven for 20-25 minutes, or until the chicken is cooked through and the internal temperature reaches 165°F (75°C).

6. **Serve:** Remove the toothpicks before serving. Serve hot, garnished with fresh herbs if desired.

Nutritional Facts

- **Calories:** 350 kcal
- **Protein:** 40g
- **Fat:** 18g
- **Saturated Fat:** 8g
- **Cholesterol:** 110mg
- **Sodium:** 700mg
- **Potassium:** 700mg
- **Fiber:** 2g
- **Sugar:** 1g
- **Vitamin A:** 2500 IU

Cooking Tips

✓ **Chicken:** Ensure the chicken breasts are of similar size for even cooking. Use a meat thermometer to check for doneness.

✓ **Filling:** Make sure the filling is well-mixed and evenly distributed in each chicken breast. You can add other ingredients like sun-dried tomatoes or mushrooms for extra flavor.

✓ **Serving Suggestions:** Serve with a side of roasted vegetables or a fresh green salad for a complete meal.

Stuffed chicken breast with spinach and cheese is a delicious and nutritious dish featuring tender chicken breasts filled with a savory mixture of spinach and cheese, perfect for a satisfying low-carb meal.

Recipe 148: Keto Lamb Chops with Mint Sauce

Prep Time: 15 minutes | Cooking Time: 15 minutes | Servings: 4

Ingredients

- 8 lamb chops (about 1 inch thick)
- 2 tablespoons olive oil
- 1 teaspoon sea salt
- 1/2 teaspoon black pepper
- 1 teaspoon garlic powder
- 1 teaspoon dried rosemary
- 1 teaspoon dried thyme

For the Mint Sauce:

- 1/2 cup fresh mint leaves, chopped
- 1/4 cup fresh parsley, chopped
- 2 tablespoons red wine vinegar
- 1 tablespoon olive oil
- 1 teaspoon honey (optional for keto-friendly sweetener)
- 1/2 teaspoon sea salt
- 1/4 teaspoon black pepper

Cooking Instructions

1. **Prepare the Lamb Chops:** Rub the lamb chops with olive oil, sea salt, black pepper, garlic powder, dried rosemary, and dried thyme. Let them sit at room temperature for 10 minutes.

2. **Preheat the Grill:** Preheat your grill to medium-high heat.

3. **Grill the Lamb Chops:** Place the lamb chops on the grill and cook for 4-5 minutes on each side for medium-rare, or longer if desired. Please remove it from the grill and let it rest for a few minutes.

4. **Prepare the Mint Sauce:** While the lamb chops are grilling, combine the chopped mint leaves, fresh parsley, red wine vinegar, olive oil, honey (if using), sea salt, and black pepper in a small bowl. Mix well.

5. **Serve:** Drizzle the mint sauce over the grilled lamb chops. Serve hot.

Nutritional Facts

- **Calories:** 400 kcal
- **Protein:** 25g
- **Fat:** 30g
- **Saturated Fat:** 10g
- **Cholesterol:** 100mg
- **Sodium:** 700mg
- **Potassium:** 400mg
- **Fiber:** 1g
- **Sugar:** 1g
- **Vitamin C:** 10mg

Cooking Tips

- ✓ **Lamb Chops:** For the best flavor, use high-quality lamb chops and let them come to room temperature before grilling.

- ✓ **Mint Sauce:** Adjust the amount of honey or use a keto-friendly sweetener to taste. Fresh mint leaves are key for the best flavor.

- ✓ **Grilling:** Use a meat thermometer to check for doneness. For medium-rare lamb, the internal temperature should be about 135°F (57°C).

Keto lamb chops with mint sauce are a flavorful and elegant dish featuring tender grilled lamb chops topped with a refreshing mint sauce, perfect for a gourmet low-carb meal.

Recipe 149: Zoodle Shrimp Scampi

Prep Time: 15 minutes | Cooking Time: 10 minutes | Servings: 4

Ingredients

- 1-pound large shrimp, peeled and deveined
- 4 medium zucchinis, spiralized into noodles
- 2 tablespoons olive oil
- 4 cloves garlic, minced
- 1/4 teaspoon red pepper flakes (optional)
- 1/2 cup chicken broth
- 1/4 cup dry white wine (optional)
- 1/4 cup fresh lemon juice (about 2 lemons)
- 1/4 cup grated Parmesan cheese
- 2 tablespoons butter
- 1/4 cup fresh parsley, chopped
- Sea salt and black pepper, to taste
- Lemon wedges (optional for serving)

Cooking Instructions

1. **Prepare the Shrimp:** Pat the shrimp dry with paper towels and season with sea salt and black pepper.
2. **Cook the Shrimp:** In a large skillet, heat the olive oil over medium-high heat. Add the shrimp and cook for 2-3 minutes on each side until pink and opaque. Remove the shrimp from the skillet and set aside.
3. **Cook the Garlic:** In the same skillet, add the minced garlic and red pepper flakes (if using). Cook for about 1 minute until fragrant.
4. **Add the Liquid:** Pour in the chicken broth and white wine (if using) and bring to a simmer. Cook for 2-3 minutes until the liquid reduces slightly.
5. **Add the Zoodles:** Add the spiralized zucchini noodles to the skillet and toss to coat in the sauce. Cook for 2-3 minutes until the zoodles are tender but still slightly firm.
6. **Finish the Dish:** Stir in the fresh lemon juice, grated Parmesan cheese, and butter. Return the cooked shrimp to the skillet and toss everything together until well combined. Cook for another minute until heated through.
7. **Serve:** Garnish with fresh parsley and serve with lemon wedges if desired. Serve hot.

Nutritional Facts

- **Calories:** 300 kcal
- **Protein:** 25g
- **Fat:** 15g
- **Saturated Fat:** 5g
- **Cholesterol:** 200mg
- **Sodium:** 800mg
- **Potassium:** 700mg
- **Fiber:** 3g
- **Sugar:** 4g
- **Vitamin C:** 25mg

Cooking Tips

- ✓ **Zoodles:** Spiralize the zucchini just before cooking to keep them fresh and prevent them from becoming too watery.

- ✓ **Shrimp:** Use large shrimp for the best texture and flavor. You can also use other seafood like scallops or a mix of both.

- ✓ **Sauce:** Adjust the amount of lemon juice and Parmesan cheese to taste. Add more red pepper flakes if you like it spicy.

Zoodle shrimp scampi is a light and flavorful dish featuring tender shrimp and fresh zucchini noodles tossed in a garlic lemon sauce, perfect for a healthy and satisfying low-carb meal.

Recipe 150: Low-Carb Beef Bourguignon

Prep Time: 20 minutes | Cooking Time: 2 hours | Servings: 4

Ingredients

- 2 pounds beef stew meat, cut into 1-inch cubes
- 4 slices bacon, chopped
- 1 medium onion, chopped
- 2 cloves garlic, minced
- 1 cup carrots, sliced
- 2 cups mushrooms, sliced
- 2 tablespoons tomato paste
- 2 cups beef broth
- 1 cup dry red wine (optional)
- 1 tablespoon fresh thyme, chopped (or 1 teaspoon dried thyme)
- 2 bay leaves
- 2 tablespoons olive oil
- Sea salt and black pepper, to taste
- Fresh parsley, chopped (optional for garnish)

Cooking Instructions

1. **Prepare the Beef:** Season the beef stew meat with sea salt and black pepper. In a large Dutch oven, heat the olive oil over medium-high heat. Add the beef and cook until browned on all sides. Remove the beef and set aside.

2. **Cook the Bacon:** In the same Dutch oven, add the chopped bacon and cook until crispy. Remove the bacon and set aside, leaving the bacon fat in the pot.

3. **Cook the Vegetables:** Add the chopped onion, minced garlic, sliced carrots, and sliced mushrooms to the pot. Cook for 5-7 minutes until the vegetables are softened.

4. **Add the Tomato Paste:** Stir in the tomato paste and cook for another 2 minutes.

5. **Add the Liquid:** Pour in the beef broth and red wine (if using). Add the browned beef, cooked bacon, fresh thyme, and bay leaves. Bring to a simmer.

6. **Simmer:** Cover the Dutch oven with a lid and simmer on low heat for about 2 hours, or until the beef is tender and the sauce has thickened. Stir occasionally.

7. **Serve:** Remove the bay leaves and adjust seasoning with sea salt and black pepper if needed. Garnish with fresh parsley if desired. Serve hot.

Nutritional Facts

- **Calories:** 450 kcal
- **Protein:** 40g
- **Fat:** 25g
- **Saturated Fat:** 10g
- **Cholesterol:** 110mg
- **Sodium:** 900mg
- **Potassium:** 900mg
- **Fiber:** 3g
- **Sugar:** 5g
- **Vitamin A:** 7000 IU

Cooking Tips

- ✓ **Beef:** Use a good quality beef stew meat for the best flavor. Searing the meat properly helps to develop a rich flavor.
- ✓ **Vegetables:** Adjust the amount of carrots and mushrooms to your preference. You can also add other low-carb vegetables like celery or turnips.

Low-carb beef bourguignon is a hearty and flavorful dish featuring tender beef simmered in a rich broth with vegetables and herbs, perfect for a satisfying and comforting low-carb meal.

Bonus Recipes

Recipe B-1: Avocado Tuna Salad

Prep Time: 10 minutes | Cooking Time: 0 minutes | Servings: 2

Ingredients

- 2 cans tuna in water, drained
- 1 ripe avocado, diced
- 1/4 cup red onion, finely chopped
- 1 celery stalk, finely chopped
- 1 tablespoon fresh lemon juice
- 2 tablespoons mayonnaise
- 1 tablespoon fresh dill, chopped (optional)
- 1/2 teaspoon sea salt
- 1/4 teaspoon black pepper
- Mixed greens or lettuce leaves for serving

Cooking Instructions

1. **Prepare the Ingredients:** Drain the tuna and place it in a medium bowl. Dice the avocado, chop the red onion and celery, and set aside.
2. **Mix the Salad:** Add the diced avocado, chopped red onion, celery, fresh lemon juice, mayonnaise, fresh dill (if using), sea salt, and black pepper to the bowl with the tuna. Gently mix until well combined.
3. **Serve:** Serve the avocado tuna salad on a bed of mixed greens or lettuce leaves.

Nutritional Facts

- **Calories:** 250 kcal
- **Protein:** 25g
- **Fat:** 15g
- **Saturated Fat:** 2.5g
- **Cholesterol:** 35mg
- **Sodium:** 600mg
- **Potassium:** 700mg
- **Fiber:** 6g
- **Sugar:** 1g
- **Vitamin C:** 15mg

Cooking Tips

- ✓ **Tuna:** Use high-quality canned tuna for the best flavor and texture.
- ✓ **Avocado:** Ensure the avocado is ripe for a creamy texture. It should yield slightly when pressed.
- ✓ **Customization:** Add other vegetables like cherry tomatoes, bell peppers, or cucumber for extra flavor and crunch.
- ✓ **Serving Suggestions:** Enjoy as a salad, use as a filling for lettuce wraps, or spread on low-carb bread for a sandwich.
- ✓ **Storage:** Store any leftovers in an airtight container in the refrigerator for up to 2 days. Note that the avocado may brown slightly.

Avocado tuna salad is a nutritious and easy-to-make dish, combining creamy avocado with protein-rich tuna and fresh vegetables, perfect for a quick lunch or light dinner.

Recipe B-2: Cauliflower Mac and Cheese

Prep Time: 15 minutes | Cooking Time: 20 minutes | Servings: 4

Ingredients

- 1 large head of cauliflower, cut into florets
- 1 cup heavy cream
- 1 cup shredded cheddar cheese
- 1/2 cup grated Parmesan cheese
- 2 tablespoons cream cheese
- 1 teaspoon Dijon mustard
- 1/2 teaspoon garlic powder
- 1/2 teaspoon onion powder
- 1/2 teaspoon sea salt
- 1/4 teaspoon black pepper
- 1/4 teaspoon smoked paprika (optional)
- Fresh parsley, chopped (optional for garnish)

Cooking Instructions

1. **Preheat the Oven:** Preheat your oven to 375°F (190°C).
2. **Cook the Cauliflower:** Bring a large pot of salted water to a boil. Add the cauliflower florets and cook for 5-7 minutes until tender but still firm. Drain well and pat dry with paper towels.
3. **Prepare the Cheese Sauce:** In a large saucepan, heat the heavy cream over medium heat until it begins to simmer. Reduce the heat to low and stir in the cheddar cheese, Parmesan cheese, cream cheese, Dijon mustard, garlic powder, onion powder, sea salt, black pepper, and smoked paprika (if using). Stir until the cheese is melted and the sauce is smooth.
4. **Combine Cauliflower and Sauce:** Add the cooked cauliflower to the cheese sauce and stir to coat evenly.
5. **Bake:** Transfer the cauliflower and cheese mixture to a baking dish. Bake in the preheated oven for 15 minutes or until the top is golden and bubbly.
6. **Serve:** Garnish with fresh parsley if desired and serve hot.

Nutritional Facts

- **Calories:** 350 kcal
- **Protein:** 12g
- **Fat:** 30g
- **Saturated Fat:** 18g
- **Cholesterol:** 95mg
- **Sodium:** 700mg
- **Potassium:** 500mg
- **Fiber:** 3g
- **Sugar:** 3g
- **Vitamin A:** 800 IU

Cooking Tips

- ✓ **Cauliflower:** Ensure the cauliflower is well-drained and patted dry to prevent the dish from becoming watery.
- ✓ **Cheese:** Use freshly grated cheese for the best melting quality. Pre-shredded cheese often contains additives that can affect the texture.
- ✓ **Customization:** Add cooked bacon, chopped green onions, or jalapeños for extra flavor.

Cauliflower mac and cheese is a delicious and creamy low-carb alternative to traditional mac and cheese, perfect for satisfying comfort food cravings without the carbs.

Recipe B-3: Garlic Butter Shrimp with Broccoli

Prep Time: 10 minutes | Cooking Time: 10 minutes | Servings: 4

Ingredients

- 1 lb. large shrimp, peeled and deveined
- 4 cups broccoli florets
- 3 tablespoons butter
- 4 cloves garlic, minced
- 1 tablespoon olive oil
- 1 tablespoon lemon juice
- 1/4 teaspoon red pepper flakes (optional)
- 1/2 teaspoon sea salt
- 1/4 teaspoon black pepper
- Fresh parsley, chopped (optional for garnish)
- Lemon wedges for serving (optional)

Cooking Instructions

1. **Prepare the Shrimp and Broccoli:** Pat the shrimp dry with paper towels. Cut the broccoli into bite-sized florets if not already done.
2. **Cook the Broccoli:** In a large skillet, heat 1 tablespoon of olive oil over medium-high heat. Add the broccoli florets and cook for 4-5 minutes until they are tender-crisp. Remove from the skillet and set aside.
3. **Cook the Shrimp:** In the same skillet, melt the butter over medium heat. Add the minced garlic and cook for 1 minute until fragrant. Add the shrimp and cook for 2-3 minutes on each side until they are pink and opaque.
4. **Combine and Season:** Return the cooked broccoli to the skillet. Add the lemon juice, red pepper flakes (if using),

sea salt, and black pepper. Toss to combine and heat through.
5. **Serve:** Garnish with fresh parsley and serve with lemon wedges if desired.

Nutritional Facts

- **Calories:** 200 kcal
- **Protein:** 20g
- **Fat:** 12g
- **Saturated Fat:** 6g
- **Cholesterol:** 190mg
- **Sodium:** 800mg
- **Potassium:** 500mg
- **Fiber:** 3g
- **Sugar:** 2g
- **Vitamin C:** 60mg

Cooking Tips

- ✓ **Shrimp:** Use large shrimp for a meatier texture and ensure they are peeled and deveined for convenience.
- ✓ **Broccoli:** Cook the broccoli to your desired level of tenderness. For a crisper texture, cook for less time.
- ✓ **Butter:** For a richer flavor, use clarified butter or ghee.
- ✓ **Serving Suggestions:** Pair with cauliflower rice or a fresh salad for a complete meal.
- ✓ **Storage:** Store leftovers in an airtight container in the refrigerator for up to 2 days. Reheat gently in a skillet or microwave.

Garlic butter shrimp with broccoli is a quick, flavorful, and nutritious dish that combines succulent shrimp with tender broccoli in a rich garlic butter sauce, perfect for a healthy and satisfying dinner.

Recipe B-4: Spinach and Feta Stuffed Chicken Breasts

Prep Time: 15 minutes | Cooking Time: 25 minutes | Servings: 4

Ingredients

- 4 boneless, skinless chicken breasts
- 2 cups fresh spinach, chopped
- 1/2 cup feta cheese, crumbled
- 2 cloves garlic, minced
- 1 tablespoon olive oil
- 1 teaspoon dried oregano
- 1/2 teaspoon sea salt
- 1/4 teaspoon black pepper
- 1/4 teaspoon paprika
- Toothpicks (for securing the chicken)

Cooking Instructions

1. **Preheat the Oven:** Preheat your oven to 375°F (190°C). Line a baking sheet with parchment paper.
2. **Prepare the Spinach and Feta Mixture:** In a medium bowl, combine the chopped spinach, crumbled feta cheese, and minced garlic. Mix well.
3. **Prepare the Chicken:** Using a sharp knife, cut a horizontal slit along the thin side of each chicken breast to create a pocket. Be careful not to cut all the way through.
4. **Stuff the Chicken:** Spoon the spinach and feta mixture into each chicken breast pocket. Secure the opening with toothpicks.
5. **Season the Chicken:** In a small bowl, mix together the olive oil, dried oregano, sea salt, black pepper, and paprika. Brush the mixture evenly over the stuffed chicken breasts.
6. **Bake:** Place the stuffed chicken breasts on the prepared baking sheet and bake in the preheated oven for 25-30 minutes, or until the chicken is cooked through and the internal temperature reaches 165°F (74°C).
7. **Serve:** Remove the toothpicks before serving. Serve hot.

Nutritional Facts

- **Calories:** 300 kcal
- **Protein:** 35g
- **Fat:** 15g
- **Saturated Fat:** 5g
- **Cholesterol:** 100mg
- **Sodium:** 600mg
- **Potassium:** 700mg
- **Fiber:** 2g
- **Sugar:** 1g
- **Vitamin A:** 3000 IU

Cooking Tips

- ✓ **Chicken:** Use similar-sized chicken breasts for even cooking. Pound the chicken breasts to an even thickness if needed.
- ✓ **Filling:** Ensure the spinach is well-chopped to make stuffing the chicken easier.
- ✓ **Secure Filling:** Use toothpicks to secure the stuffing inside the chicken breasts and prevent it from leaking out during baking.
- ✓ **Serving Suggestions:** Pair with a side of roasted vegetables or a fresh green salad for a complete meal.
- ✓ **Storage:** Store any leftovers in an airtight container in the refrigerator for up to 3 days. Reheat in the oven or microwave before serving.

Spinach and feta stuffed chicken breasts are a flavorful and nutritious dish that combines tender chicken with a savory spinach and feta filling, perfect for a satisfying and healthy dinner.

Recipe B-5: Stuffed Bell Peppers with Cauliflower Rice

Prep Time: 20 minutes | Cooking Time: 30 minutes | Servings: 4

Ingredients

- 4 large bell peppers (any color), tops cut off and seeds removed
- 1 lb. ground turkey or beef
- 2 cups cauliflower rice
- 1 small onion, finely chopped
- 2 cloves garlic, minced
- 1 cup diced tomatoes (canned or fresh)
- 1/2 cup shredded cheddar cheese
- 1 tablespoon olive oil
- 1 teaspoon dried oregano
- 1 teaspoon dried basil
- 1/2 teaspoon sea salt
- 1/4 teaspoon black pepper
- Fresh parsley, chopped (optional for garnish)

Cooking Instructions

1. **Preheat the Oven:** Preheat your oven to 375°F (190°C).
2. **Prepare the Bell Peppers:** Cut the tops off the bell peppers and remove the seeds and membranes. Place the peppers in a baking dish.
3. **Cook the Meat and Vegetables:** In a large skillet, heat the olive oil over medium heat. Add the chopped onion and minced garlic and cook for 2-3 minutes until softened. Add the ground turkey or beef and cook until browned, breaking it up with a spoon as it cooks. Drain any excess fat.
4. **Add Tomatoes and Seasonings:** Stir in the diced tomatoes, cauliflower rice, dried oregano, dried basil, sea salt, and black pepper. Cook for 5-7 minutes until the cauliflower rice is tender and the flavors are well combined.
5. **Stuff the Peppers:** Spoon the meat and cauliflower rice mixture into the bell peppers, filling them evenly. Top each pepper with shredded cheddar cheese.
6. **Bake:** Cover the baking dish with foil and bake in the preheated oven for 25 minutes. Remove the foil and bake for an additional 5 minutes or until the cheese is melted and bubbly.
7. **Serve:** Garnish with fresh parsley if desired and serve hot.

Nutritional Facts

- **Calories:** 300 kcal
- **Protein:** 25g
- **Fat:** 15g
- **Saturated Fat:** 6g
- **Cholesterol:** 80mg
- **Sodium:** 600mg
- **Potassium:** 700mg
- **Fiber:** 5g
- **Sugar:** 6g
- **Vitamin C:** 120mg

Cooking Tips

- ✓ **Bell Peppers:** Choose bell peppers that can stand upright for easier stuffing and baking.
- ✓ **Cauliflower Rice:** To make your own cauliflower rice, pulse cauliflower florets in a food processor until they resemble rice grains.
- ✓ **Cheese:** Use your favorite type of cheese, such as mozzarella or Monterey Jack, for different flavor variations.

Stuffed bell peppers with cauliflower rice are a delicious and nutritious low-carb meal, combining savory meat and vegetables with tender bell peppers, perfect for a hearty and satisfying dinner.

Recipe B-6: Broccoli Cheddar Soup

Prep Time: 10 minutes | Cooking Time: 20 minutes | Servings: 4

Ingredients

- 4 cups broccoli florets
- 1 small onion, finely chopped
- 2 cloves garlic, minced
- 2 cups chicken broth (low sodium)
- 1 cup heavy cream
- 2 cups shredded cheddar cheese
- 1 tablespoon butter
- 1 teaspoon dried thyme
- 1/2 teaspoon sea salt
- 1/4 teaspoon black pepper
- Fresh parsley, chopped (optional for garnish)

Cooking Instructions

1. **Cook the Vegetables:** In a large pot, melt the butter over medium heat. Add the chopped onion and minced garlic and cook for 2-3 minutes until softened.
2. **Add the Broccoli and Broth:** Add the broccoli florets and chicken broth to the pot. Bring to a simmer and cook for 10 minutes or until the broccoli is tender.
3. **Blend the Soup:** Use an immersion blender to puree the soup until smooth. Alternatively, transfer the soup in batches to a blender and blend until smooth, then return to the pot.
4. **Add Cream and Cheese:** Stir in the heavy cream and shredded cheddar cheese. Cook over low heat, stirring frequently, until the cheese is melted, and the soup is heated through. Add the dried thyme, sea salt, and black pepper.
5. **Serve:** Ladle the soup into bowls and garnish with fresh parsley if desired. Serve hot.

Nutritional Facts

- **Calories:** 400 kcal
- **Protein:** 15g
- **Fat:** 35g
- **Saturated Fat:** 20g
- **Cholesterol:** 110mg
- **Sodium:** 600mg
- **Potassium:** 600mg
- **Fiber:** 3g
- **Sugar:** 3g
- **Vitamin A:** 2000 IU

Cooking Tips

✓ **Broccoli:** Use fresh or frozen broccoli. If using frozen, adjust the cooking time as needed.
✓ **Cheese:** Use freshly shredded cheddar cheese for the best melting quality. Pre-shredded cheese often contains additives that can affect texture.
✓ **Consistency:** For a chunkier soup, reserve some broccoli florets before blending and stir them back into the soup after blending.
✓ **Serving Suggestions:** Pair with a side salad or low-carb bread for a complete meal.

Broccoli cheddar soup is a creamy and comforting dish packed with the flavors of tender broccoli and rich cheddar cheese, perfect for a warm and satisfying meal.

Recipe B-7: Greek Salad with Grilled Chicken

Prep Time: 15 minutes | Cooking Time: 15 minutes | Servings: 4

Ingredients

- 2 boneless, skinless chicken breasts
- 1 tablespoon olive oil
- 1 teaspoon dried oregano
- 1/2 teaspoon sea salt
- 1/4 teaspoon black pepper
- 6 cups mixed greens (such as romaine, arugula, and spinach)
- 1 cup cherry tomatoes, halved
- 1 cucumber, sliced
- 1/2 red onion, thinly sliced
- 1/2 cup Kalamata olives, pitted
- 1/2 cup feta cheese, crumbled
- 1/4 cup fresh parsley, chopped

Dressing Ingredients

- 1/4 cup olive oil
- 2 tablespoons red wine vinegar
- 1 teaspoon Dijon mustard
- 1 teaspoon dried oregano
- 1/2 teaspoon garlic powder
- 1/2 teaspoon sea salt
- 1/4 teaspoon black pepper

Cooking Instructions

1. **Prepare the Chicken:** Preheat your grill to medium-high heat. Brush the chicken breasts with 1 tablespoon of olive oil and season with dried oregano, sea salt, and black pepper.
2. **Grill the Chicken:** Place the chicken breasts on the grill and cook for 6-7 minutes on each side or until the internal temperature reaches 165°F (74°C). Remove from the grill and let rest for 5 minutes before slicing.
3. **Prepare the Dressing:** In a small bowl, whisk together the olive oil, red wine vinegar, Dijon mustard, dried oregano, garlic powder, sea salt, and black pepper until well combined.
4. **Assemble the Salad:** In a large bowl, combine the mixed greens, cherry tomatoes, cucumber, red onion, Kalamata olives, and feta cheese. Toss gently to combine.
5. **Add Chicken and Dressing:** Top the salad with the sliced grilled chicken. Drizzle the dressing over the salad and toss gently to coat.
6. **Serve:** Garnish with fresh parsley and serve immediately.

Nutritional Facts

- **Calories:** 350 kcal
- **Protein:** 25g
- **Fat:** 25g
- **Saturated Fat:** 7g
- **Cholesterol:** 70mg
- **Sodium:** 800mg
- **Potassium:** 600mg
- **Fiber:** 4g
- **Sugar:** 4g
- **Vitamin A:** 2000 IU

Cooking Tips

✓ **Chicken:** For extra flavor, marinate the chicken breasts in olive oil and season for at least 30 minutes before grilling.
✓ **Dressing:** Adjust the amount of red wine vinegar and Dijon mustard to taste for a more tangy or mild flavor.

Greek salad with grilled chicken is a refreshing and nutritious meal, combining crisp vegetables, savory feta, and juicy grilled chicken, perfect for a healthy and satisfying lunch or dinner.

Recipe B-8: Cauliflower Fried Rice

Prep Time: 15 minutes | Cooking Time: 15 minutes | Servings: 4

Ingredients

- 1 large head of cauliflower, riced
- 2 tablespoons olive oil
- 1 small onion, finely chopped
- 2 cloves garlic, minced
- 1 cup frozen peas and carrots, thawed
- 2 eggs, beaten
- 3 tablespoons soy sauce (low sodium)
- 1 tablespoon sesame oil
- 1/2 teaspoon ground ginger
- 1/4 teaspoon black pepper
- 2 green onions, sliced (optional for garnish)

Cooking Instructions

1. **Prepare the Cauliflower Rice:** Cut the cauliflower into florets and pulse in a food processor until it resembles rice grains. Set it aside.
2. **Cook the Aromatics:** In a large skillet or wok, heat the olive oil over medium-high heat. Add the chopped onion and minced garlic and cook for 2-3 minutes until softened.
3. **Cook the Vegetables:** Add the peas and carrots to the skillet and cook for an additional 2-3 minutes until heated through.
4. **Cook the Eggs:** Push the vegetables to one side of the skillet. Pour the beaten eggs into the empty side and scramble until fully cooked. Mix the eggs with the vegetables.
5. **Add the Cauliflower Rice:** Add the rice cauliflower to the skillet and stir to combine. Cook for 5-7 minutes, stirring occasionally, until the cauliflower is tender.
6. **Season the Fried Rice:** Stir in the soy sauce, sesame oil, ground ginger, and black pepper. Cook for an additional 2-3 minutes until the flavors are well combined and the cauliflower is slightly crispy.
7. **Serve:** Garnish with sliced green onions if desired and serve hot.

Nutritional Facts

- **Calories:** 150 kcal
- **Protein:** 6g
- **Fat:** 10g
- **Saturated Fat:** 2g
- **Cholesterol:** 70mg
- **Sodium:** 400mg
- **Potassium:** 500mg
- **Fiber:** 4g
- **Sugar:** 4g
- **Vitamin C:** 60mg

Cooking Tips

- ✓ **Cauliflower Rice:** Ensure the cauliflower is pulsed to an even consistency. Avoid over-processing, which can make it mushy.
- ✓ **Vegetables:** Add other vegetables like bell peppers, mushrooms, or snap peas for additional flavor and nutrition.
- ✓ **Eggs:** If you prefer, cook the eggs separately and then add them to the skillet.
- ✓ **Seasoning:** Adjust the soy sauce and sesame oil to taste. For a gluten-free option, use tamari or coconut aminos instead of soy sauce.

Cauliflower fried rice is a delicious and healthy alternative to traditional fried rice, offering a low-carb, nutrient-packed option that is quick and easy to prepare, perfect for a light meal or side dish.

Recipe B-9: Keto Chocolate Mousse

Prep Time: 10 minutes | Cooking Time: 0 minutes | Servings: 4

Ingredients

- 1 cup heavy cream
- 2 tablespoons unsweetened cocoa powder
- 2 tablespoons powdered erythritol (or another low-carb sweetener)
- 1 teaspoon vanilla extract
- Fresh berries and mint leaves for garnish (optional)

Cooking Instructions

1. **Whip the Cream:** In a large mixing bowl, beat the heavy cream with an electric mixer on medium-high speed until it begins to thicken.
2. **Add Cocoa and Sweetener:** Sift the unsweetened cocoa powder and powdered erythritol into the whipped cream. Add the vanilla extract. Continue to beat until stiff peaks form and the mixture is smooth and creamy.
3. **Serve:** Spoon the chocolate mousse into serving dishes. Garnish with fresh berries and mint leaves if desired. Serve immediately or refrigerate until ready to serve.

Nutritional Facts

- **Calories:** 200 kcal
- **Protein:** 2g
- **Fat:** 20g
- **Saturated Fat:** 12g
- **Cholesterol:** 75mg
- **Sodium:** 20mg
- **Potassium:** 100mg
- **Fiber:** 1g
- **Sugar:** 1g
- **Vitamin A:** 800 IU

Cooking Tips

- ✓ **Cream:** Ensure the heavy cream is very cold before whipping to achieve the best texture.
- ✓ **Sweetener:** Adjust the amount of sweetener to taste. If you prefer a sweeter mousse, add more powdered erythritol.
- ✓ **Cocoa Powder:** Use high-quality unsweetened cocoa powder for a richer chocolate flavor.
- ✓ **Serving Suggestions:** Pair with fresh berries or a dollop of whipped cream for an extra indulgence.
- ✓ **Storage:** Store any leftovers in an airtight container in the refrigerator for up to 3 days. Re-whip before serving if needed.

Keto chocolate mousse is a rich, creamy, and satisfying dessert that is low in carbs and high in flavor, perfect for indulging your sweet tooth while staying on track with your dietary goals.

Recipe B-10: Italian Sausage and Zucchini Skillet

Prep Time: 10 minutes | Cooking Time: 20 minutes | Servings: 4

Ingredients

- 1 lb. Italian sausage (mild or spicy), casings removed
- 4 medium zucchinis, sliced into half-moons
- 1 red bell pepper, diced
- 1 small onion, finely chopped
- 2 cloves garlic, minced
- 1 tablespoon olive oil
- 1 teaspoon dried oregano
- 1 teaspoon dried basil
- 1/2 teaspoon sea salt
- 1/4 teaspoon black pepper
- 1/4 cup grated Parmesan cheese
- Fresh basil, chopped (optional for garnish)

Cooking Instructions

1. **Cook the Sausage:** In a large skillet, heat the olive oil over medium-high heat. Add the Italian sausage, breaking it up with a spoon as it cooks. Cook for 5-7 minutes until browned and cooked through. Remove from the skillet and set aside.
2. **Sauté the Vegetables:** In the same skillet, add the chopped onion and minced garlic. Cook for 2-3 minutes until softened. Add the diced red bell pepper and zucchini slices and cook for an additional 5-7 minutes until the vegetables are tender.
3. **Combine and Season:** Return the cooked sausage to the skillet. Stir in the dried oregano, dried basil, sea salt, and black pepper. Cook for another 2-3 minutes until everything is heated through and well combined.
4. **Serve:** Sprinkle with grated Parmesan cheese and garnish with fresh basil if desired. Serve hot.

Nutritional Facts

- **Calories:** 350 kcal
- **Protein:** 18g
- **Fat:** 28g
- **Saturated Fat:** 9g
- **Cholesterol:** 60mg
- **Sodium:** 800mg
- **Potassium:** 700mg
- **Fiber:** 3g
- **Sugar:** 5g
- **Vitamin C:** 60mg

Cooking Tips

- ✓ **Sausage:** Use your preferred type of Italian sausage, whether mild or spicy, to suit your taste.
- ✓ **Vegetables:** Add other vegetables like mushrooms or spinach for extra flavor and nutrition.
- ✓ **Cheese:** Substitute Parmesan cheese with mozzarella or feta for a different flavor profile.
- ✓ **Serving Suggestions:** Pair with a side salad or cauliflower rice for a complete meal.
- ✓ **Storage:** Store leftovers in an airtight a skillet or microwave before serving.

Italian sausage and zucchini skillet is a quick and flavorful one-pan meal, combining savory sausage with fresh vegetables and herbs, perfect for a satisfying and low-carb dinner.

Recipe B-11: Buffalo Chicken Lettuce Wraps

Prep Time: 15 minutes | Cooking Time: 10 minutes | Servings: 4

Ingredients

- 1 lb. boneless, skinless chicken breasts, cooked and shredded
- 1/4 cup hot sauce (such as Frank's Red Hot)
- 2 tablespoons butter, melted
- 1 teaspoon garlic powder
- 1/2 teaspoon onion powder
- 1/4 teaspoon sea salt
- 1/4 teaspoon black pepper
- 8 large lettuce leaves (such as romaine or butter lettuce)
- 1/4 cup blue cheese or ranch dressing
- 1/2 cup shredded carrots
- 1/2 cup celery, finely chopped
- Fresh parsley, chopped (optional for garnish)

Cooking Instructions

1. **Prepare the Chicken:** In a large bowl, combine the shredded chicken, hot sauce, melted butter, garlic powder, onion powder, sea salt, and black pepper. Mix well until the chicken is evenly coated.
2. **Warm the Chicken:** In a skillet over medium heat, warm the buffalo chicken mixture for about 5 minutes, stirring occasionally until heated through.
3. **Assemble the Wraps:** Lay the lettuce leaves flat on a serving platter. Divide the buffalo chicken mixture evenly among the lettuce leaves.
4. **Add Toppings:** Top each lettuce wrap with a drizzle of blue cheese or ranch dressing, shredded carrots, and chopped celery.
5. **Serve:** Garnish with fresh parsley if desired and serve immediately.

Nutritional Facts

- **Calories:** 250 kcal
- **Protein:** 28g
- **Fat:** 14g
- **Saturated Fat:** 5g
- **Cholesterol:** 80mg
- **Sodium:** 800mg
- **Potassium:** 600mg
- **Fiber:** 2g
- **Sugar:** 2g
- **Vitamin A:** 5000 IU

Cooking Tips

- ✓ **Chicken:** Use rotisserie chicken or cook your chicken breasts in a slow cooker for easy shredding.
- ✓ **Hot Sauce:** Adjust the amount of hot sauce to control the heat level according to your preference.
- ✓ **Lettuce:** Use large, sturdy lettuce leaves that can hold the fillings without tearing.
- ✓ **Serving Suggestions:** Pair with a side of cucumber salad or roasted vegetables for a complete meal.

Buffalo chicken lettuce wraps are a spicy and satisfying low-carb meal, combining flavorful buffalo chicken with crisp lettuce and fresh vegetables, perfect for a quick and healthy lunch or dinner.

Recipe B-12: Almond-Crusted Chicken Tenders

Prep Time: 15 minutes | Cooking Time: 20 minutes | Servings: 4

Ingredients

- 1 lb. chicken tenders
- 1 cup almond flour
- 1/2 cup grated Parmesan cheese
- 1 teaspoon paprika
- 1/2 teaspoon garlic powder
- 1/2 teaspoon onion powder
- 1/2 teaspoon sea salt
- 1/4 teaspoon black pepper
- 2 large eggs
- 2 tablespoons olive oil
- Fresh parsley, chopped (optional for garnish)

Cooking Instructions

1. **Preheat the Oven:** Preheat your oven to 400°F (200°C). Line a baking sheet with parchment paper or a silicone baking mat.
2. **Prepare the Breading:** In a shallow dish, combine the almond flour, grated Parmesan cheese, paprika, garlic powder, onion powder, sea salt, and black pepper. Mix well.
3. **Prepare the Egg Wash:** In another shallow dish, beat the eggs.
4. **Bread the Chicken:** Dip each chicken tender in the beaten eggs, then coat with the almond flour mixture, pressing gently to adhere.
5. **Arrange on Baking Sheet:** Place the breaded chicken tenders on the prepared baking sheet. Drizzle or spray the tops with olive oil.
6. **Bake:** Bake in the preheated oven for 20 minutes, turning once halfway through, until the chicken is cooked through, and the coating is golden brown.
7. **Serve:** Garnish with fresh parsley if desired and serve hot.

Nutritional Facts

- **Calories:** 350 kcal
- **Protein:** 30g
- **Fat:** 20g
- **Saturated Fat:** 4g
- **Cholesterol:** 140mg
- **Sodium:** 600mg
- **Potassium:** 500mg
- **Fiber:** 3g
- **Sugar:** 1g
- **Vitamin E:** 4mg

Cooking Tips

- ✓ **Chicken:** For even cooking, make sure all chicken tenders are of similar thickness.
- ✓ **Almond Flour:** Use blanched almond flour for a finer texture and better adherence.
- ✓ **Crispiness:** To achieve extra crispiness, place the baking sheet on the upper rack of the oven for the last few minutes of baking.
- ✓ **Serving Suggestions:** Serve with a side of low-carb dipping sauce, such as ranch or marinara, and a fresh salad or steamed vegetables.

Almond-crusted chicken tenders are a delicious and healthy alternative to traditional breaded chicken, offering a low-carb, protein-packed option that's perfect for a satisfying meal or snack.

Recipe B-13: Shrimp and Avocado Salad

Prep Time: 15 minutes | Cooking Time: 5 minutes | Servings: 4

Ingredients

- 1 lb. shrimp, peeled and deveined
- 1 tablespoon olive oil
- 1 teaspoon garlic powder
- 1/2 teaspoon sea salt
- 1/4 teaspoon black pepper
- 4 cups mixed greens (such as arugula, spinach, and romaine)
- 1 large avocado, diced
- 1 cup cherry tomatoes, halved
- 1/4 cup red onion, thinly sliced
- 1/4 cup fresh cilantro, chopped
- 1/4 cup feta cheese, crumbled (optional)

Dressing Ingredients

- 1/4 cup olive oil
- 2 tablespoons lime juice
- 1 teaspoon honey or low-carb sweetener
- 1 teaspoon Dijon mustard
- 1/2 teaspoon sea salt
- 1/4 teaspoon black pepper

Cooking Instructions

1. **Prepare the Shrimp:** In a bowl, toss the shrimp with olive oil, garlic powder, sea salt, and black pepper.
2. **Cook the Shrimp:** Heat a skillet over medium-high heat. Add the shrimp and cook for 2-3 minutes on each side until pink and opaque. Remove from heat and set aside.
3. **Prepare the Dressing:** In a small bowl, whisk together the olive oil, lime juice, honey or low-carb sweetener, Dijon mustard, sea salt, and black pepper until well combined.

4. **Assemble the Salad:** In a large bowl, combine the mixed greens, diced avocado, cherry tomatoes, red onion, and fresh cilantro. Add the cooked shrimp and toss gently to combine.
5. **Dress the Salad:** Drizzle the dressing over the salad and toss gently to coat.
6. **Serve:** Sprinkle with crumbled feta cheese if desired and serve immediately.

Nutritional Facts

- **Calories:** 300 kcal
- **Protein:** 20g
- **Fat:** 20g
- **Saturated Fat:** 3.5g
- **Cholesterol:** 150mg
- **Sodium:** 700mg
- **Potassium:** 600mg
- **Fiber:** 5g
- **Sugar:** 3g
- **Vitamin C:** 25mg

Cooking Tips

- ✓ **Shrimp:** Ensure the shrimp are fully cooked but not overdone to avoid a rubbery texture.
- ✓ **Avocado:** Use a ripe but firm avocado for the best texture.
- ✓ **Dressing:** Adjust the lime juice and sweetener to taste for a more tangy or sweet flavor.
- ✓ **Customization:** Add other ingredients like cucumbers, bell peppers, or radishes for extra flavor and crunch.
- ✓ **Serving Suggestions:** Pair with a side of low-carb crackers or a slice of keto bread for a complete meal.

Shrimp and avocado salad is a light, refreshing, and nutritious dish, combining the fresh flavors of shrimp and avocado with a tangy lime dressing, perfect for a healthy lunch or dinner.

Recipe B-14: Low-Carb Chicken Alfredo with Spaghetti Squash

Prep Time: 15 minutes | Cooking Time: 45 minutes | Servings: 4

Ingredients

- 1 large spaghetti squash
- 1 lb boneless, skinless chicken breasts sliced into strips
- 2 tablespoons olive oil
- 3 cloves garlic, minced
- 1 cup heavy cream
- 1 cup grated Parmesan cheese
- 1/2 teaspoon garlic powder
- 1/2 teaspoon onion powder
- 1/2 teaspoon sea salt
- 1/4 teaspoon black pepper
- 1 tablespoon fresh parsley, chopped (optional for garnish)

Cooking Instructions

1. **Preheat the Oven:** Preheat your oven to 400°F (200°C). Line a baking sheet with parchment paper.
2. **Prepare the Spaghetti Squash:** Cut the spaghetti squash in half lengthwise and scoop out the seeds. Drizzle with 1 tablespoon of olive oil and season with sea salt and black pepper. Place cut-side down on the prepared baking sheet and bake for 35-40 minutes until tender.
3. **Cook the Chicken:** While the spaghetti squash is baking, heat the remaining 1 tablespoon of olive oil in a large skillet over medium-high heat. Add the chicken strips and cook until browned and cooked through about 5-7 minutes. Remove from the skillet and set aside.
4. **Make the Alfredo Sauce:** In the same skillet, add the minced garlic and cook for 1 minute until fragrant. Pour in the heavy cream and bring to a simmer. Stir in the grated Parmesan cheese, garlic powder, onion powder, sea salt, and black pepper. Cook for 3-4 minutes, stirring frequently, until the sauce thickens.
5. **Combine:** Use a fork to scrape out the spaghetti squash strands and add them to the skillet with the Alfredo sauce. Add the cooked chicken and toss to combine until everything is evenly coated with the sauce.
6. **Serve:** Garnish with fresh parsley if desired and serve hot.

Nutritional Facts

- **Calories:** 450 kcal
- **Protein:** 35g
- **Fat:** 30g
- **Saturated Fat:** 16g
- **Cholesterol:** 150mg
- **Sodium:** 700mg
- **Potassium:** 800mg
- **Fiber:** 4g
- **Sugar:** 4g
- **Vitamin A:** 1000 IU

Cooking Tips

- ✓ **Spaghetti Squash:** Ensure the squash is tender by poking it with a fork. If it doesn't easily penetrate, bake for an additional 5-10 minutes.
- ✓ **Chicken:** Use chicken thighs for a juicier alternative. Season with Italian seasoning for extra flavor.
- ✓ **Sauce:** For a thicker sauce, simmer longer until it reaches the desired consistency.

Low-carb chicken Alfredo with spaghetti squash is a creamy and delicious dish that combines tender chicken with rich Alfredo sauce and low-carb spaghetti squash, making it a perfect comfort food for a healthy diet.

Recipe B-15: Turkey and Spinach Stuffed Portobello Mushrooms

Prep Time: 15 minutes | Cooking Time: 25 minutes | Servings: 4

Ingredients

- 4 large portobello mushrooms, stems removed, and gills scraped out
- 1 lb. ground turkey
- 2 cups fresh spinach, chopped
- 1 small onion, finely chopped
- 2 cloves garlic, minced
- 1/2 cup ricotta cheese
- 1/2 cup shredded mozzarella cheese
- 1/4 cup grated Parmesan cheese
- 1 tablespoon olive oil
- 1 teaspoon dried oregano
- 1/2 teaspoon sea salt
- 1/4 teaspoon black pepper
- Fresh parsley, chopped (optional for garnish)

Cooking Instructions

1. **Preheat the Oven:** Preheat your oven to 375°F (190°C). Line a baking sheet with parchment paper.
2. **Prepare the Mushrooms:** Brush the portobello mushrooms with olive oil on both sides and place them on the prepared baking sheet.
3. **Cook the Turkey:** In a large skillet, heat 1 tablespoon of olive oil over medium heat. Add the chopped onion and minced garlic and cook for 2-3 minutes until softened. Add the ground turkey and cook until browned and cooked through about 5-7 minutes. Drain any excess fat.
4. **Add Spinach and Seasonings:** Stir in the chopped spinach, dried oregano, sea salt, and black pepper. Cook for an additional 2-3 minutes until the spinach is wilted.
5. **Prepare the Filling:** Remove the skillet from heat and stir in the ricotta cheese and half of the shredded mozzarella cheese until well combined.
6. **Stuff the Mushrooms:** Spoon the turkey and spinach mixture into the prepared portobello mushrooms. Top each mushroom with the remaining mozzarella cheese and grated Parmesan cheese.
7. **Bake:** Bake in the preheated oven for 20-25 minutes or until the mushrooms are tender and the cheese is melted and golden brown.
8. **Serve:** Garnish with fresh parsley if desired and serve hot.

Nutritional Facts

- **Calories:** 350 kcal
- **Protein:** 30g
- **Fat:** 20g
- **Saturated Fat:** 7g
- **Cholesterol:** 90mg
- **Sodium:** 600mg
- **Potassium:** 900mg
- **Fiber:** 3g
- **Sugar:** 4g
- **Vitamin C:** 15mg

Cooking Tips

- ✓ **Mushrooms:** Use large, firm portobello mushrooms for the best results. Ensure they are thoroughly cleaned and dried before stuffing.
- ✓ **Turkey:** Substitute ground chicken or beef if preferred. For extra flavor, use Italian-seasoned ground turkey.

Turkey and spinach stuffed portobello mushrooms are a delicious and nutritious dish, combining savory ground turkey with fresh spinach and cheese, all nestled in a tender portobello mushroom cap, perfect for a satisfying and healthy meal.

Recipe B-16: Low-Carb Eggplant Lasagna

Prep Time: 20 minutes | Cooking Time: 45 minutes | Servings: 6

Ingredients

- 2 large eggplants, sliced lengthwise into 1/4-inch-thick slices
- 1 lb. ground beef or turkey
- 1 small onion, finely chopped
- 2 cloves garlic, minced
- 1 (24 oz) jar of low-carb marinara sauce
- 1 teaspoon dried oregano
- 1 teaspoon dried basil
- 1/2 teaspoon sea salt
- 1/4 teaspoon black pepper
- 2 cups ricotta cheese
- 1 egg
- 2 cups shredded mozzarella cheese
- 1/2 cup grated Parmesan cheese
- 1 tablespoon olive oil
- Fresh basil, chopped (optional for garnish)

Cooking Instructions

1. **Preheat the Oven:** Preheat your oven to 375°F (190°C). Line a baking sheet with parchment paper.
2. **Prepare the Eggplant:** Arrange the eggplant slices on the prepared baking sheet. Brush with olive oil and season with sea salt and black pepper. Bake in the preheated oven for 15 minutes until tender.
3. **Cook the Meat:** In a large skillet, heat the remaining olive oil over medium heat. Add the chopped onion and minced garlic and cook for 2-3 minutes until softened. Add the ground beef or turkey and cook until browned, breaking it up with a spoon as it cooks. Drain any excess fat.
4. **Add Marinara Sauce:** Stir in the marinara sauce, dried oregano, dried basil, sea salt, and black pepper. Simmer for 10 minutes to allow the flavors to meld.
5. **Prepare the Ricotta Mixture:** In a medium bowl, combine the ricotta cheese and egg. Mix well until smooth.
6. **Assemble the Lasagna:** In a 9x13-inch baking dish, spread a thin layer of the meat sauce. Add a layer of baked eggplant slices, followed by a layer of the ricotta mixture. Repeat the layers until all ingredients are used, ending with a layer of meat sauce.
7. **Top with Cheese:** Sprinkle the shredded mozzarella cheese and grated Parmesan cheese over the top.
8. **Bake:** Cover the baking dish with foil and bake in the preheated oven for 30 minutes. Remove the foil and bake for an additional 15 minutes, or until the cheese is melted and bubbly.
9. **Serve:** Garnish with fresh basil if desired and serve hot.

Nutritional Facts

- **Calories:** 350 kcal
- **Protein:** 25g
- **Fat:** 20g
- **Saturated Fat:** 10g
- **Cholesterol:** 100mg
- **Sodium:** 700mg
- **Potassium:** 800mg
- **Fiber:** 5g
- **Sugar:** 7g
- **Vitamin C:** 15mg

Cooking Tips

- ✓ **Eggplant:** To remove excess moisture from the eggplant, sprinkle the slices with salt and let them sit for 10 minutes before baking. Pat dry with paper towels.
- ✓ **Meat:** Use ground chicken or a meat substitute for a different variation.

Recipe B-17: Cauliflower Hash Browns

Prep Time: 15 minutes | Cooking Time: 15 minutes | Servings: 4

Ingredients

- 1 large head of cauliflower, riced
- 2 large eggs
- 1/2 cup shredded cheddar cheese
- 1/4 cup grated Parmesan cheese
- 1/4 cup almond flour
- 1/4 cup chopped green onions
- 1 teaspoon garlic powder
- 1/2 teaspoon sea salt
- 1/4 teaspoon black pepper
- 2 tablespoons olive oil

Cooking Instructions

1. **Prepare the Cauliflower Rice:** Cut the cauliflower into florets and pulse in a food processor until it resembles rice. Transfer to a microwave-safe bowl and microwave on high for 5 minutes. Let it cool slightly, then use a clean kitchen towel or cheesecloth to squeeze out as much moisture as possible.
2. **Mix the Ingredients:** In a large bowl, combine the cauliflower rice, eggs, shredded cheddar cheese, grated Parmesan cheese, almond flour, chopped green onions, garlic powder, sea salt, and black pepper. Mix well until combined.
3. **Form the Hash Browns:** Shape the mixture into 8 patties, pressing firmly to ensure they hold together.
4. **Cook the Hash Browns:** In a large skillet, heat the olive oil over medium-high heat. Add the cauliflower patties and cook for 4-5 minutes on each side, or until golden brown and crispy.
5. **Serve:** Serve the cauliflower hash browns hot, garnished with additional green onions if desired.

Nutritional Facts

- **Calories:** 200 kcal
- **Protein:** 10g
- **Fat:** 14g
- **Saturated Fat:** 4g
- **Cholesterol:** 90mg
- **Sodium:** 450mg
- **Potassium:** 400mg
- **Fiber:** 3g
- **Sugar:** 2g
- **Vitamin C:** 40mg

Cooking Tips

- ✓ **Cauliflower Rice:** Ensure you squeeze out as much moisture as possible from the cauliflower to achieve crispy hash browns.
- ✓ **Cheese:** Use freshly shredded cheese for better melting and texture.
- ✓ **Cooking:** Cook the hash browns in batches if necessary to avoid overcrowding the skillet.
- ✓ **Customization:** Add other ingredients like diced bell peppers, bacon bits, or herbs for extra flavor.
- ✓ **Serving Suggestions:** Serve with a side of scrambled eggs, avocado, or bacon for a complete breakfast.
- ✓ **Storage:** Store leftovers in an airtight container in the refrigerator for up to 3 days. Reheat in the skillet or oven to maintain crispiness.

Cauliflower hash browns are a delicious and healthy alternative to traditional hash browns, offering a low-carb, crispy, and flavorful option that's perfect for breakfast or brunch.

Recipe B-18: Low-carb beef and Broccoli Stir-Fry

Prep Time: 10 minutes | Cooking Time: 15 minutes | Servings: 4

Ingredients

- 1 lb. beef sirloin or flank steak, thinly sliced
- 4 cups broccoli florets
- 1 bell pepper, thinly sliced
- 3 cloves garlic, minced
- 2 tablespoons soy sauce (low sodium)
- 1 tablespoon oyster sauce (optional)
- 1 tablespoon sesame oil
- 1 tablespoon olive oil
- 1 teaspoon fresh ginger, minced
- 1/2 teaspoon red pepper flakes (optional)
- 1/4 cup beef broth
- 1 tablespoon cornstarch (optional for thickening)
- 2 tablespoons water (optional for thickening)
- Sesame seeds for garnish (optional)
- Fresh green onions, sliced (optional for garnish)

Cooking Instructions

1. **Prepare the Beef:** Slice the beef into thin strips against the grain. If you have time, marinate the beef in 1 tablespoon of soy sauce for 15-30 minutes for extra flavor.
2. **Prepare the Vegetables:** Cut the broccoli into bite-sized florets and thinly slice the bell pepper.
3. **Make the Sauce:** In a small bowl, mix the remaining soy sauce, oyster sauce (if using), sesame oil, minced garlic, minced ginger, and red pepper flakes.
4. **Cook the Beef:** In a large skillet or wok, heat the olive oil over medium-high heat. Add the sliced beef and cook for 3-4 minutes or until browned. Remove the beef from the skillet and set aside.

5. **Cook the Vegetables:** In the same skillet, add a little more olive oil if needed. Add the broccoli florets and bell pepper slices, and stir-fry for 3-4 minutes until tender crisp.
6. **Combine and Sauce:** Return the beef to the skillet with the vegetables. Pour the sauce over the beef and vegetables, stirring to coat evenly. Add the beef broth and bring to a simmer.
7. **Optional Thickening:** If you prefer a thicker sauce, mix 1 tablespoon of cornstarch with 2 tablespoons of water to create a slurry. Add the slurry to the skillet and cook for an additional 1-2 minutes until the sauce thickens.
8. **Serve:** Garnish with sesame seeds and fresh green onions if desired. Serve hot.

Nutritional Facts

- **Calories:** 250 kcal
- **Protein:** 20g
- **Fat:** 15g
- **Saturated Fat:** 4g
- **Cholesterol:** 60mg
- **Sodium:** 500mg
- **Potassium:** 500mg
- **Fiber:** 3g
- **Sugar:** 3g
- **Vitamin C:** 80mg

Cooking Tips

- ✓ **Beef:** For easier slicing, freeze the beef for about 30 minutes before cutting it into thin strips.
- ✓ **Vegetables:** Feel free to add other vegetables like snap peas, carrots, or mushrooms for extra variety.
- ✓ **Sauce:** Adjust the amount of red pepper flakes to control the heat level according to your preference.

Low-carb beef and broccoli stir-fry is a quick, flavorful, and nutritious dish that combines tender beef with fresh vegetables in a savory sauce, perfect for a healthy and satisfying dinner.

Recipe B-19: Baked Parmesan Crusted Salmon

Prep Time: 10 minutes | Cooking Time: 20 minutes | Servings: 4

Ingredients

- 4 salmon fillets (6 oz each)
- 1/2 cup grated Parmesan cheese
- 1/4 cup almond flour
- 1 teaspoon garlic powder
- 1 teaspoon dried oregano
- 1/2 teaspoon dried basil
- 1/2 teaspoon sea salt
- 1/4 teaspoon black pepper
- 2 tablespoons olive oil
- Lemon wedges for serving
- Fresh parsley, chopped (optional for garnish)

Cooking Instructions

1. **Preheat the Oven:** Preheat your oven to 400°F (200°C). Line a baking sheet with parchment paper.
2. **Prepare the Parmesan Mixture:** In a small bowl, combine the grated Parmesan cheese, almond flour, garlic powder, dried oregano, dried basil, sea salt, and black pepper.
3. **Prepare the Salmon:** Pat the salmon fillets dry with paper towels. Brush each fillet with olive oil.
4. **Coat the Salmon:** Press the Parmesan mixture onto the top of each salmon fillet, coating them evenly.
5. **Bake:** Place the salmon fillets on the prepared baking sheet. Bake in the preheated oven for 15-20 minutes, or until the salmon is cooked through and the crust is golden brown.

6. **Serve:** Garnish with fresh parsley and serve with lemon wedges. Serve hot.

Nutritional Facts

- **Calories:** 350 kcal
- **Protein:** 30g
- **Fat:** 22g
- **Saturated Fat:** 5g
- **Cholesterol:** 80mg
- **Sodium:** 600mg
- **Potassium:** 700mg
- **Fiber:** 1g
- **Sugar:** 0g
- **Vitamin D:** 15mcg

Cooking Tips

- ✓ **Salmon:** Use fresh or high-quality frozen salmon fillets. Thaw completely before baking if using frozen.
- ✓ **Cheese Mixture:** Ensure the Parmesan mixture is pressed firmly onto the salmon to create a good crust.
- ✓ **Cooking Time:** Adjust the baking time based on the thickness of the salmon fillets.
- ✓ **Serving Suggestions:** Pair with a side of steamed vegetables, cauliflower rice, or a fresh green salad for a complete meal.
- ✓ **Storage:** Store leftovers in an airtight container in the refrigerator for up to 2 days. Reheat in the oven to maintain the crust's crispiness.

Baked Parmesan crusted salmon is a delicious and easy-to-make dish that combines tender, flaky salmon with a savory and crispy Parmesan crust, perfect for a nutritious and satisfying dinner.

Recipe B-20: Zucchini Noodles with Pesto and Cherry Tomatoes

Prep Time: 15 minutes | Cooking Time: 5 minutes | Servings: 4

Ingredients

- 4 medium zucchinis, spiralized into noodles
- 1 cup cherry tomatoes, halved
- 1/2 cup basil pesto (store-bought or homemade)
- 1/4 cup grated Parmesan cheese
- 2 tablespoons olive oil
- 2 cloves garlic, minced
- 1/2 teaspoon sea salt
- 1/4 teaspoon black pepper
- Fresh basil leaves for garnish (optional)

Cooking Instructions

1. **Prepare the Zucchini Noodles:** Spiralize the zucchinis into noodles using a spiralizer or vegetable peeler.
2. **Cook the Garlic:** In a large skillet, heat the olive oil over medium heat. Add the minced garlic and cook for 1 minute until fragrant.
3. **Cook the Zucchini Noodles:** Add the zucchini noodles to the skillet and cook for 2-3 minutes, stirring frequently, until just tender. Avoid overcooking to prevent the noodles from becoming mushy.
4. **Add the Pesto and Tomatoes:** Stir in the basil pesto, cherry tomatoes, sea salt, and black pepper. Cook for an additional 1-2 minutes until everything is heated through.
5. **Serve:** Transfer the zucchini noodles to serving plates. Sprinkle with grated Parmesan cheese and garnish with fresh basil leaves if desired. Serve immediately.

Nutritional Facts

- **Calories:** 200 kcal
- **Protein:** 5g
- **Fat:** 18g
- **Saturated Fat:** 3g
- **Cholesterol:** 5mg
- **Sodium:** 400mg
- **Potassium:** 600mg
- **Fiber:** 3g
- **Sugar:** 5g
- **Vitamin C:** 35mg

Cooking Tips

- ✓ **Zucchini Noodles:** To prevent excess moisture, pat the zucchini noodles dry with paper towels before cooking.
- ✓ **Pesto:** Use a high-quality store-bought pesto or make your own by blending fresh basil, Parmesan cheese, pine nuts, garlic, and olive oil.
- ✓ **Tomatoes:** Add the cherry tomatoes at the end to maintain their shape and freshness.
- ✓ **Customization:** Add cooked chicken, shrimp, or tofu for additional protein.
- ✓ **Serving Suggestions:** Pair with a side salad or garlic bread (low carb) for a complete meal.
- ✓ **Storage:** Store any leftovers in an airtight container in the refrigerator for up to 2 days. Reheat gently to avoid overcooking the zucchini noodles.

Zucchini noodles with pesto and cherry tomatoes is a light, fresh, and flavorful dish that offers a low-carb alternative to traditional pasta, perfect for a quick and healthy meal.

Recipe B-21: Keto Egg Muffins

Prep Time: 15 minutes | Cooking Time: 20 minutes | Servings: 6

Ingredients

- 8 large eggs
- 1/2 cup heavy cream
- 1 cup spinach, chopped
- 1/2 cup bell peppers, diced
- 1/2 cup cooked bacon, crumbled
- 1/2 cup shredded cheddar cheese
- 1/4 cup green onions, chopped
- 1/2 teaspoon sea salt
- 1/4 teaspoon black pepper
- 1/4 teaspoon garlic powder
- Olive oil spray for muffin tin

Cooking Instructions

1. **Preheat the Oven:** Preheat your oven to 375°F (190°C). Grease a 12-cup muffin tin with olive oil spray.
2. **Prepare the Vegetables and Bacon:** Chop the spinach, bell peppers, and green onions. Cook the bacon and crumble it if not already prepared.
3. **Whisk the Eggs:** In a large bowl, whisk together the eggs, heavy cream, sea salt, black pepper, and garlic powder until well combined.
4. **Add Fillings:** Stir in the chopped spinach, bell peppers, crumbled bacon, shredded cheddar cheese, and green onions.
5. **Fill the Muffin Tin:** Pour the egg mixture evenly into the prepared muffin tin, filling each cup about 3/4 full.

6. **Bake:** Bake in the preheated oven for 18-20 minutes or until the egg muffins are set and slightly golden on top.
7. **Cool and Serve:** Allow the egg muffins to cool in the tin for a few minutes before removing. Serve warm.

Nutritional Facts

- **Calories:** 200 kcal
- **Protein:** 12g
- **Fat:** 16g
- **Saturated Fat:** 6g
- **Cholesterol:** 220mg
- **Sodium:** 400mg
- **Potassium:** 200mg
- **Fiber:** 1g
- **Sugar:** 1g
- **Vitamin A:** 800 IU

Cooking Tips

- ✓ **Fillings:** Customize the egg muffins with your favorite vegetables, meats, and cheeses. Try adding mushrooms, zucchini, sausage, or feta cheese.
- ✓ **Whisking:** Ensure the eggs and cream are well whisked for a uniform texture.
- ✓ **Muffin Tin:** Use silicone muffin cups or liners for easier removal and cleanup.
- ✓ **Serving Suggestions:** Serve with a side of avocado, salsa, or a fresh green salad for a complete breakfast.
- ✓ **Storage:** Store any leftovers in an airtight container in the refrigerator for up to 4 days. Reheat in the microwave or oven before serving.

Keto egg muffins are a convenient and versatile breakfast option, packed with protein and vegetables, making them perfect for meal prep and on-the-go meals.

Recipe B-22: Coconut Curry Chicken

Prep Time: 15 minutes | Cooking Time: 25 minutes | Servings: 4

Ingredients

- 1 lb boneless, skinless chicken breasts cut into bite-sized pieces
- 1 can (14 oz) coconut milk (full fat)
- 1 cup chicken broth (low sodium)
- 1 tablespoon coconut oil
- 1 small onion, finely chopped
- 3 cloves garlic, minced
- 1 tablespoon fresh ginger, grated
- 2 tablespoons red curry paste
- 1 teaspoon ground turmeric
- 1 teaspoon ground cumin
- 1 teaspoon sea salt
- 1/2 teaspoon black pepper
- 2 cups spinach, chopped
- Fresh cilantro, chopped (optional for garnish)
- Lime wedges for serving (optional)

Cooking Instructions

1. **Prepare the Chicken:** Cut the chicken breasts into bite-sized pieces and season with sea salt and black pepper.
2. **Cook the Aromatics:** In a large skillet or wok, heat the coconut oil over medium heat. Add the chopped onion, minced garlic, and grated ginger. Cook for 2-3 minutes until the onion is softened and fragrant.
3. **Add the Spices and Paste:** Stir in the red curry paste, ground turmeric, and ground cumin. Cook for 1-2 minutes until the spices are well combined and aromatic.
4. **Cook the Chicken:** Add the chicken pieces to the skillet and cook for 5-7 minutes, stirring occasionally, until the chicken is browned on all sides.
5. **Add Coconut Milk and Broth:** Pour in the coconut milk and chicken broth. Bring to a simmer and cook for 10 minutes, or until the chicken is cooked through and the sauce has thickened slightly.
6. **Add Spinach:** Stir in the chopped spinach and cook for an additional 2-3 minutes until wilted.
7. **Serve:** Garnish with fresh cilantro and serve with lime wedges if desired.

Nutritional Facts

- **Calories:** 350 kcal
- **Protein:** 25g
- **Fat:** 24g
- **Saturated Fat:** 16g
- **Cholesterol:** 70mg
- **Sodium:** 600mg
- **Potassium:** 700mg
- **Fiber:** 3g
- **Sugar:** 3g
- **Vitamin C:** 15mg

Cooking Tips

- ✓ **Curry Paste:** Adjust the amount of red curry paste to control the heat level according to your preference.
- ✓ **Coconut Milk:** Use full-fat coconut milk for a richer and creamier sauce. Light coconut milk can be substituted but will result in a thinner sauce.
- ✓ **Vegetables:** Add other vegetables like bell peppers, zucchini, or snap peas for additional flavor and nutrition.

Coconut curry chicken is a flavorful and creamy dish that combines tender chicken with aromatic spices and coconut milk, perfect for a comforting and healthy meal.

Recipe B-23: Greek Yogurt Chicken Salad

Prep Time: 15 minutes | Cooking Time: 0 minutes | Servings: 4

Ingredients

- 2 cups cooked chicken breast, shredded or diced
- 1 cup Greek yogurt (plain, full-fat or low-fat)
- 1/2 cup celery, finely chopped
- 1/4 cup red onion, finely chopped
- 1/4 cup fresh dill, chopped
- 1/4 cup fresh parsley, chopped
- 1 tablespoon Dijon mustard
- 1 tablespoon lemon juice
- 1/2 teaspoon garlic powder
- 1/2 teaspoon sea salt
- 1/4 teaspoon black pepper
- Mixed greens or lettuce leaves for serving

Cooking Instructions

1. **Prepare the Ingredients:** Shred or dice the cooked chicken breast. Finely chop the celery, red onion, dill, and parsley.
2. **Make the Dressing:** In a large bowl, combine the Greek yogurt, Dijon mustard, lemon juice, garlic powder, sea salt, and black pepper. Mix well.
3. **Combine the Salad:** Add the shredded chicken, chopped celery, red onion, dill, and parsley to the bowl with the dressing. Stir until all ingredients are well combined and the chicken is evenly coated with the dressing.
4. **Serve:** Serve the Greek yogurt chicken salad on a bed of mixed greens or in lettuce leaves.

Nutritional Facts

- **Calories:** 200 kcal
- **Protein:** 25g
- **Fat:** 6g
- **Saturated Fat:** 2g
- **Cholesterol:** 75mg
- **Sodium:** 450mg
- **Potassium:** 400mg
- **Fiber:** 1g
- **Sugar:** 3g
- **Vitamin C:** 10mg

Cooking Tips

- ✓ **Chicken:** Use leftover chicken or rotisserie chicken for a quick and easy preparation. Ensure the chicken is well seasoned for added flavor.
- ✓ **Yogurt:** For a creamier texture, use full-fat Greek yogurt. Adjust the amount of yogurt based on your desired consistency.
- ✓ **Add-ins:** Add other ingredients like chopped apples, grapes, or walnuts for extra flavor and crunch.
- ✓ **Serving Suggestions:** This chicken salad can be served as a sandwich filling, in a wrap, or with whole-grain crackers for a complete meal.
- ✓ **Storage:** Store any leftovers in an airtight container in the refrigerator for up to 3 days. Stir well before serving.

Greek yogurt chicken salad is a healthy and refreshing dish that combines tender chicken with creamy Greek yogurt and fresh herbs, perfect for a light and satisfying lunch or dinner.

Recipe B-24: Cauliflower Shepherd's Pie

Prep Time: 20 minutes | Cooking Time: 30 minutes | Servings: 6

Ingredients

- 1 large head of cauliflower, cut into florets
- 1 lb. ground beef or lamb
- 1 small onion, finely chopped
- 2 cloves garlic, minced
- 1 cup carrots, diced
- 1 cup green beans, chopped
- 1/2 cup beef broth (low sodium)
- 1/4 cup tomato paste
- 1 tablespoon Worcestershire sauce
- 1 teaspoon dried thyme
- 1 teaspoon dried rosemary
- 1/2 teaspoon sea salt
- 1/4 teaspoon black pepper
- 1/2 cup shredded cheddar cheese (optional)
- 2 tablespoons butter
- 1/4 cup heavy cream

Cooking Instructions

1. **Preheat the Oven:** Preheat your oven to 375°F (190°C).
2. **Prepare the Cauliflower:** Bring a large pot of water to a boil. Add the cauliflower florets and cook for 10 minutes or until tender. Drain well and transfer to a large bowl. Add the butter and heavy cream, and mash until smooth. Season with salt and pepper to taste.
3. **Cook the Filling:** In a large skillet, cook the ground beef or lamb over medium heat until browned. Add the chopped onion and minced garlic and cook for 2-3 minutes until softened. Stir in the diced carrots and chopped green beans and cook for another 5 minutes.
4. **Add the Sauce:** Add the beef broth, tomato paste, Worcestershire sauce, dried

thyme, dried rosemary, sea salt, and black pepper to the skillet. Stir well and simmer for 10 minutes until the vegetables are tender and the sauce has thickened slightly.

5. **Assemble the Pie:** Transfer the meat and vegetable mixture to a 9x13-inch baking dish. Spread the mashed cauliflower evenly over the top.
6. **Top with Cheese:** Sprinkle shredded cheddar cheese over the mashed cauliflower if using.
7. **Bake:** Bake in the preheated oven for 20-25 minutes until the top is golden brown and bubbly.
8. **Serve:** Allow the pie to cool slightly before serving.

Nutritional Facts

- **Calories:** 300 kcal
- **Protein:** 20g
- **Fat:** 20g
- **Saturated Fat:** 10g
- **Cholesterol:** 90mg
- **Sodium:** 450mg
- **Potassium:** 700mg
- **Fiber:** 4g
- **Sugar:** 5g
- **Vitamin A:** 6000 IU

Cooking Tips

- ✓ **Cauliflower:** Ensure the cauliflower is well-drained to prevent the mash from being too watery.
- ✓ **Meat:** Use lean ground beef or lamb for a healthier option. Ground turkey or chicken can also be substituted.

Cauliflower shepherd's pie is a hearty and comforting dish that features a savory meat and vegetable filling topped with creamy mashed cauliflower, making it a delicious and low-carb alternative to traditional shepherd's pie.

Recipe B-25: Lemon Garlic Butter Shrimp

Prep Time: 10 minutes | Cooking Time: 10 minutes | Servings: 4

Ingredients

- 1 lb. large shrimp, peeled and deveined
- 3 tablespoons butter
- 4 cloves garlic, minced
- 1 lemon, juiced and zested
- 1/4 cup fresh parsley, chopped
- 1/2 teaspoon red pepper flakes (optional)
- 1/2 teaspoon sea salt
- 1/4 teaspoon black pepper
- Lemon wedges for serving

Cooking Instructions

1. **Prepare the Shrimp:** Pat the shrimp dry with paper towels. Season with sea salt and black pepper.
2. **Melt the Butter:** In a large skillet, melt the butter over medium-high heat.
3. **Cook the Garlic:** Add the minced garlic to the skillet and cook for 1 minute until fragrant.
4. **Cook the Shrimp:** Add the shrimp to the skillet and cook for 2-3 minutes on each side until pink and opaque.
5. **Add Lemon:** Stir in the lemon juice, lemon zest, and red pepper flakes (if using). Cook for an additional 1-2 minutes, allowing the flavors to meld together.
6. **Garnish and Serve:** Remove the skillet from heat. Sprinkle with fresh parsley and serve immediately with lemon wedges on the side.

Nutritional Facts

- **Calories:** 200 kcal
- **Protein:** 20g
- **Fat:** 12g
- **Saturated Fat:** 7g
- **Cholesterol:** 190mg
- **Sodium:** 600mg
- **Potassium:** 300mg
- **Fiber:** 0g
- **Sugar:** 0g
- **Vitamin C:** 20mg

Cooking Tips

✓ **Shrimp:** Use fresh or high-quality frozen shrimp. Thaw completely and pat dry before cooking.
✓ **Butter:** Use unsalted butter to control the saltiness of the dish.
✓ **Lemon:** Adjust the amount of lemon juice and zest to taste for a more or less tangy flavor.
✓ **Serving Suggestions:** Serve over cauliflower rice, zucchini noodles, or a fresh green salad for a complete low-carb meal.
✓ **Storage:** Store any leftovers in an airtight container in the refrigerator for up to 2 days. Reheat gently in a skillet or microwave before serving.

Lemon garlic butter shrimp is a quick, flavorful, and healthy dish that combines tender shrimp with a rich and zesty lemon garlic butter sauce, perfect for a light and satisfying dinner.

Recipe B-26: Avocado and Bacon Deviled Eggs

Prep Time: 15 minutes | Cooking Time: 10 minutes | Servings: 12 halves

Ingredients

- 6 large eggs
- 1 ripe avocado
- 2 tablespoons mayonnaise
- 1 teaspoon Dijon mustard
- 1 teaspoon lime juice
- 4 slices cooked bacon, crumbled
- 1/4 teaspoon sea salt
- 1/4 teaspoon black pepper
- Paprika for garnish
- Fresh chives, chopped (optional for garnish)

Cooking Instructions

1. **Boil the Eggs:** Place the eggs in a saucepan and cover with cold water. Bring to a boil over medium-high heat. Once boiling, cover, remove from heat, and let sit for 10 minutes.
2. **Cool and Peel:** Drain the hot water and transfer the eggs to a bowl of ice water to cool for 5 minutes. Peel the eggs under running water.
3. **Prepare the Filling:** Slice the eggs in half lengthwise and remove the yolks. Place the yolks in a bowl and mash with a fork. Add the avocado, mayonnaise, Dijon mustard, lime juice, crumbled bacon (reserve a bit for garnish), sea salt, and black pepper. Mix until smooth.
4. **Fill the Eggs:** Spoon or pipe the avocado mixture back into the egg white halves.

5. **Garnish and Serve:** Sprinkle with paprika and garnish with remaining crumbled bacon and chopped chives if desired. Serve immediately or refrigerate until ready to serve.

Nutritional Facts

- **Calories:** 120 kcal
- **Protein:** 6g
- **Fat:** 10g
- **Saturated Fat:** 2.5g
- **Cholesterol:** 110mg
- **Sodium:** 250mg
- **Potassium:** 150mg
- **Fiber:** 1g
- **Sugar:** 0g
- **Vitamin A:** 150 IU

Cooking Tips

- ✓ **Boiling Eggs:** For easier peeling, use eggs that are at least a week old and cool them immediately after boiling.
- ✓ **Avocado:** Use a ripe avocado for a creamy texture. It should yield slightly when pressed.
- ✓ **Customization:** Add other ingredients like chopped pickles, jalapeños, or herbs for different flavor variations.
- ✓ **Serving Suggestions:** These deviled eggs make a great appetizer or snack for parties and gatherings.
- ✓ **Storage:** Store in an airtight container in the refrigerator for up to 2 days.

Avocado and bacon deviled eggs are a delicious and nutritious twist on a classic dish, combining creamy avocado with savory bacon for a satisfying low-carb snack or appetizer.

Recipe B-27: Low-Carb Chicken Fajita Bowl

Prep Time: 15 minutes | Cooking Time: 20 minutes | Servings: 4

Ingredients

- 1 lb. boneless, skinless chicken breasts sliced into strips
- 1 red bell pepper, sliced
- 1 yellow bell pepper, sliced
- 1 green bell pepper, sliced
- 1 small onion, sliced
- 2 tablespoons olive oil
- 2 teaspoons chili powder
- 1 teaspoon ground cumin
- 1 teaspoon smoked paprika
- 1/2 teaspoon garlic powder
- 1/2 teaspoon onion powder
- 1/2 teaspoon sea salt
- 1/4 teaspoon black pepper
- 1/4 teaspoon cayenne pepper (optional)
- 2 cups cauliflower rice, cooked
- 1 avocado, sliced
- Fresh cilantro, chopped (optional for garnish)
- Lime wedges for serving (optional)

Cooking Instructions

1. **Prepare the Vegetables:** Slice the bell peppers and onion into thin strips.
2. **Season the Chicken:** In a large bowl, combine the sliced chicken with chili powder, ground cumin, smoked paprika, garlic powder, onion powder, sea salt, black pepper, and cayenne pepper (if using). Toss to coat the chicken evenly with the spices.
3. **Cook the Chicken:** In a large skillet, heat 1 tablespoon of olive oil over medium-high heat. Add the seasoned chicken and cook for 5-7 minutes until the chicken is browned and cooked through. Remove the chicken from the skillet and set aside.
4. **Cook the Vegetables:** In the same skillet, add the remaining 1 tablespoon of olive oil. Add the sliced bell peppers and onion and cook for 5-7 minutes until the vegetables are tender and slightly charred.
5. **Assemble the Bowls:** Divide the cooked cauliflower rice among four bowls. Top each bowl with the cooked chicken, sautéed bell peppers, and onions. Add slices of avocado.
6. **Garnish and Serve:** Garnish with fresh cilantro and lime wedges if desired. Serve immediately.

Nutritional Facts

- **Calories:** 350 kcal
- **Protein:** 30g
- **Fat:** 20g
- **Saturated Fat:** 3g
- **Cholesterol:** 80mg
- **Sodium:** 600mg
- **Potassium:** 800mg
- **Fiber:** 6g
- **Sugar:** 4g
- **Vitamin C:** 150mg

Cooking Tips

- ✓ **Chicken:** For extra flavor, marinate the chicken in the spice mixture for 15-30 minutes before cooking.
- ✓ **Vegetables:** Add other vegetables like zucchini or mushrooms for additional flavor and nutrition.

Low-carb chicken fajita bowls are a delicious and nutritious meal that combines seasoned chicken, fresh vegetables, and cauliflower rice, perfect for a satisfying and healthy dinner.

Recipe B-28: Broccoli Cheese Soup

Prep Time: 10 minutes | Cooking Time: 20 minutes | Servings: 4

Ingredients

- 4 cups broccoli florets
- 1 small onion, finely chopped
- 2 cloves garlic, minced
- 2 cups chicken broth (low sodium)
- 1 cup heavy cream
- 2 cups shredded cheddar cheese
- 2 tablespoons butter
- 1 teaspoon Dijon mustard
- 1/2 teaspoon sea salt
- 1/4 teaspoon black pepper
- Fresh parsley, chopped (optional for garnish)

Cooking Instructions

1. **Cook the Vegetables:** In a large pot, melt the butter over medium heat. Add the chopped onion and minced garlic and cook for 2-3 minutes until softened.
2. **Add the Broccoli and Broth:** Add the broccoli florets and chicken broth to the pot. Bring to a simmer and cook for 10 minutes or until the broccoli is tender.
3. **Blend the Soup:** Use an immersion blender to puree the soup until smooth. Alternatively, transfer the soup in batches to a blender and blend until smooth, then return to the pot.
4. **Add Cream and Cheese:** Stir in the heavy cream, shredded cheddar cheese, Dijon mustard, sea salt, and black pepper. Cook over low heat, stirring frequently, until the cheese is melted, and the soup is heated through.
5. **Serve:** Ladle the soup into bowls and garnish with fresh parsley if desired. Serve hot.

Nutritional Facts

- **Calories:** 350 kcal
- **Protein:** 15g
- **Fat:** 30g
- **Saturated Fat:** 18g
- **Cholesterol:** 100mg
- **Sodium:** 700mg
- **Potassium:** 500mg
- **Fiber:** 3g
- **Sugar:** 3g
- **Vitamin A:** 1500 IU

Cooking Tips

- ✓ **Broccoli:** Use fresh or frozen broccoli. If using frozen, adjust the cooking time as needed.
- ✓ **Cheese:** Use freshly shredded cheddar cheese for the best melting quality. Pre-shredded cheese often contains additives that can affect texture.
- ✓ **Consistency:** For a chunkier soup, reserve some broccoli florets before blending and stir them back into the soup after blending.
- ✓ **Serving Suggestions:** Pair with a side salad or low-carb bread for a complete meal.
- ✓ **Storage:** Store leftovers in an airtight container in the refrigerator for up to 3 days. Reheat gently on the stovetop or in the microwave before serving.

Broccoli cheese soup is a creamy and comforting dish, packed with the flavors of tender broccoli and rich cheddar cheese, perfect for a warm and satisfying meal.

Recipe B-29: Grilled Lemon Herb Chicken

Prep Time: 10 minutes (plus marinating time) | Cooking Time: 15 minutes | Servings: 4

Ingredients

- 4 boneless, skinless chicken breasts
- 1/4 cup olive oil
- 2 tablespoons fresh lemon juice
- 1 tablespoon lemon zest
- 3 cloves garlic, minced
- 1 teaspoon dried oregano
- 1 teaspoon dried thyme
- 1/2 teaspoon sea salt
- 1/4 teaspoon black pepper
- Fresh parsley, chopped (optional for garnish)
- Lemon wedges for serving (optional)

Cooking Instructions

1. **Prepare the Marinade:** In a small bowl, whisk together the olive oil, fresh lemon juice, lemon zest, minced garlic, dried oregano, dried thyme, sea salt, and black pepper.
2. **Marinate the Chicken:** Place the chicken breasts in a resealable plastic bag or a shallow dish. Pour the marinade over the chicken, ensuring it is well coated. Seal the bag or cover the dish and refrigerate for at least 30 minutes, or up to 4 hours for more flavor.
3. **Preheat the Grill:** Preheat your grill to medium-high heat.
4. **Grill the Chicken:** Remove the chicken from the marinade and discard any remaining marinade. Grill the chicken for 6-7 minutes on each side, or until the internal temperature reaches 165°F (74°C) and the chicken is cooked through.
5. **Rest and Serve:** Remove the chicken from the grill and let it rest for 5 minutes before slicing. Garnish with fresh parsley and serve with lemon wedges if desired.

Nutritional Facts

- **Calories:** 300 kcal
- **Protein:** 28g
- **Fat:** 18g
- **Saturated Fat:** 3g
- **Cholesterol:** 80mg
- **Sodium:** 400mg
- **Potassium:** 400mg
- **Fiber:** 0g
- **Sugar:** 0g
- **Vitamin C:** 15mg

Cooking Tips

- ✓ **Marinating:** Marinate the chicken for at least 30 minutes, but for best results, let it marinate for up to 4 hours.
- ✓ **Grilling:** Ensure the grill is properly preheated to avoid sticking. Use a meat thermometer to check for doneness.
- ✓ **Lemon Flavor:** For a stronger lemon flavor, add extra lemon zest to the marinade.
- ✓ **Serving Suggestions:** Pair with a side of grilled vegetables, a fresh salad, or cauliflower rice for a complete meal.
- ✓ **Storage:** Store any leftovers in an airtight container in the refrigerator for up to 3 days. Reheat gently in the microwave or on the stovetop.

Grilled lemon herb chicken is a flavorful and healthy dish, combining tender chicken breasts with a zesty lemon and herb marinade, perfect for a quick and satisfying dinner.

Recipe B-30: Cauliflower Mac and Cheese

Prep Time: 15 minutes | Cooking Time: 20 minutes | Servings: 4

Ingredients

- 1 large head of cauliflower, cut into florets
- 1 cup heavy cream
- 1 cup shredded cheddar cheese
- 1/2 cup grated Parmesan cheese
- 2 tablespoons cream cheese
- 1 teaspoon Dijon mustard
- 1/2 teaspoon garlic powder
- 1/2 teaspoon onion powder
- 1/2 teaspoon sea salt
- 1/4 teaspoon black pepper
- 1/4 teaspoon smoked paprika (optional)
- Fresh parsley, chopped (optional for garnish)

Cooking Instructions

1. **Preheat the Oven:** Preheat your oven to 375°F (190°C).
2. **Cook the Cauliflower:** Bring a large pot of salted water to a boil. Add the cauliflower florets and cook for 5-7 minutes until tender but still firm. Drain well and pat dry with paper towels.
3. **Prepare the Cheese Sauce:** In a large saucepan, heat the heavy cream over medium heat until it begins to simmer. Reduce the heat to low and stir in the cheddar cheese, Parmesan cheese, cream cheese, Dijon mustard, garlic powder, onion powder, sea salt, and black pepper. Stir until the cheese is melted and the sauce is smooth.
4. **Combine Cauliflower and Sauce:** Add the cooked cauliflower to the cheese sauce and stir to coat evenly.
5. **Bake:** Transfer the cauliflower and cheese mixture to a baking dish. Sprinkle with smoked paprika if desired. Bake in the preheated oven for 15-20 minutes, or until the top is golden and bubbly.
6. **Serve:** Garnish with fresh parsley if desired and serve hot.

Nutritional Facts

- **Calories:** 350 kcal
- **Protein:** 12g
- **Fat:** 30g
- **Saturated Fat:** 18g
- **Cholesterol:** 100mg
- **Sodium:** 700mg
- **Potassium:** 500mg
- **Fiber:** 3g
- **Sugar:** 3g
- **Vitamin A:** 800 IU

Cooking Tips

- ✓ **Cauliflower:** Ensure the cauliflower is well-drained and patted dry to prevent the dish from becoming watery.
- ✓ **Cheese:** Use freshly grated cheese for the best melting quality. Pre-shredded cheese often contains additives that can affect texture.
- ✓ **Customization:** Add cooked bacon, chopped green onions, or jalapeños for extra flavor.
- ✓ **Serving Suggestions:** Pair with a fresh salad or steamed vegetables for a complete meal.

About The Author

Samantha Bax, an advocate of vegan, eco-mindful cuisine, discovered her true passion in the heart of a bustling city. However, her culinary journey didn't start in a kitchen but rather in her grandmother's cozy home, where she first learned the importance of nourishing and wholesome eating.

When Samantha was diagnosed with diabetes during her twenties, her life took a turn. This pivotal moment fueled her commitment to health and well-being, leading her to become a certified nutritionist. Fate had something in store for Samantha when a close family member was diagnosed with kidney disease. This significant event brought together her two passions. Food and wellness. Inspiring her to create a niche that caters to both renal diets.

Of course, Samantha faced challenges along the way. Balancing health requirements while maintaining flavors proved to be quite complex. However, she remained steadfast in refusing to compromise taste for the sake of health. To overcome this obstacle, Samantha embarked on an adventure where she sought inspiration from kitchens across the Mediterranean region, vibrant spice markets in Asia, and sustainable farms throughout Central America.

In "***The All-New Low Calorie High Protein Low-Carb Diet Cookbook***," Samantha Bax beautifully intertwines her story with an enticing collection of mouth-watering recipes.

She strongly believes that food is not a means of survival. Also, it is something to be cherished as a way to celebrate life and promote well-being.

The main aim of her book is to present readers with a curated collection of recipes that cater to their needs while also providing them with an enjoyable culinary experience.

Apart from writing and experimenting in the kitchen, Samantha finds joy in the art of photography. She skillfully captures the essence of cityscapes, as well as serene landscapes, in nature. Furthermore, she actively leads workshops and seminars where she guides individuals on how to make food choices that prioritize taste without compromising on quality.

Other Books by Samantha Bax:

https://shop.prosebooks.com

To join her Newsletter and receive advance notification of new publications, special offers, and more, subscribe to the Newsletter for FREE today at:

www.samanthabax.com

Other Books by Samantha Bax

And more at https://shop.prosebooks.com

Or on Amazon:

Author Page on Amazon

Scan the above code to see all of the books and more...
https://shop.prosebooks.com

Thank You

Dear Reader,

As we approach the end of this journey, I want to express my sincere gratitude to you for embracing these recipes in your kitchen and, in turn, in your life. Your support means the world to me. It ignites my passion for sharing the goodness that food brings to our tables and our souls.

May the flavors you've explored and the nourishment you've derived from these pages inspire moments of happiness, connection, and well-being. Always remember that every meal you prepare is an expression of your imagination and thoughtfulness.

Looking forward to our escapade,

Warmest regards,

Samantha Bax

FREE Meal-Planner

As a FREE Bonus to all my readers, I invite you to go to my publisher's website at www.prosebooks.com/meal-planner and get a FREE Meal Planner to help and guide you along your journey to fitness and good health.

FREE Meal Planner